T0367487

A TWO-VOLUME BOOK

CONFESSIONS OF A
SURVIVING ALIEN

*A Memoir of
a Life Defined by One
Word—Vietnam*

JON MEADE

Order this book online at www.trafford.com
or email orders@trafford.com

Most Trafford titles are also available at major online book retailers.

Cover Artwork by: David Melchior

Print information available on the last page.

ISBN: 978-1-4907-6837-3 (sc)
ISBN: 978-1-4907-6836-6 (hc)
ISBN: 978-1-4907-6835-9 (e)

Library of Congress Control Number: 2016903666

Trafford rev. 12/30/2016

 www.trafford.com
North America & international
toll-free: 1 888 232 4444 (USA & Canada)
fax: 812 355 4082

This book is dedicated to my family, friends, and acquaintances. It is also proudly dedicated to all Marines, Veterans, current military and GIs, their families, and the United States of America. Moreover, this is also dedicated to all of life's warriors who fight the good fight and never give up.

A special thanks to my VA Counselor, Dr. Wahl, whose words and stories encouraged me more than she'll ever know.

Also, my college English and Creative Writing Professor, James Fetler.

Preface

*All is **not** fair in love and war.*
—JM

My whole being was seeking for something still unknown
which might confer meaning upon the banality of life.
—Carl Jung, from his memoirs

Everyone has a defining moment in life. It may be an event or an experience, or both. My defining moment in life was pivotal in Vietnam, defining my entire life before, during and after. I look upon my Vietnam experience as a dissection of my life in parts that in so many profound ways make up the whole of my being, painted in broad strokes with every color from land, sea, and sky. On a much grander scale, our country, the USA, had its defining pivotal historical moment as well—forever dividing and changing the United States. My story is intricately intertwined with the country and those turbulent times that defined a nation—and this one young American and Marine. Arguably, no one word in American history has drawn such attention, debate, controversy, division, pain, and canvases of gray more than Vietnam. Given that premise, this entire book is chronological in nature and starts from my birth in 1946 to the death of my father in 1997 and everything in between. It is divided into *two volumes* because of its size, time-frames and reader convenience.

Volume One includes Part I, Before Vietnam (BV), and Part II, During Vietnam (DV).
Volume Two includes Part III, After Vietnam (AV), and Part IV, After Marines (AM).

Volume One, Part I, covers growing up and highlights memorable aspects of my childhood, particularly those from an impressionable kid and teen. I offer possible insights into why I chose the military and serving my country before enlisting in the United States Marine Corps at eighteen and a half, going through boot camp and subsequent duties prior to actually getting marching orders to Vietnam in 1966. Part

II covers my Vietnam tour, the smallest segment in terms of actual time in my life, yet it would come to define and underscore it all—in droves!

Volume Two, Part III, entails returning to the world, as we framed it, the remainder of my four-year stint with the Corps. Part IV continues with life after the Marines and the impact of Vietnam and my service in the Corps. It describes a somewhat convoluted life that followed, but seldom, if ever, dry or boring and certainly enveloping the longest time span. This period covers more pathos than a mere preface could even whet your wildest imagination with. It also contains a deeply held family secret and a personal spiritual experience I had that defies description. Relating it will be one of my life's toughest challenges. Someone once told me my life was like a giant puzzle—a virtual smorgasbord of every imaginable flavor (my embellishment)—and quite interesting, even unbelievable. Humbly, I agree.

Many years ago, by many people, many times, I have been encouraged to write a book, especially during the college years while majoring in journalism. I actually took a crack at it, but self-imposed circumstances cut my dream short. Since then, I am embarrassed to say I became one of the biggest procrastinators on this planet or any other. I was like an alien of action and word production. I was in the great abyss of writer's block, in the vast doldrums of creative nothingness, like a detached human going around and around in space orbit with all the countless pieces of space (mind) debris. Where did it start, and where does it end? Initially, the concept of this book, titled *"USMC" (Uncle Sam's Misguided Children)*, started in 1972, with five chapters going to New York and personally delivered by yours truly to major publishers in 1977. The trip and results are revealed within these pages.

Ultimately, it ends and starts here with *Confessions of a Surviving Alien*. As I restart this memoir seriously at sixty-eight years old, I was determined to finish within months, incorporating all my other books—planned but not written—into this one all-encompassing two-volume book and salvage some dignity as a creative writer and productive human being. My days of being alien from the craft of the written word and a life I envisioned many years ago are over. My spaceship, made up of wasted imagination and contrived parts, has landed. And I'm destroying the landing and launch pad as I write. *BAM!* Gone with the swish of my hand and the cobwebs of my mind. The procrastination is over. History. I'm free and truly feel emboldened.

Well, as procrastination continued to invade my progress, it now appears that I'll be sixty-nine as this book goes to press. Plans don't necessarily equate to progress, unless it can divide and destroy that dreaded word—procrastination. The word itself seems to evoke a deadly and dark tone of division and destruction, at least in my mind. I believe it is the greatest destroyer of success than anything. I also believe it is the ultimate killer of plans, dreams, aspirations, natural talent, beginnings and progression, to name the more obvious. It is a hideous monster that delves within, looking, waiting, wanting to devour the mind and body that houses it. It feeds best on delays, excuses, weakness, and lack of confidence. Procrastination is something that we all exercise, but when it consumes you as it did me, it eats at your very soul like a rotting decay, somewhat like a decision-and-action paralysis. This book stops that decay and eradicates the poison. Now, I feel free to create, write, and share. I can't say it enough, repetitious or not. Do or die, as the Marines say, I will overcome. I am a relentless beast, with a keyboard as my feast.

But before I get into Part I, I feel compelled to explain a few things regarding this book. Firstly, I had to determine my approach. Which form of storytelling would I do, fiction or nonfiction? Or would I just fictionalize the truth? I was at a crossroads of decision for years. Why do straight fiction or fictionalize the truth? Especially if truth is stranger than fiction, especially in this case. I went back and forth, finally deciding on a nonfiction memoir. Secondly, as you will learn within the story, an inner voice years before had suggested that if I were to write the truth, every bit of it—particularly the hard-to-relate spiritual happening—that the book would be a best seller. (*Dream along with me, I'm on the way to a star—Perry Como*). Perhaps largely due to the message within, I will be humbled again. I can't lose sight of this fact. But as part of this "inner" deal, I had to be totally forthright and honest about everything, including me—no punches pulled, no quarter given or taken. This would also mean revealing deep, heavy family secrets and other very touchy topics. But the more I thought about it, the more I liked it.

Since I'm pretty stone-cold honest about nearly everything anyway, why break ranks now? So goes the ego, a potentially dangerous element of the human psyche anyway. As far as some people's names and other overly touchy areas go, I selectively protect their privacy. But as we learned in Journalism 1A and the law, *the defense to libel is truth*. There is no intent whatsoever to defame anyone, nor drag them through the mud unnecessarily. Believe me, I could have included much more had I been vindictive or operating from a platform of malice, which I definitely am not. But the truth shall set you free, so says the Bible. Therefore, writing this book will be an exercise in faith and personal release. It will be like a cleansing of the mind and soul for me, a philosophically honest account of my life and legacy for my children about their father, of which I will bare all, as surely as if I were naked. Well, maybe with a flimsy fig leaf. I will be learning nearly as much about myself and my life as the reader will. What that frankness reveals will be anyone's guess, sometimes I am sure, mine included. The connecting of my life's dots raises my own curiosity too, as I am anxious to learn more about myself and what makes my internal clock chime.

Because of this no-holds-barred frank approach, I will be sharing my story with you personally as if you were a good friend. I will share the emotions, tears, fears, humor, negatives and positives, pros and cons. This unveiling will serve me as the story purveyor, as much as you, the entertained and hopefully satisfied reader. I want the reader to be as much a part of this story as me. In all seriousness, I hope it will provide something more—something that may touch you in some deeply personal way. A way that may draw some analogy to your own defining moment—moments—in life. You see, I'm not just sharing a story but a life. And parts will not be easily conveyed, some I already dread just thinking about writing them later. In some respects of this memoir, that famous saying "The pen is mightier than the sword" shall emerge. So be it. Sometimes the sword will boomerang and stick me. So be that.

I also must add here that with this memoir, all the events, people, recollections, and history are from my memory, perceptions, and interpretations. I have gone to great (personal) lengths to ensure accuracy and honesty. The previously mentioned visions and soul-searching above would have it no other way. As it is said, *No two people looking at the same thing will have the same opinion or interpretation.* So this memoir is simply mine. I will be sharing my life, my world, my way. And of course, I do plenty of cherry picking for my topic matter, but I do just as much pulling muck from the swamp. Some things I will breeze over like a whimsical whisper over the sea while other topics that I deem more significant will get more time, garnish, deep and lengthy description like a map to an uncharted island. I like to think everything I write is done for a reason, sometimes not so immediately obvious.

As far as dialogue is concerned, it would be virtually impossible to remember someone's exact words word for word. What I have done, painstakingly, is try to capture the essence of that person's words and thoughts, given the setting and circumstances. In some rare cases, and if the dialogue is short and particularly close to me, I would like to think I got that person's words down pat; but being human, I am subject to error and can only promise I will do my best. As the Marines would say, we just want 100 percent. Well, I will attempt it, but I doubt you'll get it. If I can hit 90 percent, I'll be happy. Just read it and know it is totally sincere and from my guts and heart.

All the photos and other documents and papers are primarily meant to support the story and help to authenticate the facts.

Based on that quotient and *Confessions of a Surviving Alien*'s success, I may continue breaking those shackles of procrastination and perhaps write a sequel quickly on its heels (I already have it outlined). I will also have an accompanying Web site bearing the same title to share further with you.

That said, I will give you keys to the story and share some *Webster's* definitions based on the word ***alien***. Think of these references, and don't be alien to your own thoughts and interpretations should they be serious or not. I've selected ones I feel are fitting:

* **Belonging to another country or people; foreign**
* **Strange; not natural**
* **Opposed or repugnant**
* **An outsider**
* **Applied to a resident who bears political allegiance to another country**

* **Stranger, to a person from another region who is unacquainted with local people, customs, etc.**

And *alienate/alienation*:

* **To make unfriendly; estrange (his behavior alienated his friends)**
* **To cause to be withdrawn or detached, as from one's society**

* **Separation; aversion; aberration (of the mind); estrangement or detachment**

Sincerely,

Jon
www.JonMeade.com

Prologue

It takes an end to make a beginning.
—JM

May 1997

As the plane started its gradual descent into Minneapolis, my heart suddenly dropped with it. My feet felt like they were being welded to the floor. I felt a flush come over me and my core body temperature rise. It was an eerie feeling, almost as if I was somehow removed from the moment, not hearing a word murmured by the captain. My head turned to the opposite cabin window as I heard, "Jon, thanks for all your kind thoughts and prayers, but I'm in a better place now . . ." The invisible presence left as quickly as it appeared.

Movement in my guts told me that my dad had passed, that he was gone. I felt like reaching out to him in the vacant air, but it could hold no weight. My thoughts were buoyant, my tears contained. Even though that inner voice I heard from my dad was strong and clear, and seemed like it came out of the very clouds we were flying through, I dismissed them. They were words that penetrated my brain but didn't really sink in. In a sense, I was throwing my head and heart a life preserver.

All the way on the flight, I played Frank Sinatra and Dean Martin on my recorder, two of my dad's favorites, which had become mine. Just as the descent was announced and we were told to sever all recording devices, the song that got cut off, not finishing, was Sinatra's defining hit, "My Way." The irony of that song being stopped just before I heard my father's words consumed my emotions. I replayed Dad's words over and over again and felt like I had seen a faint image of him. But maybe it was my own mind connecting his face to his words. I thought he may have ended it with some loving words, but I was never sure exactly. What he did say left its mark, and I was surely touched.

Also along the way, I constantly prayed that Dad would hang on until I arrived. I prayed, I wished, I humbly requested that he stay alive until I got to his hospital bedside. I drank beer and coffee on the flight, as I was nervous and fidgety. I got up and went to the bathroom. Then I went back and drank some more. It went in and out with relatively no effect in between. I kept listening to music while running the gamut of emotions through my head. I just about felt guilty as I knew I was driven by a strong personal desire, an ulterior motive: the motives of release, sharing, forgiveness, love—and a deep, dark secret my father had held inside his entire adult life. One that he didn't know I knew. It was time, on his deathbed, to tell him I did and that I understood and forgave him. But it didn't happen. I was denied that destiny of revealing to him that I knew. I knew it all. And I wanted to tell him for years but couldn't. He was still too overpowering, and I didn't want to have to reveal my source, which might cause extreme problems. So I waited.

And I waited too long. Now he was gone and my opportunity with him.

Inside, I was absolutely crushed. I procrastinated again. It would have been for me—and him. But thinking back, it was his image and distinct words—delivered with such unusual softness and ease—that remarkably gave me relief and peace of mind. As I am writing this, I now recall the rest of his words, although paraphrasing a bit. He said he knew I knew (his secret) and was so touched or impressed that I was so driven to tell him, understand him, and forgive him. Almost immediately thereafter, I felt a certain serenity, enough to be a little playful with my thoughts and imagination. I opened a prayer to God, asking if he could pass along the message to Dean Martin and Frank Sinatra, who just passed away himself several weeks before, and maybe the rest of the Rat Pack. I went ahead and spoke to "them" as my words unfolded, paraphrasing.

No doubt, the rum and Coke and coffee chimed in. I was glib and mentioned that my dad loved their singing and songs and that he was a good, but tough, guy too and if they could welcome him, Dad, into their fold by greeting him through the wooden (probably not pearly) gates and show him the ropes, providing they were all in the same place. I went on a little more and felt strangely relieved by my distant encounter. Dad himself would have gotten a kick out of my playful prayer and laughed. I figuratively and literally felt I communicated with them, especially Frank, as his death just preceded Dad's. Funny, but Sinatra's name will come up again later in my story.

We were about to touch down when my pre-boarding thoughts came back with a vengeance. If I would not have gone to Greece with my girlfriend Elaine three weeks before, I could have easily made it to Dad's bedside. And I could have fulfilled my desire and destiny. I could have avoided this had I not gone. Weeks before we left for Greece—a long planned trip—Dad was feeling ill, weak, and frail at eighty. I told my mother to keep me advised of his condition so I could feel comfortable leaving. He actually starting feeling somewhat better so Mom told me to go, not to worry, and have fun. I also talked to Dad, and he strongly supported me going on the overseas trip. We did. No sooner had we gotten home to San Diego than Mom called and softly told me that Dad was in intensive care and his doctor said he could expire anytime. I got an emergency flight out and left, now feeling quite guilty.

Immediately upon those aircraft doors opening, I pushed my way upfront and out of the plane, running to the nearest phone in the lobby. I reached my mom, who knew when I was due in, and I sensed right away what my vision and Dad's words said.

"Jon," she said, "Dad didn't make it, he died this morning . . . I'm sorry."

"Really, Mom," I responded, "he's already gone?" I knew it; I was merely confirming it to myself. The walk down to baggage claim was the longest ever. Every step felt like walking through cement.

I went to see Dad's body, along with my sisters, on a gurney at the funeral home before he would be cremated. It was a little hard to believe that this bigger-than-life guy was dead. My youngest sister Joni shared her last memories of him, bedside. She said with tears in her eyes that Dad looked into her face and said he wished he could have done more—been more productive, successful, what-have-you, basically apologizing for a life he apparently felt didn't provide enough. That was very revealing, I felt, and touched every nerve in my body. Joni and Dad were especially close so that little remembrance was . . . so sad. And Joni answered him back in what I knew were soft, deep expressions of affection. It calmed me and made me feel good, hearing that. I stayed back home in New Brighton for the week, giving my father's eulogy days later at the church I grew up in, Messiah, where I had been confirmed Lutheran at thirteen. I mentioned Sinatra's song "My Way" as it was also fitting for my dad's life—he certainly did it his way, and despite all his challenges and hardships, he continued his way until the end.

I joked afterward to my mother and sisters Judy, Janet, and Joni as we left the church, saying, "Well, this was one sure way to get Dad into church—actually me too—wasn't it?" We shared a light laugh and bade farewell to John Fredrick Meade.

He surely would have laughed himself at my lighthearted humor, both for the truth of it and the levity.

Volume One

Parts I and II

The dawn looms in bright and dull.
—JM

PART I

(BV: Before Vietnam)

*Success is not final, failure is not fatal: It is
the courage to continue that counts.*
—Winston Churchill

Be patient: In time, even an egg will walk.
—Chinese fortune cookie

Chapter One

August 1946

I was born on August 11 in a Methodist hospital in Minneapolis, Minnesota, of Norwegian, Swedish, Scots-Irish (the last name) and Danish (or what I grew up thinking was Danish) parents. My father was anything but a religious man, but in the case of my birth, he insisted that I be born and baptized as a Methodist even though the faith would not be followed up on subsequently. After my birth, my mother and grandmother returned me to the family home in Columbia Heights, a close suburb of downtown Minneapolis. Years later, I found out that my father wasn't present. I was never told why, and I never pressed for an answer. From a young age—and continuing—I would ask many questions, mostly from an inquisitive nature, that would go into deaf ears, except for a few superficial answers I heard. It always was enough as I was not an insistent kid. My parents would sometimes reminisce about the past and tell me about leaving Grandma's house and moving into their first home, which was this very modest, converted old service station made into a rental house. It was a one-roomer within the city limits that they had laughs over. My sister Judy was born while living there.

My first memories, however—at perhaps two to three years old—go back to my grandmother's house, the same one that would change hands many times within the family over the subsequent years. It was just this one incident when I was very young. My aunt Christine was at the keys of the piano in the living room. I distinctly recall my mother, nicknamed "Babe" by family and friends, lifting me up and putting me on the top of the piano. My other aunt, Marilyn, both my mother's sisters, were fussing over me and smiling as Chris started the chorus for "That Lucky Old Sun" by Guy Mitchell. She played while I sang a little good hunk of the lyrics:

That lucky old sun has nothing to do but roll around heaven all day . . . Toll for my money, beg for my pay . . . till I'm crippled and gray . . . But that lucky old sun has nothing to do . . . but roll around heaven all day

They laughed while I soaked up the attention. Then I remember Chris, I believe, picking me up and putting me down on the floor, where I would choreograph the lyrics with body movements, accenting the working phrases "toll for my money, beg for my pay, till I'm crippled and gray." I remember the adoring laughter and adulating eyes. I guess I was quite the miniature entertainer at that tender age. My showbiz career was short-lived although my dad enjoyed many performances as well. But I left the stage behind—except for a whimsical stint in Hollywood many years later—to just grow up and be a typical mud-and-puddle kid. I was a huge Hopalong Cassidy fan when young and had the entire garb: scarf, cowboy shirt and hat, pant leggings/straps, and complete Hopalong double six-guns and holsters. This was just another young boy's desire to be a cowboy, Soldier, or warrior of some kind, fighting for right and justice, much like my hero example. But it was innocent as no matter how many bad guys Hopalong shot and killed, the hero always prevailed, saved the day, and the episode ended positively on a high note, always with some subtle message that good overcame evil.

Years later, my dad always brought up the story of how he lost me at around two to two and a half years of age. He would repeat this tale often over the years. It was during his full-time upholstery years around Minneapolis. As the story went, he took me with him to follow up on some upholstered chairs he had done. Although it was not like him at all, he knew he'd be gone for just a moment or two, but he left me locked in the car while he quickly ran in. He came out and I was gone. Missing. Someone could have taken me, he thought. But he quickly figured that I had watched him lock the door with the pull-up and push-down little knob and had simply pulled it up and left. Anyway, he nearly fainted as his heart dropped, realizing all the traffic on the road he parked on and the close proximity of the mighty Mississippi River.

He dashed around from neighborhood storefront to storefront, asking if they had seen a little boy with a cowboy hat on and bib coveralls. One lady told Dad she saw this little boy fitting that description running down the street toward the river, laughing all the way. He ran after me, caught me, and I acted as though it was all a big funny game. But it was a potentially fatal learning experience that my dad admittedly never got over. Even retelling the tale made him cringe, although he'd chuckle too. He said he never let me out of his sight after that. Well, as it turned out, as I grew out of that cute little boy stage, he reneged on his words and seldom seemed to know or care where I was or what I was doing.

A particular baby story he always repeated was me being stuck in the penis with a diaper pin by mom. He said even the doctor bawled her out. But I lived through it and used the penis very successfully.

Several years passed, and we lived on the east side, close to the Mississippi River dividing Minneapolis from Saint Paul, in a tiny tar paper house. It was in the fall, and while rather cold, it had not snowed yet and the river was running full strength. I was always the explorer, with my two-year-old younger sister Judy always in tow. I was probably three and a half or so. We went down to the Mississippi for a look-see—and a memory that will haunt me forever.

There was this huge angled embankment edging the river, maybe covering fifty feet. I started to walk down the embankment while Judy hesitated. I took her hand and assured her it would be okay and I would protect her from the whatever-it-was-worth-blind-coaxing-the-blind-into-unfamiliar-territory department. The Mississippi had an earned reputation of being unpredictable and dangerous as it was deep, fast, and full of buried debris. My dad and mom constantly warned me to stay completely away from it. Of course, the more they repeated that warning, the more enticing it became. Away we went down the embankment—sliding, really—until we reached the river's edge. I recall the details from this point on very vividly. I noted the water running much faster than when I was looking at it from afar. It looked scary. Suddenly, the sand on the river's edge under Judy's feet started crumbling, pulling her feet up to her ankles into the cold, murky water. As she cried, I panicked—but I reacted. I had the sense out of sheer fear to lie down against the angled embankment and dig my heels into the side's loose sand.

Now, I had both of Judy's hands and arms in my hands and held on for dear life. I'll never forget the look of terror in her face as she looked in my eyes. I felt like crying myself but didn't have time. While I continued digging in, I felt the power of the water starting to drag her lower. I knew I had to act fast and pull as if my life, and hers, depended on it. I yelled, screamed, at her not to let go no matter what. I could feel her little hands clutching mine as I kept digging my heels in and back-crawling my body up totally flat. Every inch was a fight, but I finally got her out of the water and the ensuing current. Now, despite being overwhelmed, I had to keep on my back and continue inching up. It was like it would never end, but we made it. We were standing at the very top. I can't really remember anything after that. I think we could have gotten away with our dangerous prank had it not been for our dirty, wet clothes, especially Judy's. I don't know how that ending played out, but one thing I'm sure, our folks never knew the whole story. I must have given my mom, who was home while Dad was at work, a real creative excuse because it went by the wayside, like Judy and I nearly did.

Sometime around the kindergarten age, I was ring bearer at the wedding for my aunt Marilyn and new uncle Dick, who was a WWII Veteran and Bataan Death March and POW survivor. He would later play a major part in my quest to join the military myself as soon as I was old enough. But at that time, I was content to play warlike games like any normal American kid.

Kindergarten. What innocence, that first year of school and Mrs. Lovold. She was this short, rotund woman whose heart was as big as her body. She wore glasses and was always smiling. We went to school at Irondale, this old pre–WWII built, two-story wood schoolhouse, the last one around that area of New Brighton. The old-fashioned school was for kindergarten and the first and second grades. Each of the two levels was adorned with the American flag. We always recited the Pledge of Allegiance at attention before school began. From that young age, I always felt proud and a surge of tingles in my body. I took first grade, maybe second too, from Mrs. Dodge, who instructed us on the meaning of the flag and the allegiance. If we didn't show our respects to the flag properly, she would correct you as soon as the pledge was over.

Most of us boys feared Mrs. Dodge because she took no crap from anyone, as evidenced by the measuring stick she kept at her side and used on our hands, but she probably still was the object of many boys' first crushes, including mine. Even at that age of six to seven, she looked pretty and well built. She also was responsible for kicking many roughhouse types out of class—and school. I remember one time when we were going to the circus in the morning after handing in our homework, she told three of us to finish up lunch and join the rest in the awaiting bus. She sternly said we had five minutes to finish every last bite of our homemade brown-bag lunches. I finished first and went to get up as Mrs. Dodge came back in to check on our progress. Just as she turned the corner to come into the classroom, Betty Lund, a cute but straight-faced imp, quickly slid her Hostess cupcakes on my desk and left. While Mrs. Dodge was congratulating Betty on finishing all her lunch, I had to explain my new unfinished cupcakes. I tried to explain without ratting on Ms. Lund, but it didn't work and I just gave up. Needless to say, Betty and I would never be friends even though I had to endure her company until the day we graduated high school. She always had this little grin she'd flash. Sympathy never worked on Mrs. Dodge. Never! She was tough as spikes. So I had to stay behind with this fussy little fat kid that wouldn't finish his mother's bag of veggies. But it was no wonder this kid was playing with obesity because that lunch bag of his was filled to the brim. He cried like a baby when he realized he wasn't going to the circus. I was still seething inside at Betty. I had looked forward to this trip for so long.

We both watched from the second story brokenhearted as the bus to the circus, with little Betty, pulled away. I still thought Mrs. Dodge was pretty. Well, maybe I'd changed that to okay, at least for that day. My buddy Gary, several years my senior, would later tell me his run-in with Mrs. Dodge. He said he pretended to be stuck on a math problem and just couldn't get it. Oftentimes, Gary had noticed that she would bend over the desktop to work on the problem with the kid. Gary was a boyish rascal so he couldn't resist sliding his pencil down her bra until she caught him. He spent the remainder of the day in the corner with the dunce hat on. Gary was mad at her for being punished and embarrassed, but he too still carried a dimmed torch for her. We both tried the old apple trick since we saw it on the *Our Gang* TV show, but that fizzled. I even gave her an extra apple for double brownnosing—but it didn't work. She was, however, the perfect prelude to military boot camp that we would both face years later. While a stern taskmaster, she was indeed a great teacher. I know because one time, she made me write the same word I had misspelled one hundred times and then put it in sentence form and recite it out loud over and over. Yep, she was fabulous and I'll never forget her. I always thought that if she saw an ant on the chalkboard, she'd capture and torture it. But the ant would have learned its lesson.

Oh, later in the book, I'll reveal how I got a small measure of revenge on Betty without even planning it.

Chapter Two

It was around this time we lived in a house that I absolutely loved. It was small, but a little bigger than the previous small ones as this one had a fairly big bedroom. There were two main reasons for this. First, it was up on a slight hill but sat on about an acre or so with a woods in the back, trees everywhere, including big sprawling oaks, huge treed land behind us, and a creek and spring facing the side, nasty as it was. It was here that I developed my love for nature. My Dad always did his upholstery on the side plus held one of his many blue-collar jobs. No matter what the weather or if he got a cold or the flu, he never missed work, which was quite typical back then for stand-up guys. My mother was your typical stay-at-home housewife. And Judy and I were just normal kids, forever seeking adventure, at least me.

Second, our neighbors were the Hillsdales—father George, mother Roscile, Gary, and Marlene. George was 100 percent German, and Roscile was 100 percent Swedish. George was a plumber who worked at his brother's "Copper is King" business. Roscile was like my mom—well, sort of—staying at home and keeping a perfect house. Oftentimes, I wondered if anyone lived there because it was absolutely spotless; nothing was ever out of place or even moved, compared to our house that was obviously lived in. Gary, although several years older, quickly became my best friend—more like a brother—and we were basically inseparable. There was a well-worn path between our two houses. Their place was bigger but still small and had another open and treed lot adjacent to it. Trees and woods were common. I even loved our address at 6969 Knollwood Drive, a simple narrow two-lane asphalt road that passed our utopia, which was what I actually considered this place to be. I never ever wanted to move. It was by far the happiest time of my adolescence.

It was also during this time frame that Gary and I were constantly playing war games and spending hours on end drawing sketches of paper combat. There were always two sides, us and the enemy, and jeeps and tanks and guns of every kind. Gary was a master to incorporate plenty of guts and gore with his gifted imagination and artist hand. He was like a Michelangelo of warfare while I was just a grunt on paper, drawing figures more like morphed sticks and ill-defined images. We loved it though and often kept our missions cataloged and in folders. Gary, being older, was the well-deserved general while I was along for the imagined mayhem as a first lieutenant. We both had uncles who had served in WWII and constantly watched all the war movies of the fifties. We both believed being a warrior and fighting for our country was the most honorable thing in the world, with youth dictating idealism.

But my folks had better ideas where they wanted to settle. And unlike the Hillsdales, we rented our house and it was apparently their American dream to own. My parents had heard about the first housing track of its kind in our area, but farther out in the suburbs. They loaded us up one day, and we went out there to check it out. They loved it: new bigger house, good-sized fenced yard, change, and a new beginning. I hated it: it was totally barren, no trees, no greenery, no nature, no Gary, change and a new beginning, and all the houses were the same except for their colors. Fear engulfed me like a pending tornado. But I was respectfully quiet and subdued. When we left and drove back home next to Gary's, I blankly gazed out the back window thinking, "What a name for a housing development? Circle Pines!" There were no pines. It was dull, drab, and had a blank canvas without paint. In my young mind, I thought I was sentenced to a concentration camp of sorts. I dreaded the thought. It was like being trapped in an awake nightmare.

After the new house purchase, we would have to pack up and move, but not before having to tell Gary we were moving. That drive was less than twenty miles, but it seemed like twenty thousand. Like twins joined at the hip, I dreaded telling Gary about the move, let alone more. We lived there since I was just under four. My mind thought back as if I were in some trance and my young life was flashing before my eyes.

I ran a personal movie through my head of the last five years on Knollwood Drive. I remembered them in segments. I'd never forget the tornado we were warned about that ended up coming our way, seemingly right down the street like some locomotive, but ended up quickly being the caboose. Still, it strangely made the environment dead silent as my sister and I hid behind a couch and under a table.

But it fizzled out even quicker than the strong winds whisked through. It then rained like crazy.

I recalled the fall of Gary Grable from a huge tree across the street in another woods. I was there with all the neighborhood kids, and Gary made a jump from one treetop to another. He didn't make it and fell about twenty-five feet and hit his head on a tree stump. It knocked him out and spilled blood all over. It was a terrible sight, and many of us thought he killed himself. But he didn't, and although he had a lengthy recovery process and suffered lingering problems, he went on to a normal childhood and beyond. Watching that fall and subsequent splat of his head against that stump always made me cognizant of being too careless in my adventures and risk taking although I would probably always err on the side of risk as opposed to safety. Usually. Mom would be constantly warning me to be careful not to get hurt. And while I understood it, risk taking for her seemed to always be for others, not her son. She was content to be a stay-at-home mother—common in the day—and super-protected by my dad. Mom may have been overly cautious, but she meant well.

During that time we lived there, numerous visitors, family, friends, and others would always rave about our drinking water, which came from a very deep well. We had a hand pump outside and in until finally my dad had someone come in and change the indoor one over to faucets. Even that guy raved about how ice-cold and delicious our water was. Even on the hottest days in the summer, drinking that water was a genuine treat. Compared to the city water that was running through the pipes of Grandma's house, our well water was light-years different and better.

It was during those years at Knollwood that we were all introduced to television. It was the early fifties, and the little BW box had just a handful of channels and was an incredible novelty. Uncle Milty, a.k.a. Milton Berle, was the big cheese in those days, along with George Burns and Gracie Allen, Rosemary Clooney, Howdy Doody, Roy Rogers, Gene Autry, and of course, Hopalong Cassidy, played by William Boyd. On the local channel, right there being beamed from downtown Minneapolis, was this character named Axel, who had a program called *Axel and His Dog*. Besides local commentary, Axel aired all the *Our Gang* (*Little Rascals*) shows, which all kids loved. Following Spanky and Alfalfa was like normal kid protocol.

Soon, we would be getting *Laurel and Hardy* shows and suspense with Charlie Chan. But we also still listened to radio, especially my mother, who never seemed able to get the channel on track. It always was off enough to pick up static and be somewhat muddled. But back then, I didn't care as much as I would in my teen years as I was constantly playing outside.

One day, while playing over at the neighbors who had two boys, Kenny and Wayne, whom Gary and I often played with—harassed would be more accurate—we were playing with frogs who had often adorned the basement window wells. During that time, without us kids knowing it, Mrs. Engquist, an incredibly giving lady, was sitting above the window wells inside behind her sewing machine. Numerous years later, Mom would tell me that Mrs. Engquist told her that I was coming up with all these stories about frogs and keeping her sons glued to the area. She said she was fascinated by my imagination and creative storytelling and wouldn't have doubted that someday I would become a writer or some such creative person. It was the first and most appreciated compliment early in my life, finally revealed to me by Mom when reflecting years later on the old neighborhood.

In those days, we would only be indoors for meals, chores, and sleep. Otherwise, it was nonstop hard playing and exploring. We played running games like pump-pump-pull-away in the Hillsdales' front yard. We raked leaves into huge piles and jumped into them, sometimes from low tree branches; we walked everywhere; we ran, fished at the creek, made tunnels, forts, tree houses—I even peed on Judy's head once—and a host of other rascally, boyish things that would have probably made Huck Finn and Tom Sawyer envious. We got bruises, scrapes, cuts, strains; but when we went to sleep at night, we needed no help from the sandman. We survived. And we took a certain kids' pride in that survival. Gary fell off a silo once at his uncle's farm in Wisconsin and cracked his head open, giving him a concussion. He was laid up for a few but soon returned to the childhood wars with a vengeance.

I suffered my losses too. I had two puppies that were killed, the last one being Butterball, who was hit by a train. I found him on the tracks. I was devastated. I got solace from that animal. Incredibly, I got the greatest sympathy from my dad, who explained the pros and cons of dog ownership and the responsibility therein. But, he said, sometimes things in life are just out of your control. He helped me bury Butterball with full respects. You see, he loved animals too. But his picks of pets were sometimes puzzling. During this same time frame, he had a huge pet cat named Tom (original, huh?). Judy and I were scared to death of this cat and wanted nothing to do with it. Dad defended him to us, and Mom, quite often. One time when I was leaving the house to go out and play, Tom jumped on my back with his claws out from high on a tree branch. It startled me and hurt. That damn cat acted like he wanted a piece of my flesh.

Dad would usually just say he wanted to play and wouldn't hurt us. He jumped Judy too, and she would cry and cry, being scared sometimes to go outside. Mom would be livid and insist that Dad do something. But he didn't have to. Other stray tom cats killed him, and Dad found him dragging himself home after the last of his customary battles. I said a prayer of thanks after Tom's demise. That cat was the ultimate nonstop battler. Dad got along with him fine, which just proves everyone has a soul mate of some kind. Thinking back, I believe they saw eye to eye because Tom was such a fighter—like him—and he admired that. Dad had no time for cowards.

Dad himself had the disposition of a wild animal sometimes, like shades of Tom, but my Mom pretty much contained it, bottling it like some mysterious love potion. However, he would surprise you in the other extreme with incredible passion and understanding. Like the time I swallowed a marble. I was lying on the living room floor in the evening, throwing marbles about three feet above me and catching them. Stupid, but it was something to do. Before I knew it, I lost concentration and a marble went straight up, a perfect throw, and right down into my mouth and throat. I immediately started flailing and couldn't breathe. My dad noticed my actions and moved right in, giving me a slight jar and shake. Gulp, down it went, but it felt like a big rock. I was so relieved as was Dad—and Mom. But Mom was a little mad at me for pulling such a dumb stunt like that while Dad was quite soft, understanding, and patient. He just told me to learn a lesson from it and he would sort through my fecal matter to fish it out, proving that whatever goes in must go out. As a son, it was probably the only real crap I would ever put him through.

Across the street from the Hillsdales was this unruly criminal-like teen, also named Gary, who liked to terrorize us occasionally. One time, it got out of control and this thug dragged Gary across the street and into his yard and started pounding on him. I came around after the worst of it, and together with Gary, we went inside and told Gary's father, George, who had forearms like Popeye and not an ounce of fat. He went into the closet and emerged with a shotgun and went out in his front yard and yelled at the older teen to back off and leave his hands off his son. I don't remember the rest, but obviously there was an impasse and tempers cooled down and shots weren't fired. Later, his parents apologized to George and Gary and any further personal war was averted. After we returned to Gary's house, we realized that George not only didn't have the gun loaded, but he also had no shells on his person. But his scare tactic worked, scaring us *all*.

Chapter Three

Then there was the time Gary ran away. He got into a fight with his sister Marlene about the tire swing on the big oak tree. Gary's mom, Roscile, quickly tipped off my mom—they were close friends just like Gary and I were—and Mom told me. They told me he was really mad and left down Knollwood with his cane fishing pole and a little bag of something. Mom was making chocolate chip cookies so she quickly took a handful out, bagged them, and told me to get going. I was on my way.

There were a series of three large hills on Knollwood on the way to Kettleson's Market at the top, across from our church. Gary was about halfway up so I had to run to catch up. He barely turned as I joined his side. I started trying to talk him into coming back. I also tried to listen to his reasoning for his hasty departure. He talked, I listened. But I wasn't penetrating his armor—until I took out the bag of cookies, still warm, and offered Gary some, then the whole bag. I could sense his weakening demeanor. I said, "C'mon back, Gar, and we'll have some cold milk with these. C'mon, please." We never made it back to the milk as Gary polished them off and called off his trip. How my mom's cookies were ever able to coax him back is one of life's more puzzling mysteries? My mom's cookies were . . . not good. They were mushy soft on the inside and burned on the outside, with the taste going from uncooked cookie dough to burned pastry. On the other hand, Gary's mother's cookies were to die for, absolutely the most perfect chocolate chip cookies ever made. And here's the kicker: they were made from the identical Toll House chocolate chip cookie recipe.

It must have been the oven. Roscile said it. Mom said it. But it saved the day with Gary's runaway plans so they must have had some magical ingredients that could only benefit people outside of the family. And those in great need. My Mom did make incredible ginger snaps and date bars.

But young robust boys like to eat, and we ate loads full of vegetables and fruits in those early days.

We loved green apples, chokecherries, tomatoes, rhubarb, cucumbers, watermelon, cantaloupe, and anything else on vines and branches. The only trouble was, neither my parents nor Gary's grew their own gardens although we always picked Gary's chokecherry tree naked. So we had to make visits on neighbors' gardens at night and fill up, sometimes to the point of getting extreme bellyaches, especially from green apples. We were living in an area where most everyone had a big garden. We were like thieves in the night who had to obey our parents by eating lots of vegetables, but not from our own houses. We referred to these night garden visits as raids. "Let's go on a raid tonight." It really was nice that so many neighbors shared their produce with us. Sometimes we even left our remnants behind, rinds and the like, as a way of saying thanks.

Produce wasn't the only thing I ate at home. Fresh fish, crappies, sunnies, northerns, and an occasional walleye adorned our plates, but not before we had to clean them the old-fashioned way—keeping the bones in, without filleting them. Dad was an absolute master fisherman and always, always got his limit. He took me with him once in a while, but I saw it more as an adventure in lake torture as his temper always got the best of him and me. But he would lighten up somewhat afterward when demanding I help him clean the catch. I think the only reason he brought me is so he could double the limit with my pole. There were piles and piles of fish. He actually talked to me fairly normally during the cleaning affair, and if I was lucky, I mean really lucky, he might throw me a small compliment, like a fish bone. But the way it was delivered seemed more like a reserved notion to throw back a fish—it wasn't easy for him.

Emotions with him were strange bedfellows. He had incredible passion for life and defenseless things, like animals, poor folks, old folks, and young kids. He showed those affections through his behavior. But with many emotional things, he seemed to have this internal conflict going on, like a combination of extreme sorrow with outrage. One night, in the middle of a major snowstorm and cold spell, our phone rang. It was a weeknight, and Dad answered it. I woke up because I was nearest to the phone. Judy was sleeping with the folks as they sometimes brought her in with them because she was scared a lot and was a mommy's girl. Soon, I heard light sobs from Dad, and I knew something was wrong. I got up on one elbow and asked what was wrong. He increased the kerosene in the potbelly stove and quickly started putting his socks on.

He didn't look at me but said, "My brother Wes is dead."

"What happened?" I asked.

"He's gone, he finally did it." He didn't say anything more to me, but Mom was now awake and he said, "Les (his other brother) told me he drank himself to death."

"Oh no," my Mom replied sadly.

"Yeah, it was rubbing alcohol or something. I'm going to the hospital and will probably have to take the day off." He left and that was that.

His eldest brother, Wesley, was a highly respected police officer who had just finished his exam for detective. He had a beautiful wife and three children. He was just in his thirties. But what that man and my dad and the family endured many years before undoubtedly proved to contribute to his undoing.

I think one of the reasons why my memory is so keen going back so far is because I was always trying to figure out my dad and everything related to him. When I was very young and could think, I started, and it only increased with my age. I went over many scenarios in my mind and recalled all the details over and over again. It all just stuck with me, like a massive strip of flypaper. But it wasn't just Dad and his side of the family. It was also my mom's side. My mom's mother, Hilda, was married to my grandfather, Sam Mattson (changed from Madsen), when I was very young. Sam, who came to America from Denmark, was a mason and made old-fashioned blockhouses. Grandma would also say that he came over with some wrestling contract but wouldn't follow protocol or cooperate.

After Dad and Mom got married, Dad would sometimes work for him and often remarked how difficult he was to work with. Talk about the kettle calling itself black. Grandpa Sam always wore a scowl on his face and was built like a tree stump, solid and strong. He was much older however and old-school, set in his ways in the extreme. He ruled over the house, Hilda, Marilyn, Mom and Chris like a hardened taskmaster. It seems I was his favorite when I was a little tyke. He put little wheels on my old potty chair and watched me chase the family dog, Tippy, around the front room. They told me it was about the only time he laughed. He would sit in his easy chair with a corn-cob pipe, watch me chase the dog relentlessly, and laugh like crazy.

According to Gram or Mom, or both, after Mom had her tonsils out and was recovering in the hospital, Sam went there, picked her up, put her head and upper body in a gunny sack, and flung her over his shoulder and took her home, against the hospital's wishes. As the story went, the neighbors feared what happened as blood was coming out of Mom's mouth and it was going down the back of Sam. It must have been quite a sight. As he got older and I was still a young kid, one time I found him in this old wooden chair in the backyard, his body all slumped over and looking dead. I ran into the house and told Gram. She just said the old chute was drunk and to not worry. I went across the street to tell a friend and then play. The neighbors were sitting on the steps saying they wished the old buzzard would just die, as everyone would be better off.

He would recover and just retire to the house he made for himself out in the garage. He wanted to live by himself. He would also die by himself not too many years later when he drove his car off a bridge several stories down and landed on the railroad tracks. He was in his late seventies, but the fall didn't kill him; pneumonia did shortly thereafter. He was highly intoxicated when the accident happened.

The day arrived when we were all packed up and ready to move from Knollwood to Circle Pines.

They got their wish to buy this new house for around $10,000, including appliances. It was the day I dreaded. It was here. How would I say farewell to Gary? I had this big wooden chest that I had put my play stuff in and really loved it. But I decided to ease the tension and give it to Gary. He knew I loved that chest and refused to accept it, but I insisted. The rest is a little hazy, but I remember trying hard not to ball as I looked back to see Gary crying himself with his elbows on the chest and head cupped in his hands. This was virtually the first time in five years that we didn't have contact. It was the saddest day in my entire young life, even worse than losing Butterball, and my parents knew it. I could feel their awareness, but our wheels were on their way to Circle Pines as I took a last look at all the neighborhood trees.

Settling down in Circle Pines was a challenge. The houses were ridiculously the same, except for entry doors on opposite sides and a small variety of colors. Not a single tree in sight. Every house was barren and boring. All houses were elevated up from the streets, which were designed as if someone dropped ropes of asphalt from the sky. The folks set up bunk beds in our bedroom, and the house had a stone-cold block basement, which to me was its only saving grace. But it still wasn't Knollwood, and I knew it never would be. Gary and the old neighborhood seemed planets away.

I got into fights, especially with two bullies—John Buhl and this Butch character. I actually became pretty good friends with John, but he was always picking on smaller guys and I felt continually compelled to straighten him out, usually with two to three punches to the face, next to his house. Butch, I wouldn't have been surprised if he became a criminal later in life. He was one year older than me but looked ten years older. A rough little punk, and I first approached him my very first day waiting for the school bus. He was terrorizing boys and girls while waiting. Then the bus came and he literally pushed everyone aside as he got to the front of the line. I started screaming at him to stop and I forgot what else. Some kids took me aside and said that I should be careful because of his family, not to involve them because Butch would get revenge. I kept it up and he sneered at me and said, "Do you know who you are talking to?"

I said I didn't care and he better stop what he was doing, or else. Well, the bus driver let him in with no comments, and nothing else was said by either of us. But he never pulled that same stunt the same way again. His whole family was plain weird. His brothers were into racing cars and motorcycles, and they were the first family to move into that development, according to them. Even Butch's mother was, well, a real character. The father was never around, and word had it that he was serving time, which should have been the case with the whole clan. And they were a clan. There were neighborhood clashes, police calls, and constant problems surrounding that home, if you could call it that. Instead of "home sweet home," it was more like "home bitter home." I'll tell you though, it did make me appreciate my own home more, and my parents—even Dad.

Even though I never started any fights, I was confident in my ability to defend myself. Dad, who was a huge boxing fan and quite fast and athletic, taught me the basic moves from a young age, but it was more in teasing than in constructive instruction. He would jab me and move around and slap me in the face with light swipes, then retreat to the side. I went after him, and he loved it as I never caught him. He would just keep that jab sticking in my face and head while I chased him with a vengeance. The madder I got, the more he laughed. I learned that even though it was totally frustrating, it was yet harmless. If it taught me one huge lesson besides the boxing, it was how to be relentless.

I had my first formal girlfriend at eleven. She was really cute and loved to kiss, so much so that on the school grounds she wouldn't let me go and the principal called us on it and we both had to go to detention. Meanwhile, at home one day alone while the folks were away shopping at Piggly Wiggly supermarket (first big shopping venue of its day in that area), this drop-dead gorgeous older girl down the street who loved to raze me found out I was home alone from my sister, whose friend was also her friend, and she came over and knocked on my bedroom window, then forced herself in through the opening. I was dumbfounded. She literally threw me back on the bed while kissing me and started ripping my clothes off. She was laughing the whole time but seemed to be also aroused. I was in full panic mode as despite this jaw-dropping beauty trying to get me naked, I was more scared of my Dad and what he might do if they walked in. She would nearly rip a piece of my clothing off, and I would desperately put them back on. I finally started yelling at her to leave while still trying to be nice about it. Finally, I just had to push her out the same window she slipped in. This was the first time I was made aware of my imploding maleness. I never forgave myself for that behavior. I should have given her, her way. I mean, at that age, how long could it have lasted? She was like a dream for a kid like me.

For years thereafter, I promised myself that if a girl ever did that to me again, especially as breathtaking as her, I would be on her bones like a young orthopedic surgeon.

Chapter Four

Circle Pines maybe wasn't so bad after all. Still, I always heard Knollwood calling me back, even the trees and the woods.

Soon thereafter, I discovered a huge never-ending woods across from the development and Highway 10. We attended church occasionally at this Lutheran facility, and it was sitting there by itself, surrounding by a woods—forest—so big it made the old neighborhood one seem pale in comparison. It was like a gift from God. I loved nature and soon found myself spending tons of time there with various friends or just myself. I also went small game hunting with a pump BB gun, shooting birds and whatever else was moving. I set traps and caught some small prey. One day, after catching this huge bird, I put him in a small box I had and brought him home. I guess I was somehow looking for some kind of nod from my dad for being a good hunter, as he went hunting occasionally and often brought back pheasants, ducks, even deer.

But I was in for a surprise. Dad was full of them. He saw that the bird's leg had been broken by my trap and very gently and compassionately told me that I couldn't eat this kind of bird, so why trap him, injure, and kill him? He told me all about the bird having as much right to live as people did. And that hunting should be reserved solely for food and necessity. He picked the bird up and softly examined it, saying, "Jon, we are going to have to put this poor guy out of his misery. The leg is too broken, and he seems to be in shock."

The tears started streaming down my cheeks. I sobbed while trying to catch my breath. I knew he was right and started apologizing to the bird. And to Dad. He was genuinely touched and told me to leave while he took care of the bird. Another lesson learned about hunting, life and death, priorities and Dad. Some days he would explode like a madman over nothing, other days he would exhibit the biggest heart and patience in the world. This day, it was the latter.

At eleven, I also played little league baseball. I mainly played catcher but sometimes the outfield. I was one of only two little league players that hit a home run that year. The park was unusually big and the fences a long way away. The biggest compliment I ever got back then was when I came to bat. I heard the buzz from parents and other little league followers saying, "If this kid can straighten out his swing and quit pulling the ball, watch out." Well, easier said than done. I had the power, all right, but broke more people's car windows that were parked along the street outside the left field fence than anyone by a long shot. Sometimes the men would get up from the bleachers and run to their cars to move them when I got up. It was actually funny, but not. I did, however, manage to straighten one out and get that home run.

That home run though was not my most predominate memory. It still hurts to this day, if I think back to it. I was playing catcher this particular game and warming up our number one pitcher, a kid who could really throw the heat. I was down in position, and we were going back and forth warming up.

I looked away for just a second or two to the bleachers—probably a pretty girl—while he blazed his final rocket to me. As my face returned to the front, the ball hit me straight in the face, knocking me end over end. I lay there dazed as the blood just poured out of my nose. My manager took his hankie out and put it over my nose, hoping to stop the river, but it filled it and other players rushed some towels over. It was a mess and hurt like all get-out with my nose completely numb and my face a balloon of pain.

The manager acted mad because I had to leave the game. He showed no remorse and seemed upset only because he'd be short a player. I don't remember going home. I don't recall my parents attending this game because if they did, Dad would have no doubt jumped from the bleachers and went after the manager, and the scene would have been much messier. I just remember Dad acting cool and patient and helping me lie down on the floor at home, where he helped me raise my legs and put them on the hassock. He then told me to breathe through my mouth and let the blood in my nose coagulate. I fell asleep, and when I awoke, my nose was completely shut as my nostrils were filled with hardened blood. I freaked at first, but Dad told me to relax and start to easily pull the blood out of my nostrils. I did it too fast the first time, and it started flowing all over again. Dad just smiled patiently and told me to lie back again and let it harden up. Next time, he said, "do it the way I said." I did.

That final attempt was something I'll never forget. I grabbed a little edge of the hardened blood in one nostril and gently started picking and pulling. As this long red licorice rope came out, I thought that my nose and face were coming apart. It was the weirdest feeling. And it hurt my entire sinus cavity as well. I then carefully pulled out the other rope of blood and took a sigh of relief and breaths through my nose. It was like life was being pumped back into me again. Dad said it was a miracle my nose was not broken, or worse.

After that experience, I did not return to little league the next year nor would my belief and confidence in team sports ever be quite the same; although there would be some team sports played later, my preference would be individual sports.

That eleventh year could be described in one word: pain. No, I mean three words: lots of pain!

Not long after the baseball incident, I experienced another painful experience. I got an abscessed tooth and was so weakened by it that my parents called Dr. Corn, our early lifetime family dentist. They explained it all to him and he said to rush me to his office. It was Sunday and was considered an emergency. I started walking to the car and literally fell into Dad's arms. He picked me up like a baby and put me in the front seat. I was really in a bad way. When Dad brought me into Dr. Corn's office and chair, he took a long look inside my mouth and said the front tooth was badly abscessed and would have to come out immediately because there were three large pus bags on the roof of my mouth and were slightly leaking. He said he would have to very carefully break them and remove them because of the deadly bacteria, which had been forming around the tooth for days. I got tons of Novocain and was in la-la land during the lengthy procedure.

Afterward, he told us that if Dad hadn't brought me in when he did, the pus bags could have broken on their own and been swallowed. He said that amount of infection and bacteria could have poisoned and even killed me, given my size and the large amount of infected area. Because of the rush on Sunday, Dr. Corn's dental assistant and receptionist couldn't make it; so as we left his office, Dad stopped at the desk and waited. Dr. Corn came out and said, "You can go, John, I'll send you a bill and set up more appointments for the false tooth and plate."

"No," my dad said, "I'll pay now like I always have. I don't like bills and debts."

Dr. Corn seemed taken aback and with great hesitation replied, "Okay, John, okay, if you insist."

He went into the desk and pulled out the receipt book while looking up at me. "You know, your dad, your dad . . . if all my patients were like him, I could probably retire in half the time." Dad just lightly grinned while I was tired but was content with the thoughts. Dad whipped out the cash without a blink and thanked him for taking me in on Sunday. Dr. Corn profusely thanked Dad as well. I sensed it was my turn to be polite so I thanked the dentist too through my half mouth full of cotton.

There were different versions on exactly what caused the abscess. Could it be a delayed reaction to being hit in the face by that baseball? One was my mother's angle that a heavy lock on the door to my father's portable fish house in the backyard I was playing in hit my tooth. The other was mine, which I kept to myself at the time, was that first girlfriend of mine had a twisted sense of humor and gave me a box of cookies for my birthday and one contained a small rock. I bit down hard on it, and it immediately produced a deep sense of nerve pain. That was the end of our brief relationship. I could never figure why she could do such a thing. Maybe she was just starting her menstruation cycle and took it out on me. Who knows, but it cost me a tooth.

Later, I learned from Dr. Corn that the X-rays showed upon close examination a tooth growing inside of a tooth, which turned out to be the first of its kind in Minnesota and among only a few in the entire recorded dental world. It was so rare that Dr. Corn contacted the University of Minnesota, and they in turn wanted to encase it and put it on display at the university. We gave Dr. Corn and the university permission and up it went. I never did see it as I figured I needed no reminders of what I went through with it. So with that revelation, it put a new twist on the cause of my abscess. Maybe it was a lock, or maybe it was a rock, or a little of both, but the tooth-inside-a-tooth thing made me a celebrity of sorts, according to Dr. Corn, at least at the university and in dental school. The trade-off wasn't worth it in my eyes. I would have preferred my tooth back in all honesty, damn the notoriety.

Even though our parents didn't like it, Gary and I biked to each other's house for sleepovers, having to pedal along Highway 10. It was quite a dangerous journey, and we ended up doing it very little. But because I was so motivated to visit the old neighborhood, Dad actually offered to drive me once in a while. My folks realized I was miserable, and even my sister missed her girlfriends back around Knollwood. Dad could have at least planted a tree or so but didn't. He just put in plain grass like everyone else. More and more, I'd venture across the highway to the big woods, sometimes just walking with our dog, Duke, a springer spaniel, down along the woods' infrequent dirt roads. It seemed like I never saw anyone there, and I loved it. It was like my salvation moving to Circle Pines. Duke was this incredible dog that Dad had brought home from the railroad where he was working as a crane operator. Duke was a stray that everyone loved, and Dad adopted him. But it seemed that Duke must not have liked Circle Pines much anyway as he ran away. Another dog lost and another reason to hate Circle Pines.

Not long thereafter, upon leaving my old beat-up bike in the driveway one day, Dad came home from work, saw it, obviously got mad, picked it up, and threw it across the entire yard where it landed against the fence we shared with our neighbor. It was broken and twisted. That was that. He yelled at me for being lazy, and it always accompanied this rabid dog scowl that was scary. After a while, he would calm down and act nice, his way of being sorry. I was just glad he was out of that funk of his despite losing my bike. I walked everywhere after that. It was a good chance to reflect and think. I was always thinking, always dissecting life in my own young inexperienced mind. I loved life for the most part, but I'd appreciate it a lot more back where I considered it home.

My mom's sister, aunt Marilyn, took me all alone to downtown Minneapolis one day to see the big hit movie, *The Ten Commandments* with Charlton Heston as Moses. She bought me a new suit, and we made our way to the State Theater on Hennepin Avenue. That movie seemed bigger than life and made me in awe of what God did and what he could do. I loved the idea of good overcoming evil. I also felt that life wasn't a rose garden but more of a huge challenge, and it was up to us individually to rise to the occasion. I felt up to it; I relished the fight and felt uplifted and strong after that film. Marilyn treated me to a nice restaurant down Hennepin after the movie. I was ten years old. This was the first really nice thing that Marilyn did after us moving to Circle Pines, knowing my misery index was quite high.

Another time, Mom, Marilyn, and Chris took me and Judy to downtown Minneapolis to see Dean Martin and Jerry Lewis. Live shows were the venue then, and the prices were reasonable. Other than Dino singing and Jerry doing his shtick, what I remember most was outside the theater after the show.

Way up high, obviously from their room, they had their window open and were throwing out photos or something. Dean was all smiles, and Jerry was Jerry, yelling and screaming and being a comic lunatic. Talk about entertainment spontaneity.

The second nice thing came a year or so later, when Marilyn and Dick bought me this high-end fully loaded, expensive Schwinn bike. It was so nice that I just about felt guilty riding it. It was this pretty red cruiser that had no equal. I was elated and protected and watched over it like a father rooster. And I never put it in harm's way, totally away from the driveway and anywhere close to it. At this same time, Dick gave me his extra box of medals from the war. I didn't want to take them, but he insisted. I cherished and would keep them until I went into the military myself years later, when they seemed to mysteriously disappear. Looking back, I always felt they were so generous because they knew how much I missed our old home and neighborhood and Gary.

I did start watching more TV during those Circle Pines days. I mainly followed westerns and war movies and Disney stuff like Davy Crockett and Daniel Boone, but also the Mousketeers. Let there be no mistake though; I watched that goody-two-shoes program for one glaring reason: Annette Funicello. I also watched with regularity *American Bandstand* with Dick Clark. It was a new rage and very popular. All the participants and dancers seemed so perfectly choreographed and dressed. And their confidence and coordination on the dance floor was impeccable. They were quite intimidating and took the starch right out of my own legs and feet, as far as dancing was concerned. How could I ever measure up? I didn't quite realize that I wouldn't be on TV like them, being watched by millions, but only by a few in my own dancing domain. It made no difference. I never really tried during school dances as I was too self-conscious. I would have rather had another abscessed tooth pulled out. I guess my self-esteem in those days was low, very low.

My absolute favorite TV show back then was *Mutual of Omaha's Wild Kingdom*, the insurance company, hosted by the famous Lowell Thomas. It always followed westerns on late Sunday and often canceled out any plans for church. It was filmed primarily in Africa and sometimes other faraway places like India and the Amazon. I loved the big animals of the jungle and how they lived and interacted with their pristine environment. Anything that remotely threatened their existence highly agitated me. My parting thoughts of any infringement upon these beautiful animals, especially things like molesting the Amazon for developments, would stay with me forever: *how dare mankind disrupt the delicate balance of nature?* I thought that if this was man's progress, at the expense of animals and nature, it wasn't worth it, at least in its extremes. Now that would have been a great sermon for church: why did societies feel compelled to ruin what God had created? Even at that age, my mind was forever philosophizing about life and our existence. I didn't just want to see the gray but all the colors as well. I liked to interpret most things through my own filtered prism. I'll give Dad credit for that approach since he was often in that prism.

Just before we left Circle Pines, emergency newscasts came over the Minneapolis radio and TV stations. Several brothers had committed serious crimes in the city and were in a getaway car coming down Highway 10, right past our area. Police advised all citizens to retire to their houses as these brothers were armed and dangerous. Naturally, that just peaked most of the braver people out and closer to the highway, me being among them. I can't remember exactly, but I'd imagine my mom was having a cow.

Anyway, their speeding car was soon in our midst, and shots could be heard in the distance. The cops were in hot pursuit with a string of vehicles with flashing lights and sirens. It was exciting if for only a few minutes as they passed us. They eventually caught them, and it was front-page news for days.

When I returned home and for days afterward upon watching the news, I would make comments about their robberies and what bad guys they were, more than willing, it seemed, to kill cops or anyone else in their way. I couldn't really conceive people being that evil, and I shared with my parents my thoughts openly. Mom would always agree softly and shake her head. Dad didn't say a thing or make any response except making a slight gesture with his mouth. It seemed somewhat out of character for him since he expressed his opinions and views very indiscriminately and without reservation.

Chapter Five

I was twelve when we moved back to the old neighborhood, but in another new house that they paid in the low teens for. It was a nice split-level, and I immediately assumed the lower section basement bedroom. The house was at 2463 Fairchild Avenue and only four blocks from our old house and Gary. While it was on the very edge of this new housing development, it had a separated large lot, older houses surrounded by trees and bushes across the street. It was also on a road that dead-ended right at the railroad tracks and the start of a massive woods and Rice Creek. I was happy again, so after a brief time, I showed my appreciation like any good red-blooded boy would—I ran away.

We had a gang of four—me, Gary, Roger, and Bruce. We all had our reasons to run away, all no doubt shallow, insignificant, and meaningless, except perhaps for mine with my father frustrations. Mainly, we wanted to strike out on our own and be some kind of soldiers of misfortune. Our plan was to leave on Sunday morning when there would be less traffic and ride our bikes over fifty miles up Highway 10 to Fergus Falls, on the edge of Wisconsin. We had no intentions of ever returning. We brought just a few bucks and figured we'd find work, and things would somehow magically work out. They didn't.

The bike ride was quite grueling as we had very little road shoulder, which was gravel, to ride on and had to go with the traffic. It was also a little cooler than we planned, and none of us had jackets. Roger was the eldest and the definite leader. About halfway up, Bruce started whining about his bike not pedaling right. He claimed his chain kept coming off and we all had to stop. Roger would go back patiently and try to help although sometimes he'd pass us upon returning to the lead, only to say he didn't see the chain off. Gary and I were mad and fed up with Bruce. We'd stop and start again many times. Sometimes Bruce would be nearly a half mile behind, but Roger always got him back up to speed. I have to say that I had ridden Bruce's bike once or twice, and it was the biggest dog I had ever tried to pedal. But when we realized he was crying and trying hard, we all relinquished our pace. We finally made it, all fifty painful miles.

We were all very hungry so we had a meager meal at some cheap hamburger place. Why we didn't bring more money is anyone's guess, but none would make sense. Soon, it was getting dark—and cold, much colder than we ever anticipated. That night, we all made this ball of bodies in the middle of the park, close to the waterfalls, to keep warm and tried to get some sleep. We didn't as we were too busy freezing and shaking. It was a nightmare. Finally, we did fall asleep just as it was getting light. Suddenly, we heard these loud manly voices above us, kicking our shoes and telling us to get up. It was the police, two of them. They demanded we get up and go home, thinking we were locals. We went up the edge of the park and gazed at a local eatery serving breakfast across the street. We coined our funds together and had enough to buy a couple of egg sandwiches to share. It didn't make much of a dent as we now were forced to evaluate our plans and day.

Bruce blurted out that he wanted to go home to be able to make his Monday paper delivery. What? We couldn't believe it? This was supposed to be a lifelong venture, and here we were with our plans disintegrating in front of us. He said he already missed Sunday's paper delivery, the biggest of the week, but thought he could salvage his life and paper route by making Monday's delivery, starting the new week. Roger was understanding as Roger always was, but Gary and I were livid. We all stood there debating and arguing. Between the stomach growls and being bone tired, we all decided to throw in the towel and start pedaling back home. After several miles and Bruce's bike miraculously working better, I got to thinking.

I was wondering what my dad would do when I returned. I started counting the hours it would take to get home and realized we wouldn't make it before he got home from work at 3:30 p.m. It was then that I had a burning desire to pedal ahead and try to make it home before he did, figuring I would rather be in the house already when he returned from work, downstairs waiting for the wrath of Dad. I told my runaway buddies what my desire was and proceeded to force myself to pedal that bike as if my life depended on it. I started to pull away and kept going at a breakneck pace. The more I thought of Dad, the harder I pedaled. The harder I pedaled, the more I thought of Dad.

I made it with an hour to spare, and my mom greeted me and was upset with me and briefly bawled me out and told me to go down to my room and "wait for your father." That warning seldom came from Mom, and if and when it did, it seemed like a death sentence.

It was one of the longest hours of my life. Another surprise. After me hearing him upstairs walking around, he finally called down to me. "Jon, c'mon up here. I want to talk to you."

Here I go, I thought. I was too scared to even say a quick prayer. My life was much too short.

I kind of hung my head in front of him and quickly said, "Sorry, Dad, I'm sorry."

He just looked at me for a quick moment then said softly, "You shouldn't have run away like that. You had us worried sick."

"I know, I know, I'm sorry."

"I talked to Ma (his mother, my grandmother) last night," he related, "and she reminded me of when I ran away and that she thought it was pretty normal for boys to do that. She said boys will be boys. And that I shouldn't punish you." He even had a slight grin on his face, but Mom didn't as she seemed much madder, but paused to talk, as if she was thinking.

I felt like my life had been spared, and a huge weight just left my body and departed like mercury running down my legs and out of my tired feet.

"Just don't do that again. Don't put us through that, it's pretty thoughtless . . . Okay?"

"Don't you think he should be grounded, John?" my mother said to my father.

"Yeah," he said. "Jon, you can't go anywhere tonight, and let this be a lesson."

I quickly departed the room and went downstairs. I plopped upon my bed and thanked my lucky stars above. I said to myself, *Never again, never again.* Until next time. After the dust cleared, the Hillsdales invited me along to a trip to Wisconsin to visit family. Gary had told me about this incredible ride that was up there made by a farmer and which was only five cents. It was called the Otter Slide and had a reputation as being for thrill seekers. Since Gary knew no fear and loved speed and flying, he said I wouldn't believe this amusement park on this wheat farmer's land. It sounded so bizarre, this amusement park up in farm country with nothing around it. But Gary was the (older) leader, and I always followed suit. Gary's dad was to drop us off one day, and we would visit this place and go on the ride.

When I saw the place and its run-down condition, I nearly laughed. There were signs of former rides and other primitive amusement elements, but it seemed it was all buried in time. But there was this one thing remaining, the famous Otter Slide itself. It was way up this steep hill, more like a small mountain.

Gary told me you pay the farmer five cents, and he will put you in this broken-down-looking open railroad car thing and take you to the top. Even in those days, five cents was like the deal of a lifetime. I couldn't believe it was so cheap when the normal rides at the Minnesota State fair, which we went to every year, were going for twenty-five cents. The ride up there alone took twenty minutes as the cables on the car had to catch on the rails each leg of the way, inching along quite slow—but steady. When we finally got to the top and got out and looked down this rickety slide, I started freaking out. It was an unbelievable drop down to this big area of hay. Gary raved about how fun it was. He said even his sister Marlene loved it. Really? There was a flimsy stack of old rugs, and Gary told me to grab one. He said you would get on the rug, give yourself a push, and down you went. It was old beat-up tin for the bottom slide portion and five-inch broken, bent, warped wood as sides to keep you on track. The design of it looked like a big looping snake.

I was scared out of my wits while Gary was licking his chops. The farmer gave us some rules to follow: Just stay on the rug and don't pull anything cute. Gary was first and took off. I noticed how his whole body completely left the slide as he went down and then picked up great speed until he hit the hay. It was freaky. I hit the slide with my rug and went down, but it seemed to be going much faster now that Gary paved the way. How lucky for me. When my body went off that slide and into the air, my eyes shut as I came back down hard on the slide, barely fitting within the rails on the side. One more body departure and crash down, and I was landing suddenly in the hay and okay. It was fun in a morbid way.

If I didn't think otherwise, it just about seemed like a contrived trip and plan to scare the crap out of us by our parents after our running away. But that couldn't be because it was our idea; Gary loved it, and I tolerated it. I still think the farmer should have paid us to go down that rattletrap of horror. Gary told me years later that someone was seriously hurt on the thing and they shut it down. Why wasn't I surprised?

Shortly after, Dad took me downtown Minneapolis to see the first closed-circuit broadcast in Minnesota at the famous RKO Orpheum. It was heavyweight champion Floyd Patterson defending his title against Swede Ingemar Johansson. Dad loved the fact that a Swede was fighting for the title since he was half Swede from his mother's side and was elated when Johansson knocked out Patterson. I don't know why, but I fought back the tears as I felt so bad for the champion, who got knocked around so severely. Afterward, Dad took me down to Bridgeman's, the hugely popular ice cream parlor, where he treated me to anything I wanted. We talked about the fight and ate ice cream, which seemed like a chilling combination. I didn't realize it then, but I came to believe later that Dad was trying to bond with me more after that runaway. It certainly helped at the time and made my father a little more human, but it also solidified my own interest in boxing.

My twelfth year was very active and productive. I had my very first job picking radishes and strawberries—a nasty, filthy way to make a buck. Gary and I, always the pranksters and always looking for a laugh, entertainment, and easier money, devised a plan to get a bigger yield from our daily grind. We noticed that as the rows were picked and bushels were left in the rows, the flock of pickers and the farm supervisor, the daughter of the farmer who owned this huge operation, was always up front with her notepad, writing down the bushels as they were picked and recorded. Gary and I were always joking with her, despite her being a much older teen, and figured we'd get on her best side, complimenting her on her looks and personality and generally schmoozing her to the hilt. We kissed her ass so much I wouldn't have doubted that the symbolic saying somehow penetrated her tight jeans and tattooed her skin. When we felt we had her in our dirty trouser pockets, we planned our move.

We would joke and kid around when first starting out picking, purposely dropping back in the flock. The lady I'll call Ann just shook her head, laughed at us, and said, "If you want to just have fun and not make money (yeah right, it was like slave labor), fine." We just laughed and moved like we had cement in our pants. But there was a plan and scheme to our madness. After the other pickers moved way ahead of us, showing bushels and bushels behind them while we had just several, we waited until Ann was not paying attention and went several rows over and pulled those bushels over behind our rows, and we started catching up. When we got much closer and added many bushels to our rows, we went up to her and told her that we were catching up and wanted to record our progress. She seemed puzzled but looked way back and saw our added bushels in our rows and recorded them. Her smile was broad as she said she knew "we could do it." Standing way up there and looking back, you virtually couldn't see the lapses in the other rows as they were staggered and irregular. It worked like magic, and Gary and I still got a respectable bushel count and a regular payday. It worked for a month, on and off, but then Ann changed supervisor positions; and the new supervisor, her brother, was much more mistrusting and watchful. Our gig was up. Gary's sister, Marlene, who also worked on the farm, knew we had pulled something but couldn't figure it out. How could we start and move so slow and end up with so much. Ingenuity, Marlene, ingenuity. Gary and I laughed so hard between us after we got home that our stomachs hurt. We only made $2–5 bucks a day so we didn't feel too guilty. *Boys will be boys.*

Money becomes a driving force early on in life. I remember oftentimes on Saturdays when Dad's brother Lester, all six feet three inches and over 250 pounds of him, would drive down from the city and he and Dad would always do the same thing: sit at the kitchen table, clear everything from the top, and bring out their money, both from their pockets and their wallets. Lester would sound like a token machine on a bus as he walked because of all the change he carried, which was all nearly real silver in dimes, quarters, half-dollars, and dollars. Many were very old and valuable. He also had wads of $100 bills in his wallet, sprinkled with twenties and fifties. Dad didn't carry change like Lester, but he had a fairly respectable stash of cash in his wallet too, but nothing like Lester. Neither, at the time anyway, believed in or trusted banks.

They always encouraged me to join them as they counted their money, mainly concentrating on Lester's piles. They would joke and raze each other endlessly as they were entertained by watching me wither in my chair and foam at the mouth with envy. Once in a great while, Lester would push a silver dollar my way or some quarters. Dad didn't. He was as tight as a leather drum. Dad would sometimes slap his hand down over Lester's coins to tease, and Lester would just smile while he effortlessly peeled up his fingers and removed his hand. Dad would look at me and say, "Can you imagine somebody, a lot of somebodies, trying to take Les's money? I'd pay to see that." I never saw my dad laugh so hard, as well as Lester, always called Les by my dad, unless he was pissed about something with him, which was rare but usually happened over fishing, especially ice fishing, which they did all the time.

Dad had told me a little about Lester's past in World War II as a paratrooper in the Army Special Forces. He said he was a hero on the beaches of Anzio in Italy and was wounded. I sometimes asked Lester about those days, but he refused to say a word no matter how hard I pursued my interest. The most he would say was, "Oh, you don't need to hear that. It was nothing." During those times at the table, Lester would often be picking his face, the cheek areas, like he was popping zits or something. Years later, I found out it was shrapnel he was picking out, with small pieces oozing out from his body after all those years.

Every time Lester or the war came up, I would always ask my dad why he didn't go in. He would always say something about having to stay home to take care of his mother or that they wouldn't let him because Lester was serving. He would always cut the conversation short. He would usually switch to talking about how tough Lester was as a kid. Dad said he was so skinny that Mabel, his mother, my grandmother, nicknamed him "Fat." As the story evolved, Lester got into many fights with a bigger bully type, named So-and-So Baker. Often, Grandma would also talk about it when we visited her for Sunday dinners. Baker would start things, and the two of them would go across the street to a vacant lot and fight and fight, sometimes for hours. Lester, Dad and Gram said, always prevailed. He returned home a bloody mess but continually the victor. They both said there was no quit in that boy, really no quit in any of the Meades, including Grandma. It all ended one day when Gram heard a knock on the door. There stood the Baker boy with his father.

"Look what your son has done to my boy," the father said, upset, his boy cut and bleeding and clothes ripped from his body.

Gram yelled for Lester to join them and put her hand on his thin frame. "Do you mean my skinny rail of a kid Lester beat up your big strapping boy? Your boy towers over him and weighs a hundred pounds more." She laughed and slammed the door in their faces. Although I never heard Lester say it, but Dad and Gram always referred to that kid as Cock-Eyed Baker, as a result of what Les did to the big kid's face. Grandma Meade was nobody to fool with herself. She was a strapping Swede who was six feet tall and had a look on her—I wonder where Dad got his—that could scare anyone. Her eyes were fierce as if she was upset. My mom often said she was scared to death of her back then. But she said she had her reasons. I always thought she was the greatest as my dad would always refer to her as "Kool-Aid Mabel" for her incredibly good, better than most, Kool-Aid, always cherry. Years later, I found out her "secret" for superior Kool-Aid. She doubled the recipe—twice the sugar, twice the cherry. It worked. When she prepared Sunday dinner for our family, it was like the feasts of all feasts. There were two to three main courses, salads, breads, vegetable dishes, fruit dishes, and another two to three selections of desserts, all made from scratch. I always felt Mabel had the warmest and most infectious smile I had ever seen, next to Hopalong Cassidy, and was a great grandmother.

At that younger age, I knew a little about the Meades' background but always had a hard time learning all the facts in detail. Seems that Claude, my father's dad and my grandfather, was a renowned horse trainer—even having had a hand in the training of the famous horse Dan Patch—and also raced sulkies with the low small carriage behind the horse. Dad and the boys were raised in that environment in downtown Minneapolis when barns and horses were still on the streets. It was their whole life, horses and races. What I did know was that Claude was in a barn after a big race victory at the fair and someone came up behind him and shot him in the back of the head, killing him.

This was during the Depression years, and times were tough. Dad would say that he had just run away from home and was riding the rails with buddies, at fifteen, when he sensed that something was wrong at home. He thought the stars were somehow telling him to go home—quickly. His friends thought he was nuts. He jumped off the railroad car and hopped another going in the opposite direction. When he arrived at home, he saw the aftermath of his father dying in Wes's arms. Wes, his older brother, had been the sulky racer who had won the event. That was the extent of it when I was younger. Gram, I guess, went crazy herself and tried to get neighbors together, according to Dad, to go get the killer and hang him. It never happened, of course, but Mabel was never the same. In the freezing winters of Minnesota, she had to get a job at a rag company and walk to work over the Camden bridge to make $1.50 a day, enough to barely feed the boys. It would be hard to conceive what was more bitter back then, the weather or their minds.

Little else was said about the subsequent years. That's all I knew about the Scot Irish grandfather I never met—in little bits and pieces—until years later. But I had many other questions back then too. Dad's jumping from job to job always made me wonder. I remember one time he took a test for some job, scored higher than anyone else, but didn't end up taking the job. He always had his excuses, but nonetheless he always had good blue-collar jobs and sometimes wanted to vie for more and was qualified off the charts in terms of IQ, but they didn't materialize. It was always mystifying. No matter what else, he always did upholstery jobs on the side and weekends and made great money as he had an impeccable reputation, which I admired. He always seemed like this perfect citizen who would never even break the speed limit (oh, he drove so slow it drove me nuts). He always stressed to me the importance of being a good kid and not getting into trouble, which seemed to be about the only thing he did ever advise me about.

More often, I saw him as this hands-off distant father despite his ever-present volcanoes of behavior, whose primary targets were my mom and me. His bad was bad, real bad, and his good was real good, even hard to believe. The whole time growing up, I was usually in this stupor of wonderment, trying to figure my father out. On top of that confusion was the fact that Dad had the sense of humor of a stand-up comedian. I'll call him a very gifted sit-down comedian. Since he was sharp as a tack, his humor was also very quick and creative. I took after that trait in him, in my own fashion, and it certainly helped me during those years. I always found it amusing that Gary never had a clue about my dad's behind-the-scenes behavior early on. Dad always kept his behavior behind closed doors, for the most part. I kept it to myself in a similar manner except in venting some years later with Gary and certain friends.

Chapter Six

During this twelfth year, I also started my lifelong quest for fitness. It kicked off by watching Roger at his home working out with weights. He had already developed quite a muscular physique and was very strong. Because I looked up to Roger, about Gary's age, he was very influential. While I did follow his lead and workout in his bedroom, I couldn't afford my own weights yet, so I turned to the comic books. I believe it was the Classic Series and *The Red Badge of Courage* and Charles Atlas, who sold his "Dynamic Tension" course on the back cover. I used it religiously at home in my bedroom. I even doubled some of his exercises, especially the dips between chairs. Dad would continue his teasing boxing tactics with me, but I was getting closer to tagging him so it became less frequent.

When it came to building muscle and strength, I was of the persuasion that it would serve little to any real purpose unless it was tied to practical application to sports or athleticism. Just doing it for purely aesthetic reasons seemed empty and totally superficial. I felt that a strong muscular physique should be able to be backed up by action, not just appearance. Within a short time after picking produce—perceived produce, that is—I was able to purchase my own weight set and progress even more. I accompanied the workouts with reading everything I could about bodybuilding, strength, fitness, baseball, boxing, and other athletic endeavors.

The bottom line, however, boiled down to what normal, healthy boy wouldn't want to look better, more muscular, and strong? It goes back to the caveman days without the clubs, but the females were to be the main benefactors and were entrenched in the picture. It was probably why 99 percent of all boys had this same picture focused in their young minds. So much for the mindful idealism. Besides the farm work, I also added select babysitting with immediate neighbors, who apparently liked and trusted me. I used every dollar on more weights and materials to make and duplicate equipment I saw in the muscle magazines. I made my own bench and squat racks. One day when I was doing benches and squats, I felt strong and kept adding weight until the bar was full. I ended up squatting with 225 pounds and benching with 160—for reps. I realized I was much stronger than I thought. It no doubt didn't hurt that my mom and dad were very strong, as well as my whole family, who were quite large and physical. The genetics were on my side, so from that point on, I would always push myself to the max. In short order, I surpassed Roger but always downplayed it and kept it to myself as he was the one I was emulating. He was my ideal role model, and I just about felt guilty.

Gary, meanwhile, was more content to hone his skills as the paper war artist. Now, however, I noticed he was adding much more planes to the battles. There was as much in air combat as there was ground. I'd try to copy his artwork, especially the aircraft, but I could never come close to reaching his skill level. So I concentrated on the ground combat, which I preferred anyway. I liked the idea from the get-go of getting dirty and being a grunt. I could not muster up the same love Gary had for aircraft, but I tried to appease him. We did share the same passion for poker, as we were big fans of the popular TV series *Maverick* with James Garner. We both bought the *Maverick* book of poker and likened ourselves to becoming card-playing experts. Gary's growing love of aircraft only got more intense. He apparently heard about the Civil Air Patrol, an ancillary of the Air Force, and asked me to tag along. This seemed obvious since Gary and I were in the Cub Scouts together for two to three years.

Gary liked what he heard and signed up, later getting his parents' approval as well. Naturally, he wanted me by his side, so I signed up too although I was under the age of thirteen, their minimum. I lied.

We both started as airman cadets and once a week would have to hitch a ride with older cadets in our area down to the University of Minnesota. The evenings were about three hours in duration and encompassed classroom instruction, marching, and basic military protocol. All the learning was acclimated toward airplanes, flying, and subjects like dead reckoning. We had uniforms nearly identical to the Air Force except for the patches. We both really got into it and had a lot of fun, and certainly learned a lot. After about three months, in the summer, the CAP flew us down to Scott Air Force base in C-119s— flying boxcars—to Illinois.

We had to go through a simulated Air Force boot camp for two weeks, which was quite something for kids our age (I was twelve, Gary fourteen) even though it seemed tough at times—about five to six kids locked their knees at attention and blacked out. Nasty. They told us repeatedly to stand a certain way and not lock our knees, but some guys just can't listen. After seeing a few of them crash face-first on the deck, we were glad we listened. Otherwise, we had downtime and it purposely wasn't quite as hard as regular Air Force boot camp, and we enjoyed every minute, especially at the pool. It was then that Gary and I formulated a future plan to join the Air Force together after high school graduation. We shook on it and felt confident about our decision. Our future to serve in the military was sealed. Just the thought of it, which occupied our minds frequently, was inspiring.

After our return, our battalion captain devised a recruiting campaign whereby the cadet bringing in the most new sign-ups would win a new stripe. We had one week. I took the challenge literally and went to school and recruited all the warm bodies I could. I was an extreme extrovert and talker so the event fit right into my demeanor. Gary, on the other hand, was an introvert and rather quiet. Considering we were such close brotherly friends, we were direct opposites in many ways. At the end of the week, I had parents dropping off their boys to my house, front yard to be exact. Forty-three of them! The problem was I had no idea what to do next. I never thought how I'd get them there. I had one extra car coming, but they never expected how many newbies I recruited. Everyone was shocked, especially my parents.

My dad was puzzled and pissed, but I don't know why because all they were doing was standing on the grass and monkeying with the mailbox and shrubs and anything else within a hand's reach—as they waited. Our sergeant came and called from the house—oh, Dad loved that—and got three to four more cars to come. The whole thing took about an hour, and it seemed like my dad was counting every minute, just like me. I can't recall if Gary got one or not.

When we all got to the building and fell out into the auditorium, the cadet brass simply couldn't believe their eyes. I won the contest and was promoted, not one stripe but two, to cadet first class, the equivalent of a sergeant, just like Gary, who was already two stripes ahead of me because he was such a crackerjack in the classroom. Our captain said it was a recruiting record he felt confident would never be broken. My chest grew that instant by several inches in pure oxygen. When those flags, including Old Glory, were paraded in front of our formation, I felt proud and felt it give me inner strength. More important than that, I was now on par with Gary, certifying our joint plans down the road.

My uncle Dick who was in the Army Air Corps, later called just the Air Force, had a uniform from his active days similar to my CAP one despite us being worlds apart. He was the hero from World War II who was captured at Corregidor and then went through the Bataan Death March, where he would be a POW for three and a half years. He was an incredible inspiration toward joining the military one day, and I also had many talks with him—although limited about the war—including ones about my father. He said very little in response except to respect him as much as I could and try not to take too much too seriously. We no doubt shared a certain closeness because I admired him so and Dick and Marilyn never had any kids of their own, so I was like some surrogate son.

I always kind of thought Dad may have been slightly jealous toward him 'cause he shared some memories with me, and Lester, whom Dad claimed was more quiet and modest about his experiences, never did. To Dad, that was somehow more honorable. While I greatly admired Uncle Lester, I never really saw it that way, and I don't think Lester himself would have either. Dad was driven by jealousy in his life quite a bit. Mom and aunts Chris and Marilyn related stories about my father's insane jealousy over my mother. Dad would get into fights, sometimes with more than one guy at a time, and fare better than them. He apparently was a vicious fighter by all accounts. Even Dick one time told me with his unreal background that he would never want to get in a fight with Dad. That was one front he would never want to face. That camaraderie I had with Dick was also another reason for Dad to be jealous. And it seemed like the more I'd bring home little vignettes about the war from Dick, the more I'd wonder why Dad didn't serve and sometimes repeat my burning question. It was just a boy's natural inquisitive nature. I never pressed the issue that much, really, but it always seemed to be a protected bone of contention.

My particular aspirations related to me and Gary's plans joining the Air Force changed soon thereafter, if only to myself. We had this sergeant whom we all loved and was this great cadet and leader who told us that one day he was joining the Marines and would be leaving. We just about laughed as this sergeant was hunky and out of shape who hadn't heard about the toughness of the Marines, but he joined and was soon gone. Months passed and it pretty much left our memories. Then one day, there was this green-like figure standing next to the wall in front of our formation. Our captain introduced him as this sergeant who had just graduated from Marine boot camp and wanted to recognize his accomplishments and wish him a hearty congratulations. It was our cadet sergeant, and it hit us like a brick wall. He stood so tall, looked so slim and tight, and seemed very rigid, standing ramrod straight.

We all rushed around him, especially those like Gary and I who had him as our platoon leader. Close up, we noticed this large reddish long scar running down the side of his face, from eye area to chin. He explained that during bayonet training, the scabbard that held the bayonet had ripped his face open. I don't know about Gary, but I thought it was the greatest scar I ever saw and right then I knew in my heart I wanted to be a Marine. The transformation in the guy was incredible. But at the same time, I knew my allegiance to Gary was paramount. We spent a total of two and a half years as CAP cadets, and the training we knew would serve us well in our records and training later in the Air Force.

During that time, we also went flying a lot in small planes, sometimes through the CAP, sometimes on our own. I never had the stomach for it like Gary. He would always want the pilot to do flips and other stunts in the air. I didn't. One time it backfired on him with this much older CAP leader that was a pilot and had his own Cessna. He asked us if we wanted to do aerials, and Gary quickly said yes. I cringed. He did all kinds of stuff including stalls and rollers and flips, and I felt super sick. I tapped him on the shoulder and asked him to quit. He didn't. He just turned his head a little and smiled. He and Gary got a big kick out of it. I didn't. I threw up all over this pilot's back and didn't realize a human being could hold so much food in their guts. It smelled—oh, it stunk. There was no doubt that I had the last laugh although I couldn't laugh.

During our teen years, particularly the earlier ones, while I was at Fairchild Avenue, we continued our garden raids; went ice-skating— our smoke and skate—four to five times a week at the creek by me, sometimes in (way) below freezing temperatures, but bearing the harsh

Minnesota winters without complaint; started smoking (Camels and Lucky Strikes); often shared the same girlfriend; played poker; went down to the Stenhoffs', Roger's place; and continued living life to the fullest as defined by us. We went swimming bare ass down at the bullhead hole, fished, visited the mysterious old mill and the caverns full of water while always attending Messiah Lutheran Church nearly every Sunday, and even whizzed a bottle of vino out of the church office one time. In church, we both went through Catechism for three years to get confirmed (having to take a final 250-question test). But we sometimes got called out for pulling pigtails on girls, sticking gum under the pews, and leaving wrappers from our candy stash. At the same time, everyone, the detached parents anyway, thought we were two of the nicest and most polite kids around. We were. And respectful. But on the flip side, we were hellions with manners. But it was pretty innocent, and no one got too hurt.

Gary and I also loved outer space, particularly at night. We'd spend many nights, usually on the side of my house, lying down flat on our backs and staring up at the sky, talking about the stars and cosmos. We would pick out the star constellations and then come up with the origins questions and try to comprehend the whole creation of the outer atmosphere and everything else under the dark sky with luminous stars. We accepted our teachings of the Christian Protestant faith, but we loved to speculate a little too, especially with other scenarios. Related to that, we would pose the question to each other: What was eternity like? What would it be like for the afterlife, for example, to never end?

We quickly realized that to really try and understand this hypothesis, one would have to get into a higher and more pure mental state.

You had to totally clear your mind to get yourself on a clearer, less cluttered plane of reasoning, thinking, and understanding. Only then could you see a more defined picture of what eternity might be. To think about something, anything, never ending, having no conclusion—forever—is mind-boggling. If you can reach that mental clarity of thinking, it can be scary. The *what-ifs* always piqued our interest. What if your eternity was horrible? What if your eternity was beautiful? What if your eternity was undefined, yet existed? What if your eternity was alone? What if your eternity included others? What if your eternity was utopia? What if your eternity was not? We always erred on the side of our biblical teachings in the simplest terms in the end, accepting faith. But studying the *what-ifs* and all possible options was also fascinating and challenging.

For me, it was a little deeper. I saw the sky and stargazing as an escape from reality. I saw the cosmos as something much bigger than me and my dad. And by looking into the vastness of it all, by seeing the universe above me, I was able to downplay any negatives and unhappiness in my own life into a more acceptable package of my existence. I saw a certain nobility and honor in accepting my fate and knew it was minuscule compared to the universe, that it was nothing in a world of nothingness. Sometimes I would say a little prayer to myself, in a personal message to God, and simply thank him for everything and admitted my own shortcomings. It was always personally soothing, and I always felt compelled to say that little prayer after viewing the sky and cosmos.

The Cobb girls also went to our church, and Mary had a crush on Gary. But Gary couldn't be bothered by her as I guess he didn't want to be tied down. Anyway, the Cobbs were the wealthier people in the neighborhood and lived in a big house at the edge of Rice Creek, which was where Gary and I spent a great deal of time year-round. One day upon hiking down and around the creek from my area to theirs, we realized that the Cobbs had a large number of chickens, chicken coop, and yard. It was also quite away from the main house. Our reconnaissance gave us an idea. Since we both had BB guns, we thought we'd come back just before sunset and take some target practice. We positioned ourselves within the surrounding brush and started taking potshots. When the BBs hit the chickens, we would hear a loud thud, but nothing else happened. So we kept firing, hitting the same chickens over and over again. We went through rolls and rolls of BBs. We never saw one drop, and after quite some time doing this and hitting maybe a dozen chickens, we got frustrated and went home.

The next day, the neighborhood was abuzz over all the chickens that were shot and killed at the Cobb place. Some neighbor had seen us leave the scene and told the Cobbs, but the Cobbs never called the cops. They just called us and told us they knew we were the culprits, and it changed their positive impression of us—forever. They also suggested we pay them for the loss, but that never came to pass. Our reputations were now tainted and our perfect boy impressions ruined. Although we did feel a little bad, we also knew that a lot of chickens fell after all. It also killed Mary's crush on Gary.

But that wasn't the only Mary that had a crush on Gary. The people that lived right next door to us on Fairchild had the mother's younger sister come to babysit for the summer. When Gary was sleeping over one night, we met her on the way while we were walking down to the creek throwing frogs high in the air and watching them fall. We felt we were doing the community a favor because the frog population was out of control. Sometimes Mary would ask us where all the blood came from on our clothes. We made up some harebrained story that made us look somehow tougher. Gary and I went google-eyed over her, but she seemed to pay more attention to Gary. I felt a little jealous, but Gary was older so I just stepped back and let nature take its course. We hung together a lot, but Gary would find an opportunity to get her alone and they'd make out. I would excuse myself and let them be.

The following summer, however, Mary had a crush on me and not Gary. At the same time, Gary had a crush on her and I couldn't stand her. Love is fickle, isn't it?

The next summer, Mary had a crush on both of us, and both of us had a crush on her. Our frog-killing days were over, and we were becoming more mature and grown-up, somewhat, in some ways.

Because I lived right next door, I did have certain advantages, like talking to Mary through my bedroom window. One day, she told me she would be alone all afternoon and asked me to come over. I told Mom I was going out and would be back for supper. She seemed to look at me a little funny as I left, but I didn't take it very seriously. I soon would. After going next door to Mary's, the baby was asleep so we began making out on the couch. Just as we were really getting into it, there came a knock on the door, which startled us. Mary looked through the tiny peephole and said it was my mother and that she seemed very mad.

I quickly scrambled into the closet and hid. It was just an impulsive thing I did at the moment because I didn't really know what else to do. I had an uncomfortable feeling about Mom obviously storming over here. Why? I was a young teen, not doing anything more than a little harmless kissing.

While I was held up in the dark little closet, I thought Mom must have heard us talking through that window and then making plans for a get-together at Mary's place. Still, what was the crime? I didn't get it, but I soon heard my mother say some negative things to Mary and they bantered back and forth about me being there. Mary kept her composure and continued to deny I was there, and Mom finally left after saying some choice departing remarks.

I was in a near shock. What just happened here? I apologized to Mary over and over again and said I admired her strength. She was about the coolest cucumber in the bushel while Mom was the hottest pepper in the batch. I waited for quite a while before I went home. Mom just looked at me with long eyes, saying nothing, and I went straight to my room saying nothing. It was weird. But that incident caused me to be leery about ever having anything to do with girls or having a girlfriend, at least around her and the neighborhood. The discomfort I felt stuck with me many years later until I got married. As far as my mom was concerned, I was just content to be a boy, have zero interest in girls, and hang out with Gary and other buds. Probably because of the way my dad was, I always liked to think my mom was just being overprotective. Way overprotective.

Chapter Seven

Just before I turned fifteen and had a burning desire to get my own car, Gary and I ran away again. This time we did it with another kid, Darrel, who was having issues at home and talked us into it. His idea: to leave Minnesota and the greater Midwest and venture to cowboy country in Montana and get jobs as ranch hands. Darrel was a fun kid, a little unruly, but came from an upper-middle class family on Spring Lake. We both liked him but felt that he was a little more *out there* than us, but cool and had plans much bigger than our neighborhood could handle. Not long before leaving, I had put him up in the basement crawl space in the dirt for several days and secretly fed him during another one of his runaways. My mom suspected something and apparently called his folks, who had their plans to quietly come over and get him. He left before they got there, but they ended up getting him and taking him home. Foiled again, he undoubtedly said, because this time he wanted to escape from his strict parents who were very religious (but great parents) forever. We all had some money and jackets and struck out by hitchhiking west.

We got as far as the eastern part of South Dakota the first day, having hitched two rides with local and over-the-road truckers. That first night was rough as we slept in this old abandoned cement building. The next night, after making it to the western side of the state, we hunted for large vacant cars and slept in them, but were found and kicked out twice.

In the morning, one of the car owners called the cops, and they came to interrogate us. After sensing we were just wayward boys, they drove us out of their county, stopped their car, and said, "Don't ever come back this way." A little surprising since we thought for sure we would be arrested. These cops, we thought, were cold and just wanted us out of their hair and state. It was at that point when Gary got cold feet and wanted to return home. I was more than willing to go on, but Gary was my best friend so he ruled the day and the trip. I told Darrel I was sorry—Gary didn't bother as he was fed up—and Darrel went his way west and we went our way back home.

Not that we were greeted with a ticker tape "Welcome back home," but the only penalty we got from our parents was a ban on Darrel—for life. So we weren't that good at running away, but we did beat our old record by one day and about two hundred miles—not bad. Darrel continued having problems, and we said hi in the school hallways occasionally, but that was it.

Gary already had his driver's license and now it was time for me. Just about as soon as I got it at fifteen and a half, I wanted a car because I knew my dad would never let me touch, let alone drive, his car. It wasn't too uncommon in the day. Gary's dad wouldn't let him take his, but unlike me, Gary did not want the perceived responsibilities of car ownership. I did. So I bought an old '53 Ford Fairlane. It had the incredibly reliable flathead engine but was the slowest dog on the road. I didn't care as it spelled freedom to me. My interest in boxing had grown, and I seldom missed the Gillette Friday night fights, which I first started watching with Gary, who appeased me on this one. In 1962, we watched the championship fight between Benny "Kid" Paret and Emile Griffith. After a furious battle, Griffith backed Parrot into the corner and pounded him senseless. He dropped like a bag of cement and was hauled away on a stretcher. He died the following day. Gary wasn't a boxing fan like me so that fight pretty much severed his interest permanently. But with my latent warrior spirit, I was just beginning and I wanted to now pursue boxing as a sport. I went down to the downtown YMCA and joined for one year as I heard they had a boxing gym and full-sized ring. The fee for a student was $12.

There was more to the boxing interest than pure sport. I also wanted to learn how to fight more than the light sparring with my father. I had the ulterior motive of revenge. Several years back when Roger got his first car, he, Gary, and I went joy riding on Central Avenue toward Minneapolis. We were going through a rough area on the south side. As we approached a stop light, we noticed this car, several of them actually, in like a caravan on the other side of the medium, and the lead car looked long at us and honked loudly.

Before we knew it, a car came up on our back bumper at the stoplight, and both Roger and Gary were dragged from the car like rag dolls. I looked back and saw Roger in the middle of a circle fighting for all he was worth. Gary was in front of the car somewhere haplessly standing by. I started to get out of the passenger's side when I was greeted by this tall, much older teen. At that age, the difference was like David versus Goliath. He quickly swung back and hit me with three rapid-fire punches to the side of my jaw. He then looked surprised and shook his hand out and hit me one more huge shot.

I took them all, didn't fall, and didn't drop an ounce of blood. I guess I had a hard head. The guy just opened the car door and threw me in and wouldn't let me out. But soon the fight would be over.

At that precise moment, I realized I could really take a punch—many punches, not necessarily a good thing if a person had pacifist inclinations, which I didn't. Following that brief thought, Roger, who obviously didn't either, jumped back in the car, as did Gary, and we peeled out.

Roger was a sight to behold. Although Rog was primarily fighting the gang leader, other gang members got kicks into his head, face, and body. His face was covered in blood, masking bruises, cuts, and even foot imprints on his chin and neck. His lips were swollen, and he could barely open his mouth as we drove away. We got clear of the area before we stopped and assessed the damage. It was incredibly bad. It turned out to be so bad Roger could not have his photos taken that year for the school yearbook. His mother, Iris, cried so hard when seeing him I thought she'd never survive. Roger's father too was shocked. Everyone at school was also, and talk was going around Mounds View High School that revenge was in the works. Roger was quite popular. It was learned that the gang on Central was led by a bully named Bucky, who had a reputation of getting into fights and biting hunks out of guys' cheeks. Appropriately, the gang was called the Animals. Despite talk circulating for quite some time, everyone willing to step in and meet them in a gang fight, it didn't materialize. Not for a long time anyway.

Sometime later, I heard that a muscled-up state champion wrestler from Mounds View, Larry Leigh, evened the score by beating Bucky up like a cheap rug on a clothesline. Roger's horrible ordeal was justifiably revenged, at least that was how all the boys saw it. Larry didn't need to be any more a hero than he already was. For me, I vowed to myself that I would learn how to fight and never let something like that happen to me or anyone I knew again. And it never did.

Joining that Y turned out to be a real learning experience. I had to take a long bus ride to get there. It was on the third floor, and virtually no one used it. I would go there and train on the light and heavy bags, do calisthenics, jump rope, and do other boxing exercises all alone, except this one particular day. I was hitting the light bag and had laid my training routine on this floor mat. This much older guy, slightly shorter but well built, came over to me as he passed the mat. "I noticed your training schedule calls for sparring—if possible. Do you want to spar?" I stopped and looked him over. He looked thirty if he looked a day. I was fourteen. My pride was already heavily ingrained and I knew what I promised myself, so I hesitantly said okay. We got the gloves and entered the regulation ring. We didn't have a bell, but I'd soon be hearing one anyway.

We maneuvered around the ring, and he had a stopwatch on and timed it like a regular fight at three-minute rounds. At the end of the first round, I caught him with a classic one-two combination of a left jab and a right cross. He was against the ropes and was definitely hurt. I threw a few more punches but then backed away toward the middle of the ring. I didn't want to hurt him. Just then, he landed a left hook and a tremendous right haymaker that caught me flush on the face and literally knocked me out on my feet. My head was spinning, and I couldn't focus on him anymore because I virtually couldn't see through the stars that were spinning in my head. But I didn't go down. Despite his continued punching, I weathered the storm until his watch indicated time to stop. I was still seeing stars when we approached each other for the second round. But it didn't materialize as he said, "Let's wrap it up, kid."

While he took off his gloves, he said sternly, "You had me going, kid, you could have knocked me out, no doubt . . . but you backed up and let me go. Don't ever do that again if you are serious about boxing. Ever, under any circumstances. Damn, son, you have serious skills and killer power. But you need to add that killer instinct."

With my head still hurting, especially my nose and entire face, he added, "Do you understand me, kid? When you are fighting and you have your opponent hurt, you don't back off, you go in for the kill."

"Yes, I understand," I replied respectfully.

"But you also took my punches like a pro. Honestly, I would have just stopped short of knocking you out if I could have. But I couldn't.

You can take a punch as well as you can give one. But stick with the giving instead of the getting . . . okay? You got me?"

Oh boy, did I get him. He went on, "Just so you know, I fought as a pro—a welterweight—and I was pretty good too. I'm thirty-two now, and retired." We thanked each other for the fight, me for the lesson, shook hands, and parted ways as he left the gym, saying, "Keep going on and don't forget this lesson." I didn't. I also didn't forget what it felt like to be knocked out on your feet and to see stars—not too heavenly.

I met another famous old-timer who was in his seventies at the time but in terrific shape. Someone else told me about his notoriety. He was also a pro boxer who had fought in the Jack Dempsey days. I was all eyes and ears as he taught me the rudiments of the ring, inside and out. We put the gloves on too, but I didn't exhibit my newly acquired "killer instinct" to his person. But he did feel the sting, I guess, of my punches and complimented the power and accuracy behind them. We had this interaction for perhaps several months— which he loved because very few people ever stepped into the boxing room, let alone the ring—and he greatly enjoyed the sparring. It didn't hurt that I was such a receptive learner and participator. About the last time I saw him, he encouraged me to enter the Golden Gloves. He said he knew the new coach there who had actually partaken in several of the last Olympics as coach or assistant coach. His name was Verne Agnus, and the particular gym was way down in south Minneapolis at the Unity, a neighborhood house it was called in the day for disadvantaged youths in depressed areas. This old-timer just faded away, and I never saw him again. He was certainly another very positive influence on my young existence, and I always thought I missed saying goodbye.

I waited to go down to the Unity and check out the boxing program until I got my license and a car. Since I lived in the exclusive white suburbs of north Minneapolis, I had to drive all the way through my area and on the edge of downtown to go over the bridge to the "other side of the tracks," which turned out to be a half-hour trip and thirty miles away. I parked my car three to four blocks from Unity. I quickly was introduced to Mr. Agnus and subsequently signed up for three months of membership, even cheaper than the Y. The first session was easy as we went over rules, ring, Golden Gloves, and Unity protocol.

Right away, he said I'd be fighting as a middleweight on the team, if I made it, and he felt I had a naturally long reach and jab, as well as power behind my punches. He encouraged me by saying that if I trained hard and listened to him, I could go a long way. I was stoked to be sure. But that night upon the drive home—on a school night—I realized what a challenge I faced—not in the ring, but in the four-day-a-week schedule.

The round-trip drive alone, especially in the winter months, which was the season for Golden Glove boxing, and the expense seemed overwhelming. There were no city buses from my suburb area around the various legs of this drive. I felt however that I could not pass this up as it was my true heart's desire. Since Gary and I had upped our career aspirations to ground row pickers under the Twin City Speedway's bleachers and now made seventy-five cents an hour, plus some change in the dirt, I thought if I was frugal—real frugal—I could cover all the expenses. I had saved nearly everything from my summer efforts. That would be an understatement of my neophyte boxing existence.

The first guy I had to fight for team qualification was a short, stocky brute named Steve Silver, probably a ring name. He was scary. He looked much older than I, had established a reputation in the ranks, and was highly respected. He also had four missing teeth in front; short, curly greasy hair; and looked like he could chew the chrome off my car's bumper, missing teeth or not. He was no doubt a mixture of several races that were all radically different than anything I had ever seen or met. I had trained for weeks before this shot. Since Coach Agnus, whom I greatly respected, said my perfect jab was my "cake" punch and my powerful right cross was my "frosting punch," I was told to concentrate on that combination.

In preparation for the fight, he told me to twist my right arm behind my back and hold it there while I threw jabs—a thousand of them—at the heavy bag. In addition, he told me to move laterally, from side to side, left to right, right to left. I figured he was involved with the Olympics, and I wasn't about to question him. I just took some deep breaths and started. After being satisfied with my start and progress, he took off to help others. When he returned some time later, he seemed surprised I was still doing what he said.

"Gee, Jon, how many have you done now?" I stopped for a moment.

"About four hundred, I guess," I replied, breathing hard as I dropped my left arm, which felt like an iron beam.

"Well, I was just saying that hypothetically. I didn't mean for you to actually do that much," he said with a grin as he directed me to take a break. That's how determined I was to make the team and excel. Agnus could see that and seemed to definitely take me under his wing. In that fight with Silver, the coach instructed me to jab, jab, and jab some more. "Only throw the right when you want the frosting," he quipped, "but keep your mind on the cake. The cake is just as important as the frosting."

Over the next week, I thought my left arm would drop off; it was so incredibly stiff and sore. Remarkably, following that weekend, my arm and jab felt like a battering ram. It not only recovered but did so with increased strength and accuracy. I bragged about it to the coach, and he just smiled broadly.

That's exactly what I did, and Silver, the extreme aggressor that he was, tried as he might, could not land a single punch to my head; but his head, meanwhile, was bouncing back and forth like one of those bobbing doll heads with such regularity that it seemed monotonous. His eyes and forehead were swelling before my eyes, and I just about felt sorry for him with all the cake and frosting I was laying on him. But I didn't. We were instructed to stop short of any knockouts as these were the trials. I got the nod handily. As Silver left the ring, he said to Agnus through slightly bloodied lips, "I think you got yourself a keeper there."

"You did exactly as I said, Jon, great job," he said. "My job is to assess your strengths and weaknesses and help you take greater advantage of those strengths. You definitely have the tools to be a good fighter . . . even more." With those inspiring words and Silver in my gym bag, I felt well on my way.

My next fight was against a classic boxer who was very tall. He was an Indian named Jerry Buckana and, again, was *much* more experienced and older than I. Despite having to switch to a more aggressive and slugger style, which coach Agnus advised, I was able to do well enough to advance on.

After a few more forgettable fights, I had basically secured a spot on the team. I think Agnus was actually more excited about that than I was, which was saying something. My personal gas tank was still on full, but my car's tank was struggling to have enough. I read old boxing books and the current crop of fisticuffs magazines as a way to keep motivated and inspired.

The driving across town to the roughest part of Minneapolis through cold and snow four school nights a week demanded it. I told no one of my boxing experience and what I was doing, not even Gary, especially not Dad, even though he sparked my interest in the first place. The only person who knew was my mom's mother, Grandma Hilda, because I stopped at her place to have dinner quite often—big steaks and chicken—on the long drive home. I loved that old family home where I was born, one block to the railroad and all the related buildings for parking and repair. I loved the sounds and the smell of linseed oil always hanging in the air. But Gram Hilda was such a giver and helper. Upon my request, and something I had read, she also helped me secure some raw calves' blood from a local butcher, who lived right around the corner.

Some of the historical old-timers said it was good for the blood and gave you a certain "hungry, aggressive edge." I drank it three times and nearly threw up, shelving the idea. But it obviously worked for dogs as they seemed to follow me after my half-hearted calf-blood consumptions. Primarily, I shared my situation with Gram because I couldn't make up any other excuse for my nightly schedule. I just told my folks that I was "working out," and since they were used to that scenario, it worked. Grandma also often slipped me a few bucks to help. She was always an "escape mechanism" away from home, and she and I became very close as I acted as her chauffeur when needed. But her giving to me and others could never be equaled. She always sacrificed a great deal for her family, but I guess we established this special bond that usually is reserved between grandkids and grandparents.

That next week, coach Agnus took me to an auditorium where the Golden Gloves were starting. We watched the entire card, but the one kid Verne kept talking about was this middleweight, who was coming up. He looked good, I thought, but the coach kept pointing out negatives to me; and upon many keen observations, Verne looked at me and said, "I think you can easily beat this kid. He's the one who is favored to win the championships because he's been around a while." I looked at him and nodded.

I watched, thought, and said, "Any particular way I should fight him?"

"Yeah, just relax and be yourself. Move laterally and serve him up plenty of cake and frosting. You don't have to hold back like with Silver. You can go for the knockout," he said nonchalantly. "Put a big cherry on top," he quipped, chuckling.

When I look back, I don't know how I was able for those months to drive across town in that clunker of mine, with its heater problems and makeshift fuel pump. Some nights by the time I got to Unity, I was beat tired, and my eyes were strained from driving through blinding snowstorms. Grandma slipped and had told Mom and Dad about my boxing, and Mom was constantly telling me I should quit. She said it was way too far away, took too many school nights, and I'd probably get hurt or worse. I told her I was the one who was doing most of the hitting and hurting and I seldom got tagged. Her badgering continued. My dad said nothing. I was surprised because of his own interest in boxing, but he was totally mum on the subject. I too said nothing. I felt no one from home was in my corner. Because I was such a respectful kid and I didn't want to make my mom feel the way she did since she put up with so much from Dad, I told her I'd quit. Ever since that time, I always believed I didn't follow my dream. I never really forgave myself.

It always gave me a certain resentment. I told Mom over and over that I would only pursue this if I was really good and didn't get my face messed up. But she just couldn't understand why I would want to partake in such a "violent" sport, especially with all the bad press boxing had received over the years. Mom simply was not a risk taker herself and didn't like the idea of me being one either.

Next, the hard part—I had to call the coach, who had all this confidence in me, and tell him the bad news. I had a hard time sleeping Sunday night, the night before. I rehearsed what I was going to say and was more nervous about telling him I had to quit than entering the ring in the first place. Finally, I did. Instead of showing up for ring practice, I called coach Agnus at the end of the evening and broke the news. He acted shocked and disappointed, even borderline mad. I explained all my reasons, the main ones being the distance, time, and expense. While saying he understood, he kept pushing for me to find some way to make it all work, even tapping into my parents more. I felt embarrassed so I didn't mention Mom's influence. He asked me to think on it some more and call him the next day. I did, and despite him complimenting me on my skills and being convinced I could easily win my weight class in the finals and championships, my answer was the same.

I not only felt bad for quitting, but I felt just as bad about letting him down. He was a great guy and fantastic coach. I left by saying I thought I learned things from him that would stick with me forever, and I appreciated it. I mean, he was involved with the Olympics. Done but never out of my memories. I had studied boxing and read everything I could on the topic, including all the heavyweight bios, plus others. I knew I would grow into a heavyweight one day, and if I had any aspirations back then, the only one I recall was someday winning the heavyweight championship of the world. Talk about lofty goals, but they stuck. I think I felt this way for two reasons, both Dad-inspired. One, Dad's consistent prodding, pushing, and jabbing my face, never hurting me but creating this inner desire to retaliate and score jabs and big shots of my own—never able to do so with Dad. Second, I wanted so bad to land just one compliment from him and felt that the only way I might accomplish this was by winning something big in boxing, like the crown jewel heavyweight championship of the world, the same one he took me to see with Johansson and Patterson as a kid. Dreams and secret aspirations are a huge part of growing up, their ambitions usually far exceeding any realistic practicality. This was one dream that never drifted from the private confines of my mind, but while there, it never lacked vivid details and dimension. And it stayed intact for years.

Chapter Eight

Having made close friends with Tom Booth by this time, I started more weight training in earnest. Tom was this infectious ball of energy and humor who was also a high-level varsity wrestler. I shared a little of the boxing challenge I had just left, and he too thought that long drive that often alone on school nights was extreme and too hard to overcome. Tom and I both had this mutual love for bodybuilding, powerlifting, and weightlifting. We attended the *Hercules* movies with Steve Reeves in the day and were always taking vitamins, drinking horrendously terrible, chalky soy protein shakes. They were gagging, but we consumed them religiously. I think if anything, they may have given us a few bumps of muscles, along with our training, but they also helped us got a few new bumps of zits. We had a lot of laughs, and it all helped school days go by quicker.

Tom even entered an AAU weightlifting contest and won his weight class. I held his gym bag during the event and his trophy after his victory while he got dressed in street clothes. As proud as I was for Tom, inside it hurt because I knew I may have experienced the same fate as Tom had I continued with Golden Gloves boxing. And then on to bigger and better things. I had my visions.

During this time, Gary, who was not into sports and fitness like me, was more busy reading at home, so Tom and Roger filled in the gaps. Roger was in the new work-school program, owned a fancy convertible, and backed off the barbells while picking up the bottle. He was hanging out with some rough types down in Minneapolis and was drinking so much whiskey he was keeping the empty bottles in his closet. But occasionally, he would venture downtown to the gym he sometimes frequented, the American Health Studios on Seventh and Hennepin. While I ended up joining, Roger never went again, as he was too busy partying. But I became somewhat of a fixture down there from that period until the time I joined the Marines. It wasn't nearly as far as the boxing gym at Unity, and I probably went there on and off, two to three times weekly, with more visits during the weekends and summers. It also had a lengthy but interconnected bus line. The gym was a hotbed of world-class powerlifters like Don Cundy, Mike

Carroll, and Ed Ammerman, in addition to professional wrestlers--whom I also later called mat Thespians--like world champion Verne Gagne, Crusher, Bruiser, Igor, Harley Race, Eddie Sharkey, and others. There were even a few newbie pro boxers that were blended in. One was the up and coming heavyweight with the last name Bobick, brother of Olympian, Duane. He was tough, I guess, but didn't go too far, but he went a lot further than me, didn't he?

I usually always did some boxing on the heavy bag there when it was up, but mainly I concentrated on bodybuilding and powerlifting, even setting a few supposed "unofficial" bench press and squat records at the teen (16) and 165-pound class. But my main claim to fame came about primarily from being called "skinny legs" by Cundy, who had legs like thick, mature oak trees. Also, some attention and laughs from an upper-body (didn't care about legs) bodybuilder who worked at the studio with incredible arms and torso, as an assistant manager, who refused to put the gloves on with me because he "didn't want to get any bruises on his chest or arms." Verne Gagne, whom I knew had also been a Marine, recognized me quite often at the gym, encouraged me to take his son Greg—just several years younger than me—under my wing and teach him a little about working out, which I did enthusiastically over a month or so. Greg became an accomplished pro wrestler himself years after.

But in those days, that gym was just as much known as a chick magnet hangout as this basement health studio that was started years before by a Mr. America, Alan Stephan. In some ways, on some days, it would be like a home away from home. I used it as a springboard for numerous chance encounters and friendships far from the quiet suburbs up north. After having my self-esteem knocked down so often at home by Dad, going down there not only pumped up my muscles but also my mind and self-confidence.

Another close friend I met there was another gym manager named Paul. Paul had a hugely muscled physique, had a cutting-edge sense of humor, and was perhaps one of the biggest characters I had ever met, or would ever meet. He came from a tough background as his father flew the coop when he was young. Paul, who was Polish and proud of it, was obsessed with bodybuilding and had this incredible, unreal appetite. It wasn't strange for him to polish off two full chickens for lunch. His mother, who looked like this broken-down, worn-out wench, was always bringing him food at the gym. She'd bring him bags of stuff, stop at Woolworth's and get more, and hobble downstairs to the gym. Paul always tried to get the food and shovel her out the door real quick as if he were ashamed. The biggest memory from Paul was when I took him to McDonald's for lunch. It was before they had everything built in and the customer would just walk up to window and order, even in the winter.

It was quite cold that day, but Paul wore his tight-fitting T-shirt anyway. It was red and showed off his huge arms to best advantage. He was in front of me and ordered first. "Let's see now," he started with his hand rubbing his chin. "I'll take eight hamburgers stacked up with no buns, hold everything else, and two large chocolate shakes." Me and everyone around me nearly stopped breathing. The order taker, this young black lady, after a great delay and a priceless reaction and look, said, "You can't get hamburgers here without the buns, mister. You can only order them the way they are offered."

Paul just made a cringe of a smile and shook his head. "Well, I just did and I would like my hamburgers now, please. Thank you." I thought of Wimpy in the Popeye cartoons.

I put my hand on his shoulder and said, "C'mon, Paul, why don't you just take them the regular way?"

"No, it is quite a simple order. It's like they normally make them but without the buns or the condiments, simple. I don't want the starch from the bread. It's bad for your body. I have my rights and I want my hamburgers. Holy cow, lady, it's simpler for the cook to make them 'cause they are just a pile of meat," Paul responded. One patron started acting impatient behind him, and he just looked at him and the guy froze.

The lady yelled for the manager. He was there in a flash, recognized Paul, and told the lady he knew him and to give him his order as he ordered it. The manager was falling over himself apologizing. Paul grinned shyly, flexed his pecs and arms a little, with a naughty little smile in his eyes.

When the order came out, right there at the window, Paul took the stack of bunless burgers out of the bag and positioned them between his index and forefingers. He then shoved the sides of the burger stack into his mouth and proceeded to take four large bites out of the stack, finishing eight burgers. He then took a napkin and gently dabbed his lips. Then he drank down the first shake by literally inhaling it and quickly grabbed the other and did the same, once again meticulously dabbing his mouth with a napkin like some knight in King's Court. I started giggling, and then the others there did the same. It probably made their day, week, year. Paul was full until the next feeding hours away. Years later, I ran into his brother, Pete, and found him to be the same exact image as Paul—same humor, same muscled-up physique, and same unforgettable character. To be around Paul and Pete was to be entertained 24-7. I loved those guys and found out that both became well-known and respected attorneys who seldom lost cases, especially Paul. If Paul brought his unique personality into the courtroom, it was no wonder he was such a winner. I have enough Paul stories to make a book, but his inclusion will have to stop here.

During my high school years, every Christmas, Dad would get stone drunk and come home on Christmas eve and make a scene. At the very least, he was fall-down drunk; sometimes he was in such a stupor he had to be dragged out of the car and into the house. There would always be stories or excuses along with the drunkenness, including his fights, but the result was always the same—it ruined our Christmas. Christmas eve was being drunk; Christmas Day was recovering and being sick and nasty along with apologetic. Christmas apparently kicked up deep-seated emotions. Those two words together—Dad and emotions—made for a volatile combination. I always thought it could have been much worse and was grateful it wasn't. It wore on my mom and sister Judy much more. Maybe I got a little pleasure seeing Dad yanked out of the car and dragged through the snow, bumping into walls, falling over steps.

Judy had her own drunken episode when she was a teen. Right next door to us lived the Walkers. Nice people with several young kids. Judy was hired as their babysitter this particular night and ended up asking her girlfriend Linda to assist her for the evening. But they had more sinister plans than mere babysitting. Judy and her accomplice found a bottle of vodka in the cabinet and proceeded to get drunk, so much so that they went outside in a snowstorm and romped around in the white stuff and passed out. As the story went, the Walkers came home, found the girls in the snow, and called Mom, who told Dad. After hearing of this story, my first thought was, is Judy still alive, tongue-in-cheek somewhat. Seems that Dad rushed to their rescue, picked them up, cleaned them up, hair frozen in vomit and all, escorted Linda home, and nursed Judy to recovery.

According to Mom, Dad didn't say a terse word or have any particularly bad reaction. Instead, he showed nothing but patience and love. Judy, by the way, wouldn't ever be babysitting for the Walkers again, but she was not any worse for the wear and learned a valuable lesson in drinking. I often wondered what would have happened if that were to happen to me with dad? And my gut response is probably the same, but I never pushed that envelope because I didn't want to see.

I remember the evening I came home from Unity House and boxing training. I had hit the heavy bag so hard that I pushed all the knuckles of my right hand up to the top middle of my hand. It happened just before the training night was over and I didn't want to bring it up to coach Agnus, so I kind of hid it and went home, not knowing what to do or how to do it. Dad somehow noticed it and wore a broad smile. "Looks like you messed up your knuckles a little, huh, Jon," he said calmly.

"Sorry, Dad . . . What am I going to do? It hurts," I said, worried. "Am I going to have to have surgery or something?"

"Probably not," he replied, still wearing that grin. "If you let me help you."

"Okay," I said reluctantly.

Dad took my hand in his and with his other hand quickly and strongly pulled. The knuckles were pulled across the top of my hand and magically went into place. He did it so fast, not giving me much of a chance to think about it, and it was over without extreme pain. Later when I got to thinking about it, I couldn't believe how those knuckles were jerked out of their new position back to the original spot.

It hurt much more thinking about it afterward. The lesson here was how powerful and dictatorial the mind really was, that the mind often led the body. Dad left the scene by simply saying, "You'll be fine."

Shortly after, I joined the church softball team and did quite well, so I knew the knuckles healed fine. One of the huge benefits of belonging to that church team was watching this one teammate get a hit and run the bases. She had huge hooters and couldn't help them from bouncing like balloons with the air being let out. The only trouble was that she couldn't hit for crap and seldom was able to provide that busty show.

Chapter Nine

Just as I concluded my sophomore year, Gary told me he had joined the Air Force and was leaving for boot camp in several weeks. I was dumbfounded since we had plans to join together when I graduated.

I can't recall his exact reasoning, but for the first time, I was really upset with my brother-like buddy. I felt that perhaps he wanted to get the jump on me, and that hurt like a betrayal. However, I soon got over it and bade him farewell and insisted he write me a lot and keep me abreast of everything about the Air Force. He did. My mother had her last child about this time, and I privately prayed for a boy, a brother.

But my prayers weren't answered, and I ended up with a third sister, Joni, to add to Judy and Janet. All of us kids had first names starting with *J*. Even Dad's name was John, with the *h*. Mom was the only outcast on the name front, with the first name Imogene, nicknamed "Babe." Dad teased her quite a bit with the Imogene, but usually only used it when he was upset and wanted to drill home a point. His mixture of humor, teasing and then flipping to viciousness, could happen quite effortlessly.

About this same time, Roger joined the Navy—which surprised me—and also soon left for boot camp. I was now left with my workout buddy Tom, some thugs down at the gym, and Roger's younger brother Jerome. Jerome and I became fast friends, and I probably spent, oh, 75 percent of my life down at his house playing pool (and smoking), going through car magazines, listening to the top 40 hits of rock 'n' roll, watching comedies, mysteries, and *The Tonight Show* with Steve Allen.

We also went hunting for pheasants, rabbits, and ducks, but the latter saw us quit altogether when our duck boat sank and we had to swim to shore holding our rifles above our heads (perfect for survival training). I think those days contributed to me being a pretty model kid, as I always got along with Mom just fine, and Dad was Dad, from being the greatest helpmate in the world to being a man-beast, with an uncontrollable temper, with me being the recipient more often than not (not to take away from what Mom took). One of the best examples of his behavior went back a few years when Mom took one of her seldom ventures away from home. Mom's sister, Aunt Chris, talked her into going somewhere, and both Mom and I paid the price. She would not be there when Dad returned from work and not there to prepare supper.

I returned from school around three in the afternoon, and seeing the note that Mom had left with Chris and would be home later, I took the steak out of the freezer and put it in the sink to thaw. I also got a few other items down from the cupboard. Dad came home at around three forty-five so I thought my help toward dinner would assist Mom avert any potential disaster. When Dad came home and walked in and saw the note, his facial features took that radical transformation, suggesting there would be hell to pay.

He mumbled a few things to me then shut up while wearing his mask of destruction. I would have rather been beat up any day, compared to that look of his. It was that scary.

Soon, I unwrapped the big steak and put it in an awaiting frying pan. "What are you doing?" Dad said.

"I'm just helping getting supper ready," I replied, just cringing, guessing what reaction that would bring.

Then the barrage started as he called me many four-letter names with such nonstop viciousness that it drew tears from my eyes, and they were so heavy they dropped into the frying pan and sizzled. But I kept standing there overseeing the steak and taking the verbal attacks, 90 percent directed at me, with some potshots thrown at Mom. I was afraid to say anything else because I would be damned if I did—doing Mom's normal duties—and damned if I didn't, being complacent or defending her as he would see it. I tried my best to ignore him while scampering around the kitchen getting dishes, glasses, and the like. When Mom finally got home, I informally excused myself and went down to my room and shut the door. I would hear lots of screaming, and when supper was called, Dad was stone quiet, now sulking.

Behavior like his was commonplace. He always worked hard, fed us the best, and provided all of us kids school lunch and needs without delay—but it all too often was under a roof of tyranny. That's why I escaped so much to Jerome's place as the Stenhoffs' home offered another safe harbor. During the winter, I would still walk down to Jerome's a mile away, even in the harshest storms, and then walk back home, always combining a cigarette with inhaling the freezing air, easily averaging five to six nights a week. Those walks home also caused me to think about leaving home one day to join the military. Leaving home, the neighborhood, and Minnesota for greater horizons and adventures was on my mind nearly every spare moment. Success in boxing also played a paramount part in my thinking: win, leave.

Because I went through two to three clunkers by the time I was a junior, Lester just handed me his car keys one day and said, "It's yours. Your dad will never let you drive his, so take it. I'm sick of driving anyway." I couldn't believe it, nor could Dad, but I had Lester's car, another Ford, but this one was like a hot rod. It had a three-speed column shift and peeled out like nobody's business. Since Dad never gave me anything, this was a real shot in the arm from Dad's brother Les. But the luster of that generosity would soon be erased by one day in late November 1963.

I was in Mrs. Jensen's English class. It was late in the morning, approaching lunch break. Suddenly, the principal came on the loudspeaker and told us that President John F. Kennedy had been shot in his motorcade down in Dallas, Texas. Everyone gasped out loud, sending the same sound bouncing against the schoolroom walls. Just as erupt was the deadening silence following that, like the echoes sliding down from the walls and into and upon the floor. The principal closed his shocking announcement by saying he would report right back to us with further details. Lunch became a mirage.

His next report told us, "I am sorry to convey to you, students, that President Kennedy was fatally wounded and despite all attempts to save him, died at 1:30 p.m." This time, there were both sighs and sobs, quickly followed by "I have ordered all buses to be immediately dispatched to the school, and classes will be dismissed until further notice."

Normally, early school dismissal would be time for celebration, but this was no day for happiness. It was a day and a time for great remorse. Everything and everybody seemed to be moving in a morbid, exaggerated slow and methodical manner. Levity and normal interaction and communication were on hold, as if it were bound in an endless big bowl of thick sludge. I got home and barely remembered the bus ride. I joined my mom in front of the TV, watching the news live. My dad would soon be joining us as we were all glued to the stream of events as they unfolded, including the police officer who was shot outside a theater. The only newsman I remember was Walter Cronkite, probably because they kept replaying Cronkite looking up at the clock, swallowing hard and fighting tears, as he announced Kennedy's passing. It would, of course, become a timeless classic of live breaking news. It also put an immediate end to Camelot. And the world knew it and mourned.

The second biggest shock—an aftershock if you will—close on the heels of the assassination, happened right before all of our eyes. The apparent assassin, Lee Harvey Oswald, was shot and killed while being transferred from one area to another. He was soon pronounced dead, and the saga and drama dug in their heels for an extended stay. It was so nonstop that it was hard to even leave to the bathroom. And it went on and on, with one scenario and endless revelation after another. As the relentless pounding of the story and grief went on, it became a story you wanted to also put to rest. But in totality, couldn't.

That summer while staying with my grandmother just outside the city, I had landed a great job at Warner Hardware in downtown Minneapolis as a mail boy. It was quite a big operation and was housed in a six-story building. They provided hardware items for the entire upper Midwest. As I made my rounds with mail, I enjoyed talking with different types of the rank and file, especially this one much-older woman. She was like some impossible dream for a kid like me, but served well for fantasies of different circumstances. Her whole womanly package exuded sex appeal and had most guys' eyeballs and tongues dragging around like lap dogs. She was the secretary to a company big shot, and I found myself running into her as I delivered my mail quite often, especially in the elevator, alone. One time, after checking me out pretty thoroughly from stem to stern, she reached over and stopped the elevator, saying she needed to go down instead of up. She brushed against me as she did this, and I felt that I was about to go up despite what floor I would be going to, not that I was paying attention.

What I missed most about that summer stint was that sultry lady, if only in my dreams, sleeping or awake. She would forever more be used in my head as the perfect example of what a truly sexy and attractive woman was or should be. Just another story of the trials and tribulations of growing up a boy with increasing levels of testosterone. Minnesota's chilling winters seemed to stifle that somewhat, but after that summer, any excuse would work to chill the desires.

Chapter Ten

During my senior year of high school, I felt that I just had to make more money, so I secured an occasional job with this janitorial company and filled in for no-show workers. I did a good enough job where they offered me my own little company to clean. At seventeen, I was the youngest employee they had ever hired by a long shot. It was slotted as a weekday position that was paid out for three hours for one person. But there was a lot of variety built in the time since the job itself would vary based upon different factors, related to the dirtiness of this meatpacking home office. Normally, I could handle the job myself. Sometimes I had to have help and the janitorial company would call me and send them over.

This particular night, it was still raining hard and the company called me and said they were sending me help. I was the one with the master key so I waited in my car outside the side of the building. A car pulled up and this black guy got out, extended his hand with a big smile, and we strode to the doors, exchanging pleasantries. I was a little surprised since the only minority I had ever met was down at the Unity neighborhood house in south Minneapolis. We were on the edge of Saint Paul in a businesslike industrial area. The guy, whom I'll call Fred, was very complimentary, saying he couldn't believe they would entrust anyone with this job and its security at such a young age. He said their normal guidelines were twenty-one or older. We kind of hit it off right from the beginning. He was so cordial and outgoing.

Just then the shock. It was like a bolt of runaway lightning. Two cop cars pulled up and told us to freeze, which we quickly did. Three cops approached us, and as they did, they gathered around Fred and pushed him against the car and told him to "hold up your hands and spread 'em." I was left alone standing there in sheer amazement. They grilled us, checked my master key, and called the janitorial company to confirm who we were. This all happened while Fred was still leaning against the cop car.

After a while, they released Fred and told us to be on our way, with no apologies or anything. I was pretty upset; Fred wasn't.

He just smiled widely and said, "A person like me just gets used to this. I wasn't hurt or anything. It's okay, son." I couldn't believe his response. Compared to the cops, he was about the coolest guy I had ever met, and he did it with this measure of class that even my age picked up on. He was so nonchalant about the whole thing that I felt the cops were the ones to look so bad and low class. We talked about it a little longer, and I apologized to him profusely and he would thank me back and leave the issue by telling me about himself.

He was in his late thirties and been married since twenty and had five kids, three boys and two girls. He added that he had a full-time job plus this part-time position, filling needs the company had. He also said his wife was a housewife and had her hands full watching over the kids. He said in some context I can't remember that they loved their kids and everything was for them. I somehow couldn't picture my own father ever saying that to anyone about his kids, but who knows. I know I never personally heard anything like that, but that was probably par for the course in those days. He also asked all about my life and seemed genuinely interested.

Fred was not only a great guy, but he was also a relentless worker and we were able to leave the building within two hours. I called the janitorial manager the next day to compliment Fred and say how wrong it was for this to happen to him. I told that manager how lucky they were to have such a man as Fred in their ranks. They agreed and thanked me. It was an experience that will always be at the forefront of my memories. It also was an incredible lesson in human honor, class, patience, dignity, and work ethics.

I've always used Fred as one of my main benchmarks for men I would look up to, try to emulate, and use as a comparative example for judging people. That would really be saying something considering the whole experience and impression happened over a period of two and a half hours.

Later, when more employees added to that company's job roles and increased our workload, another person was assigned to me; but before that happened, my mom expressed interest in the job with me, and they let her come aboard. Had it not been me, Dad would have never let her leave the house, especially in the evening, and do this. I wasn't crazy about the idea, but it all worked out fine and lasted for an entire season. Despite Mom's resistance to trying the floor buffer that cleaned and waxed, I pushed her to just try—once. She really had this aversion to risk in practically any form. I was determined to have her try this and overcome this fear of hers. I showed her how it worked and how the handle switch maneuvered and how to simply let go of the handle if it started to whirl out of control.

She was ready, she said, but I had my doubts for some reason.

She finally started the machine, gripped the handle switch, and it immediately started whirling out of control. I thought she would have a heart attack so I stepped in, more like ran in, and simply took her hand off the handle switch. If I didn't know better, I would have sworn her hand was welded to that handle. I laughed so hard I couldn't contain myself, and she joined in, good sport that she was, but her laughs weren't nearly as robust as mine. From that point on, Mom stuck to cleaning the desks, tables, and other easier jobs.

As a senior, I also met my uncle Oscar Hansen for the first time, who was Grandma Hilda's brother. He was this huge, huge Norwegian who had the most extreme northern Minnesota, North Dakota accent. He also was cut from the same cloth as Hilda, being very easygoing, hardworking, bighearted, soft, and generous. He was retired as Mayfield North Dakota sheriff and was content just traveling around and spending time with family and friends. My mom's side of the family owned farms up in North Dakota and were all big hearty people. I used to love to go up there and feed the chickens and yank bales of hay around. Farm life seemed very honorable to me. I also liked all the land and privacy, with your immediate neighbors being farm animals. It was a super hard life, especially in the winter. Farmers would always get up at four-thirty in the morning and be finished in mid to late afternoon, plus emergencies. During the planting, growing, plowing, and picking seasons, it was seven days per week.

I heard many stories of the Hansen household—all thirteen kids—and how tough it could be. Mom always told me Grandma never left a food scrap behind because of their upbringing. The boys went out in the fields and did all the work while the girls stayed home and did all the cooking. Since the boys were all so large—and hungry—there was never enough food, so oftentimes the girls had to let the boys eat all they could while they had nothing but the scraps left. It always explained why Grandma cleaned the chicken bones right down to the grizzle and ate that as well. She did that her whole life.

Oscar's past was quite colorful too. He was this big strapping farm boy who was called out by this sideshow wrestler at the carnival. After much razing, pushing, and encouragement, Oscar took the challenge and went up to the ring and beat the pro quite handily. He won some money and a job doing the same thing. After that, he ran for sheriff and won. While being mild and effective with people, he was voted back as sheriff numerous times. People knew that he could also hold his own with the rougher crowd if need be.

Even though we had this huge age difference, Oscar and I became friends, which would last until I joined the Marines. He took me to the pro wrestling show once, and while there, his wallet was stolen.

He said he had a hundred dollars in it, but took it in stride. He was so easygoing and just rolled along with life like a big log. Having a close friendship with Oscar as I did helped me tolerate Dad at home as his calm demeanor helped circumvent Dad's rage. Oscar was another positive example and influence for me. I can't recall the branch of military service, but I'm fairly certain he served his country as well. He was from that great generation.

I was not a very good student over the years, hanging with a small group of boys who prided themselves with doing nothing in class or out, and just skimming by within a hair of failing. I may have only cracked my books open in high school enough so they wouldn't rot. I was deeply into that "zero" element of student application. In my junior year however, I started waking up to the fact that I was not proud of myself and my performance. I didn't want to fall back on the excuse that it was very tough at home. I gradually started changing and doing better. By the time I graduated high school, which my mother insisted I do—and I never assumed I wouldn't although Dad said he didn't care and that I should just work—I had upped my overall grade average to mainly As, Bs, and some Cs. I also was called out for designing and making a steel piece of exercise equipment in shop class and designed a subterranean home—three-fourths underground—in architectural class. More importantly, I discovered my love for communication, particularly writing.

It happened in English class with Mr. Feyereisen, where I surprisingly ran across my writing talents. We had a theme paper due and I realized I hadn't touched a pen to paper yet, so I stopped at the library in my free hour before class to pound out something. I can't remember what I wrote about, but it was two pages long and was somewhat messy. Feyereisen picked it out of the pile of papers, got up to sit atop of one of the desks that he was famous for, and started reading my paper. I was embarrassed beyond belief. Red came to my face as surely as a stint at the gym. After he read parts of it, he put it down and looked at me. "Did you write this?"

"Yes, I did," I responded as I explained my library-stop story.

He looked rather bewildered. "Okay then, did you copy it out of some book?"

"No, I didn't, Mr. Feyereisen. I've handed in papers before, can't you kind of tell this is mine?"

"Well, I do recognize the messy writing and some minor punctuation," he replied, with a slight grin.

I got an A from him in my final English class, and I was elated. I always heard that Feyereisen had been a boxer in his earlier life and always wanted to talk to him about it but never did. I have to say, along with most classmates, that he was about as cool and easygoing as any teacher could be. The boys in the class also sensed that they shouldn't ever mess with him. Funny, but years after, in a Catholic Church close to my old high school, I ran into him. I was attending mass along with my then wife upon a visit back home from California. He was still the same quiet, cool guy, but I had to ask him about that theme paper incident with me. He couldn't remember, so I refreshed his memory and he somewhat remembered small parts of it, smiled, and we parted ways. Before he left though, I told him that the second-guessing of his of my work and then the obvious subsequent complimenting of it in that offhanded way encouraged me to write more and even pursue a degree in journalism in college. I thanked him and felt that both of us felt good about it. It's noteworthy in life how we often learn lessons that end up serving us well. More than that, I was very happy I finished high school on a positive note and was so influenced by this man, who never fully realized how he impacted me.

On that graduation day and on the school grounds, someone got some boxing gloves and said that Betty Lund's boyfriend wanted to box me. He was considered a tough guy, I guess, but someone I never had any problems with. We put the gloves on just because some guys wanted us to. I sparred with him, landing punches at will, especially the jab, but in reality held back as there was no reason to look tougher than him. I just wanted to do enough. He said afterward that he couldn't land a punch or get to me because my arms were so long. It was true and okay. He was a good guy. But it was Betty—Miss Hostess Cupcakes—that gave me my payback and satisfaction. I was smiling inside. If I would have had a cupcake, I would have celebrated right there, unless she took it away again.

Chapter Eleven

I took a two-week break from graduation before I took a job as a welder in Saint Paul. A friend's father got me the job after a test and ended up giving me my own night shift. I was the youngest hire again. I busted my ass when there and got a raise from $1.50 an hour to $1.85. I felt rich as I got some overtime too. I traded in this classic 1949 totally restored Oldsmobile I had for a practically new Chevy Corvair with four-on-the-floor. They gave me a large amount in trade because the Olds was old, but like new, with many original upgrades. I never forgave myself for that trade. I was just young and insane. I was dating several young ladies, but none in my own area, all in Saint Paul and Minneapolis.

My gym buddy, Ed Ammerman, a world-class lifter and older, lined me up with this friend of his girlfriend. Ed said she was a sure thing, and that's what I wanted. And boy, did I get it. Within the next day, at work, when I urinated, I got this searing pain in my penis. It was so extreme I had to grab the pipe coming down to the urinal. I wanted to scream in pain but couldn't because I was at work. It was like a slow penile torture. I weathered the storm until my night shift the next day. I picked out a small clinic far from home thinking I could assure privacy. Wrong again! Oh, so wrong!

I filled out some paperwork and walked up to the window. An old nurse read it, puzzled. I probably didn't get an A on that theme because I hedged around the truth with nonsensical explanations. Then emerging through the back door came this beautiful young nurse, a little older than me. It was a girl that I had just started dating and had very high regard for, like that special girl in a young guy's life you want to preserve for better things. She saw me, was very surprised, then joined the older nurse reading my form. I felt my legs giving away, like all the blood in my upper body was draining down. I probably turned white. Just then, with about three people in the waiting room behind me, the older nurse blurted out, "So, it looks like you may have gonorrhea. Do you know what that is?"

I just learned, the hard way. And everyone else did as well. I died many times over. My potential girlfriend left and closed the door behind her rather hard. I waited a few more minutes and was called to come in. I was shown to a room by the older nurse. She wasn't exactly a diplomat. "You got the clap, kid. You must have been playing with the wrong girl. How old are you?" I didn't answer. I just thought about my good buddy Ed. With friends like him, I didn't need enemies. "You have to get two big shots of penicillin, maximum strength, one in each hip so you can walk afterward. You have a pretty good case," she said in rapid fire as she left. She must have served in the military or war, or both, 'cause she was hardcore, pulling no punches and sparing me no embarrassment.

I waited and waited for what seemed an eternity. Finally, the door cracked open, and guess who walked in. If it was that drop-dead gorgeous gal with a face and body God could have only seldom created, you would, of course, be right. She said nothing as she slowly drew the needle back into the chamber and tested for fluid. She told me to stand and drop my pants. I did, just in enough time to get that huge needle nearly thrown into my low hip. Still saying nothing, she did the same to the other hip. They were like javelins of pain, spears of torture, cattle prods of revenge. I deserved it. And I'm sure the young beauty thought so as well. My mind already felt the loss. There she went high into the air and space like an angel going back to her heavenly perch.

"You can pull up your pants now," she said with a twisted grin. "You may have a little hard time walking and moving for several days, but it will soon go away. Gonorrhea is treatable, and you will have a complete recovery."

I may have been able to recover from the clap (why would something so gross and painful be referred to in such a congratulatory way?), but I never would recover from this experience as far as learning a hard, painful, remorseful lesson. Before I left, like some damaged animal with his tail between his legs, she had some parting remarks.

"And to think, Jon, that I was raving to my girlfriends about you," she remarked before taking a long, long pause. "You can go now and never look back."

Did she have to use my name? I was frozen in reaction and words. I just looked at her with cow eyes as she left the room and slammed the door. I left, paid my cash at the window—no bills at home for me—and left quickly like a thief in the night. I had to drive to work and continually lift my butt cheeks as I made the trip. They told me I didn't need any meds for pain. Yeah right. It seemed fitting. I stopped dating as a punishment and just worked and went to the gym. That was until I met *her*.

"*Her*" was a cheerleader from high school. In any season, her name started the summer. Months after graduation and my "clap" incident, I only wanted contact with wholesome, decent, "good" girls.

I always thought this particular cheerleader was the prettiest of the lot, and she had this classy air about her, a dignity, and had an impeccable reputation. I called another classmate who was friends with her and asked her to mention that I was interested in possibly dating her.

When I talked to her again, she said this girl said it was okay for me to call her. I was immediately excited. I soon called her and had a great conversation. I had never talked to her before as she seemed to be on a different plateau than me. Everything about her was perfect, even her sweet, unassuming voice. She also seemed quite intelligent, which I loved, and she shared some proposed minor plans for her future with me. I was a little surprised when she gladly accepted my date invitation as I couldn't believe she wasn't taken or had a boyfriend. I later found out that boys shied away from her, probably for the same reasons I did.

When I went to pick her up at her house in New Brighton on Tenth Avenue, I was invited in to meet her parents, who were of solid German stock and very nice, although her dad gave me the man-to-boy eyeball look over. Since I was raised to always be respectful and polite with high-grade manners, I usually was well liked and accepted by parents, as was the case here. While meeting them was pleasant, I couldn't resist staring at this gorgeous model of a young lady. She had this incredible smile and perfectly groomed, natural blonde hair that was worn up in a tight bun. She also had a femininely athletic figure.

As this initial date was to be strictly an introductory get-together and I was so in admiration by her I can't remember a thing about where we went or what we did. I just recall being in awe of her as I put my very best foot forward. I guess it was good enough to get another date. Her face, figure, and demeanor were now firmly planted in my head. She was no doubt my first real love, but I didn't realize the full extent of my feelings at the time. Even more, I didn't share them with her or anyone else.

A short time previous to our burgeoning relationship, I joined the Marines. I was so focused on her that I can't remember if I shared my enlistment with her or not. Joining the Corps was no cakewalk. One day when I determined it was time to join the Air Force and follow in Gary's footsteps, I went down to the federal building in Minneapolis to sign up. I sailed through everything until it came to blood pressure. Mine was high, and I got rejected. I got another try and failed again. I was absolutely crushed. Oh well, me and the Air Force probably wouldn't have been compatible anyway. I would have thrown up on some pilot's back. They told me to wait for a few days and come back and try another service, maybe I'd be luckier. I wasn't. I failed the Navy physical too. They told me at that time I was basically 4-F, unqualified for military service. I thought, I'll show them, I'll show them all, Gary and the world. I won't be denied. I went back for a fourth try. I picked the Marines, which I really wanted anyway. And while sailing through the physical as before, I failed the blood pressure test again. I was so anxious to get in and so upset with myself, I felt like I was living this nightmarish horror that would never cease.

The Navy doctor who failed me this last time sat me down and with deadly serious eyes said, "Do you realize that you are signing up for the Marines, the toughest of all the services . . . especially boot camp?"

"Yes, I do, Doctor."

He just sat there studying my eyes. "I've never seen anyone try so hard to get in as you." I was silent and frankly somewhat embarrassed. "You do know you qualify for 4-F which means you can get up and walk out of here. Some guys would probably kill for that. You tried and there's nothing dishonorable about it."

"Yes, sir, but that's not me."

"Obviously," he said. "I'll give you a break and retest you in forty-five minutes. Maybe if you relax and reduce your anxiety, your blood pressure will go down. And if so, I'll sign off on your medical and enlistment."

It wasn't easy, but I calmed down and forced away all my pent-up negative thinking. Before I knew it, the doctor was strapping the blood pressure monitor on my arm and declaring it was fine—normal. I felt like doing a somersault on the examining table. The doctor laughed at my excitement and said anyone with my desire deserved to join the

Marines and that the Corps loved guys with guts, even if they were a little crazy.

I was now a tentative Marine (actually far from it), but signed up two months before I would leave for boot camp. And all this for the princely sum of around $70 per month. I think it is safe to assume none of us young men back then signed up for the income opportunities. I remember my recruiter asking if I wanted to apply for any particular career designation. Career designation? What? I just wanted to be a regular ground Marine, which I would later learn was a *grunt*. The recruiter documented my work history, including my current job as a metal fabricator and welder. I thought nothing more of it.

I had another date with *her* before Gary would come home on leave, and we enjoyed a double date together. That second date was rather unusual as I had asked her if she was up for something different. She was so I took her to the Saint Paul Auditorium where we saw the Crusher and Bruiser wrestle in a tag team match, besides my gym acquaintance Eddie Sharkey. She seemed highly amused, and after dessert somewhere, we ended the evening on another high note. But it was that double date later with Gary that changed everything with *her*.

After we wrapped the evening up, we returned to Gary's house, where his parents were out for the night. Gary went inside with his date to watch some TV and do some smooching. I stayed out in the car with *her*. We did a little smooching ourselves but mainly just conversed. I realized at that precise time that I had to distance myself from *her*. I couldn't see her again. I didn't say anything to her about it; I just knew inside my heart it was the right thing to do. Maybe someday again down the road (who was I kidding?), but not now, not after joining the Corps. My thinking may have been somewhat noble but flawed as far as trusting my hunches and the hearts of both *her* and me. She meant so much to me I didn't ever want to hurt her, figuring as a Marine I could go to war and didn't want to put her through any heartache in case I got killed. That's why I didn't want any serious girlfriends, especially an extra special one. Although I did a good job of eliminating her from my life, I never eliminated her from the back of my mind. Between the nurse and the cheerleader (*her*) situations, I left the double-female fiasco behind me, of which I was totally responsible for myself. I messed up one and severed the other.

Looking back, it was a little premature, but my future wasn't the best at that time to get serious anyway. I doubt how good a provider I may have been. It wasn't until I became a Marine that I would really wake up and get motivated, go to college, and become better suited to a productive existence, especially for someone like *her*. She deserved the best, and I didn't think I was there yet.

Chapter Twelve

When late April of 1965 rolled around, it was time to get myself ready to leave for the Marines. I said my goodbyes all around, and Dad drove me downtown to the federal building on his way to work.

I remember the last song I heard on that AM radio as "Eight Days a Week" by the Beatles, quickly flashing a memory of the Beatles invading America on *Ed Sullivan* the year I graduated in '64. I never liked the Beatles much, but I would come to love and always remember that song as it defined the time I left home to be a man. Dad offered his hand, we shook, and he wished me well as I thanked him. I met three other young guys who were joining with me from Minneapolis, and we were driven off to Wold-Chamberlain Airport where we would catch a Western Airlines prop job to San Diego.

What can I say about Marine Corps boot camp that hasn't already been said, resaid, analyzed, and documented a thousand ways to Sunday? I guess there were a few things that impacted me in particular, other than capsulizing in three words the experience: "It was tough." And the DIs exemplified those words by being the toughest of the tough, even while we were checking in, being indoctrinated, and starting the receivership of gear.

Before getting the famous haircut, we stripped off our street clothes and checked all our personal items into a bag, including wallet, keys, money, everything. Upon going through my wallet and emptying it, the DI found a lonely condom, as in rubber, as in trouble. He looked me up and down while I was standing at attention and shaking in my stocking feet, still in typical shock from entering the sacred halls of Marine Corps Recruit Depot.

"What do we have here, Private?" he demanded with his eyes glaring. "Well, answer, you lowlife."

"A condom, sir," I answered with bated breath.

"No, sunshine, we say, 'Sir, condom, sir,'" he said.

"Sir, yes, sir. Sir, condom, sir,"

"And what are you doing with it? Did the Marine Corps recruiter tell you it was okay to bring a condom with you!" he yelled. "Did he suggest you would have girls galore and be able to bed them in your spare time, maybe over a candlelit dinner with wine?"

"Sir, no, sir, no, sir," I said, flustered.

"One no is enough, twinkle-toes. Just what is this condom for, Private?"

"Sir, condoms are for sex, sir," I said, not knowing what to say or how to say it.

"Is that right?" he said. Then he moved next to one ear and yelled, "Are you fucking kidding me, maggot! Are you trying to educate me? Are you suggesting I don't know that? Are you insulting me?"

"Sir, no, sir!"

"So entertain me, Private. Do you always walk around your cozy little neighborhood back home with a condom in your wallet, lover boy? I suppose you carry one around just in case you get lucky, huh? Huh, lover boy? Okay, tell me again, what is the purpose of a condom, a rubber, a raincoat, a banana peel?"

"Sir, condoms are used for protection against disease . . . and birth control, sir." I thought to myself, *Did I really just say that?* Life and fate has its ways of paying you back, and I was getting my share of payback. I deserved this browbeating, I figured; I really did. Like losing that nurse, potential girlfriend back in Minnesota wasn't enough?

"I'll accept that, lover boy. But the one thing I don't get—and, boy, you better have the right answer for this or your dick will be in a sling—do you plan on using this condom on your travels around my Marine Corps base while you are here for vacation?"

"Sir, no, sir," I barreled out.

"Are you sure?" he asked.

"Sir, yes, sir!" I screamed out louder.

He picked up a garbage can, hit it hard on the floor a couple of times, and made a gesture to pick up the condom and throw it away. "Now get on your way, lover boy, before I put that condom over your head and make you run a couple of miles." I scampered down the line and hoped that nickname never stuck. Thankfully, it didn't. I took fate's punishment, and it ended there.

Beyond actually being tough, however, was the perception of being tough. Or on the flip side the perception of being weak. And this realization reared its head many times in boot camp. Sometimes the toughest appearing are the weakest and the weakest are the toughest. When it comes to true strength, guts and will, the cover of the book, doesn't always necessarily ring true. For example, by far, the toughest-appearing recruit in our platoon, was this big, tough looking guy who wore a motorcycle jacket with emblems and filthy jeans.

But from that time, his days were numbered. The DIs had it out for him, but he brought it on himself. Sometimes our demands were kicked up, and we were given the impossible command to take "one minute to shit, shower, and shave." Who knows if we ever made it—how would it be possible?—but we tried like hell. The motorcycle tough guy, I'll call him, was trying so hard under the pressure that he cut himself badly shaving, causing blood to ooze from his face. He was last to finish because of it. While we were all lined up "asshole-to-belly-button," as the Corps called it, the DIs positioned him at the door opening of the head—Marine jargon for the bathroom—at attention, mocking him. They told us to hit the recruit in the stomach if we wanted. Some recruits did, others didn't. The ones that did probably felt that way because he caused us extra punishment a lot because of his screwups. I felt sorry for him and wanted to give him a break so I didn't hit him. Also, it was a cheap shot. It all happened so quick you weren't called out for it if you didn't. His face was a bloody mess, and the towel wrapped around his waist was too.

A little more time passed, and our resident tough guy was weakening more. We were in one of the WWII–era Quonset huts, where we were housed back then at MCRD, being schooled on Marine topic matter. He messed up on something, and the senior DI, a highly decorated Korean Veteran, had quite enough. We always carried steel-rimmed buckets around with us to class and other assignments. We used them as chairs and always had to jump through many hoops before they'd let us sit down on them. Up, down, up, down until we got it right. They used to say they wanted to hear the unison smack of nuts as we sat before it was accepted.

Sometimes your testicles would hit the steel rims hard and they were sharp, and if you let out any sounds of pain or discomfort, you would be punished. That's what happened to our tough guy one day. The DI made him stand at attention while he put the bucket over his head and repeatedly hit the bucket with the butt of the tough guy's rifle. We sat still, and waited, and waited. Finally, it was over. You could hear some stifled sounds coming from beneath the bucket like sobs, sniffles. Another DI dismissed us to our huts to study the Marine Corps manual and clean our M-14s.

We never saw the motorcycle tough guy again. Some recruits thought that they sent him to motivation platoon, where they would bind your ankles and wrists while carrying a twenty-pound sledgehammer. They dressed them in prison-like stripes and still demanded the same from them as regular recruits, only more like busting up large rocks. It was all designed to make the troubled recruit straighten up and fly right and appreciate the rigors of regular boot camp and their platoon. Others thought he was taken to the brig or the hospital. I didn't care. I just felt bad for him. He was a good guy but just couldn't take it. About seven others also dropped out. One in particular was this tall, lanky recruit who started strong for the first several weeks then started dropping out of runs and whining all the time. It got worse where he started talking to himself and always had this faraway stare to him. Instead of kicking him out right there, they put him on mess duty. We saw him when he went to chow, and he was even skinnier. His head was constantly shaking. He totally lost it and had to be taken away in a straitjacket and ambulance.

Another dropout was way overweight (his recruiter did him a huge disservice). He was a very likable kid and tried so hard to keep up on all the runs and physical training, but couldn't. The DIs were on him like termites on rotten wood. It got so bad he couldn't do anything right. One night, he went AWOL over the fence between MCRD and the San Diego International Airport. A night-watch recruit reported him to a DI, and he was sent to motivation platoon. We all thought he would literally die in there, but the darn kid got through it and was sent back to our platoon, somewhat smaller for the wear.

But it was just not to be.

Within a short week, his face now distorted in defeat, he went the same route over the fence to the airport. This time, no one saw him and he made it all across the runway to the hangar area, where he was caught the next day. Our DIs later told us he was taken to the brig, would face a court-martial, and probably get six-six and a kick, which means six years' hard time, six years' forfeiture of all pay, and a dishonorable discharge. Back then, with no alternatives to the sentence or records, a guy's life would be shit, as they told us. The one DI seemed really hurt by it all but kept a strong demeanor, of course.

Like the DIs would always say, boot camp helps prepare you for combat, and it wasn't as tough as combat yet it was their job to make it as close as possible. It was their job to make us or break us. At some point in the process, every recruit is broken; sometimes the tougher you are, the more breaking it takes. So in a sense, that recruit would go through more. We had some little guys that seemed so fragile and weak, but got through everything and excelled against all odds. Perceptions can be as strong or weak as our imaginations can dictate, but reality is always the common denominator. I was broken down just before the rifle range at about week three. I missed several cadence counts when marching—it didn't take much.

It had been raining, and there were mud puddles everywhere. This one sergeant who liked me about as much as a Sailor took me out of formation and brought me over next to the bleacher stands. He told me to stand in this puddle and do five hundred up and on shoulders, which means raising your M-14 straight overhead, then down to front shoulder position, then up again and down to back of shoulders, and so on. Having a command to do five hundred of them was like a death sentence. I was to count each movement as "sir, 1-2-3-4-5, sir" and on to five hundred. I recalled the one thousand jabs I tried to do in Golden Gloves and made less than half but survived. So I just started and was going along quite well when the DI increased the demands by saying I had to also double-time in the water while doing the rifle, shoulder exercise. I went on, and after doing in the mid-hundreds and not giving up despite stumbling and barely able to move, he seemed to get frustrated by it all and me and told me to return to formation.

One time, this former football player and star athlete in high school was pulled aside for getting a box of goodies sent to him by his parents. It was primarily candy and cookies, lots of them, enough for him and all his buddies. Yeah right. The higher-ups let that box through the gates purposely so the DIs could have some fun and teach someone a lesson. They told us the first few days to write home and tell your parents NOT to send you anything but letter, envelope, and stamp. Obviously, someone didn't get the word.

The DIs know full well there are goodies in a box, so they use all their comical skills, which can be considerable, to formulate a game plan of learning and discipline. This one started with a call to the duty hut, where a recruit goes through hell trying to get permission to enter. The muscular kid finally got his permission for entry. Then we heard more yelling and screaming than a football game. Finally, the DI came out with the recruit and the box. He directed the recruit to the famous sandpit, where exercise, discipline, and punishment are stablemates. The DI had his nose pressing against the recruit's nose while he was yelling and saying his mommy and daddy just broke Marine Corps rules and their little baby boy would have to pay the price. The DI jumped out of the sandpit and told the recruit—maggot, I should say—to get down and give him one hundred push-ups for a warm-up, counting each one in typical Marine Corps fashion: Sir, one, sir, sir, two, sir, and on. When he finished, he yelled out loud, "Sir, I am finished, sir!" The DI went crazy, absolutely mad.

"Did you say you were finished, you scumbag! You haven't even begun. Now get on your face and get that dirt in that pie-hole of yours! Gimme a hundred more, this time singing 1-2-3-4 I love the Marine Corps!"

"Sir, yes, sir!" he yelled as he went down and he started his singing push-ups. When he was done, now full of dirt and sweat, he stood back at attention and said nothing.

"Well, shit-for-brains, have you completed your punishment for your parents' fuck-up?"

"Sir?" He seemed confused.

"You just don't get it, do you? I'm in charge here and don't you ever, ever forget it." The DI picked up the box, opened it, and said, "What do you know, cookies and wrapped candy bars! How sweet. I bet these cookies are homemade by your momma too. She probably put lots of love in the ingredients for her little boy who is away from home. Is your mom-ma a great cook, or just a good cook?"

"Sir, she is a great cook," he answered proudly.

"I bet she is. Are these peanut butter cookies your favorite?" the DI questioned.

"Sir, yes, sir."

The DI quickly looked over the inventory. He picked up two huge tins of cookies, opened one, and took a couple of bites. "Yes, I would agree with you, Private, these are very good cookies. I could probably even eat the whole tin myself, but unlike you, I have manners so I will let you eat them all yourself. But it just wouldn't be right if I didn't provide you with some water to wash it all down."

The DI took the canteen off from the private's cartridge belt, turned it over, and emptied it then said, "Excuse me for a moment, Private, while I go into my hut and get you some clean, fresh, warm water."

When he returned, he said to the private, "Now, while you are double-timing, I want you to eat every cookie she sent you. After all, you don't want to disappoint your mother, do you?"

The recruit took the first big tin in one hand and started double-timing. The canteen was next to the sandpit waiting for drinking. He would eat a bunch then reach for the canteen. We were allowed to watch but remain perfectly quiet. After he started eating the second tin, he greatly slowed down and started moving like his feet weighed tons. His face was taking on a chalky appearance and soon he would be throwing up. The drill instructor was grinning broadly and watching him carefully as he threw up a stomach full of cookies and warm water. The DI told him to stop. The private stopped and was literally standing in a sandpit full of vomit.

"No, Private, I didn't mean for you to stop exercising, just stop eating the cookies. I don't want you to mess up my sandpit anymore."

"Sir, yes, sir," the private said through trembling lips full of vomit strings hanging from his mouth. He kept double-timing.

"No, no, Private, let's change the exercise to full squat thrusts because you can kiss the ground better instead of beating my sandpit down so much. I want to see another one hundred. Begin."

That display not only taught the private a lesson he'd never forget, but it also drove home the point to every one of us in the platoon. He would survive just fine, and we were all quietly—more like morbidly—entertained. Along with him, we'd probably be seeing large volumes of vomit hurling through the air in our dreams—in color.

Chapter Thirteen

Earlier on in boot camp, we had simulated bayonet training, which are called pugil sticks (long, thick sticks with hard cushions on each end). I was matched up against this extremely tall and thin black recruit. Within a short period of time, I knocked him down hard and backed off, thinking it was over. One of the DIs that had the eyes of a madman, and didn't seem to like me, came up to me, took the pugil stick out of my hands, and hit me hard on the side of the (helmeted) head several times.

"This exercise is about killing, Meade. You don't knock him down and let him be. You have him hurt and you go in for the kill!" he said, screaming. Other recruits had won their match, went in for the simulated kill, and backed off, ending the confrontation, so I didn't quite understand why I was being singled out. The DI shoved the pugil stick back into my hands and yelled, "Go in for the kill!" Suddenly, I had a muddled flashback to the YMCA boxing days and my lessons on going all the way for the knockout. I knew and liked this recruit, but the "killer instincts" enveloped my thinking and body. He was up again so I knocked him down and, this time using slicing, slashing, and poking gestures, knocked him around on the ground, giving him a pounding and drawing blood. The DI then stepped in and pulled me off, looking satisfied. I had known this private from the first days we were coming into the base and receiving barracks.

Because we were short of bodies to make a platoon, we had to wait nearly two extra weeks to formally start boot camp, during which time we cleaned, shined brass, did physical training (PT), and sometimes would have to just stand and wait for hours at a time at attention in full sun. As a result, we all got severe sunburn on our necks and especially the tops of our ears. They would be so burned and peeling that cracks were formed that oozed blood. I remember this black recruit's ears bleeding just like mine.

Even though I felt bad, I never second-guessed my "killer instinct" again.

Sometimes the DIs were so funny with their unique brand of put-down humor; it called upon every nerve in your body to hold in the laughter. That was one of their mechanisms to test your will, it seemed. Break a laugh, grin, snicker, or even a hint of one, and you were toast. My biggest test came one day during a rifle inspection. I produced the rifle at port arms for him to grab. He looked it over and shot it back. Then looking at my hairy chest, he said, "Are you a damn ape or something, Private? Where did you get all that nasty hair? Look at my chest. Go ahead, move your beady eyes to my chest." He folded over the top of his T-shirt. "There's no hair on my chest, is there?"

"Sir, no, sir," I said.

"You know why, Private Ape Man? Because hair don't grow on steel."

Another time, it was all about breaking you from individuality. The DI had lit the smoking lamp for one cigarette, and after earning the right to smoke by doing gobs of push-ups, he noticed that I wasn't smoking and came rushing over. "And who do you think you are, Private, the surgeon general or something? I didn't recall giving you permission not to smoke, did I? May I be in charge here? Thank you." He took out a cigarette and shoved it in my mouth and said, "Light up with another private's lighter. And if I were you, I would appreciate me giving you the liberty to smoke." I had quit over a year before in high school, and here I was lighting up again. I quit again after boot camp and ITR.

Going to newly constructed Edson Range for rifle training and qualification was quite demanding. We combined all aspects of M-14 training with plenty of long runs and reams and reams of PT. One day after a couple of boots couldn't quite keep up running in the hills south of Camp Pendleton, our DIs punished us all by putting us in the sandpit. It was a very hot day, and we were all sweaty and completely covered in dirt. Shortly after, I had to request a sick bay visit because of extreme swelling and pain on my right shin. The doctor there had me strip and soak in a whirlpool tub. I had a lump on my shin about the exact size of a cut-in-half tennis ball. It was *huge*. They took X-rays and found a severe fracture going across the entire front part of my lower leg.

The doctor held up the X-ray to the light and said I would have to go to the hospital for surgery. He explained that the only way for the injury to heal properly and fully was to reset the bones and get complete bed rest. He said I would probably be laid up for a month and have to be set back in boot camp to the very first day when I returned. The doctor recited what the Marine Corps says: if you miss something, anything, you make it up and start from scratch. The doctor said they would start putting the paperwork in. I hesitated and asked if there wasn't some alternative to the hospital. He said no because the extreme training we underwent wouldn't allow for healing on its own. He also stated that the pain would be unbearable.

Well, I decided right then to bear it—to grin and bear it. There was no way I was going all the way back to the first day, with a new platoon and new recruits. Now, I just had to find a way to convince the doctor, who seemed very soft and wimpy. I talked and talked and begged and begged, and finally he relented. "If you really want to try and go back, you can, but don't be surprised if you end up in the hospital anyway and in worse shape than you are now. You have about six to seven weeks of boot camp left. I just don't see how it is possible."

I was now relatively cleaned up and grabbed my rifle to leave. "Sir, thank you for all your help. It's better . . . much better. Everything will be fine." The corpsman present looked at the doctor, and they both made frustrated gestures as I left. Right then, I was determined to overcome this fracture and pain and go on. When I went back to my platoon, I was given a light duty chit for several days but didn't take up the rear of the platoon like a few other boots with light duty. I just figured if I was going to overcome this, I had to start right away. I just tried to put less weight and pressure on my right leg and thought totally positive. I said practically nothing to anyone because I thought that would plant seeds of doubt and negativity in my mind. I would overcome. And I did. The pain continued, sometimes throbbing pain especially after long runs and PT, but the swelling eventually went down and the pain lessened. It decreased enough where it became bearable. I never could figure it out myself, but it sure seemed like it proved the old adage, mind over matter. I never experienced any residual problems after boot camp or my four-year stint. Or since.

There were some other things that weren't very *average* or *normal* about boot camp. After returning to MCRD from the rifle range, our platoon, 327, was ranked as the worst platoon in the Third Battalion. This was based on rifle qualification, PT scores, written tests, general military subjects, close-order drill, and overall Marine Corps protocol. Because of this, our DIs had a bigger challenge on their hands and we went through more than any other platoon. They pushed us harder, PT'd us longer, ran us more, punished us more, and drilled us into the ground. But in the end, 327 made a 360-degree turnaround and became *honor platoon*, the best in the battalion. Even the DIs said it was a miracle. I felt I added to that by having my own (medical) miracle.

Shortly after, in a loose formation around our senior DI, he gave us all our MOSs, which equals military job assignment and description. Recruit after recruit was given an 0311 designation, a basic infantry— grunt—duty, with some given artillery, radio operators, and other support combat classifications. The difference between the Marine Corps and the other services according to our DIs was that every Marine, no matter what his MOS, was a basic rifleman and could always be called upon in that area. They also told us the Marines wanted their "own" to have these supportive positions because their level of training and discipline would always complement the infantry and grunts, the backbone of the Corps. The only exception would be on the medical side where the Navy took the honors, such as doctors and corpsman.

I wanted to be a grunt, nothing less, nothing more. I was somewhat shocked when I joined and realized that all Marines weren't grunts. It was really unsettling for me. I thought of my hero uncles, one being in the artillery and the other an army grunt. I was fairly sure I would get that 0311 number as well. After all, I had no training except in high school and a blue-collar job. I felt like the rest of these guys that got the grunt call. However, I felt something in my guts churn. Just then, the DI yelled out, "Private Meade, . . . you got 1300, engineers. You'll probably be working and welding on bridges."

My heart sank. My head hurt like someone punched me. Some of the guys congratulated me and said I was lucky. I didn't feel "lucky." I felt betrayed, disappointed, frustrated, denied, double-crossed.

I managed a smile and even a thought of relief, but then felt immediately guilty. I felt like yelling out to the DI as loud as I could, "I don't want to be an engineer! I want to be a grunt just like most of the guys here!" But I knew I couldn't or at least I didn't dare. We were readying to graduate. Several of my closest buddies all got infantry, including Private Lopez, who had the largest, toothiest smile I had ever seen. When I looked at him now, I somehow knew that smile would be short lived. I just had this eerie feeling. Many years later, I saw his name on the Vietnam wall. Despite the current course of events that day being very upbeat, I was down, confused, and not feeling like I should. This day would twirl around in my head like an out-of-control Tilt-A-Whirl.

The last day just before graduation, our platoon and the entire battalion took seats in the auditorium where we would be schooled on the next step and the future. The base (Christian) chaplain gave his benediction. We were also congratulated, called Marines for the very first time, and given a motivating speech. After that, we broke up somewhat inside where our own DIs took over. The talk that stood out was by Corporal Scull (real name). He was as black as coal, and everyone feared him with a vengeance. He personified tough and took us to task more than all the rest. He never showed a smidgen of emotion—until this day. It was either him or another DI that said most of us would be going to Vietnam and some would not return.

My mind slipped back to mid–boot camp when our senior DI jumped up on the drill podium on our company street and stated, "I have good news for your privates. Congress has just declared Vietnam a *police action*, which means we can go in there and kick ass and take names!" I remember being marched to chow after that announcement. We always lifted our boot toes high and dug in our heels when marching to create this thud in unison as it bounced off the metal Quonset huts around us. But this particular day saw our desire to engage in combat so high we dug our heels in even more, causing more noise than ever. My heels dug in the pavement like everyone else, and I can't remember a single twinge of pain. This time it was more like ego than mind over matter. My pride soared to infinity.

As we left the side door of the auditorium, Corporal Scull wished each one of us well as we passed him standing in the doorway. His eyes were beet red. He had tears running down his cheeks. It was an unforgettable moment. I was eighteen years old and ready for graduation outside of the auditorium. Out in front of the auditorium on the world-famous grinder, we went through the ceremonies. When colors were presented before us, to think that I would have the opportunity and honor of serving those flags of the United States and the Marine Corps and my fellow countrymen and women caused a rush of pride from the top of my head to the soles of my feet.

My grandmother Hilda, along with two of my aunts from California, attended the ceremonies. They even took an 8mm movie film, which I still have. We had a four-hour break after graduation on the base, where you could either go to a modest PX, where they had light lunches, or you could go to one of the picnic areas around the perimeter of MCRD. I invited five to six of my closest buddies to join my family for eats and treats at one of the picnic areas.

After that brief break, we would be loading up our gear and bussed to Camp Pendleton about an hour's drive from MCRD and San Diego. There we would go through one month of ITR, infantry training regiment, before getting our first leave after four months of training. But now, we were Marines, and we earned the right to get weekend liberty if they saw fit to give it to us, which they normally did every other weekend. After training on all weaponry and running up and down, Old Smokey, a famous killer of a mountain with snake holes and rain ravines, covering many miles, we earned our first liberty. Many of us chose to go to Orange County and Disneyland. All this newfound money was burning holes through our pockets, which were pretty shallow.

Five of us went in together to get a double bedroom outside Disneyland. But before the night was out, about seven to eight more newbie Marines were holed up with us as they ran out of cash. Four of us took the beds while the rest pulled up some nice shag carpet. It was so crowded we could hardly move. The bathroom was in constant use as we were drinking beer—all of us underage but a couple—and we would eventually get into trouble with the management. It was a mess, but it somehow worked out so we didn't get into trouble with the police, who were summoned at one point. Even though things were much cheaper back then, our pay was so meager that it was simple to spend the whole, slender wad in one liberty day or weekend. Like a DI once said, "Marines don't need money, they just need courage and guts. Money will just get you in trouble anyway." He added that if your head was right—gung-ho enough—he would be proved right. No one questioned him then—you couldn't—but the jest of his words had merit, in the most Spartan way.

Money has a way of muddling your mind, at least for a hard-charger Marine. Many things on the base like Pendleton were free anyway. The movies were normally ten cents or free on certain nights.

They sold popcorn and soda, and that was dirt cheap. If you stayed on the base on your weekends, food and entertainment was free, other stuff a near giveaway. But staying on the base, in your barracks, would be the challenge despite being gung-ho to the max. We were still human, for the most part. Even if you did venture to Oceanside, paid ten cents for the bus, you could go to the USO for entertainment and food, where snacks were free and meals were extremely reasonable. They also had girl escorts there, but the USO had very strict guidelines for troops and girls alike. My money always lasted, and I had no complaints so I guess I was gung-ho according to that pronouncement by the DI.

Chapter Fourteen

My biggest personal thrill in ITR was the moving target range. There were about a half-dozen small mounds that ran down this course. The object was to run down to each mound, hit the deck, and quickly shoot the moving targets that would emerge on the relatively close perimeter horizon. I felt I did good, and at the end, several of these course sergeants were yelling for the Marine that ran down line two or whatever it was. It was me. "Damn, boy, what's your name?"

"PFC Meade (I got promoted during ITR)."

"Well, PFC Meade, you got more than two times the number of targets than anyone else. It's a course record. You also set the record for time. You're a dinger. Join me over here on the side for a moment."

"Tell me, Marine, how did you do so well? Were you a hunter back home or something?"

"To be honest, sergeant, I had to use the head really bad, and the quicker I finished, the quicker I could go."

"Okay, Meade, then the secret with you or anyone like you is to send them out on patrol or combat and deny them a head call first, huh? To deny you peeing is to deny the enemy from living? But I know you are holding it pretty good now, PFC, so get out of here."

I ran to the head and did my business, probably setting a record of sorts there, too, for accuracy and delivery time.

Upon leaving the head, since I was now behind, they quickly pushed me along to the bus and the next combat exercise despite that sergeant yelling for me to come back. Who knows what that may have resulted in? Could they recant and put me in the grunts or make me a sniper? Or maybe they put me in recon? But my thoughts would linger as I left the area. There were many more Marines going through ITR now because of the call for troops in Vietnam, and it was pretty chaotic. I kept thinking, why didn't that sergeant run after me, pull me out of ranks? Maybe I should have run back to him.

Soon ITR would be over, and I would be going on my first leave. I received my first duty station order for Camp Del Mar, just outside of Camp Pendleton right on the beach, outside Oceanside. The outfit was called Shore Party, *The First to Land*. But first before the *First*, a free, standby flight home to Minnesota. That did excite me.

But it wasn't all that exciting. I did my rounds with family and friends, including a trip back to high school and my gym, to show off my Marine uniform; but since I cleaned my slate of girls, I completely missed that relationship reunion. I actually looked forward to leaving and going back to California. Back then, trains were common, going all over the country; so I left a few days' early, wore my uniform to get a huge military discount, and was on my way across the country. While the uniform got me a military ticket discount, it didn't help not being ID'd for age and I was denied beer the whole trip. I couldn't believe it despite the drinking age being twenty-one. I was nineteen, serving my country, and here I was being denied a simple beer, or two, or more, which was probably the problem: us young military upstarts couldn't be trusted not to overdue or get in trouble, as some always would. So I went beerless the entire journey, flirted with girls, drank Pepsi, ate sandwiches and Hershey bars—but imagined slugging down some cold ones in my underaged mind.

I loved Camp Del Mar. It was situated so close to the Pacific Ocean in order to train for amphibious training exercises. It was also adjacent to the highway, running up and down California. I quickly made friends, this corporal in particular, who took me under his wing. He talked a lot about foreign-duty stations he had been to with that salty swagger talk and said I should accompany him to Tijuana someday, laughing that there were no drinking age restrictions down there after hearing my tale about the train. He didn't have to ask me again; we planned on going the very next liberty weekend. And what a weekend it would be.

My buddy tipped me off to all the ins and outs of TJ. He took me first to the (then) famous Chicago Club, said to be the most controversial hot spots on the TJ club circuit. Anything of a sexual nature went on there, and frankly, all was shocking. But with enough beers, you just blended into the crowd of primarily GIs (Marines), college students from San Diego and Los Angeles, and tourists.

If you were shy or reserved in any way, it would be dragged out of you, like it or not. Most of us liked it, in a perverse naive way. The action always exceeded one's imagination, and then some. One thing for sure, both your money and your sperm would be totally spent and left behind if you didn't exercise self-control. Even if you did, you'd leave with a lot less than when you first walked through that front door.

One of the warnings the corporal made was to put a good hunk of money deep down in your socks, close to the bottom as a precaution. I put twenty-five bucks down there and felt confident about my stash. He told me that TJ's objective—much like a military mission—was to strip you of all your money before you left or as close as they could get. More accurate words could not have been spoken. He also stressed over and over again that the last place you ever want to be taken was a jail in TJ or anywhere in Mexico. He also advised me that if we got lost in the web of deception they had there, to always make our way back up to Revolution Avenue—the main drag—and hook back together up there. And that's exactly what happened.

We got separated and I found myself back up on Revolution, so I walked down the street just checking stuff out. I was near totally sober and well aware of my surroundings, until this nice-looking, sexy-dressed Mexican woman took me by the arm and dragged me through a nightspot door and curtain. I'll never forget the name: the Black Cat. She plopped me down in an open booth against a wall, screamed at the bartender something in Spanish, and within a minute, we had a beer and her drink in front of us. Just about as fast, I was seeing double, even triple, and this gal was rubbing me in the front while working my wallet out of my back pocket. I was constantly catching her just before it was about to slide out. I had enough sense and wherewithal to catch it. Soon, she got so flustered she stood me up and walked me out the door. I truly was in lull-la-land, and I don't mean in some fantasy ride at Disneyland.

Soon, she stopped at the corner of the building and flung me around the corner—right into the arms of two *federales*. There was a short, fat one and probably the tallest Mexican I had ever seen, but also quite thin. They asked for my ID. I took my wallet out and handed them my Marine Corps ID and liberty card. They spoke in Spanish and looked back and forth at each other while occasionally looking at me. Finally, the fat little troll said, "You no pay girl, senor?"

Suddenly my senses were coming back like a light switch was being turned on. I thought quick and answered in a way dictated by the circumstances. "Yes, I paid, I paid."

They thought for a moment and spoke softly. The approximately five-feet-three-inches 240-pound *federale* said with a straight face and serious look, "Well, American, no, prostitution is illegal in Tijuana. This will cost you a $26 fine for breaking the law."

I was quick to respond, "You gotta be kidding me. I did nothing wrong, and I don't have twenty-six bucks."

"How much do you have, gringo?"

"I have $10 in my wallet, but I need three of that for bus fare back to the base. I can give you seven." I knew I had that $25 in my sock and felt oh-so-cocky.

I was now in complete control of my facilities and didn't want to cooperate with this setup any longer. I took my opened hands together and clapped my ID and liberty pass right out of the fat man's hands and ran. My close-cropped haircut was standing on end as I ran. I ran a couple of blocks down Revolution and took a turn down a side street, but realized I was running the wrong way, deeper down away from the main drag and tourist section. I thought I heard shots above my head—two to three loud bangs following me—but couldn't confirm, so I just ran faster.

Down the sidewalk, there was another huge Mexican selling tacos from a wheeled cart. He heard the whistles blowing, saw me coming, and spread his arms and legs across the sidewalk. I ran through him like some bulldozer, knocking him and his stand all over the sidewalk and street. I smelled a burst of tacos and condiments as surely as I could gunpowder back on the base. Tacos or not, I kept running. Finally, I felt clear and out of danger, so I saw this little club and ducked in.

Just as I passed the doorway and sighed a deep breath, numerous hands cupped my shoulders. It was three other *federales*, and they had me. My mind was running. I didn't want to go to a Tijuana jail, but even more, I didn't want to get in trouble with the Corps. I just couldn't believe the jam I was in. I was more mad than anything and felt like I wanted to fight my way out of this situation somehow—but how?

They brought me up to Revolution, right in front of the Chicago Club where it all began. Soon, my corporal buddy would be walking toward us, and I thought he would save the day. Wrong, he took the arm of some girl and walked right past us. I yelled out to him over and over again, and he acted totally oblivious to the whole scene. As he disappeared down the sidewalk, I yelled out, "Semper fi, Marine, I won't forget this!" A *federale* paddy wagon pulled up along the sidewalk. I knew now that I was in serious trouble.

I was wearing a heavily knitted sweater, and feeling there was no hope, I rolled up my sleeves and said to the officers, "I know at least one of you can hear me so I'll repeat—I did nothing wrong. I broke no Mexican law that I was aware of, that was legitimate anyway, and I'm not getting in that paddy wagon. I'll fight you right here first." They talked among themselves for what seemed an eternity while I maintained tight jaws and my fists clenched. It drew a lot of attention on the street, just as I wanted.

The next thing I know, they released their grip and let me go, saying, "You are released. Leave. Leave Tijuana."

"Thank you, I will," I said in shock, the kind of shock that is so pleasant that a feeling of elation comes over your being, like an angel dropping lucky dust over you. And this was one *lucky* I appreciated like the very smoggy air I was breathing. I walked away quickly, not believing my good fortune, and picked up speed as I walked toward the bridge where a person enters TJ. Before I got there, another *federale* grabbed me from a blind alleyway and said in perfect English, "You broke the law, senor."

"What law now?" I said, not believing this was happening.

"You spit on the sidewalk. I saw you, you are littering."

I flung his hand away and pushed him down hard upon the alley street and ran even faster than before. I quickly got up to the bridge entry point, but not before being accosted by about a half-dozen kids who were selling Chiclets, those tiny packages of gum. They grabbed my legs and arms and were trying their best to stop me. I was flinging them off and away like so many little chickadees. Suddenly, out of nowhere a car stopped, opened the door for me, and sped off quickly, leaving TJ. They were Sailors, and I was forever grateful and lavished praise and thanks on them. We had some laughs, and they dropped me off at the American bus station.

After I returned to the base and bitched out that corporal big-time but eventually forgave him, I said, "I will never ever go back to TJ." Not until the next time anyway. I went back there within two weeks; but the next time, I was armed with much more experience, knowledge, and savvy. I never did return however with my corporal friend, as I told him, "I would have never left you behind like that, so I still consider you a barracks buddy, but that's it."

Chapter Fifteen

My first visit back to TJ, I went solo. I enjoyed the food and stayed on Revolution Avenue. In the early evening, I thought I'd catch this dancing girl bar, which was also quite small and quiet. Two girls were up on the little area just behind the bar, and they would exchange spots with two other dancers as the night progressed. And as that progressed, dancing to popular American hits of the day, providing a very relaxing atmosphere, I was getting pretty tanked on beers. It seemed like I was being treated extra nice, even getting a free beer here and there. What I didn't know until much later as told to me by one of the dancing girls was that the main dancer, who did Tijuana proud with her radiant good looks and majestic figure, had put a piece of gum on the back of my head at the neckline. That gesture told the house that I was hers and all hands off. Talk about being flattered; bar girl or not, she was ravishing. Other than gazing at me and winking a few times, I didn't really notice the special attention.

Approaching midnight, she finally talked to me, very quietly at the bar, and said she was attracted to me and wanted to invite me down to her villa by the Mexican beach. And to think I was on a long seventy-two-hour pass. But a big but, she had to find a way to break a date with the owner of the bar and many other bars, on the main drag we were on. Just then, this huge—by far the biggest Mexican I had ever seen—walked in and started talking to one of the girls. Then suddenly, he turned toward my beauty and told her he wanted to go dancing at some place down the street.

As they left amid all the noise and patrons talking to the owner, she looked back at me and called out the name of the place they were going. As they left, I ran back to the men's room. As I was standing at the urinal, two Mexicans came in behind me and closed the door. I immediately sensed I was in trouble. Both were smaller than me but rough-looking guys. I made a split-second decision to act quick and turned around and took one by the neck while squeezing and rammed him into the door and purposely put on my bad-man game face. They let me go, even opening the door for me, and I left, virtually running out of the place.

Wow, I thought, that was a close call; but I had better things to do, like find this dancing place. I actually saw the couple—the guy's size was impossible to miss—so I just followed them from a distance. I caught the woman looking back my way and knew that gum she planted on me definitely had some meaning, and I certainly didn't want to dishonor her interest. It took forever for them to make progress down the sidewalk because the big guy stopped to talk to numerous folks. After I entered the place, they were already on the dance floor, but it was sparsely being used so I could tell she did not dare look my direction. I ordered a beer and sat over at the end of the bar, behind some patrons. As I left the place behind me, I had asked one of the other girls if they were serious, and she replied no then gestured for me to pursue her. Here I was, trying to figure out how in the world this could go down without me going down.

I was lucky if I got one glancing look from her as they were dancing. After having several beers and spending an hour waiting in the wings, I thought about my chances; and as much as I hated to, I decided to leave. It was obvious this big guy was dominating this woman's attention, and she seemed very apprehensive about leaving his side. I justified my departure by seeing the matinee-like beauty in his arms and thinking that the residual gum behind my ear had dissolved despite her own apparent desires. Besides, the risks were as gigantic as the bar owner was.

My next visit to TJ came about through my own mother. She was talking to the mother of my close friend from high school who had joined the Navy and was also stationed in San Diego. My mother passed along David Glubka's contact information, and before I knew it, we planned this get-together in TJ. I brought a Marine buddy with me, and Dave also brought a friend. We met at a famous bar on the main drag in Tijuana that had been used in many films, including John Wayne's westerns called the Long Bar. The dominating theme at this hot spot was an overwhelmingly large—and long—bar. It was all lit up and not your typical TJ dive, but an obvious hangout for tourists and college students.

We somehow locked up with this stray Sailor Veteran, an Eskimo from Alaska, and he joined our group. We tipped many beers, and when we left after many hours, we knew we had a full night of fun.

There were five of us as we walked to the bridge just before the border. The bridge was shaped like a partial moon, with the two ends lower and the middle much higher. As we got up toward the middle, we were being approached on the same side of the bridge by a very large group that looked like college students. There were perhaps fifteen to twenty of them, and as we got to the exact same point, something had to give. We all stopped. Their apparent leader, the proposed tough-looking guy in the middle, said we had to move out of the way. I responded with my own equal demand. Suddenly, he raised his hands in a defensive fighting stance, and I quickly took him by both wrists and turned them over, going radically down. His wristwatch popped—flew—off his wrist, breaking apart as it hit the concrete. No need for me to waste a punch. He was shocked as I spread my arms out to make a path, and we all walked through as if the Red Sea had been parted.

After several months of purposeful training related to Shore Party, the word came down that orders were canceled for Vietnam, at least for the foreseeable future. I was let down. I went through the proper channels and transferred to an engineering battalion that I heard was soon going. It was First Engineers, which was in that same First Marine Division, making the transfer easier. I left beautiful Camp Del Mar behind and joined the ranks at Camp Pendleton, virtually across the highway. There I was befriended by Lance Corporal Harry Parmer, who was this big strapping kid from Pennsylvania.

We hit it off immediately, and I quickly found out that Harry was a prankster, besides always trying to wrestle around with me. One time, while I was away—we shared the same bunk area—he got me good. He taped my master lock with surgical tape, and it took me virtually hours to finally get it open.

Another time, he hit me hard on the shoulder and I hit him back and we went back and forth. Next, we locked ourselves around a square wood pillar in the hallway and made up some stupid game of hold, release, and hit each other in the shoulder. It was brutal, but Harry always maintained this smile. I was more serious as I thought the whole thing was childish. But here I was doing it. We did this for about fifteen minutes until neither one of us could raise our arms. The pain traveled down your arm and nerves into your entire upper torso. We just released our grip and quit. Harry said he played football in school and enjoyed strength challenges. I said I had done some boxing and quickly threw out a measured left jab toward his nose, coming within a whisker of landing. We both smiled broadly and walked off together with our arms around each other's shoulders. It took a week or more for those shoulders to return to normal. I joined Harry once, more in friendly support, put one over on this other Marine. He had been out late the night before and didn't respond to reveille, so Harry thought he'd prank him. He took a black felt pen and carefully drew some glasses, an uplifted mustache, and a scar on his face. No one shook him to get up until a few seconds before we fell out for formation. He had no time for anything, threw on his cover, and dashed outside. We just happened to have an inspection that morning, and it was like some movie comedy to witness—out of the corners of your eyes—as the colonel stopped in front of our newly crowned pirate after he did a classic double-take from a distance. The colonel just stood there dumbfounded, studying his face.

"And who the hell would you be, Marine, for lack of a better term—a near-sighted Captain Hook?"

"Sir?" the poor guy replied, having no idea what he looked like.

"Captain, since I do outrank you, run inside to the head and look at your face."

As he ran inside quickly, the colonel said to the lieutenant and sergeant next to him, "Report to me after formation."

After Captain Hook ran back to the formation and assumed his lance corporal status, scan all markings, he blurted out, "Sorry, sir."

"Company dismissed," barked the colonel, with a slight grin on his face. Have you ever held laughter inside you that hurt, only trying to come out in closed-mouth bubbles of oxygen? We all should have been given medals of self-restraint, especially Parmer as he held it in so expertly.

Soon, Harry would be inviting me to come up to Pasadena with him and spend a weekend with his aunt and uncle. He said they lived in the nicer area of Sierra Madre up in the mountains, and he'd never asked anyone else to go with him before, indicating his respect and trust in me. We went up there by bus and had a ball. And returned many times. One of those times we hooked up with two girls that had *serious* written all over their forehead. We met their parents, mine being this strict former chief petty officer, and they were good girls. Right away though, I knew this could not continue, as did Harry.

So we broke it off and just enjoyed our bachelor ways. His aunt and uncle were superfolks and were secondary big shots involved with the Rose Bowl. They owned a local funeral home, and Harry and I used to joke about it all the time, at one time even bringing our dates there around the time of the Rose Parade. We got great seats because of our contacts and used it to our best advantage.

Shortly thereafter, back at the base, First Engineer Battalion had their orders to Vietnam rescinded.

Some Marines were relieved; others like me and Harry were not. Before I knew it, Harry had put in for a transfer to Ninth Engineer Battalion, which was leaving to Vietnam in weeks and was gone. He did it quickly, right under my nose. I was right behind him as I requested mast to see our commanding officer of First Engineers. I told him I requested to be immediately transferred to Ninth. He pulled my record and noticed I had just left Shore Party, as their orders were canceled. Now it was First Engineers. He asked me several times if I was sure of this transfer request and said something like, "Maybe after all these cancellations, going to Vietnam isn't in the cards for you, son."

I answered short and quick: "I want the transfer to Ninth, sir, and I want to go to Vietnam."

Chapter Sixteen

I got transferred to Ninth Engineers just days before they were to pull away from San Diego Harbor.

The battalion was being sent there with all its equipment and was to make a major amphibious landing on the beaches of Vietnam. It sounded exciting to me. I checked into one of the large barracks that haphazardly held the troops. It was totally chaotic with all the preparations that were going on. I checked into service company—I hated that non-combative name—and met my immediate platoon and squad. I was going around meeting the squad guys, Kuhlmann, Lewis, Paret, Pat, Uncle Pete, Reynolds, and Rucker. I was told that one of the squad members was in the advanced Shore Party, a California surfer turned Marine, Chris Angie.

Suddenly, this bald head popped up from a prone position on a rack (bed), jumped off the top and came over to me, and introduced himself. "My name is Staff Sergeant Bee and I am your squad leader." We shook. The rest of the guys kind of gave this funny look and some—mainly Rucker and Uncle Pete—made a smirk.

Our squad leader was hardcore Marine, very short (must have gotten a waiver to get in the Corps), had his head shaved so tight you couldn't even get a hint of hair stubble, kept his lips very tight, almost lizard-like, and had huge ears that looked perfectly perpendicular to his head. He rose up on his toes when he walked, somewhat like a bantam rooster. After Staff Sergeant Bee excused himself and walked away, several of the guys whispered, "His real name is Sneezy, you know, one of the seven dwarfs." Well, it wasn't his real name, of course, but it certainly was fitting, I thought.

I couldn't find a rack with the squad so I had to be separated until we left just days away. It remained this way until we actually pulled up off the shores of Vietnam. I was one of the last lingering check-ins for the battalion. Soon, we'd all be saddled up and leaving the barracks, departing on buses to the docks where the USS *Ogden*, a huge equipment and troop transport vessel, was waiting.

While we were waiting on the dock, I made my farewell call back home. My mom answered. We exchanged a few words before she said sadly, "Uncle Lester just died . . . I'm sorry to tell you like this before you are going far away, but I must."

"You're kidding. Just like that, huh? How old was he, and how did he die?"

"He was only fifty-one. He died of a heart attack. I hope this isn't some kind of bad sign?"

"What did you say, Ma? I could hardly hear you."

"Oh nothing, Jon, I was just saying this is not good news to send you off with, sorry."

"I know, Ma, but don't worry, everything will be fine with me. Try not to worry, I will be okay."

Mom put Dad on the phone, and I gave him my heartfelt condolences. We wished each other well and said our goodbyes, and he passed the phone back to Mom.

"We love you, Jon, and please take care of yourself. Don't take any unnecessary chances."

"Okay, Ma, love you too, and I'll write soon. Would you keep my personal stuff I left behind safe?"

"Sure, sure," she said.

"I better go, they're calling us to come aboard the ship. See ya, Mom. Bye." I couldn't stop thinking about Uncle Lester. I thought the heroism of his life, all the sacrifice for the country and his fellow Soldiers and humanity, would be forgotten and buried with him. I paid an inner tribute to him in my mind and heart. I just wished I could have seen him before he died and talked to him and shared more.

The next thing I knew, I was boarding the ship all alone, without one other squad member. They kept pushing us on and up we went. When I got aboard the ship and saluted Old Glory, I joined the crowd and stood on that massive ship deck with full marching pack, combat gear and rifle, all weighing about 120 pounds. I looked back at the San Diego docks as our ship slowly maneuvered out of the harbor. San Diego was by far the furthest place I had been away from Minnesota. As I saw many Marines and Sailors waving goodbye to their loved ones, I realized going to Vietnam was worlds away and I had no idea what to expect. But whatever it was, I felt ready.

Months before, I had volunteered to leave First Engineers to take an advanced infantry training. It had an unlikely name of "The

Regimental School." It was said to be tough enough where it was hard to get volunteers to partake in the thirty-day course, especially if a Marine was not too far out of boot camp and ITR like me. But Mr. Mac Marine just had to raise his hand and be picked. It was not far from my engineer unit on Camp Pendleton. The school was designed and run by Major Hiram Walker III, a recon Marine and Vietnam Veteran. He was also one of the heirs to the Hiram Walker Whiskey empire. As legend had it, the old man told his two sons that to someday realize their share of the family fortune, they had to prove themselves in some significant fashion. One son went on to form a hugely successful law firm, and the other chose to attend West Point and become a Marine Corps officer.

The school was much like ITR but more intense, strict, and demanding, with shades of boot camp all over again. We fired every weapon imaginable, took long runs on tough obstacle courses, played war games, PT'd until we puked, did book studies and took tests on different methods of warfare as it related to the Corps, and went through the gas chamber three more hellish times. Whatever he demanded, he also did, and probably more. He seemed skinny, but when he took his top off, we marveled at his ripped, muscular shape. Not a centimeter of fat. Solid grit. This guy bled Marine Corps green. He was also quite famous for celebrating his birthdays. He would put on his full dress blues and go up in a small plane and parachute out. Upon landing, he would hit the deck, disarm his chute, and do one hundred push-ups, plus his age, which at the time was in his late thirties. He was a hard charger and couldn't care less how it looked, as in some circles he was the talk of the town, at least the towns outside of Marine bases like Pendleton. But an equal number thought he was just plain crazy, over the top, and an attention monger. He would always explain this last one as being good for drawing that attention to young men as a recruiting tool. I thought he was all of those. But I liked and respected him, character that he was.

Maybe to understand someone like him, you had to be there and see the whole operation, where you had to get special permission from Marine Corps headquarters in Washington, to exist. The regimentation was much like boot camp, but with much greater emphasis on combat training and survival. For the overwhelming most part, I enjoyed it. I envisioned parlaying the training into something much more than the engineers. Every morning we were awakened to garbage cans being thrown hard upon the floors.

We had minutes to get up, make our racks, use the head and shave, and fall out with our weapon for inspection.

As we ran down the flight of stairs, there was a huge—10 × 10 foot poster of General Chesty Puller, whom Major Walker would emulate. Puller was the Marine Corps version of the Army's George Patton, and they were actually cousins. Chesty was by far the most highly decorated Marine—led by five Navy Crosses—than any leatherneck in history. He was more than a legend. He was the consummate Marine. The biggest two lessons I learned from the Regimental School was what Major Walker referred to a lot, especially upon any inspection: The first was *Immediate Corrective Action*. The second was *Attitude Adjustment*. Both need no explanation. I was proud of the diploma I received and framed it for a lifetime.

Unlike boot camp, we got two weekends off like ITR, making the month go pretty quick. My first weekend saw me venturing to Los Angeles where I wanted to visit Muscle Beach in Santa Monica. After spending the day on the beach I found a restaurant that I had read about owned by a former fighter and trainer/manager. The name of the place was Duffy's, and it was right down by the beach. I found the guy, and we talked a little about boxing. He took me in the back room and told me to put my dukes up and wanted to see what I had. We danced around, dodging punches and throwing some, with me throwing my signature left jab. He was impressed enough to invite me to visit him again after the Marines and voiced a desire to take me under his wing. It never came to pass as his establishment went under and he was nowhere to be found.

My last liberty weekend in Oceanside saw me get a going-away tattoo. It was quite small, but it sealed my devotion to my trip to Vietnam and the Corps. Across my upper right arm, it read "U-S-M-C," and it cost $4, $3 for the outlined and lower blue section and $1 more for the small upper red part. Many years later, I heard that tat went for over $90. I went to the USO and mingled a little then found a nice steak house over in Carlsbad and treated myself, like a last meal and testament.

Looking out from the ship's deck, I was staring fate right in the eye and felt a new chapter—by far the biggest of my life—about to unfold. I was so ready and motivated I felt I could have jumped off that ship and swam to Vietnam. Well, at least in the left part of my brain where dreamy thoughts are on the ready. My mind was there well before my body.

Politics of any kind never entered my mind as there wasn't any room left with all the patriotism consuming it. I also never heard a political utterance of any kind coming from any other Marine's mouth. Now, that certainly wouldn't remain so, but at this point it was. We took great pride in just being Americans who were going to a foreign country to defend another nation's sovereignty and liberty, at the possible expense of our own lives. Maybe some of that was naively superficial but sincere. We were told in briefings beforehand that we were going to help the South Vietnamese overcome communism and help them win their freedom. How often have we heard that freedom isn't free? It made sense to me so I never questioned it. Like what the Marine Corps would always stress, *Don't think, just do.* I also improvised like the Corps always stressed and did both. I thought and I did.

We weren't just trained to *kill!* We were trained as Marines to adapt and overcome and represent our country in the finest traditions of courage, honor, and valor. Strength of character is not only measured by toughness, but by selective tenderness in tough situations. One of our stated goals as Marines in Vietnam was to win over the populace and show them we weren't just there to fight for and with them, but to help, support, and encourage them in their quest for independence and democracy. Idealistic for sure, but realistic in its good intentions. Some Marines saw it all as what they humorously called happy horseshit; most took it more seriously, including me.

I stayed on the deck and saw the San Diego harbor slowly vanish in my viewfinder. When I saw the tiny little figures of family still waving in the distance, I felt glad that I severed ties to any and all girlfriends. I was alone, and that's exactly what I wanted. I was engaged and married to the Marines, and if they lost me, it would be an honor of the highest order to be counted among those other Marines who gave the ultimate sacrifice. I certainly had no death wish and highly valued my life, but I felt that my mind was right. Whatever may happen, it was a consequence I was more than ready to risk. Who wouldn't, when pondering the philosophy of what makes a Marine, a Marine? Not once did I think I was going there as an engineer and not a grunt. I think that if I did in my own rigid mind, I would have been less gung-ho and motivated, as silly as that may sound. But at this point, there was nothing to suggest we weren't going as the infantry. After we were out of the harbor, the brass started pushing us all to go below deck and get squared away.

I found a sergeant and asked him. "I've been separated from my platoon and squad, so what should I do? Where should I go?"

"Don't worry about it, Marine, just follow the group and get downstairs and pick a rack. We can't be uptight about perfect logistics right now. You're in the line for starboard side, so just join the rest."

I went down to the starboard side, picked a rack in the middle, and arranged my gear while securing my weapon against the wall. The bunk area was about one foot above your prone body and had a teeny light adjacent to it. It was tight but cozy. It was like your own 6 × 2½ foot body print of privacy. Later, I overheard the Sailors on board kid about our "slave" quarters being so perfect for Marines. What did turn out to be such a pain was the shower area, which often had problems and didn't work properly. The toilets, too, had some water and flushing issues; it worked if you *worked* with it. Go with the flow, flow with the go.

Despite every effort, my being on the starboard side on this huge ship totally disconnected me from my platoon and squad. I had briefly met my immediate squad back at Pendleton and remembered a few faces, but with them all obviously on the port side, we never connected until the final last few days of the cruise. Yes, for me, it turned out to be a cruise. I never did understand how or why, but I was totally on my own, and I took full advantage of it. Who was I to argue? I was just a private first class pee-on.

According to the Corps, *Yours is not to ask why but to do or die.* Mine was not to ask why but just eat it up and lie. I had to take leave from my grunt thinking during the luxurious cruise and lie around on the back deck's cushy life rafts and sunbathe. It was tough, but I had to do it. I would lie there for hours and hours just looking at the endless ocean and the big ship print the vessel made from the massive props in the back, leaving an agitated ocean for as far back as your eyes could strain.

The weather for most of the trip was near perfect. I would go have morning chow, then go back to my tiny cubicle, write home, and read. Then I would drag myself all the way back to the ship's mess hall and have a large lunch, after which I would go up to my favorite spot and soak up the rays. I actually had to go to the PX and buy suntan lotion as I was getting crisped up. Sometimes while passing the chow hall in the afternoon I would grab a chocolate shake and some popcorn and return to my perch. I also ate hundreds of crackers to avoid any possible seasickness.

Compared to us, those Sailors on the ship ate like kings. And for the majority of the cruise, I was forced to be a Sailor—on leave—with all their extra perks. The chow, food as it were, on the cruise was suburb. I'd probably rate it a 4 out of 5 in the context of restaurants and ship cruises although I had never been on one. I would have rated it a perfect 5, but I had to go down to the chow hall; it didn't come up to me. I must have gained ten pounds because my web belt had to be loosened about an inch.

I did do my share of recon and surveillance while on that back deck sunbathing. I would gaze out as far as my eyes would stretch and look toward the hazy line of the horizon. There was nothing out there but our ship, the water, and the sky. Honestly, the serenity of it all I would never forget. The scene brought me back years before to lying down outside at night to stargaze, study the cosmos, and reflect on humanity and eternity. It was without a doubt the cruise of a lifetime and all gratis of the United States government and the Marine Corps.

En route, however, my routine was somewhat interrupted by stops in Hawaii (where I enjoyed further vacation time), Philippines, Okinawa, and Guam, hitting the waters of the South China Sea outside South Vietnam exactly twenty-four days later. Just four days prior to that, my platoon's warrant officer found me and wanted me to engage with the others down in the 120-degree well deck of the ship, doing PT and rifle training in full uniform. Since we were so far apart and the well deck couldn't accommodate all Marines in a single session, I was told to *try* and make it on my own. Yes, sir, I thought I would do my best to do just that, but I guess in the end I was still put off by being an engineer and would rather settle for my deck recon and surveillance rafts.

I just couldn't make it through the jungle of that ship, so I had to be satisfied with my own lookout post. No one was any wiser. Sometimes I swear, when some Sailors saw me there on my own looking rather somber, maybe they thought I was there on some assignment. It was one of those unusual situations where no one ever questioned me. If they had, I was always ready to saddle up and turn Marine. I had a clear, defined mission in my head to change from ship cruise dude to leatherneck at a moment's notice. That notice never materialized. I would have never retreated, but rather regrouped as the Marines would call it.

PART II

(DV: During Vietnam)

Vietnam was more about enabling a people, friendships, buddies, camaraderie, life and death, sacrifice, courage, and the frailties of humanity . . . than anything Washington and American culture would try and define it as.

—JM

Chapter Seventeen

The first thing I noticed was the extreme heat, with incredibly high humidity. It was as if we all just landed in this big strange sauna and everyone was drenched in sweat, which would not change much during the scheduled thirteen-month tour. It was May of 1966, and the clock in everyone's head was ticking and would never stop. I had since hooked up with my squad and was a full-bore Marine again.

Before our first dusk, Staff Sergeant "Sneezy" Bee gathered us together for a last-minute briefing. His eyes were large and fixed, his lips razor thin. He looked off into the distance toward the shore as he spoke, his eyes focusing like lasers and his lips so tight you couldn't have pried them open. The squad was all ears. Finally, with an inflexible sternness, he told us that reports from intelligence indicated we could be hit by the enemy from both sides and the front upon landing on the shore. He told us to make sure we had all of our personal effects, gear, ammunition, and flak jackets in place and in ready. He ended with, "And don't forget to have your dog tags on your necks." That statement made me realize this was for real. This was not like playing war games as a kid back in home-sweet-home America. I was so glad.

Our first night in Vietnam was greeted with a pitch-black sky. The air smelled different than I was accustomed to, but I couldn't identify the aromas, except that they were intriguing. The ship was anchored about one mile from shore. Just as the sun had set, jets were streaming overhead and in the distance. Way off in the mountains, you could see smoke billow up and hear the faint sound of explosions. Helicopters also flew over the ship and then off to unknown destinations, adding to the activity level surrounding the ship. When that perfectly dark sky hit, it was greeted by a constant siege of flares, lighting up the sky like the Fourth of July, which was months away.

When excitement is mixed with anticipation and anxiety—on whatever level—it produces a funny, almost intoxicating brain cocktail. I felt somewhat high on that volatile mixture. But it was also like being scared, apprehensive, of walking somewhere as a kid; you just didn't know where you were going or what to expect as the adrenaline powered you forward. I loved that risk, that unknown, the hole to nowhere as you were walking into the unknown. That night before nodding off below deck, I said a prayer I had learned as a youngster, word for word, with all the sincerity I could muster, and asked God for my soul to be saved in the event my body was taken. I also asked a few favors for my family and friends. Additionally, I added a caveat to the prayer by asking for protection for the battalion, my squad in particular, and myself. Corny as it may sound, I asked for no favor and just wanted a blessing to be the best Marine I could be, an unbreakable jarhead. I repeated this last prayer part in a number of ways. I guess I wanted to ensure priority delivery.

As dawn was breaking, I gazed up into a sky with clouds that looked the same as back home. We were lined up to climb over the edges of the ship onto nets thrown to the water's edge. Some bursts of gunfire and explosions still slightly lit up the air off in the distant mountains. We climbed down the nets and into Marine amphibious landing crafts. I had heard them sometimes be referred to as "floating coffins." With the landing crafts full, you now realized where the term "asshole-to-belly-button" may have originated. You were literally packed in there like boatfuls of mackerel going to market. This exact same amphibious landing on a foreign shore was the same used in World War II and Korea. I was one proud mackerel.

Actually, most Marines and other military forces landing in Vietnam did so by airplane. Our major landing, like some John Wayne movie, was rather rare, but we were there somewhat early in the war and were landing an entire battalion, gear, and equipment.

Here I was about to set foot on the foreign soil I had volunteered for. Chu Lai was up along the ocean in the northern sector of South Vietnam, not far under Da Nang. It was said to be inland from the ocean at the foot of a major mountain that had absolutely nothing there. The only previous troops, Marines, were embedded deep in the jungle, beyond and around the mountain and famous Ho Chi Min Trail, the major enemy supply line that stretched from south to north.

With just under one year in the Corps, I had volunteered for virtually everything I could to further my chances as a ground-pounding Marine. There's an age-old saying in the military that goes (paraphrased): *Don't ever volunteer for anything because you will be sorry.* That obviously did not apply to me as I never regretted raising my hand, from the extra infantry training to the constant requests to transfer to a unit going to Vietnam. That same mindset would play out many more times during my enlistment. I always felt it was my destiny to be a hard-charging Marine and constantly pushed for nothing less. Anything less to me would be like a form of denial. I loved facing things head-on, damn any negative consequences. I always admired actions over good intentions. To me, and many others like me, volunteering to step over the line to earn the right to become a Marine—or any other service member—to defend America's principles, ideals, and allies was the greatest honor that could be bestowed upon a young man. It was like an unwritten personal belief and code that while not wearing it on our sleeves, it existed strongly in our impressionable minds. American and military history would humbly push those beliefs to anyone receptive enough to accept them. I insisted to be in that line. And of course, the Corps did more than their part to ensure my high level of patriotism, which I accepted with outstretched arms.

I suppose I was like the ultimate recruiter's dream. This wet-behind-the-ears eager kid who walked in and wanted nothing more but to become a Marine. But as time passed, I saw my volunteerism as some form of a magical shield protecting me from harm no matter what I raised my paw for. I came to resent it. It seemed the more I stepped over the line, the more I was spared. And the more I was spared, the more I stepped over the line. Frustration and guilt related to all these beliefs, and the partial lack of execution therein followed me like a weary hound dog throughout Vietnam and beyond. Way beyond.

As the door of the landing craft came slapping down against the sun-drenched water, I was ready to run out and tackle the shoreline as we had been trained and as the war movies had portrayed. But just before that, I saw no signs of bullets or expositions coming in. The only thing that registered as pain or discomfort was my dog tags entangled in my chest hair. Even before that, I kissed those tags as a way of saying I was ready, like a reverse farewell to arms. The only thing reminiscent of a war movie was that it wasn't true. Right away, I sensed we were as safe as waiting in the doctor's office back home. The landing at Iwo Jima it was not. We walked out to the shore without a hint of a cloud overhead. It was one of the more pristine beaches I had ever seen with blinding pure-white sand. I hated it.

Then I saw the entire beach before us. I saw hundreds of wooden crates parked upon the perfect sand, not even coarse enough to hurt your undersoles. There were bodies everywhere around the crates, some just lying there relaxing and drinking beer. The only thing I had to dodge from the front and both sides were pull-top tabs from Budweiser and Coors cans. From that point on, I viewed Sneezy—"Sneeze" as a makeshift Americanized version of Napoleon or Mussolini, as they shared the same short stature and grandiose narcissistic egos.

To view Sergeant Bee walk off that landing craft was priceless, what with his artificial swagger and the .45 pistol bouncing rhythmically on his hip. I would have given my next month's pay to see inside Sneeze's mind at that precise moment. If you didn't know better and squinted your eyes tight and used some imagination, you may see MacArthur coming back to the Philippines after promising, "I shall return." I laughed inside to the degree where the levity put the landing in proper perspective. I immediately relaxed and put any thoughts of legendary Chesty Puller on hold.

But leisurely (hot) beer drinking—*amber-colored liquid*, as Major Walker would warn us about back at the regimental school—would be short-lived and a distant mirage as the order was passed down to saddle up and get ready to man the WWII–Korea vintage troop trucks and move out. It was still hard for this Minnesota boy to realize he was nearly thirteen thousand miles away on the South China Sea. We were packed again like mackerel in the open trucks in convoy to make the caterpillar-like trip from the water's edge through several miles of expanded beach and patches of dense, yet intermittent jungle. At the end, we would reach the distant mountains where our base camp would be.

Chapter Eighteen

As we made that dredge in the boiling heat, I first witnessed the people—peasants, really—of Vietnam and how a war environment can bring out the worst in some individuals, just like it can bring out the best. It's the *worst* during the convoy that stuck in my mind like a bad headache. A few Marines on my truck certainly didn't make any friends or help to win over the local populace, including not winning over me. Often, it's not what good you do that's remembered but usually the bad. I can honestly say that the first enemy I faced was not the Viet Cong but fellow Marines, at least on the initial superficial level.

At this one point where the convoy would take one of its many stops, a colorful group of a dozen or so Vietnamese were walking along the dirt road in unison, young and old alike. As they approached to pass our truck, this one Marine whipped out his goods and urinated on the top of this umbrella. As the urine spattered and ran down over the sides, this old man looked up from the umbrella as if to check if it were raining, and he too got hit. Just then, another Marine joined the other and added his urine. If looks could kill, we would have all been dead. The old man's eyes were like bullets of disdain and hatred, as were the rest, especially the older ones.

"What the hell are you doing?" I yelled loudly. I said some other choice things but can't remember exactly what. I was pissed, in a way, as if I were urinated on. The first one that started it all—whom I always referred to as the "Yellow Rainmaker"—said something back to the effect they were only gooks and to mind my own business. I told him I was making it my business, and it created some definite tension on our truck. A couple of other Marines grabbed me casually and suggested I ignore them and forget about it. I did but very reluctantly. I figured it would take two quick punches to knock this clown off the truck, but I didn't. I didn't want the trouble, but more than that, I didn't want to hurt my fist. It wasn't just this idiot's actions that bothered me so, but his facial expressions and penetrating, disgusting remarks. Lastly, I wondered how he would have reacted had some complete stranger urinated in public on his father? If it would have been my father, for example, the young Marine wouldn't have made it to twenty-one, or if he did, he would have the scars to prove it.

I had to be content to look at the beautiful countryside as we made our way closer to the foot of the emerging mountains. I was fascinated with this new country and the war it hosted. But I kept thinking of being an engineer. Deep in my mind, my lingering belief was that the only Marine was a grunt Marine 100 percent of the time. I revisited the fact that had I fully realized otherwise, I probably wouldn't have joined. It still didn't make much difference to me that the Marine Corps wanted and needed their own for all logistics and support. That basic premise that all Marines were basic riflemen and grunts would only be called upon if the situation dictated it didn't appease me. At this point, I could only hope that situations *would* dictate it.

Here I was ending our convoy journey and ready to dig in like any good grunt but knowing I would be assuming duties shortly as an engineer, which seemed far removed as we encircled our convoy and equipment like a modern-day wagon train inside a large patch of barren land and stacked layers of barbed wire. Our first task was to dig our own foxholes and help with platoon trenches for defecation.

After setting up two-man tents, we enjoyed our first meal of C-rats. We washed it down with warm water that we drew from steel water buffaloes. We also started taking our malaria tablets. My tentmate was one Peter Kuhlmann, whom later would pick up the nickname "Pistol Pete" by another member of our squad. Staff Sergeant Bee would make his rounds to ensure we were following proper protocol and following the Marine Corps manual in dig-in techniques. For being a big cluster fuck, as the Marines called it, it was pretty organized.

That first night in-country was a little surreal as we didn't know really what, if anything, to expect. Pete and I escaped perimeter-guard duty that first night because it had already been established. We were still instructed to be on fifty-fifty alert, meaning we would do alternate sleeping through the night. The dark sky greeted us with a near-constant barrage of flares, across from our positions, behind us toward the jungle and really 360 degrees around. Sneezy was probably in his tent counting his pistol rounds and thinking, *Okay, I was a little late, but maybe we're going to see some action this night.* The only action we got was constantly slapping away at attacking mosquitoes.

They attacked from every flank and swarmed at us individually and collectively. Their combative counterparts were flies who obviously loved these American C-rats.

The first thing the next morning, we had a big formation and was schooled on our upcoming schedules, what not to do with the locales like giving them C-rat cans or anything else as they could be used against us as small booby traps, and other Marine stuff in relation to our mission in Vietnam. They also told us to try to ignore all the Vietnamese people trying to sell us stuff over the barbed wire. The entrepreneur in the locals came out when we assumed our new home as many had never made contact with any Americans. The kids in particular would guardedly bring out decks of cards that depicted sex in every way imaginable. Apparently, that was their first impression of Americans: they wanted sex pictures. These little imps would pull a deck out of their pockets and say, "You want fuck pictures, GI?" Right behind that were offers for bags of pot. And other assorted trinkets. I got a big charge from it all, but bought nothing and just grabbed a few peeks of the sex cards.

After three days, we moved from two-man tents to larger tents pitched over dirt. There were big enough to house two squads. We also got cots, sleeping bags, and mosquito nets. Our entire squad was now together, and Sergeant Bee couldn't be more pleased as he had complete control. Well, not entirely.

Our squad leader, informally, was Lance Corporal Rucker, who was from the East Coast and had the humor of a New York comedian. He was rapid fire with his tongue, and nothing or nobody escaped his wrath, especially those deserving souls. He had come from a well-to-do family with corporate and political ties and joined the Marines in defiance of all that.

To further his defiance, he got a large snake—in full color—tattooed on his arm. Sneezy immediately got us busy with our first duties, making shitters and pissers out of fifty-gallon drums and empty bomb shells. At first we worked directly under the grueling sun on twelve-hour shifts. To say he was a slave driver would be an insult to the slaves. We would return to our tent after a shift completely spent—often nursing metal burn holes and marks all over our body—only to find we had to fight the heat, flies, and mosquitoes to get some sleep. You'd get under your mosquito net to protect you from the hordes of bugs, but quickly realize the heat and humidity did not dissipate with the setting sun. To lie there in a heavy layer of sweat and dirt was hard to get used to, but as an engineer, who the hell was I to complain? Working in that sun along with the heat from the welding we were doing, the smoke going directly up to your lungs, hour after hour, day after day, with that first few weeks was a genuine challenge, made worse by Sneezy's gung-ho, charge-the-hill-with-welding-rod-in-hand approach. We got to resent him. He may have stood only five feet four inches, but his big man's ego was on trajectory to the moon.

Rucker, in particular, was seething. He too, I'd find out later, was another denied, frustrated grunt. And Sneezy's behavior drove it home like so many piercing welding rods. Every day, we had to report to our superiors that we were keeping our tents and trash cans totally clean and policed. One day, Rucker, like he often did, made a grand pronouncement, rising up on a garbage can to address the squad, complete with dramatic gestures. He said anybody could keep their area cleaned, but it would be far tougher to see how dirty we could get ours without emptying the trash or lifting a finger. The range in his voice went way up and then down like some military hero going into battle. Was that an understatement? Within days, after contriving ways to avoid prying eyes, we were ankle deep in trash and were literally fighting off battalions of flies and squads of rats, big and small. The word got out, and the next thing we knew, the battalion medical officer was at our door. Someone yelled out "attention," and the Navy doctor entered. He was obviously disgusted as he made sounds and gestures of a revolting nature. Just as quickly as he entered, he departed, saying, "This tent is condemned and you Marines are on report."

Sneezy's squad was now the buzz of the battalion, and we slept under the stars for a couple of days, having lost our tent and grounds. But because we were urgently needed for the P & S detail, as well as making poles for electricity from those same empty artillery shells, we were let off the hook and allowed to pitch another tent. Led by Rucker, we had belly laughs at night so loud we were told by our superiors to tone it down or we would once again lose our tent. Sneezy was called up before the Man and, while not saying much to us verbally, worked us extra hard and seemed to detach himself from us as human beings.

We loved it, but that was short-lived as he sent his right-hand man, Lew, our formal squad leader, into our tent to bunk with us. Corporal Lew was just one of the guys, but around Sergeant Bee, he gave new meaning to brownnosing and working your way up the ranks. In a way, it couldn't be helped as Sneezy's ego needed someone close to him so he could belittle and berate that poor unfortunate soul and look bigger for the effort. Lew accepted that call as squad leader, like it or not. We also had to guard the perimeter of the camp besides work duties. Sneeze saw to it that we did more than our share as he probably wanted to make amends with his superiors over our behavior. Sleep was in short supply, but I always was first in line for guard duty, thinking it may bring some action.

Chapter Nineteen

One night in particular, I was in a bunker, sandbagged roof and all, with my two-man-tent bud Pistol Pete. We were on fifty-fifty alert, which was quite common, and it was my turn to sleep on the dirt floor with my helmet as a pillow. Suddenly, screams woke me up, and I instinctively grabbed my rifle. Pete was standing there looking like he was being shocked by bolts of electricity, arms and legs flailing, eyes in panic. "A rat crawled up my leg!" he yelled, barely audible. I noticed that he did not blouse his boots and they were loose. Pete caught the critter around his crotch and, probably in desperation and fear, squeezed and held the rat in place. I yelled at him to let him go, but instead he ran out of the bunker and up upon the perimeter itself, running back and forth like a madman, holding that rat in his pants. Since I was in Sneezy's squad and was conditioned to see humor in everything, I couldn't help but laugh. At the same token, I thought if there were any enemy out there, they would surely see this wild-eyed Marine as a moving target on the skyline and he'd be taken out, rat and all. As I told him to get down and come back and let go of the rat, he came down—alone. The rat episode was over, but not forgotten.

After the dust settled and Pete went to sickbay, it had to be determined if the puncture wounds on his upper thigh were bite or claw marks. The attending corpsman couldn't tell for sure but recommended that the full array of rabies shots in the stomach should commence. Pete wanted no part of them and insisted he take the risk and only get a tetanus shot. If he made the wrong decision and more time passed and he did get rabies, it could mean his demise. His hunch paid off as the tetanus shot did the trick. He would never forget to blouse his boots again. The rat was probably scared off to Da Nang.

Another night on guard, a couple of the Marines got bored and started shooting flares over the grass huts on the edge of An Tan, the village adjacent to our camp. Their aims were good as several straw roofs of the huts started fires. Although I was well down the perimeter and had nothing to do with the mischief, I couldn't help but laugh as the burning roofs would awaken the residents who would come out screaming in panic and put out the fires. The officer of the day wanted to write them up but couldn't prove who the guilty parties were. Some roofs were partially lost, but no one was hurt. Just one more night in a bunker.

Shortly, we upgraded living accommodations with two-by-four framed tents, with risen wood floors. The sides of the large tents had side flaps that served as sun awnings. Everything else was the same as far as cots, mosquito nets, and sleeping bags went. Except for guard duty, we were now off the dirt. We even had a large basin ten feet out our door for washing, shaving, and dental care. Just to do something positive, I started a ritual of brushing my teeth and gargling three times daily. While there, I did calf raises holding the basin until I couldn't stretch them anymore. My brushing got me accolades from the dental team, and my calves became etched like diamonds. It was just something to mark time as I often looked out toward the jungle and wished I were in the thick of things.

About the same time we assumed our new billets, our company commander gathered us together for a talk. Basically, he was saying how important our mission was in building roads, infrastructure, bridges, and churches. He also said our mission would be expanding away from the base camp and it may be fraught with dangers, especially for land mine engineers. So as a kickoff to that and in celebration of having our camp reaching completion, he said he would allow some light liberty in the adjoining village of An Tan, determined by our squad leaders. For us, that meant Sneezy. And for Sneezy, that meant power, control, and working us to the bone to earn that liberty.

Meanwhile, Sergeant Sneeze was getting commendations and being called out by the brass for the incredible amount of work we were producing. Sneezy would sometimes tell us there's work done by a normal high-achiever engineer and welder, and then there's the Marine version. We were Marines. We always rise above the rest. Rucker, forever the wise-ass, blurted out, "We are the Marine's version of combat welders then?" Sergeant Bee sensed his sarcasm and just tightened his lizard lips as he left. But during this high time for Sneezy, he gave us liberty in staggered shifts and also had me promoted to lance corporal. That meant along with the standard of just over $60 per month for combat pay and $16 for overseas pay, my increased rank meant my monetary riches were going up. I sent practically everything home, and Dad said he would invest it for me until I returned.

The major also gave us a speech like a father figure about the dangers of liberty in the village. The worries were hollowed-out booze bottles—whiskey and beer—that were refilled with tiny glass particles, small booby traps, and worse of all, the "black syph." He said if we contracted that from a local whore, the strain of venereal disease was so bad we might be listed as MIA (missing in action)—seems like an oxymoron now—and sent to Okinawa, never to return home. It scared the crap out of me, and I vowed right then to keep my goods to myself. This was despite all the saltpeter they swore they put in our hot food, which was to negate our sexual appetite. But how about all the times we ate C-rats? No matter, I usually woke up with enough morning wood in Vietnam to build a house.

Even though those dire warnings kept me celibate, others threw fate to the wind. I did risk having some beers, however. And after wrapping up liberty, we were walking back to camp and passed a long line of Marines standing outside of a hooch. We went behind the grass shack and peeked through the wide cracks. There was this skinny little Vietnamese girl—woman—with a Marine striding her body and her son or young brother holding a cup next to her, collecting the $10 from each GI. While this jarhead was getting his jollies, this gal would turn her head, moan, and take a bite out of a big apple. We had a laugh as I nicknamed her the "Apple Eater" and swore I wanted nothing to do with these women.

As a prelude to that first liberty being issued, Ninth Engineers had its first casualty. And he was without doubt considered to be the safest of us all, our mess—food—sergeant. He left our enclosed compound and went a short distance down the only road going through Vietnam, the two-lane dirt Highway 1. He went down in a jeep armed with his .45 cal. pistol and the driver and his M-14. Their duty was to deliver food before dawn to engineers working on a bridge. They were ambushed by Viet Cong, wounded, and their vehicle set on fire, where they died. Staff Sergeant Friddle was not scheduled to finish his Vietnam tour as he was in line to retire. He had a large family. They later dedicated the mess hall in his honor. It was somewhat of a wake-up call for all of us as it showed we really were in danger and that anything could happen at any given moment. Thank God.

I often wondered about our camp position right at the foot of the mountains. We were surrounded entirely by the back and a little of both sides, about 180 degrees of jungle. Looking at it, you'd swear we would be prime targets for the Viet Cong, rockets, mortars, small arms fire, and even assaults. The Cong probably figured they would let us off the hook since we were doing so much good for their area. Nevertheless, I figured guard duty was always a possible way to engage in combat; that's why I volunteered so much for it.

At one point, I was working the welding shifts while standing guard, sometimes double shifts. I was getting little sleep but feeling good at the same time until we had a full-on alert for possible insurgence that would take away any sleep for two to three days. Added to my already-exhausted state, that overall eleven-day period made me a near zombie.

One day, while standing in the extended chow line, I came up to one of the big metal cans that held red-hot water and the little stove and pipe to heat it. We dipped our mess kits—metal dishes, canteen holder, and utensils—into this scalding water to disinfect everything. While standing there, I fought my eyes from closing, but they eventually did and I fell against the hot pipe and burned my arm and a small portion of my chest with its hair singed right down to the skin. I jumped awake in pain. Incredibly, it happened again only it wasn't as bad. I was so tired I skipped chow and went back to the tent to grab some shut-eye. I learned my lesson of trying to be Super Marine and accepted my fate, at least for a while.

After I got rested up and once again had it with Sneezy's combat welding, evolving more now into I Corps area, which was the main area of First Marine Division, and infrastructure, roads, and bridge-related duties, I volunteered for one week of the shit detail. I was truly crazy. The shit sergeant, as he was known, was a lifer who had a minuscule amount of brain cells to rub together. But he was a hardcore Marine who did everything by the numbers, including taking his duties as NCOIC of waste disposal—the formal reference—very seriously. Upon introduction to the detail everyone dreaded, and what he expected, his first order of business was demanding allegiance to the task.

"I want those drums so clean after the final step that you could eat your chow out of them." He was serious as we would soon find out.

He went over the process with us in minute detail. First, we would take an open-ended, cut-in-half, fifty-gal. drum (which our squad had made), fill it to a certain point with kerosene, and light it. After the top of the waste was burned down, we would take a shovel and scoop out the remainder then repeat the final burning step. Each outhouse had anywhere from three to six stalls that were contained under the seats behind a trapdoor. We wouldn't start this procedure until we had filled a dump truck load of shitters. Then we would take it way out of the way and line them up and start the black smoke flying.

It was such a nasty duty that the brass couldn't even talk the Vietnamese villagers, who were hired to do menial jobs as goodwill for the community on our base, to do it. They refused to burn our shit, even with offers of more money. Part of this was hard to believe since they said they would do anything for money to help their families, but they absolutely, to a man or woman, would not touch our defecation. They obviously drew a line in the shitless side and wouldn't cross it. I thought, *Whew, these peasants are smarter than they look while other Marines took a near-offended posture.* The shit detail ended up in our hands, and our shit sergeant would see to it that the duties were done within the highest standards of the Marine Corps. But he was no better than a shit Nazi with his barking orders and heartless leadership. It still was a nice break from Sneezy.

After about three days of taking his shit, the five of us had our fill. What could we do to make this Marine not look upon these barrels as mountains to conquer in combat but as cans full of crap? One guy had an idea. You had no choice but to go along for the ride. His plan was simple: We would start talking with the sergeant about his favorite subject—him. And then we would ask questions about his second favorite topic—his Marine Corps career. Then with the cooperation of the truck driver, the truck would be readied to quietly dump the entire contents of the load down upon his head. It was a mission fraught with danger and risk, but we felt it had to be done. Probably the biggest and hardest aspect of the mission was getting the truck close to him without disrupting his thinking, which was strictly on a single track. We inundated him with compliments about his leadership and questions about all his duty stations, especially the one he held dearest, Japan. As the driver somehow started the truck bed to be quietly dumping, we kicked up our voices and drowned him in attention.

Then it happened. The whole load of barrels full of shit came tumbling down as the driver quickly drove forward. Everything dumped over the sergeant's head, and as the last barrel hit him in the head, remnants of shit poured over the same. He had absolutely no response as he took off his cover, with turds and toilet paper dangling from his forehead and nose. He shook off his cover and put it back on, walking away casually, saying nothing. I felt sorry for him because that last barrel really hit his head hard. But no harm done, it seemed. While this would be one story he would undoubtedly omit from his career exploits, the incident humbled him, and he apparently put the shit detail in proper context and treated his Marines much better. So our actions saved and benefited all shit Marines in the future, at least during his tour—which he extended by six months.

Unlike the shit sergeant's lack of response getting hit, we could not contain ourselves. We lost it and were laughing so hard we were crying. We thought the sarge wasn't so bad after all because he could definitely take a lot of shit and not take it out on us and have us all busted. I personally felt bad enough about it all to volunteer to stay on an extra week, but with a unique twist. I easily sold him on the fact that he could get some good praise and credit by dressing up the shithouses. So I was now in a special services category of the waste management detail. I went to supply and made wooden signs for each large head we had in the company area. One was the "Honey Hut." The other was the "Sugar Shack." Both were painted in Marine Corps yellow and red and were innovative in their letter creation and application. When completed, it drew a lot of laughs, including the Officer Corps, and was well received.

Chapter Twenty

Upon leaving the waste removal duty, I applied for and received R & R (rest and recuperation) in Hong Kong. I brought exactly $250 and was determined to make that last for the five days, although I had heard others say they spent over five hundred bucks. We wore our khaki uniforms and flew out of Da Nang.

Up in the Pan Am flight—besides just "asshole-to-belly-button" Marines—there were three to four stewardesses working the flight; one was a drop-dead-gorgeous brunette who had it all. When she served me my meal and drink, I noticed she had a Scandinavian accent. I told her I was Swedish and Norwegian and was from Minnesota, and it opened the door for me since she turned out to be from Bergen, Norway, where my grandma's side was from. She would frequently stop next to me and make small talk. Try using your charms and seduction abilities in front of a plane full of hungry and horny Marines? Now that's a challenge worthy of a promotion. But there wouldn't be enough promotions to compete with an officer sitting up front, who was also trying to hustle this girl.

She seemed to be going back and forth between me and him, at one point sending a fellow stewardess back to check me out. I felt confident that there was enough chemistry going on to quietly ask her for a date. I actually wrote the request on a piece of paper and slipped it to her as I visited the restroom. Hong Kong soon was in our landing sites. I don't know which one I was more excited about, Hong Kong or Miss Norway, but I would have settled for the latter.

The plane landed, and we were deplaning. The back was emptied first as we were all the rank-and-file troops. As I was ready to leave, the gorgeous stewardess showed up just as I was walking off. I sensed trouble. "I'm very sorry, Jon, but I guessed you were outranked." I left and didn't look back. I had been sitting with this black Marine who had just come off a major combat operation up north to go on R & R. We hit it off, shared our plans, and ended up booked at the same hotel. But he was rather uptight, in a nice way. We wished each other the best and said we'd reconnect upon the flight home. There was a time when I didn't know if I would make that flight. But that's behind all the fun.

Hong Kong was big, like a huge dragon that would swallow its American prey if you didn't watch your p's and q's. The British still owned and controlled this commerce capital, and my first thought was to go out browsing to find a British girl. After all, we were on I & I (intercourse and intoxication) leave, not R & R. First, I had to dress right, so I did the customary thing that all previous GIs talked about after coming back from Hong Kong. I summoned a tailor to come to my room and measure me for a handmade suit. It was like $50 and included everything. I talked him down from $80 and felt like a good American negotiator. It looked much more expensive than I paid so I was happy and set.

Talk about false confidence. I went to this swanky hotel that I heard were full of Brits and started my search. Who was I kidding? With my short haircut and suntanned features, not to mention if I opened my American mouth, I was red-flagged like a cheap lot under construction. The whole British community and their families probably forewarned any female that the Marines and other service members were pulling R & R in Hong Kong and to be mindful. We weren't there as diplomats. I remember capturing a few glances from young ladies as I devoured the hotel, but mainly they looked at me with this bewildered wonderment, like I was some alien. And I was but a harmless one.

As I left, I realized that my fate was in the hands of bars and whores like every other GI. I quickly found out that prostitutes were a different breed in Hong Kong and there were several approaches to take. The first approach was meeting a bar girl, as they called them, and if there was a positive connection, she would be your "girlfriend" for the entire stay. The second approach was along the independent route where you spent time with more than one girl. I liked the indie approach and quickly found my first girl and brought her to my room to spend the night. In the morning, she excused herself and said she hoped to see me again soon. Although she was certainly Asian, her eyes were pretty wide, her body shapely, and her face quite pretty, and she was a great lover—but I had indie on my mind.

After giving myself a huge treat by having lunch on the famous floating Hong Kong restaurant noted for instantaneous fresh-netted seafood and Chinese beer, I was ready to rumble. I picked up my second girl that night and brought her home.

Before the night was over, I had a knock on my door. It was the first girl and said she thought we were girlfriend and boyfriend for the week. I apologized, and for an instant thought I may have to referee a fight between the two, one in bed, the other at the door. Words were exchanged, and they weren't well wishes. She said I was a butterfly and that many girls like her didn't like butterflies. And so it went for the remainder of the week. I would be called a butterfly wherever I went—that huge city seemed so small—but I still ended up with five different girls during my stay. I was not into prostitutes for sure, but Hong Kong sure had it down to a fine art, making the experience seem natural, not contrived. They really did act like a loving, giving girlfriend and took great pride in it. The city of Hong Kong highly regulated them and conducted physical tests on them every three to five days. But I did yearn for a regular girl and found one in the afternoon at a wine and tea club. While there was a mixture of both prostitutes and escort girls, as they were called, I picked one that just looked at me nice.

She turned out to be a university student majoring in medicine and spoke near-perfect English and was very articulate. But she made it very clear, very quickly, that she was not a bar girl, but a good girl. I was impressed enough with her to spend hours in her company. Working there was just a way to make extra money for school and expenses and supplement her father's allowance. She wasn't beautiful or anything, but she was attractive and quite deep and intelligent. She was keenly interested as she asked dozens of questions about my being a Marine and an American. She was timing our visit together so I wouldn't have to spend too much money on her tea. Each cup was timed so she made sure I got maximum time per cup.

I kind of felt I was parked at a car meter, but I appreciated her generosity and enjoyed every minute.

The next day, after dismissing my "date" for the evening, I went back to the "Tea and Wine Palace." There, I spent another day with Lee, as she finally told me her name, and she seemed to be falling in love with me. I knew it was real, and it scared the stuffing out of me. She was stumbling over herself apologizing for not being professional and "liking" me too much. She started sobbing slightly and coyly covered her face, saying she couldn't let anyone see her. I didn't know where to take this. I was dumbfounded.

Okay, Jon, I thought to myself, *you wanted a "normal" girl and here she is.* She said all the things she saw in me and said she had never talked so freely and openly to anyone like that before, as I was a "unique American." I charmed and complimented her too much, maybe, as it appeared to melt her down significantly. She was so incredibly sweet and feminine. But I had to end this before it went further so I spent some more quality time with her and excused myself and said I would see her again the next day. That day would not come.

I felt a little guilty, but damn, this was I & I and I had a reputation as a butterfly to live up to so it was cruise time again. The working girls were going to the bars, and I was in the hunt. But this was the final night, and I wanted to step way out and do something different. I had a few quick beers, washed down with a rum Coke—double-doused—and I saw a rickshaw and wanted to catch a ride and see the sights.

We were instructed upon R & R to only stay on the Kowloon side of Hong Kong and not venture to the Hong Kong side. It was strictly off limits. After the rickshaw driver took me to the renowned outdoor sculpted walls and paintings of wars and strife and the history of Hong Kong—not far from movie star William Holden's house—I was feeling pretty good so I told him to take me to the best whorehouse in Hong Kong, not fully realizing just what I said. It was a long, long ride; and when he stopped and let me out and quickly took off, I knew I was in trouble. What have I done now? I wished I was sitting back at the tea palace with Lee.

Maybe this was karma paying me back. My mind was racing, but one thing was for sure; I was on the Hong Kong side, and it was all around me. There were no other round eyes to be seen, and the Chinese on the sidewalk were staring at me with daggers in their eyes. *What the hell did I do?* I thought. *It seems I am surrounded by enemies—more than in Vietnam—and I'm just a young man looking for fun.* I was perplexed, but what the heck, I was here and I was a butterfly and I was going to find a place to land whether they liked it or not. I took on a don't-mess-with-me attitude, which I had learned and applied in Tijuana.

It worked. I landed long enough for a quickie—but I used double raincoats (condoms)—and after walking down this long, dingy stairway with people smoking opium or some such thing, on the steps, I called for a rickshaw. I told the guy to go as fast as possible back to the Kowloon side. He was younger on this leg so I tipped him good after he made it back like an Olympian. I was now back in the "safe zone" and visited the very first bar when I arrived in Hong Kong and ran into my first girlfriend. We made up, enjoyed a final night together, and I finished my five-day adventure on a high note. Except for one negative.

I loved my suit and thought I'd wear it back on the return flight to Vietnam. I laid it out on the bed as my girlfriend watched. I put the pants on first, and the seams in my butt burst open. She said she could bring it down to the hotel office and they could fix it. Okay, fine. Just as she was readying to leave, I put the jacket on and the arm came right off. The back also split up to the shoulder level. I took it off, threw it on the floor, and grabbed the pants and did the same. We laughed and I would tell my buddies later I called it my five-day suit. I gave my girlfriend a tip for her great company and left for the pickup point with $20 still in my wallet. I was on top of the world and ready to spread my wings back to Vietnam.

I ran into my flight-over friend, and we shared our stories. Seemed that his was a little more hairy than mine, which was hard to believe. After a heavy night of drinking, he had some disagreement with his girlfriend and picked her little body up and hung her upside down from her ankles outside the window from the sixth floor. People talked him into letting her down, and after she got inside the room again, she beat the living snot out of the guy. The management figured she beat him up enough so they didn't call the cops. He even had a few marks on his face to prove it, but he was laughing hard. He said it was a misunderstanding and it was his fault because she reminded him of a Viet Cong. Aren't wars hell?

In a way, Hong Kong reminded me of Tijuana because I deposited both money and sperm in the working girl community and their local economies. I was a contributing American to world peace and harmony.

Chapter Twenty-One

When I returned to Chu Lai and Ninth Engineers, I was determined to wear a new face for Sneezy, Sergeant Bee, that is. I would try my best to find his good qualities, despite them being buried somewhere within his short stature.

The squad was busy as ever making telephone poles and related tasks. We finally had a tarp cover for a portion of the outside work area, but it gave little relief from the relentless humidity. Whatever weight I had gained on that cruise was long gone, plus about ten more pounds. The heat and humidity plus the smoke and burning heat from the welding created a volatile mix. Even with just one man—me—going on R & R and not working for five days, it was taking a toll on the rest of the men.

Uncle Pete, a black Marine who was our unofficial leader of sorts and greatly loved by us all, didn't seem to be himself as the heat had ravaged his energy and attitude. He had to drag himself to work, and his fatigues were much wetter than the rest of us. His zest and humor were gone, as Sneezy constantly called him out for not being more of a NCO leader, as he was a senior corporal. The more Sneeze dragged him down, the more we picked him up. We knew something was drastically off because he didn't even care about boom-boom (the symbol for sex with hands clasped together making a slapping motion) in the village anymore.

The very next day when assuming my shift, I picked up a welding helmet and started welding. But something didn't seem right with the lens or something. Since we were under the gun all the time, I just worked on. Finally, I stopped as my eyes were burning bad. While it seemed the darkness of the protective lens was awfully light, I still couldn't understand it. All other helmets were being used so I went on. Not long however. I got mad and ripped the helmet off my head and closely examined the lenses. I noticed heavy scratches on the inside, impacting the protective portion in places. It appeared the scratches were man-made and purposely done. My eyes were now in full pain mode, feeling like I had pebbles in them, causing me to barely be able to keep my eyes open. If any light hit them, it would make them worse. It was excruciating.

Sneezy rushed over since anything concerning welding was his baby and looked at my eyes and said, "Arc flash. Arc burn." He showed them to Lew, who was now a new sergeant, and they both said they would take me to sickbay. The corpsman and doctor quickly assessed the eye damage and said I would have to go to the hospital up at First Marine Division Headquarters. After arrival, I was issued hospital blue pajamas and escorted to a framed tent and given a cot. A doctor treated me with ointments in my eyes and wrapped my eyes for three days, where I was totally blind. They made sure I got my malaria pills and brought me portable food to my bedside. With everything dark, I just relaxed and slept.

After the three days and the wraps coming off, it was a slow recovery to full vision, but when it came back, the colors in particular were extra vivid, contributing greatly to my immediate environment.

Being admitted to the military field hospital in Chu Lai was like a lethal dose of beauty and the beast. The *beauty* was in the setting, which was like another tent city—with added Quonset huts—but nonetheless breathtaking. It was situated high upon soft inclines and cliffs that blended in from the pristine white sandy beach. Small outcroppings of sparse green vegetation spotted the terrain between the hospital and the oceanfront. It was to become strangely serene yet disturbing during my nearly two-week stay. My particular tent was right near the edge of that scenic view, with my cot having a spectacular vantage point.

The *beast* was lingering in and around me at that hospital like some caged wild animal waiting to jump out at the slightest opening of that loosely closed cage door. This beast, the animal, was the overwhelming presence of death, near death, and profound injury. Despite the clear blue skies, it permeated through the environment like dark daggers in an otherwise dreamy day. The smells, noises, sights, and sounds invaded my being like sharp, long claws, penetrating me deeply and constantly but without drawing one bead of blood. I felt like this detached casualty who wasn't directly attacked.

When I first checked in, there were only three to four cots taken, out of several dozen, but in short order, every cot was filled. I did not feel deserving of mine. And I could never quite bring myself to tell others exactly why I was admitted. I usually just said I got an eye injury after telling one Marine and his response being, "Arc what?"

Because I was ambulatory, I had the freedom to walk to the mess hall for every meal, which was considerably better than back at Ninth. Most nights, they had open-seating outdoor movies. It was incredible observing all the wounded hobble in from the tents to find a seat. I always felt honored to be able to help some Marines arrange their wheelchairs or crutches as they settled in for some entertainment. Others were holding thick plastic bags close to their chests that acted as artificial stomachs while others lying prone on their hospital beds were wheeled into the seating area with their IVs hanging overhead.

To witness this merciless parade of souls blending into the crowd of staff and doctors and then laughing and having fun at the movies like everything was totally normal was a surreal sight. Some of the wounded had multiple limbs missing and were wrapped with fresh gauze. As I studied the audience, I felt like I had the eyes of a cat in the dark, only making a move if I felt it was safe and I wasn't being seen. Guarded caution would be the two most accurate words. But the one word, even though I didn't cause it, was *guilt*, which kept creeping into my being, even if by just the slightest cracking of that caged door.

Several days after my bandages were removed, my eyes were greeted by this Red Cross nurse in her alluring full dress uniform. She came into the tent and immediately made a beeline to me as I was lying down in my cot. She sat down in the vacant cot across from mine. It was a time of the day where many residents were out and about or getting treatment in one of the many specialty tents. As she sat on the depressed cot, her skirt went way up to her upper thighs, and her legs happened to be in the killer category. She put her hands over one crossed leg and rocked back even further, nearly exposing herself. Her round eyes were impish and her pretty facial features laminated as if they were etched by an artist. She was immediately comforting although I made it quite clear that there were others that legitimately needed her attention much more than me. She didn't seem to think so.

She was extremely outspoken and frank with a hint of bitterness about the war in her voice. After some personal conversation, and with a straight face and not so much of a waffling of her words, she said, "If the time and circumstances permitted, I would like to jump into that cot with you and make love." I was speechless and taken for a loop. Me! She went on and told me all about the big Red Cross ship parked in the harbor directly across from the hospital and my tent. It was all by itself like some marooned vessel in distress. But the only distress was on board.

The nurse went into a vivid description of how that ship was like a huge floating emergency center, tackling the worst of the worst. She said she was wrapping up her tour on that ship and it was like hell itself, with blood awash upon the floors like wax and bodies everywhere with missing limbs, faces, and hideous wounds. Her eyes looked away toward the ship. She turned back to me in momentary silence, studying my face, then continued. She said when the choppers brought in fresh bodies from battle, it was so chaotic you couldn't tell the dying and dead ones from the mere wounded. She related that young men nearly always cried out for their *mommies* when dying. Sometimes, she said, a dying Marine would just yell out that he wanted to touch, hold, and kiss a woman before he died, sometimes with a little different verbiage.

It was hard to break that seriousness of the moment, but it happened. Suddenly, a younger Red Cross nurse started to enter the tent and swung the screen door open. As it hit the cot behind it and she looked down, she saw an asleep Marine with an erection poking through the front slit in the pajamas. It looked like some hastily pitched tent with the pole protruding through the center that was partially collapsed. She screamed loud, waking the poor leatherneck up and probably making him think we were being attacked as he scrambled around his immediate area looking for his nonexistent weapon. He had no idea that the only weapon around him, at least according to that young innocent nurse, was his manhood. The older nurse across from me laughed and said she needed that wake-up call to overcome her naivety. And with that, she looked deep into my eyes, wished me well by professing I would be fine, and left, joining the young nurse who was still upset outside the doorway.

After she left, I felt somewhat drained and couldn't take my eyes off that parked massive hospital ship with its big RED cross that was embodied on each side, against pure white. It was ironic that she had said the ship should have instead been painted deep red with a small white cross on it. She had remarked that the ship was unlike any hospital in existence and was really a floating death ship. She said all this with practically no emotion whatsoever, just matter-of-fact, as if she just wanted to get it off her mind and share it.

Shortly after, as incredible as it seemed, an old boot camp buddy was admitted to my tent with an extreme case of dysentery. Seeing Corporal Clute before me was simply remarkable, but not hearing what he was about to tell me. He had this distant, wayward look with reddened eyes that seemed like they never blinked. And his mouth never closed, with his lower jaw just hanging. His lips were deeply cracked and heavily chapped. He had dirt, the kind of reddish dirt you'd often see closer to the jungle, ingrained on his smorgasbord white face and deep into his scalp. We briefly hugged, but he was totally detached. He just kept shaking his head and looking at me, deeply, and saying, "Jon . . . Jon, you are so lucky, so incredibly lucky, you just don't know, man." He repeated the word *lucky* over and over again. I never heard that word mean so little before. Dropping the word to "luck," it seemed more like a dirty four-letter word. It seemed obscene. Who was I to be issued any luck?

He then told me that many of our boot camp comrades were killed when their battalion landed on the shores between Chu Lai and Da Nang. He mentioned a few names and one in particular who had just gotten married before leaving for Vietnam and was to become a new daddy. He was decapitated by an artillery round during the landing. Now, my jaw was dropping. But I certainly didn't feel *lucky*. I felt sad and at a great loss as I pondered my existence and fate. I kept thinking how I was one of the few that didn't get a direct infantry designation in boot camp. I remembered every second of that exact time and how they were practically handing out death certificates to everyone except a few "lucky" ones like me. But it was still a proud time as we were all gung-ho Marines ready for combat and anything the Corps would challenge us with. This would include the strange companion of guilt, justified or not.

Chapter Twenty-Two

During my hospital stay, I also learned about the ingenious but hideous torture methods the Viet Cong used against their captured Americans. One was utilizing beautiful young women as bait and working the GI up, literally. Then they would force a glass rod up his penis and break it with a hammer or something hard. They would usually bleed to death. The second was hanging a captive upside down between two large bamboo trees, each being tied back. Then they would cut the ropes and the trees would go in opposite directions and literally split the GI in half. The other things they did with small and large booby traps, which we had information about on the ship, were ever present, and many of the wounded I was around were victims of their dubious methods. Suddenly, the jungle seemed less alluring and the engineers more attractive. But that gave me another form of guilt.

To accent my thinking, I got a visit at my bedside from Sneezy and a few others wishing me well. He was incredibly nice and voiced his concern for my recovery as well as his puzzlement about how those scratches got on that helmet; he actually apologized to me and said he was still trying to get to the bottom of the incident. Fatherly as he was, his words were not consoling as it just further reminded me I was an engineer with more welding rods on my person than weapons. My mind went back and forth.

After a week of being hospital-bound, I was fidgety to do something rather than embrace the prone position in pj's and read the enemy KIA and American casualty list in the *Stars and Stripes* newspaper. So I got my regular Marine Corps green utilities on with boots and just started walking, like going on an aimless tour of the hospital grounds. With being just another number in my tent, with far less challenges than even the least wounded or recovering from whatever malady, I was on a very long leash, with near-total freedom to come and go as I pleased.

This fact, combined with the environment I was in, merely put added fuel to my growing-inside feeling of guilt, with the dirty four-letter word of *luck* dangling with it. It wasn't like I was always thinking about it, I wasn't. But it was manifesting itself deep inside me like a malignant cancer. And I was about to literally stroll into the hellfire depths of this manifestation on this hospital tour.

After browsing casually around the grounds seeing more of what I had become accustomed to, my insatiable curiosity took me away from the tent area that housed most of the patients and personnel. I soon found myself opening the door to the first of a long row of Quonset huts. A burst of air-conditioning greeted me like a long-lost friend upon a visit. In the heat of a typical Vietnamese summer day, it felt so incredibly good I wanted to just savor the moment, so I stood in silence and reaped the incredible comfort. I quickly realized I was in an IC unit, normally reserved for the most extreme cases, like that Red Cross hospital ship on the ocean. It seemed like this IC unit was vacant until I was about to turn and walk out. Something summoned me to walk in more toward the very back of the ward.

I thought I had seen someone lying on a back hospital bed, but it seemed relatively small unlike a patient lying there, so I nearly dismissed it.

Nearly.

As I approached the bed, I was awestruck by the fact that it was a person, but not a full person. At first, I just stood at the foot of his bed where his medical record was hanging on a clipboard and stared.

I was totally mesmerized. It was a black Marine who was lying on his side. He had tubes everywhere on his upper torso, with no legs or hips. Both his arms were missing, including the shoulders. The top of his head, which looked almost flat, was heavily wrapped. Because he was positioned mostly without covering, it was very plain to see his entire body, or at least what there was left of it. There were numerous small puncture-type wounds on his chest and endless smaller abrasions all over his chest and face. He showed no signs of life but was still obviously breathing. I had an almost eerie feeling that he somehow knew I was there without a sound or move being made. I picked up his record and read that he had been shot first, with a machine gun or rapid-fire bursts, and subsequently fell down and ignited a land mine, blowing him up. I read enough.

I kept walking around him until a sight stopped me in my tracks.

I saw what must have been a dozen or more large half-dollar-like holes in his back, with some going all the way to the other side, making exit marks. Some had tubes in them; others were just open and gaping. Nearly every centimeter of his back was also covered with bloodied marks, wounds, although smaller. The back part of his head—a protruding of the skull—appeared partially missing. I simply couldn't believe he was alive. I returned to the foot of his bed, just staring at him.

I methodically said a prayer that basically asked God to just please take his life without further agony. On his behalf and in proxy, I asked for the traditional forgiveness a Christian would request prior to someone's imminent death. And I even threw in any and all indiscretions he did as a person and Marine. I also asked for all this for his family's sake. I could not conceive by any stretch any loved one seeing their son, brother, relative, boyfriend, buddy, or Marine this way.

He deserved to die, I thought, soon and without further suffering.

After my special prayer, I stood there frozen for minutes in silence, again feeling that this fellow Marine brother, whose eyes were tightly shut, sensed my presence. I felt it in my bone marrow. I gave a nod of my head and turned and walked to the door to leave. Just as I was about to leave, the door burst open and two corpsmen entered, carrying a wounded Vietnamese woman on a stretcher. She was screaming in these horrific outbursts. As one corpsman left, he transferred his end to me as I stood there dumbfounded.

As he pulled over a hospital bed to the side of the stretcher, the remaining corpsman yelled out, "She was run over by a tank!" Blood oozed from beneath the white sheet that covered the frantic woman, probably in her thirties. He yelled at me to help him lift her to the bed at the count of three. I grabbed her upper arms, and she immediately grabbed mine, creating a locking together of both. The corpsman took her feet and ankles, readying for the transfer. Her screaming had now reduced to moans. I had no time to think but only to follow his commands.

As we lifted her, she yelled out at the top of her lungs an American swear word. The visible blood from the sheet became instantly saturated as she virtually came apart in two in my arms. It felt as if we were pulling apart human taffy. The sensation of her separating like that was impossible to describe. She died instantly. Her head flopped over heavily. Her hands had dug into my upper arms during the transfer and were nearly embedded into my skin. They slid down slowly as if it they were the last part of her that gave up. I remember how she looked at me in desperation and clutched my arms. But I had no time to ponder as yells for me cut through the chilled air. My body moved, but my mind didn't. The total chaos enveloped me and the ICU area.

Shortly after, in what can only be described as a frenzied hospital, I found myself running around the immediate emergency area. The only thing I remember during this onslaught of endless casualties from a major combat operation was the constant yelling of "Incoming! Incoming!" referring, of course, to the arriving wounded. They were like incoming shells of bodies. Running around in and out of the main emergency admitting area, I took quick note of a Marine holding his eyeball in and the vision of a Vietnamese mother squatted down in some hallway, holding her limp little boy and screaming and crying. The child's face was horrific, obviously the victim of napalm, and was nearly totally melted. The mother lightly shook and rocked the boy, probably two to three years old, thinking and wishing he was still alive.

He was not. He probably died right there.

I recall all the blood on the wooden door handle. I also remember being yelled at by a nurse to go wash my hands in the sink like a doctor would. As I was doing it, a doctor came up next to me to scrub up with his emergency outfit on and surgical mask. "What the hell are you doing back here in surgery, Marine? You don't belong back here."

"A nurse just grabbed me and told me to do it and wait for further instructions to help, sir."

He said nothing as he quickly left. The emergency area was awash in blood and complete panic.

I remember nothing else except staying around throughout the night until the sun broke in the morning. Sometime earlier the next day, I was exhausted and feeling like I was in some kind of ether. I rambled around and bumped into an enlisted man's club. The door was open so I went in.

I went to the vacant bar and sat, feeling like I was in some emotional and mental stupor. When the Sailor showed up, I ordered a beer. He bent over the bar top, getting real close to my face: "Hey, jarhead, there is no fucking beer." He then quickly turned around and opened one frig door then another, and another. I saw the soles of boots before me. Many boots. He said, "We ain't got no room for any beer and won't for a few more days. Too many casualties."

I quickly turned around and left.

Strangely, I wanted no more *luck* when I left that hospital. The four-letter word disgusted me. I wanted action. I wanted to be in the deepest jungle and do as a grunt Marine would do, what I knew I was trained for. But I also wanted to leave my *guilt* at the checkout tent as I felt it was consuming me. And as I went through that mental process, I thought that maybe luck wasn't such a foul word after all. But that would kick off my feelings of guilt. I had strong mixed feelings that would visit my head like a returning nightmare. It was a constant resident of the frontal part of my brain.

Chapter Twenty-Three

When I returned to my squad tent back at the base camp at Ninth Engineers, I shared my stay and experiences—most, not all—with my buddies. I was a little surprised as about three to four guys seemed as anxious as me to get out of what we humorously called our "chicken outfit" and get into the heavy shit.

However, when I detailed all the carnage, they backed off, opting to just stick out their engineering stint with Sneezy, except one, Rucker. He was in a similar mindset as me.

While I was in the hospital, I received a letter from Gary, who was stationed down south at Tan Son Nhut Air Force Base in Saigon. He said he was going up through my area and wanted to stop and visit me. I never had a chance to respond as he came through when I was still hospitalized. About the same time I was in the hospital, which was on the ocean side of First Marine Division Headquarters, word spread that there was a Viet Cong somewhere inside the area, sniping shots at the Marines who were raising and lowering colors. It got to the point where one Marine was wounded and one killed, if reports were accurate. The hunt was on. It was discovered, much too late, that the Viet Cong was a young girl working at the area PX. She would find this perfect locale high up in a palm tree and perpetrate her deadly deeds until she was found and killed. When it came to guerrilla warfare, which the Viet Cong element primarily was, this was a prime example of it, and its potential could rear its ugly noggin practically anywhere.

Before I really got fully integrated back into the work schedule because of the sensitivity of my eyes, I was given liberty almost immediately. I went to the village next door myself, the only friend being my M-14, cartridge belt, and ammo. I found this tiny eatery named "Susie's Place." It was a ten-by-ten grass hut with a dirt floor. The sign was crudely painted and made me somewhat suspicious of their "American menu." I sat down, kept my rifle close to me, and was joined by a smaller dog, who sat at my feet. I ordered their classic hamburger with fries and a bottle of Coke. The wait was quite long, but when it came and I took the first few bites, I was pleasantly surprised. The hamburger was unlike anything I had ever tasted.

"What kind of beef is this?" I asked, smacking my lips. It took them a while to understand until an older man came out.

He pointed at the mutt under my feet and said, "It dog meat. It dog."

I couldn't believe it, but the taste was indescribably delicious. Incredible. I felt funny eating that burger with such fervor, especially with potential hamburgers sitting under the table, but I simply couldn't resist. It was the same with the french fries. They were in a class by themselves as the potato taste was elevated to heights of pure culinary delight. While the guy was lingering around, I asked, "These are potatoes, right? I mean, I know they are, but how can they taste so good?"

That one took a little longer for an answer. Finally, it came, with wide eyes. "The potato, the French fries, come from over there, yes, they grow there," he said, pointing to the massive field where the villagers defecated. At first, I couldn't believe it. But I also couldn't believe how good they were, so I ate every fry and wished I had more. I did feel bad for that dog clinging to my feet as I left. *Sorry, doggy*, I thought. *You'll have to appeal to the doggy gods for this one.* I would rather assume he wasn't a high enough meat grade for those hamburgers and was just a pet.

During the first week of my return, I spent most of my time on guard duty, assigned and volunteered. For several nights, we supposedly got word from Washington and President Lyndon Johnson that we were to recognize a cease-fire and only defend ourselves if need be, if we saw the "whites of the enemy's eyes." Hell, I couldn't even find any enemy eyes to find the white in them. Another high government directive said we couldn't fire off any flares unless it directly affected our "immediate security." Since we were being entertained at night deep from within the village from "Saigon Sally" recordings and loudspeakers, telling us to give up, lay down our arms, and just enjoy Vietnam without fighting; it seemed like such an irony and conflict of sorts.

This order outraged the entire perimeter and bunkers surrounding our camp. Word was passed around that the end bunker would shoot off a flare, then the opposite end would, followed by the middle, and on and on. The sergeant of the guard would then have to write a report of the reasoning for the flare, as ordered by top brass, along with all the rest of the absurdity, including sign-offs by the officer of the day. It worked like magic. The first one summoned the sergeant right away with his pad and pen, but not before the second went off and called him over there. He was running back and forth as the ranking officer was on his heels. Soon, it stopped, out of utter frustration and impossibility, and we were told to return to normal operations.

We were all talking about the stupid politics behind it all, and it was perhaps the only time I can recall discussing Washington politics in any appreciable way, other than select barbs and arrows that we would always fling. The thing I thought about during this alleged "cease-fire" order was the Marines and other troopers like Soldiers deep in the jungle having to conform to the politicians' insanity while their existence was in harm's way 24-7. That scenario just outraged me so I can only imagine how it made the jungle grunts feel.

Following this, I volunteered to go on convoys into adjacent jungle areas up north toward Da Nang.

But other than that, I was called in for a special assignment based on the sign-painting success I had with the shit sergeant and the outhouses. Seems there was a big USO show in a few days, featuring Nancy Sinatra and some other nondescript acts. I was ordered to paint a sign for Nancy's personal outhouse with simply, "Nancy." I used the same Marine Corps colors as I did for the company shitters and applied creative handmade lettering.

A huge stage had been built for her arrival, and the battalion announced it would be FREE beer night as well. I joined the rest of Sneezy's squad in bleacher-type seats for a night of what would become near-total unadulterated mayhem. Beautiful round-eyed Nancy, clad in a super short miniskirt, and looking too good to be true, was coming fresh off her big hit, "These Boots Are Made for Walking." Those lyrics would just about come back in reverse to haunt her as *our boots were threatening to walk all over her.*

Nancy, the daughter of legendary crooner Frank Sinatra, would only get off about three songs before the troops went into an absolute frenzy and charged the stage, totally out of control. At first, it seemed like blurry-eyed fun, but soon it became dangerous as chairs and fists were flying. It was turning into a riot, and soon Nancy's entourage, along with the obvious help from security Marines, were frantically scrambling to exit the stage and protect the celebrity guest. Nancy was heard to say as she left or immediately after getting to her helicopter that she "would never entertain in front of those Marine animals again." Or something to that effect.

Who could blame her? What *could* be blamed was the volatile combination of unlimited free beer and a sexy American miniskirt. What the brass saw as innocent entertainment for the troops nearly ended in a horrible catastrophe. Later, some wiseass jokingly asked me if Nancy had used her outhouse. "How would I know? I didn't check. Ask the shit sergeant," I said sarcastically.

Other USO shows wouldn't go off as this one. We had visits from country pop singer Sue Thompson ("Paper Tiger," "Norman"), of whom I had the pleasure of brushing my bum against in the "asshole-to-belly-button" chow line, and Martha Raye, whom I missed but heard that she jumped down into the bunkers with the guys and was a fearless, fantastic giver and helper. Ms. Thompson would sing "Norman" indirectly to our squad sergeant, Sergeant Norman, and we had fun razing him for the next few weeks. Those were great shows, along with Korean entertainers, and always gave the troops a shot in the arm. Bob Hope was said to be scheduled at some point, but never made it. Maybe he heard about Nancy's plight visiting Ninth Engineers?

After my eyes recovered as much as they ever would, I dove headfirst into my welding and engineering duties. Since the telephone building was now just residual work in support, and shitters and pissers took little time to make, I joined the rotation taking place at the rock crusher down a little south from the camp. Our job was to replenish rows of welds to the barrels that evolved within the huge machinery that crushed the larger rocks down to a size suitable for covering the roads. It was somewhat of a scary job as you had to wiggle your way into a small area right in the center of the crusher and weld numerous beads in a row across the tumblers.

You barely had enough room to move except for your arm to do the welding. The constant smoke would go straight up, right through and under your helmet, mouth, eyes, and nostrils, as it found an exit. We did it at night, in complete darkness except for some area lights, and our own weapons. Naturally, the Viet Cong never attacked us because why would they hurt the hand that helps them and their country so much? If they did have the gumption to attack, our defenses would have been minimal. We would work one person at a time as the others haphazardly stood watch, rested, and got fresh air.

When it was your turn, you just dreaded being trapped in that little space with tons of machinery surrounding you. The oxygen was limited, and the heat and smoke were miserable. We did it night after night, day after day. At the same time, with little break or exception, we did our daily work as well.

Sometimes we would get the call for a day assignment if the tumblers were particularly worn down. It was then we ran into little "Rock Crusher Anne." She was just nine years old and supposedly was, what some called, a nymphomaniac, a charge I found, like most, to be totally outrageous, disgusting, and cruel. How could any young girl like that be a nymphomaniac? If this was humor, it wasn't funny.

Where did this claim come from, I thought? I learned it was borne from the rumor that Anne would be known to jump down into foxholes or bunkers and let some GIs take advantage of her. I always said if I ever heard that while I was on duty and there was evidence of such acts, I would step in and take protective action. As the story went, Anne got to enjoy the encounters to the extent that she increased them and was more than a willing participant. Sick scuttlebutt! I didn't give a damn if she was or not; it was wrong and absurdly abusive, and I wouldn't be a party to it. But if all that were true, it never happened when I was on guard duty. Still, I thought of my own sisters back in the States and our role in this country, and it caused me plenty of inner turmoil.

When she was around the rock crusher, we would be entertained somewhat because she was this very bright little girl who was interested in everything, and she jabbered constantly with a lot of cute mannerisms. Sometimes she would innocently jump on my lap and ask many questions about many things, especially things about America and American life. Her level of intelligence for her age was rather incredible. And she wore a smile that spread from one ear to the other. She was this ball of nonstop energy that was endearingly cute. I simply couldn't imagine Marines taking advantage of her. It was nearly impossible to believe. I always hoped it was just a sick bit of twisted humor.

Anne was about as much a part of our terrain as we were. She seemed to be everywhere. Every time she saw me, her smile and eyes lit up and she would come running to me in outstretched arms. I never could quite understand why she never seemed to be at her home, her grass shack, wherever that was.

There were other engineering duties other than the rock crusher. One time, right in the middle of the night, we were called out for an emergency bridge repair. It was in about the same area and portion of Highway One where our first casualty took place, mess sergeant, Staff Sergeant Friddle. Because of our relentless schedule, we were all beat, and Sneezy was fighting to get enough welders to go down there. I just got up and volunteered. Oh, here I go again. But the thought of possible engagement lured me in. After all, I was a welding warrior.

I was one of four Marines, aside from Sneezy, that made the trip. It was a small riverbed that supported beams and a bridge, going right beneath the highway. The welding rods that we grabbed had gotten wet on the ship over and were missing huge portions of flux. Someone said they were probably leftovers from WWII and that may have not been a stretch as the Marine Corps often had to accept equipment that was old and tired. Yet we were expected to do more with it just because we were Marines. Whatever the case, they were pathetic. Our hip boots had leaks in them so we'd quickly be standing in wet mush. We were also connecting rods for electricity.

This was another situation where you couldn't help asking yourself, "We are like sitting ducks, how come these Cong don't take advantage of the situation and attack us?" This riverbed, more like a stream, was murky so if some of those little gooks wanted to, they could have swum down to us and jumped up with a knife or something. So we would take shifts while several were welding; others would watch with M-14s at hand. The other incredible red flag we gave off was these huge—two of them—high-powered searchlights that were planted on the outside edge of the riverbed. They illuminated with tremendous power as we needed them to see properly. We were out there in *nowhereville* and were dead giveaways, like illuminating targets at the state fair shooting gallery.

When you struck your welding rod against the steel of the bridge in those boots and with those rods, you got zapped as surely as being shot. It sent shivers of electricity through your body and was scary as hell. Those rods were so messed up they couldn't hold a proper arc so you had to continually stop and start, all the while you were getting continually zapped. We were all more concerned about the impossible welding conditions more than we were worrying about a possible enemy. It became so unbearable that a few of the guys started blaming Sneezy for not ensuring we had proper equipment and safeguards. But he responded by saying he couldn't help it; he and Lew had to grab what they could when the emergency call came in. Okay, Sneeze, we understood, but it didn't help our attitudes that were being nearly fried. But we were Sneezy's welding warriors and fought on.

It was so bad that we started joking about it all, led by Rucker who tore down Sneezy, the Marines, the engineers, Vietnam, and everything within his mind, which was considerable. His humor was always biting and sarcastic and very reminiscent of notorious Jewish comedian Jack E. Leonard. The noise we must have made was loud and echoing. We no doubt woke up every human within earshot.

But apparently not the Viet Cong. Sneezy refereed our behavior, but even he realized the difficult position we were thrust into and backed off. We did the job, Sneezy got the praise, and another engineering task was complete without any enemy fanfare.

I did feel *lucky*, but the humor erased all my thoughts. When we finally hit the rack as the sun was rising, we all nursed numerous burn holes in our uniforms and skin from all the hot flying metal. They itched and smarted. I could still feel remnants of those electrical-like pulses going through my body from the previous water-intense welding. I even seemed to be a little aroused despite being bone tired. I guess I was boned-tired.

The very next night, I was on guard duty again, facing Highway One. When the night ended, word had it that Army units were moving in with their refrigerated trucks full of steaks and chops and all assortment of incredible goodies we just couldn't believe. They were to assume the farthest northern point of the Chu Lai defense perimeter that was directly across from our farthest northern point of Ninth Engineers. They were an infantry unit and were to take over guarding of that portion in the northern sector. Within three days after the Marines' handing over the duty, Viet Cong infiltrated the sector and stole some equipment and made breaks in the double barbed wire. The Marines came back in, and all was fine again. I knew the Chu

Lai defense perimeter stretched all the way down farther than the rock crusher, away from Ninth Engineers, and it always seemed like it was barren and intriguing, especially as it went down to protect the eastern quadrant of the Chu Lai airstrip. For now, I was entrenched at Ninth Engineers.

Back at the squad tent one day, a Sunday and a day off, along with another letter from Uncle Dick, giving me advice on tents, I received a package that came from my grandmother Hilda in Minnesota. It was full of goodies, including candy, cookies, snacks, and boxes of Bugles. I opened them up and shared them with the tent. Rucker, as was in character for him, stood on his cot and proclaimed the day to be in honor of "Meade's granny and all the prizes." To celebrate further, Ruck suggested that we wash it all down with booze. Since we couldn't secure anything else, we got our hands ahold of numerous bottles of local rice wine. We cleared the floor and put several helmets in the middle and poured the wine inside. We then ate the goodies and lapped up the wine with cupped hands. We went on partying well into the evening, where after Rucker put us to sleep by laughing so hard in our cots, we were exhausted and passed out.

Before we passed out, Rucker was throwing his sometimes weird and bizarre humor around and said we should all break open the Botch box, which was this beautifully made wooden box, raised up on metal leg stilts and painted black and red, made by Pete Kuhlmann, a.k.a. Botchman, a.k.a. Pistol Pete.

The Botchman nickname was given because Pete had a bad sinus condition and he used to spit goobers on his overhanging tent flap adjacent to his cot. They stuck and hung like bats in some nasty closet. Ruck used to call it botching it. Rucker was great on nicknames so hence Pete's. The tamer Pistol Pete nickname came from the fact that he collected antique pistols at home and was some kind of developing expert on the subject. Rucker wrote all of our names that day upon the rafter immediately above each man's rack.

Mine was pretty tame, "Minnesota Hulk Meade," followed by "Pussy Paul," "Ang the Pang," "Too Tall Reynolds," "Uncle Pete," "Purring Paret," "Shit-piss-suck-fuck Ruck," and of course, "Botchman."

The outrageous things Rucker did and instigated were all driven by his constant reference to "showing and putting down the phonies in his family."

Rucker seemed superficially envious, even jealous, of Kuhlmann's smart and ingenious ideas to improve his designated area, especially by making the Botch box, as he named it, which under lock and key held canned foodstuffs and other goodies. Pete did hoard it, but he just said it was his own personal stash and it was his little secret getaway, so to speak. None of us had any trouble with it except Rucker. He ridiculed where Pete got the materials, especially the paint and lock and goodies.

So when Rucker jumped back upon his cot and declared, raising his voice dramatically, that it was time to open the Botch box and discover his secrets, we all reluctantly chimed in, with booze clouding our thinking. At least half of us were totally against it, but Rucker got a bar and pried the lock off by himself. After he opened it, he started a feeding frenzy like sharks in the waters. He ate or broke open everything, eating what was edible and smashing the rest. He then threw it on top of Botch's rack, wrapped it all up in his sleeping bag, and threw it out of the tent on the dirt, but not before urinating on it for good measure. We all just kind of watched on in measured displeasure. Yet drunk as we were, we laughed and never stopped it. That Jackie Leonard critical put-down humor would always win us over, if not in full, in part. This was all possible because Pete had to go from welding duties straight to guard duty. He would be gone for many hours.

Sometime later that night, Pistol Pete was returning from guard duty and was coming back in the dark to the tent. Suddenly, despite our drunkenness, we heard yelling as Pistol Pete returned to his rack with a flashlight only to find it not there, but out in the sand in a disgusting pile. Before we knew it, the sergeant of the guard and officer of the day entered the tent and turned the overhead lights on. Pete was now entering the tent with the old man, the major and commanding officer of service company.

He called us to attention and we couldn't quite get up like Marines should, so he turned over a few of our racks. He was a sight, and was he pissed! He only had his camouflaged towel on, wrapped around his waist and protruding stomach, held in place by his holster and .45 caliber pistol. He had his shower clogs on but no cover.

We were all standing before the Man naked: me, Rucker, Paret, Uncle Pete, Reynolds, Angie, and Paul. Because Rucker declared he was sleeping bare ass because of the heat, humidity, and lingering increased body heat from over-drinking, we all followed suit. The major was outraged, livid, and nearly steaming from the ears. He walked down the line, saying things in total disgust. When he came to "Too Tall Reynolds," a black star basketball player in high school, he grabbed a towel off a rack and threw it to him. "Cover up, Marine, you are disgraceful."

Reynolds could barely raise his head as he covered himself. "Yes, sir." His head kept dropping, and the major kept demanding he keep it up. After the last time this happened, Reynolds erupted like a volcano and threw up, trying hard not to, but hitting the major's shoulder and upper chest. It came out in great volume and speed. The major stormed out while yelling back, "You Marines have finally gone too far and are on report and you'll be sleeping in the sand tonight and for the foreseeable future."

The next morning, Monday, was hell as we all had hangovers and Sneezy tore us all a new one, claiming we were now the laughingstock of the entire battalion and would have records because of it. He worked us with no slack that day, and it was pure torture. But other than losing our tent for a few days and nights, everything was back to *abnormal*. They probably figured no one worked harder than us and accomplished more. When we got mad and disgusted, we worked harder, strange but true. Rucker sort of apologized, and Kuhlmann sort of accepted. Angie, a surfer dude from California and somewhat of a hellion himself, told Rucker that he had gone too far and he didn't want something like that to ever happen again. Both Rucker and Angie went out between the tents and worked out with makeshift weights with another squad buddy, Lenny Rinaldini, a trucker. Lenny's drive to work out no matter what the circumstances was always inspirational. He was this old-fashioned bust-ass worker in every sense of the meaning. During this time and after I joined them a time or two, my muscularity and strength from genetics and earlier years of working out caused my squad and others to nickname me "The Hulk" or "Hulk" for short. I certainly didn't view myself as any kind of *Hulk*, but the name would stick, at least during Vietnam.

Meanwhile, back at the tent under the shade, Pistol Pete would say there would never be another *Botch box*. Thank God—again.

Chapter Twenty-Four

Shortly after all this happened, Sneezy was promoted to gunnery sergeant. Upon a joint liberty in the village one day, a bunch of us saw him walking down the highway going through An Tan with a fellow sergeant. His bantam rooster walk and the rise up on his toes seemed even more pronounced than usual. Even his ears seemed bigger, but no match for his bigger-than-life ego. He immediately exercised his new rank with our squad with renewed gusto, leading Sergeant Lew around as if he had a leash on him. Poor Lew was always the middleman/Marine, and it was tough. But when he overheard our words that day, I thought he was going to die laughing. The more he contained his laughter, the more it burst out.

We were joking about the fact that it would be more fitting for Sergeant Bee to wear 60–10s in his holster rather than his .45 cal. pistol. Sixty-tens are commonly used welding rods. We envisioned Sneezy as he walked down that dirt highway carrying his rods rather than his pistol, and we made up many stories related to that. Rucker, of course, led the comedy and pictured the scenarios, including pulling his welding rods out when confronting an upcoming hunk of enemy metal. Again, we were laughing so hard all of us developed a six-pack of abs. Sneezy's squad nearly all had six-packs right down to the last man. Sneezy was indeed the ultimate welding warrior.

But after returning from that hospital, the humor started bothering me, festering on me like a boil. The very thought of having welding rods in your pistol holster instead of a pistol made me want to leave the engineers right there and then. To that end, I requested mast through the chain of command to see our company commander, a major. Actually, I had done the same before this major took his post and stood before the Man and complained, using perfect Marine protocol, of course, to recite why I thought Sergeant Bee was not living up to his stated duties as squad leader. The rest of the squad couldn't believe what I did. And here I was doing it again, but this time I was going further. I mentioned a few critical things about Sneeze, but also said he had gotten a lot better.

I told the major that I wanted to transfer out of the engineers and "just be a regular, ground-pounding Marine." He was a pretty tough-skinned officer but seemed to respect my gumption and guts, saying something mildly to the effect. He pondered for a moment and came back with something I wasn't expecting.

"Well, Lance Corporal, I know an officer with First Recon, and maybe I could talk to him and see if you could be transferred over," he said. "You would certainly have to be trained and indoctrinated to recon's mission, but maybe with a motivated Marine such as yourself, it could be done. What do you think of that?"

I undoubtedly showed my enthusiasm as I said, "Yes, sir, that would be great. I happened to have gone through the regimental school at Pendleton run by Captain Walker, who was a recon officer in Vietnam. Thank you, sir."

"I will keep you advised, but in the meantime, learn to work within your command and realize that Sergeant Bee has accomplished tremendous things with his men, including you. Be proud and be on your way."

I had some hope now. My spirits were lifted. But weeks would go by without any word coming down through the command for any transfer. Nothing. Just as I started wondering if the major was saying all that recon stuff just to scare me or something, word was going around that headquarters First Marine Division were looking for men to fill spots with First Marines, Fifth Regiment, an infantry unit, as some of them dropped back from jungle operations to assume the perimeter of Chu Lai and the airstrip. I wasted no time, and in frustration waiting for a questionable recon transfer, I volunteered and was accepted. I packed my sea bags, said my goodbyes again, and was told Ninth Engineers would remain my parent company, providing paychecks, daily malaria pills, and maintenance of my military records. Not knowing the exact situation, a few of my buddies thought I was crazy while several others, especially Rucker, seemed envious. I had heard through the grapevine that the east, or beach side of the airstrip, constantly had action receiving mortar and rocket attacks and combat engagements. I would be on the opposite side, the west, facing the jungle, not far down from Ninth Engineers. Perfect, I thought.

Before I left Ninth, however, I had to work a few more shifts making telephone poles and pissers, which were made out of empty rocket and artillery containers that held six rocket chambers, perfect for peeing into. They were then buried halfway at an angle. A small patch of small rocks were at the other end serving as a buffer as the urine was absorbed into the soil. The last shift I pulled saw Uncle Pete approach me. He was wearing this twisted grin and could barely keep eye contact.

"I'm sorry, Jonny, about your eyes. That was supposed to be me. I scratched the helmet lens the night before, but the next morning you grabbed it, not me. I couldn't think of a way to stop it. Sorry." He dropped his head. "I just wanted to get away from Sneezy for a while. At least you did." I quickly forgave him, and we shared a good laugh.

Camp at the Chi Lai perimeter guard detachment was sparse. There was a very small batch of tents in the middle of white sand about a thousand meters inside the perimeter. No wood floors, just dirt and canvas. Our sleeping gear remained the same. We even had a little tented wood mess hall, the same size as our tents, where outside mess cooks would bring us one hot meal daily, sometimes two. Sometimes none. The other meals would be from C-rats. We were on a six-day guard rotation, with one night off, unless conditions and security dictated otherwise. Sometimes there would be tiny inside patrols or special details or convoys. For the overwhelming most part, it was all about guarding the First Marine Division perimeter and the Chu Lai airstrip.

We would leave as a small unit from the base camp well before sundown, with flak jackets, plenty of ammo, a few hand grenades, and the other traditional combat garb of rifle, helmet, cartridge belt, and water. We would then disperse around the perimeter, find a foxhole, or dig a new one, and usually share the night and watch with another Marine. Occasionally, quite rare but it happened, if we were short of men, you would be in a hole by yourself. Hopefully, you had gotten some sleep during the day because you'd be up all night in the dark; but when that happened, there usually wasn't any warning so it could end up being a tough night to stay awake.

Unless we were on *condition red*, which meant extra alertness, 100 percent, for possible penetration and no sleep, we were usually on *condition white*, which equaled 50 percent watch, a half night's sleep, and some semblance of a casual watch. Our posts were regularly checked by ranking Marines and officers, so being lax wasn't possible.

We always had to use perfect protocol on duty with the famous "Halt, who goes there?" If anyone came upon your position, no matter who, you could be written up and court-martialed if you didn't comply. We were more concerned about getting in trouble with our superiors as we were the enemy. Therefore, it was a very tight perimeter, and this fact was said to be well known to the Viet Cong and helped create a psychological barrier of sorts. It was like there was this invisible sign facing the jungle that read, "Marines on perimeter, proceed, and lose your life."

When the morning broke and full light was apparent, we were relieved and marched back to base camp and our tents, where we'd grab some real shut-eye. Later, we'd be either free to visit the local village or beyond or be on various slop-shot work details or related 1-5 (First Marines, Fifth Regiment) duties. And so it went the first month, with me and a few others volunteering to stay on. Every day was basically the same, with practically no incidents more challenging than snakes (vipers that can kill very quickly), flies, mosquitoes, mice, and rats, especially during the monsoon when they would share your hole and cracker crumbs. Sometimes during the downpours, you would be entertained by rats swimming in your foxhole as you assumed your post. They didn't wear swimsuits, but at least the dirty little varmints were getting a bath. Some of those suckers were as big as small cats. Fixing bayonets was one sure way to keep them at bay. They were the only enemies on our side of the Chu Lai perimeter that we had to fight, and the fight was ever present.

For some reason, I never really questioned why the few of us from Ninth Engineers stopped getting malaria pills after we left. We were out of sight and mind from Ninth, and the pills just went to the wayside, totally a foregone conclusion. We were like marooned on the outer edge of the airstrip just waiting, looking, waiting, and looking. While we were getting no action, the direct opposite of us on the east were. There were numerous firefights, mortar and rocket attacks. You'd think just by virtue of the perimeter layout and airstrip that our west side facing the jungle would be catching the hell and not the east side facing the ocean. It made no sense to me. In my idle thinking on guard, sometimes I'd think that it was because I was on the west side of the perimeter along with my *luck* that was protecting us. I always was thinking my luck was like a curse and not a blessing. If it were a blessing, why me?

One time when I had to man a foxhole without a partner, it was miserable during the monsoon and I was sitting outside the foxhole on the front sandbags. I had gotten mad because of the rats and literally tore the foxhole apart. My head kept bobbing around trying to stay awake. Suddenly, I was startled so much I fell back into the hole after feeling the massive *swish* of an apparent artillery round sail right past me as it made its way to a distant mountain target. Obviously, it came from a naval ship parked offshore and was called in for by Marines. As it passed my head, which felt inches away, it seemed to suck some air right out of my ears and they were ringing like crazy. I appreciated it though because it kind of woke me up, preventing me from being caught off-guard napping.

With the incredible heat in that country, I never thought I'd ever get cold. Remarkably, at night, with the high humidity in Vietnam and the endless drenching rain, the cold penetrated your body like icicles. Sometimes in bad storms, your foxhole would literally cave in, including the little makeshift roof, and really upset the mice and rats and cause quite a disruption. You would just have to tough it out until the next day, with hopeful help from the sun.

One time, a fellow Marine in another foxhole had his transistor radio ruined from the mess. He nearly lost his mind over it. I suppose he felt he lost his only little friend for that one hour of Armed Forces Radio that he wasn't even supposed to bring with him. A little noise like that carried through the dead night air like a loudspeaker, and if there was an enemy out there, they could focus right in on you. Maybe I should have gotten a transistor radio myself and played James Brown. That may have drawn the enemy in for some holiday jamming. Our entertainment was sparse, but we laughed at the craziest little things, like our own misfortune and that of others. It was like double-checking your humanity.

Chapter Twenty-Five

And then it was Christmas Eve, December 24, 1966. There was a break in the monsoon, and it was supposed to be a temporary cease-fire. It may have been declared temporary, but the dreary evening gave me a lifetime memory.

There's just something about Christmas that spells *home*. So when you are away from home, it's difficult to replace those missed feelings, especially if you are in some dark, wet, lonely dirt hole worlds away. The rain had finally broken and left me and my holemate bailing water out with our helmets. It was cold for Vietnam and miserable. We had heard that Ninth Engineers down and across the road were having Christmas dinner. After we got our hole somewhat dry again, we both sat on our helmets and talked about what our favorites at the Christmas table would be. Nevertheless, I ended up with C-rat boned chicken and chocolate pound cake, issue B-1. It was my favorite canned chow. My partner had ham and lima beans, his least favorite (and mine). But that was the luck of the draw.

As the dark progressed, my partner offered to take the first three-hour watch. Since we were on a loose fifty-fifty condition white alert because of the alleged cease-fire, I could sleep. I spread out my poncho on the wet dirt for a makeshift mattress and used my helmet and some built-up dirt for a pillow.

I could slightly hear the Christmas entertainment from Ninth Engineers, and it was soothing as I knew many Marines were having a nice war zone Christmas. I was quite content as the moon was nearly full and the air was bone-dry.

It is always alarming to wake up from a terrible dream, everything seemingly so real, even if it was convoluted. That's what I thought, as I jumped up from my prone sleeping position and instinctively grabbed my M-14 rifle and helmet and lock and loaded a magazine. I posed at the ready at the edge of the foxhole. I thought we were being attacked or overrun as my heart was pounding in my chest. It was confusing at best as I saw bursts of gunfire and tracers zooming back and forth in front of me on Highway One, as well as bodies running hundreds of meters away. It all happened so fast I literally couldn't follow it all accurately. Suddenly it stopped, as if a curtain was drawn down. Our foxhole was the very first one in our sector of the airstrip, right on the corner of two intersecting roads. The next foxhole down was quite a distance away, so it felt we were practically alone.

In all the instantaneous confusion from a dead sleep, I realized my partner was gone. He simply was not there! Now, I was really taken aback. Whatever happened before must have involved him?

But one of our general orders was to never leave your post, so I held steady and waited. And waited. Then like a dark cloud in a blue sky, I saw someone approaching our foxhole. I took off my safety and chambered a round. About 150–200 meters away, I yelled out, "Halt! Who goes there?" I advanced him to be recognized and immediately knew him as my partner. His face looked twisted and crazed.

As I relaxed my weapon, he swung his up and pointed the muzzle inches away from my forehead, then touched it. I felt that circle of cold steel against my skin and knew—Marines just know—that his weapon was ready to fire. With the help of a widening moon, I could barely see his eyes, but what I did see was freaky as his eyes seemed forced open beyond their sockets by expanded pupils. I spontaneously acted by moving the end of his muzzle away from my head with a free hand and loudly burst out, "What the hell are you doing?"

I was really upset as he just stood there looking at me, rifle hanging at his side, his eyes still ablaze.

"I'm your damn partner, I'm not the enemy, you asshole," I said.

He paused and spoke beyond me, like he was talking to someone in the distance. "I just killed another Marine. By mistake."

"What," I replied, stunned. "How?"

I was still upset with him for sticking his weapon in my face. I couldn't fathom why he would do that? Has he totally lost his mind, I thought? But then I cooled down as I realized he was all hyped up, his adrenaline on some delusional high.

He told me in halting sentences that while he was on watch, he observed two dark figures in the distance going toward the perimeter fence around the airstrip. He yelled out for them to halt, and the figures, clad in black pajama-type outfits—much like the Vietnamese wore, even the Viet Cong—started running toward the fence as if to penetrate our perimeter. He claimed he fired a warning shot over their heads and kept yelling for them to halt, but to no avail. So he took aim at one thinking they were Viet Cong and shot. He hit his target and he went down and held the other at bay while he ran to his fallen foe. As he approached the two, the other figure started yelling and crying frantically with raised arms.

My partner quickly realized they were Marines dressed in black. As he told the story, the two jarheads—who were part of the Chu Lai defense perimeter on the east, ocean side—didn't want to stay in their foxholes on Christmas Eve, so they thought they would dress in black and pull unauthorized liberty in the village and find some girl and drink action. Before it was all over, they found death and destruction. The one that was shot died instantly with a wound to the kidney. The other Marine went crazy and had to be taken away in a straitjacket. Their night out backfired. What could they have been thinking? What absolute insanity to dress in black and try to penetrate their own Marine perimeter?

Now, I got to thinking. Aside from all the assumptions he made, I had my questions. Before the sunset that evening, we were talking while sitting on the front edge of the foxhole. During our conversation, he took aim to the horizon with his rifle and moved it slowly along its path. He kept doing this over and over again, finally saying, "All's I wanna do is find the enemy, shoot him, and watch him squirm." He kept repeating the same desire in assorted ways over and over again. I was not amused, just amazed at his near-sinister tenacity.

I asked him about all the other tracers flying and frantic activity coming from in front of a truck in the road. He said some shots were fired from Ninth Engineers across the street and could have hit him, and some MPs from the shack at the road junction were involved as they had his back. His explanations were all over the place, but he said he was the sole shooter. First, he said he fired one warning shot, then two, plus the fatal shot. He said they were wearing black pajamas yet when explaining the scene at the edge of some lying monsoon water, he said the shot hit the Marine under his web belt and trousers. It couldn't have been both.

We checked his watch and found the time at 0040 in the a.m. He was supposed to wake me at 2400 (midnight) since his watch started at 2100 (9:00 p.m.). When the shooting actually took place, he was standing my turn at watch. My mind was whirling. Would I have reacted the same? Something in my gut told me I would have perhaps handled it differently. The whole scenario was strained. The night was still young, and I had to share the foxhole with this guy, who still seemed in shock. I felt sorry for him if he was just doing his duty, but I had so many reservations. Was he just trigger-happy and overreacted? His dry target practice on the horizon seemed sort of weird, especially now. Until we were relieved at 0700 in the morning, I have absolutely no recollection of that remaining six and a half hours with him that night in the foxhole. As hard as I tried over the years to remember that time frame, I could not recall a single second. Still.

My memory kicked in again when our officer of the day, a captain, gathered us together and said a Marine from the adjoining perimeter across the road had been shot and killed by someone from our sector since no enemy had penetrated the airstrip. He asked to smell our barrels and check our ammo.

My partner quickly stepped forward and said, "No need, sir, I did it." I certainly did admire his honesty and accountability for whatever that was worth.

Our circle of Marines went dead silent as the captain counted his ammo and found one missing round. One! He told me he fired at least one, possibly two warning shots. He must have had an extra round or two with him. I certainly witnessed more than one shot. Yet the math just didn't equate right.

I know what I saw, and I know what he told me. But it didn't change the fact that there was a dead Marine going home and another probably being medically discharged for psychiatric reasons. I nearly questioned my own sanity as my mind was so muddled about the experience. Christmas Eve would never ever be the same.

There was an ensuing investigation, and all the facts of the shooting were officially confirmed by First Marine Division Headquarters and put to rest. The sergeant of the guard that night actually said in his report, which we got wind of, "At least ONE Marine was doing his duty that night." My partner, it was rumored, was found innocent of any charges. We never saw him again. And no one ever said a single word about it. The exact truth and circumstances were buried with that unfortunate Marine. I was the only one who was privy to the incident, and it would have to stay in my head, unresolved. It would be many a night before I could sleep fully again. Later, I heard the Marine went back to his parents as "killed by friendly fire (mistake)." The last thing I would call it was "friendly fire." I was more inclined to call it "questionable fire." But like the sergeant said, maybe he was just doing his duty. Maybe he was.

After several more months of mundane perimeter guard duty, I was getting hit by that guilt again, but this time it was different. This time, the guilt not only came from the feeling of not doing enough, but from feeling somewhat lucky, the very word I had despised. Obviously, I felt lucky over the Christmas Eve incident, but immediately following that, I also felt lucky that the major at Ninth didn't materialize that transfer to recon. That would be short-lived, however, as I went a good distance away on a small makeshift patrol I had volunteered for.

There were reports of Viet Cong in this tiny little village next to a river. Although it had evidence of prior Cong presence, none was uncovered while we were there. The patrol to me was more like a dark stroll. However, while we were there, I felt their presence. A few of the women wore faces of worry, nearly horror. The villagers had this particular avoidance and detachment. They had this little dock there, and it seemed like the perfect launching pad for covert activities and also perfect for them to surround us as we were boxed in. It would have certainly been a hairy situation and close-in combat had time gone on just a little more.

I just knew they were there somewhere, possibly in spider holes under the numerous baskets that littered the ground, but it was getting dark quickly and we had to double-time back to our own perimeter. Days later, they asked for volunteers to leave the airstrip perimeter and go closer inland toward the ocean to be part of a special guard detachment that would be providing security for an American civilian engineering compound. I had no idea what to expect, but I thought maybe it would be more dangerous and challenging. Hopefully more than that little patrol.

It had gotten so boring in those foxholes at night that sometimes we would ignore the perimeter and just talk and sit in the hole. Some of the guys put up trip wires with empty C-rat cans on the end in case anyone, including Marines, came upon our positions. I can say I never had those same grizzly thoughts about killing like my old foxhole partner had that fateful eve, but I did crave action on any and all levels. I never thought of any consequences; if I did, I would have gladly accepted that as my fate and destiny. Other than that, my foxhole thoughts usually started and ended with the three big Cs in revolving order: cheerleaders, cheeseburgers, and chocolate malts.

It was probably this train of thought that kept me away from all the pot numerous Marines were smoking although I certainly wasn't totally innocent. One time when a bunch of guys had gathered in one small foxhole to smoke dope, I stumbled upon them when walking the perimeter. When I raised the poncho from the hole opening, the smoke barreled out. They quickly yelled to close the door and join them. There were five jarheads in that tiny hole, and I quickly wanted out, taking just one drag to be a good team player. I told them I didn't need more because the hole was so full of smoke that you could barely breathe. I stayed long enough to get my lungs filled. When I got outside in the fresh air, I suddenly felt quite high. The guys told me they were smoking the strongest weed they could find, and since I was quite clean, it apparently didn't take much for me to get an effect, a pretty big effect.

I looked out toward the outlying perimeter and swore I saw large pink elephants, each one holding the other by the tail. It was like a cartoon or something. The gang of smokers got a big bang out of that and I would join their laughter, but I quickly came down to earth and literally ran back to my foxhole, never feeling comfortable about pot again. Nonetheless, I thought the rumors about the strong Nam pot were true.

So this new duty would break that boredom and hopefully provide some kind of action, as in war, combat, or anything. But soon I would find out that the action I would encounter would fall under the *anything* category, as in not war or combat, but *anything.*

Chapter Twenty-Six

Our small security contingent was housed in wood-frame tents, with floors again, just like Ninth. It was nice compared to the constant waiting-for-action foxhole living although a far cry from the digs we were guarding for the American and Aussie engineers. It was a definite upgrade nonetheless. Too nice an upgrade, I thought, providing just another excuse for guilt.

I quickly abandoned my guilt over feeling lucky and renewed my straight guilt over not doing enough. My hate for that disgusting word called luck was reinforced totally by this new assignment. I knew it the first time I ate in their first-class civilian mess hall. It was quite large and under a Quonset hut roof and was even referred to as a restaurant. Fancy that. I nearly fainted when I opened the door and was greeted by air-conditioning. I sat down and chowed down like a wild man. They had everything, and it was beyond belief wonderful, comfortable, and relaxing.

And I hated it! Not for all those pleasantries, but despite them. I thought about how my luck was treating me and that old boot camp buddy in that hospital, what he said, and what I subsequently saw; and I got a new wave of guilt. Marines, leathernecks, jarheads, warriors are not supposed to experience this, I thought. Period.

But I must say I did have one close encounter with danger at that engineers camp.

From *overeating!*

Yes, overeating, pigging out, sloppy overindulgence ugly American-style. A bunch of us, loving this king's ransom of food, decided we would have a steak-eating contest. I was the biggest gluttonous Marine at that table that day, eating eleven full steaks (New York's, probably six ounce each). The runner-up was this big black Marine from the South who thought he would be the sure winner as back home he won barbecue sparerib-eating contests. He choked down seven steaks. Part of the contest, however, included servings of all dishes. In about forty-five minutes of serious table combat, I consumed three plates of French fries, piles of corn, green beans, creamed spinach, plus thirteen rolls with butter. Dessert was three Jell-O delights with gobs of whipped cream. All before me was washed down with eleven glasses of iced tea.

The looks on the Vietnamese workers watching these loony Marines was like they were in shock, like seeing crazy King Kong scale a building for the first time.

If they were giving awards for that table combat victory, I would have surely won a *silver* spoon, fork, or something. Or if they were handing out citations for table valor, I most certainly would have won for displaying the greatest disregard for my own health and well-being by leaving that table under my own accord and walking out. Further, not being content with being the best glutton, I also proved I was the most gung-ho Marine at that table by not walking—taking the dare—and double-timing (jogging) to the barracks without barfing, crapping in my drawers, or dying. I think the older civilian engineers who also witnessed this torturous table combat would have referred to it—and me—in different terms like immature testosterone run amok!

Other than that flirt with danger at the table, the duty was safe and uneventful. Quonset hut after Quonset hut was filled with Vietnamese workers, civilians, peasants working within the camp doing different tasks. My main duty was standing guard over their rice-hall, as we called it, for lunch and dinner. There were some Chinese workers melted into the flock, among them two girls in particular that seemed to take a shine to me. One of them was studying to be a doctor and the other a scientist. When they walked up to the rice-hall, they were like giddy little schoolgirls as soon as they spotted me, but were twenty and twenty-one respectively.

The doctor-to-be one was sharp as a razor and sweet, speaking fluent English. The chemist was much prettier, super shy, modest, and incredibly quiet. Both were very attractive and stood out from the crowd. I was very open and worked my charm, accented with respect and manners, and it apparently worked. I was doing my best to advance American international relations. They paid me compliments, too, by saying I was the nicest and best-looking Marine and American they had met. I would also use humor although some of it went over their heads, but the stuff that didn't had them laughing their way into the rice-hall. While they were inseparable, it would soon become apparent that I had to walk a fine line between them as a little green monster would emerge and had to be handled with kid gloves. But that's the challenge of international diplomacy. My attempts at equal treatment and male-to-female adulation served the situation well.

Occasionally, one of their male school friends would accompany them, and after establishing some trust, he asked me everything about my life back in the States, part of it for the girls, the other part for himself. Eventually, he asked if he could have my parents' home address and phone number. I thought about it and gave it to him, thinking he would never use it. On the other hand, if the girls had it and ever visited the States, I would welcome them with open arms although I would get married shortly after discharge. But then, they served as distant fantasies when I was bored, thinking if I couldn't separate them, maybe I could enter into a polygamist state as I helped them pursue their American studies. Oh, what young men's minds can conjure up, especially when eating civilian food without saltpeter.

The only other concern besides watching for the Vietnamese workers stealing food out of the rice-hall was the genuine concern we had over the possibility that at least some of those workers were actually Viet Cong in disguise. While they had an early curfew at night—when guerrillas do their thing best—sometimes several of them wouldn't make it or not even show up. Our only job was to turn them in if they were delinquent, nothing else, as the whole camp was civilian and not military, except our recent deployment as security. The civilian engineers played the public relations thing to the hilt, much too much in our opinion. But they were the ruling authority.

The workers' sleeping quarters were all bunched together, and they had to always come through our checkpoint Charlie, where we checked ID, asked a few questions, and looked them over, searching lightly only if absolutely need be, which was very seldom. They complained to their engineer bosses quite a bit about our strict tactics, but the civilians never questioned us more than a passing wonderment. It was during some of these ID checks and questions that some of these Vietnamese seemed quite suspicious, at least if looks and behavior were used as the sole measuring sticks. Some of these men and women looked at us with pure resentment and hatred. They were the ones we always wondered about and kept an extra eye on. My buddy, another Lopez, and I both felt the same way as we had our suspicions.

There was only one time when the workers were ready to rise up and cause problems, maybe even a potential riot. It came on the heels of President Johnson's comment about not wanting American boys to do and die for Vietnam instead of their Vietnamese counterparts. It was just Johnson's way of dealing with the incredible frustration he faced about the whole Vietnam dilemma. It happened during my guard stint at the rice-hall. This rather large Vietnamese worker came up to me and started reciting some of Johnson's words. He said something to the effect, how dare our president say such a thing. Right away, I told him how could *you* say and think such a thing. It really pissed me off, the very balls of this worker who had so much given to him by this American work camp. I was joined by a few other Marines who were much more upset than I was; and at the same time, numerous Vietnamese gathered around our group as our voices were rising.

I quickly realized a negative tempo was building and a couple of the Marines were getting highly agitated, and I wasn't far behind them. But there were the Chinese girls, watching my every move, with no expression other than holding their hands to their mouths. They just about seemed to be crying.

As a way to appease them as much as the situation, I somehow defused the drama and the crowd dispersed. The girls were smiling, and the others just left. The thoughts of that day stayed with me as it defined our duties there as our rotation replacements arrived and we left.

Chapter Twenty-Seven

After I returned to the airstrip perimeter again, I only stayed long enough to pack my seabags and return to Ninth Engineers, as my tour time in the foxholes was complete. I didn't look forward to returning to the Engineers one iota, as my heart was in the jungle. So I volunteered to guard another convoy that was going far up north and deeper into the jungle area. Because I volunteered for so many different duties, I can't recall exactly if it was at this approximate time or before.

Anyway, it was either the convoy I was on or one just afterward, but several of the trucks hit a land mine and blew up with tremendous force. Numerous Marines were wounded and about six to seven were killed, dispersing their body parts up into the palm trees. I didn't witness any part of it personally, but saw a full array of photos immediately afterward. One of the Marines who was present took photos and had a friend up at First Division Headquarters Marine Corps develop them.

Most all of the photos were of the killed Viet Cong that were uncovered after the blast in this small village that the Ninth Engineers had ordered be leveled and destroyed. The innocent villagers were cleared out, only leaving the underground tunnels that were discovered under the village. A search-and-destroy mission was conducted, and the enemy were all killed and thrown into a dump truck, where their bodies were thrown out along the road to show that the Marines weren't ones to be taken lightly and to scare those Viet Cong sympathizers in particular. The bodies were hideously shot up, with holes and missing limbs and heads. Some of the photos showed kids just standing there looking on in amazement. It was Ninth Engineers' single biggest loss.

And I, of course, felt lucky, and guilty.

Although I was greeted with open arms by my squad buddies, our fearless squad leader Sneezy seemed to hold me in great disdain as I had gone to the Man one too many times over his leadership and was the only one who took action like that. I was most certainly number one on Sneezy's shit list.

I took Rucker's number one slot but only because he had transferred out to a company within the battalion that were responsible for land mine clearing, a very dangerous duty. In some circles, they were called *super-grunts*. Rucker and I were always on the same page as we both wanted more action and did whatever we could to make it happen. I knew right then I had to follow Rucker's lead and immediately do something to get out of this platoon or battalion, or both.

So another request mast up to see the major. I explained my desires, but the commanding officer wasn't too patient with me anymore, and while not mentioning anything about that alleged recon offer, he said he would approve a transfer within the battalion to Delta company. I went back to my tent to bid farewell to my squad, but skipped Sergeant Bee. He would find out soon enough. As I was packing up my seabag again, I was told that Rock Crusher Anne had been killed. She was run over by this sergeant in his big tracker. The news greeted me like a hard punch in the guts. How could this be? I nearly couldn't believe it. But it was true. She was gone, that beautiful little girl.

After picking everyone's brain, I found out that Anne had been kicked out of her house by her parents and she was spending practically all of her time around our camp. Some sick scuttlebutt said that she got pregnant, but most everyone thought that was just a ridiculous rumor. Most Marines I was aware of were equally upset by some of their brothers who may have taken advantage of her out in the bunkers, but not enough and not to the extent that something should have been done. As the story went, Anne was riding her bike along the narrow dirt Highway One and got hit by this sergeant, whom I never much liked. He ran her over and killed her. Big *tough* Marine.

Angie and Kuhlmann, among others, were also deeply disturbed by this report. It particularly hit me hard, especially when I heard the sergeant who hit her didn't express much, if any, remorse. There was plenty of shoulder along the road so I just couldn't understand it. Every time I saw her riding her bike, she was way over, off the road on the shoulder. Maybe it was an accident, maybe not? I was certainly *not* the only one who felt this way. Many Marines were outraged by her death. Whatever the outrage from the rank and file, the sergeant was not charged on anything. He got off scot-free.

I used to pray nearly every night, especially early on. It was simple. I admitted all my shortcomings—sins—and asked for forgiveness. I declared my belief and faith and hoped that maybe my meager life could have some meaning to someone else. Ending, I asked that his will be done. My final prayer request was for Anne's little innocent soul and her family. I can't recall praying again during the remainder of my Vietnam tour or for some time thereafter, except for, I guess, once in a while.

As I joined D company, the whole battalion was having an IG (inspecting general) inspection. I remember, remarkably, that an $8,000 special generator that had not been formerly issued—but traded for something—was buried underground to hide it from the IG team. Naturally, it ruined it. At that same time, despite the US government's issuance of $5,000 to Anne's family for her death, her grandmother visited our main gate with a grenade under her clothes, hoping obviously for revenge. Whatever her intent, it was averted, and with that, a conclusion to the entire horrific tale.

My big challenge at D company came with my (unknown) ability to repair greatly damaged trucks that had hit land mines. I volunteered to try fixing one and with my success proved that such a deed could be done to work within the bare-bones budget given the Marine Corps in the field. Most of these trucks were Army hand-me-downs from World War II, some with wooden planks and sandbags for floors. I quickly got promoted to corporal by Gunny Buck, a hard charger I knew from Camp Pendleton. Along with the difficult repairs on the truck, especially the frames, I busted my ass making gym equipment from a heap of scrap metal for the troops. It made me an instant expert and friend. But I didn't need that; I worked so hard just to try and get little Anne out of my mind. And the woman who came apart in the hospital. And the Marine killed across from me on Christmas Eve from—unfriendly fire.

I also volunteered for another convoy and trips into the field on welding assignments although I only landed one to two of those. I would be atop a truck again in full combat gear, only to run again into nothing but good luck, that oftentimes distasteful four-letter word. But I came to accept it, for the most part, sometimes even embracing it. The Vietnam experience had matured me in many ways and made me appreciate living and life.

Chapter Twenty-Eight

I was now a short-timer with only thirty days left in country. Despite the rule that short-timers are not to venture out in harm's way, I managed to volunteer for a few more days in the field, usually doing some bridge work and jungle equipment repair. But suddenly, I felt anxious to leave Vietnam when I finally realized there was nothing more I could do to put myself deeper in the war. My guilt even subsided and temporarily went into the doldrums. No sooner had this feeling soothed me than our battalion asked for volunteers from the short-timer ranks to leave the country, by ship, and leave two and a half weeks early. Since I was the resident expert in volunteering, I raised my hand and found myself soon packing my sea bags for the final time in Vietnam.

I checked in my rifle and gear, bade my farewells, especially to my old squad, and jumped on a troop transport truck with others to Da Nang. *I've never looked back except for the last forty-eight years.*

We were taken to a large holding area around the airline hangars just outside the Da Nang airport, not far from the shipping port. The first day there, we were gathered by this captain who gave us overnight liberty, saying we must check back in at 0700 the next morning and prepare to board the ship later that day. He told us we shouldn't need liberty passes and if we were asked, to just say we were waiting to board a ship back to the States and Captain So-and-So authorized it. How wrong this captain was. We knew this captain was very anxious to return home and told us over and over again to go to Da Nang and kick up your heels and have fun. We did and we paid the price, especially me.

I caught a ride to Da Nang with a friend from Ninth, nicknamed Crazy. He was another character and up for anything. But his pay didn't catch up with him before departure, so I let him borrow $150, a lot back then, at least it seemed that way compared to the $5 I had weeks before borrowed from Pistol Pete. We were both on our honor to pay it back someday. Da Nang was like a regular city, something I didn't even realize existed in that country. I thought it was all grass

Jon Meade

shacks and peasants, but then I never did a tourist check beforehand either.

We essentially treated Da Nang like R & R, or I & I as it was actually known and applied. First, we got gassed up on cheap beer and whiskey, after which we visited several city brothels. Crazy did his thing, I did mine, which included exceeding my Hong Kong butterfly count from five ladies in five days to five ladies in about fifteen hours. I guess I threw my worries about the black *syph* our commanding officer had warned us about out the window. That's not the only thing that went out the window. In this last brothel, the ladies, for lack of a better term, threw the used condoms out this one window. They then hit the adjacent building less than a foot away and slid down the stone wall. It was all done nonchalantly, and they seemed to get a real kick out of it, like it was a contest or something. I looked over and down *very carefully* and saw hundreds of used condoms. Too bad they didn't have plastic recycling bins back then. It all added to the outrageous environment we were in, yet enjoying every minute, or I should say, every condom.

Then it happened. The place was raided, and it turned into total confusion. The girls herded us under beds and in closets. Wait, I thought, we were given overnight liberty, so since when is it wrong to contribute to a local economy as GIs? We soon found out how wrong we were. We were caught, handcuffed, and taken into custody by the Marine MPs. After they processed us at the Da Nang MP headquarters, they returned us by jeep to our holding area first thing in the morning. Along with us was a full array of charges, including unauthorized liberty, unauthorized danger zone, no weapon, and resisting arrest based on intoxication and unruly behavior. As the MPs were escorting us up to the holding area office, there were signs everywhere with my name on them: "Corporal Jon Meade, report to officer of the day immediately." Some of the signs would include "emergency" in the message.

The MPs turned us in to the officer of the day, who was this hardcore, battle-weary Marine mustanger, one having been promoted from the enlisted to officer ranks under a battlefield commission, which I had been told about later. The MPs dropped their paperwork charges on a nearby desk and left. Then with Crazy now gone, the officer marched me over to one of the huge holding hangars, where

172

they were having an embarkment formation. There must have been 1,200–1,500 Marines gathered together. This officer said practically nothing as we joined the formation, with him at the helm and me in the middle—alone, standing before everyone. My knees were literally shaking. He called us all to attention and walked over in front of me. Then he called parade rest to all the rest of the Marines.

This mustanger was an old salt, and he was so mad his face was red and his mouth twisted in disgust. I had no earthly idea what this was about as the officer circled me, assessing my person. Why wasn't Crazy here? I thought. Why was I being singled out? The officer stopped in front of me, nearly touching his nose to mine.

He yelled with echoes of his words bouncing off the tin walls, "We have been looking for your sorry ass all night, Marine, and I use that term lightly!" He then backed up, did a 180-degree turn, and quickly stopped. "It seems that, Mr. Party Man, Mr. All-Night Delinquent Scavenger, that while you were having fun in town, your father back in the States had a heart attack and complications and may not even be alive anymore."

My heart dropped to my toes. I swallowed hard again and again. The officer went on. "And here we are babysitting for your pathetic ass. You could have been out of this snake pit last night when headquarters Marine Corps first contacted us and been on a plane, probably close to getting back to your father right now. But NO, not you, you'd rather be partying in some whorehouse all night."

Even though all the troops were at parade rest, you couldn't have heard a round drop. I was so stunned I was in a stupor, but of course, I couldn't show it. I stood tall and took the verbal abuse as he continued circling me with his fists now clenched tight. Suddenly, a thick-necked Mac Marine–looking sergeant major, highly revered in the Corps, approached the officer who was much smaller and asked him if he could back off. I could barely hear him. It seemed to have no effect on the officer.

Next, the sergeant major walked up to the officer, close to his ear, but didn't whisper. "Sir, this Marine has been through enough already and is facing a lot of grief. I think you've said enough, don't you, *sir?*" The "sir" was said with a certain amount of respectful disrespect. The sergeant major's jaws were tight.

The mustanger became quiet and his demeanor changed, as he dismissed me and said the office would have my travel orders drawn immediately and I would be leaving by air as soon as they could get me on a plane. While briefly waiting, I learned it was more the sergeant major that was the combat warrior, hero, and not so much the officer. The fact that the sergeant major shook my hand when I left made me proud to be a Marine despite leaving under stressful conditions. I also left feeling my *luck* was with me somewhat and appreciated it, but hoped it would continue and even produce a little miracle. I recited a tiny prayer for my dad's soul and recovery.

I left on Pan Am again and was flown with a plane full of high-ranking officers and other unnamed dignitaries. I felt a little out of place but sat back, enjoyed the air conditioning and food and drinks and service and life. I covered my dad with a short prayer and waited for the plane to touch down after the twelve-hour flight to the United States. Even the name sounded so sweet and welcoming. Before we landed in San Francisco, the pilot announced that there were unconfirmed reports that hordes of hippies and demonstrators were waiting at the airport and may cause troubles, even violence. What, I thought? Weren't hippies supposed to be all about love and peace?

In those days, there were no Jetways, and the planes parked on the tarmac and had stairways brought to the doors. When we deplaned, they had set up a heavy steel fence as the walkway from the plane to the airport building. There were relatively few of us enlisted men on that flight. As I walked off, I heard some "baby killing" yells emerge from the distance and other derogatory remarks, but I ignored them.

Many Marines and other service members had told of being spat upon and called filthy names. I told myself if some guy got close enough to that protective barrier and tried to spit on me or anyone else, I would grab him by his shirt and pull him to the fence and grate him through it like a piece of cheese.

The only cheese I would be grating was in my mind, somewhat still stressed and on extra alert. I looked at the clouds, felt the cool moisture in the air, and inhaled a deep breath of America. It seemed a little foreign, like I wasn't welcome or something. I was on American soil but somehow felt like an alien in my own country, like a surviving alien from a distant, faraway planet called Vietnam.

I was home, well not quite as I still had to catch a flight to Minnesota, but for all intents and purposes, my tour in Vietnam was over. My travel orders included an emergency thirty-day leave and orders to my next duty station, Camp Lejeune, North Carolina. I was happy, but I was sad.

Baby Jon and Big John.

The grandfather I never knew, Claude Meade—later assassinated in horse barn—with granddaughter, Flossy.

Uncle Lester, dad's brother, WW II hero, poses with two Italian boys at Anzio.

Talk about a good-looking couple and
parents, John and Babe.

Judy and I dressed up—Mississippi River on other side of woods.

Grandma Mabel Meade with mom, baby Judy and me.

Book ended by Judy and me, my uncle Richard W. Bartz, two-time
Silver Star recipient, decorated by MacArthur's Chief of Staff.

Me on left with Butterball, Gary, right.

Meade and Hillsdale kids, from left, Gary, Butterball,
sister Judy, Marlene, baby Lorrie, me, baby Janet.

Gary strangling me.

Hitting the heavy bag in the dingy back room of
the American Health Studios at 18.

Family Portrait after boot camp: Top, proud Marine, Judy;
Bottom, from left, mom, Janet, Joni and dad.

Me with boot camp buddy, another Lopez (Vietnam, deceased).

Chu Lai (village), South Vietnam, (apx.) July, 1966 (19 years old)

Chu Lai (tent, base camp), South Vietnam, (apx.) June, 1966 (19 years old)

Bunker in front of 9th Engineers where Pistol Pete had rat run up his leg.

Me, right, on Chu Lai defense perimeter and airstrip, with good buddy Lopez.

Me in village with kids, little Anne on knee, right.

Visiting John F. Kennedy's grave at Arlington National
Cemetery, Washington, D.C., 1967.

Hills of Heroes at Arlington

The Iwo Jima flag rising memorial at Arlington.

My baby—my Corvette—just before departure from
Minnesota to Camp Lejeune, N.C.

Flat tire at 110 mph in the Texas Panhandle,
en-route from North Carolina to California.

Corporal of the Guard, Marine Barracks, NAS Lemoore, clearing weapon.

Best man at Terrible T's base chapel wedding.

Me and Marie at the Marine Corps Ball.

Transformation from Marine to civilian, 3 months.

California Boxing License: Boxing aspirations still in my blood during college.

Sick boy Alex in my arms.

One grandfather, one dad, two sons—pre divorce.

Me with my darling girls, Chrissy and Jenny, before divorce.

First of many holiday full turkey dinners for kids—post divorce.

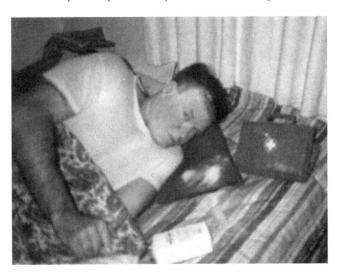

Youngest daughter Chrissy was a part-time doctor—here I
abruptly awake after talc powder surgery—post divorce.

Chrissy the doctor was also a cowgirl—post divorce.

In Salt Lake City hotel after pizza with kids and alleged "kidnapping."

Several years after divorce in San Diego visiting Elaine.

My apartment complex in Sherman Oaks (LA)
after infamous Northridge earthquake.

My unit, upper back.

Me and Elaine, a great lady, early 90s.

Me with eldest son, Alex, hotel, post divorce.

With son Adam, hotel, post divorce.

Visiting my old boot camp Quonset hut at MCRD, San Diego, early 90s.

Escorting Jenny to plane for trip home after tearful visit.

Down memory lane visiting MCRD San Diego receiving barracks, early 90s.

Dad in his last few years.

Outside Athens, Greece, ruins—52 years old.

My "Shackled in Greece" pose at Aegina, the ancient,
breathtakingly beautiful Greek island that welcomed me.

Volume Two

Parts III and IV

The sunset lingers on the edge.
—JM

PART III

(AV: After Vietnam)

Those who dare to fail miserably can achieve greatly.
—John F. Kennedy

Chapter Twenty-Nine

The farther I got away from Vietnam, the closer it became. My mind simply couldn't stop racing, and the sweat marks combined with dirt under my arms had dried on my khaki shirt. It reminded me where I came from. I was now getting ready to land in Minnesota and hoping my forty-eight-year-old dad was still alive, but had no inclination either way. There were no antiwar demonstrators when I landed in the Twin Cities. But if there were, I was so ready for them. I looked around me as I left the terminal. Someone in my family picked me up and quickly whisked me to the hospital, explaining that Dad was still alive.

Upon arriving at Unity Hospital and embracing my mother, who was standing by Dad in vigilance, I found him barely clinging to life, in a semi-coma in a private extensive-care room. The heart attack, I was told about, was just an aftermath of a series of medical mishaps, resulting from a routine gall bladder operation gone amok. This was all underscored by a bizarre reaction to standard medications for the procedure and a discovery of a rare blood disease, discovered by chance by our family doctor. The disease was so rare that very few medical practitioners had even heard of it—porphyria, which was also known as the "royal blood disease," shared by the King George III bloodline and Queen Elizabeth, and the "vampire's disease," as was named in some corners of Europe.

It was said to intermittently, radically affect behavior and be impacted by things like stress, alcohol, medication, and the sun. Our doctor was fascinated by the disease and diagnosis and wanted to do more tests and research. Although I didn't dwell on this information, it did register in my head and caused me great inquisitive thought. For now, I was concentrating on Dad's condition. I went to his bedside and saw a man with tubes coming out of every part of his body. His large size was dwindled down to a shadow of his former self.

Mom bent over and told him, "John, Jon is here. He just arrived from Vietnam." His hands that were folded on his chest started nervously bouncing up and down while his eyes and cheeks started fluttering slightly.

Dad's Wellington boots were perfectly situated under his bed and shined like dimes. The nurse told me she was starting to remove them from his bedside, and he stopped her with practically no movement but a strong voice. She then shared that she had a feeling that the death certificate paperwork on her counter would not be needed. The doctor arrived and filled me in on Dad's incredible experience and then his diagnosis. He confirmed that he had reached a very dangerous 106-degree body temperature, and to save him, they put him in a tub of ice, which contributed to his heart palpitations and dangers. He said that the more medication they gave him, the worse he became. They were effectively killing him without any idea as to why. It was then the doctor followed a hunch he had from reading some medical research papers years before. They immediately stopped the stream of medications, and he immediately improved.

The doctor said it was a miracle the whole ordeal didn't kill him or cause major, if not fatal, brain damage. He said, "Your dad has the strongest constitution and will to live than any patient I have ever had. He is a real fighter. Incredible as we all find it, I would not doubt your father may well make a full recovery."

As well he did. When he became totally conscious, he looked at me, studying my face. Mom had told me how at times while going under Dad would say he saw the Chinese and Vietnamese doing terrible things to me and in his mind, which was greatly impacted by his body temperature and other complications, was hallucinating. He was delirious. He shared with me that the visions of the Asian attacks on me were very realistic. He also said he had an out-of-body experience and saw that "white tunnel." The nurse said perhaps him hearing his son was coming home gave him hope despite his life-threatening condition, and it may have helped in his recovery. Within the week, we were picking up Dad and bringing him home. From all the incisions and tubes everywhere he had, he could not lift his head up as he had to walk with his head totally down. He was thin and walked like a dead man, but he was very much alive.

While he was in the hospital, I took the money I sent home to him and purchased a five-year-old 1962 Corvette, with many extras. It was in this guy's garage and was in perfect condition. It was white with a black interior, and I absolutely loved that car. The seller gave me a deal at $1,800 because I was in the service. I purposely carried a $250 loan on it just to help build my credit. My payment was $25 per month, but I paid it off within five months. Full collision insurance was dirt cheap. I felt like a green mean Marine driving machine. Watch out, world.

As soon as I purchased this car and before Dad was discharged, I picked up Gary, who had just gotten discharged from the Air Force, and we went to the Frost-Top Drive-In for root beer and burgers. My top was down, and we took in all the environment around us, including these two pretty girls in another car. We ended up hooking up. Gary would eventually take the hookup to the point of getting married within the year. In the second double date we had, my mom was not home and left a note she'd be gone for two to three hours, during which time we stopped at my home. We had been drinking beer, and all of us used the bathroom. The next day, Gary told me his girlfriend had something that was causing severe itching. Not to be outdone, that night in the shower, I was itching badly and noticed a little brown discoloration around my genitalia area. I freaked.

The next morning, I went to the VA and they discovered I had the crabs. They took a sample and put it under a microscope to show me what these buggers looked like. I couldn't believe my eyes. They were like these hairy-legged, nasty-looking mini-monsters. The VA did that to scare me and it worked.

After the doctor had a good laugh at my expense and I told him where I got them—Vietnam, in the whorehouse—he gave me some salve and said they would be eradicated in several days. These minuscule Viet Cong I brought back with me were a huge embarrassment all around. Gary's girlfriend and future wife Sue took it all in stride and understood my night out in Da Nang. Meanwhile, I had scrubbed the toilet and seat at home so much I nearly took the porcelain off. I can't remember the exact timing of all this, but obviously my luck visited me again and this time, I was very thankful.

Gary and I would spend many a day laughing about this, but wasn't so sure about Sue. Remarkably, my date, Barbara, was not accosted by the dark brown visitors from a war zone. Another miracle, I guess. The real miracle, however, was Dad not being home quite yet. I couldn't imagine him picking up the little Viet Cong intruders off the toilet seat. That would have been a disaster beyond disasters. But at the same time, in a twisted way, it may have been a little funny too. He survived that terrible medical storm, so this would have been just some additional crown jewels. Kidding aside, I would have never forgiven myself.

When Dad came home, I took him for a little ride despite him not being able to lift his head. I drove like a sane man although it was tough. He said to take it to a local car wash and he'd treat me. As we were waiting in line, some big fancy new pickup truck cut in front of us. Dad could see enough out of the corner of his eye to respond. He told me to wait a minute and he would see what this guy thought he was doing. I tried to stop him, but he was up and out. He walked over to the big, much younger guy and told him, "What the hell do you think you're pulling? My son here just came back from Vietnam—he was ahead of you." They exchanged more words, and as Dad was walking back to my car, the guy yelled out, "Go back to your son, bald old man, before you fall down." Oh, brother, what now? I was readying to get out of the car and go to Dad's aid although I'm fairly certain he wouldn't have needed it despite his incredibly frail condition.

Dad turned and went back to the driver and challenged him to get out of his truck and "he'd show him an old man." Dad's old scowl came back and was in peak form as he stood his ground, continuing to challenge the guy to get out and "settle things." Suddenly, there was silence, and Dad returned to my car and we got out of the car wash. That altercation loosened up Dad's head somewhat, and it seemed to pump him full of fight and adrenaline, maybe even helping his recovery along faster. As I often found myself repeating to myself over my lifetime, "Why me?" No complaints, just wonderment.

During my leave, my kid sister Judy was pregnant from the "most likely to succeed, best athlete" in high school. This whole assorted affair was a real rock under my sandals, but I tried to contain my protective anger as there was a marriage proposal in the works somewhere. She was actually overdue and having some challenges with the pregnancy. I figured I'd help her by taking her out in the Vette and gunning it. As we drove, I popped the clutch and nearly gave her whiplash, but no baby popped out.

I meant well, but how stupid was I? Judy couldn't stop laughing and was a great sport about it and shared the experience with nearly everyone. Who knows, maybe it helped things along as in a few days she gave birth despite continued complications. The baby, Brian, was a very large kid and must have contributed to the difficulty.

Poor Judy, she had to leave in the middle of her senior year as a straight-A highly praised student to give birth. But she still got her diploma in the hospital bed. She had won awards from the University of Minnesota for her final project on Minnesota history, about a foot-thick incredible piece of work, especially for a high schooler. So as it turned out, I had my tooth-inside-of-a-tooth on display at the U Dental College while Judy had her project displayed in the history department.

Gary also cared for Judy a lot as a teen and later as well. They dated but were just not compatible enough. The high school star meanwhile who impregnated Judy, later marrying her and giving her another child, Heidi, joined the Marine Reserve and went to boot camp. I figured he got his just desserts.

In the waning days of my leave, I visited my old gym in downtown Minneapolis and found out that my mentor, Mike Carroll, champion powerlifter and successful physique competitor, had committed suicide. I was shocked. He was just twenty-four years old but had self-esteem issues as his father abandoned him and his mother when he was quite young. He had it all: intelligence, good looks, muscles, strength, and was easily the most popular guy in the gym. Apparently, he didn't have enough. Some people never do.

Another old bud walked by me and said, "Hi, Jon, welcome back." I knew him, but he looked totally different. When I left for the Marines two years before, he was quite thin. Now, he was huge. Under his breath, he said, "Steroid pills, Jon, steroids. You gotta try 'em."

I never did. It went against the grain of physical culture, the very motivating factor that got me started in the first place. I thought it was unfair, especially if you were to compete athletically, and unhealthy since it wasn't natural. While it was nice seeing him again, I didn't like the bigger, faker version.

Since my parents had bought a house in older New Brighton, only several blocks away from the cheerleader's house, I just couldn't get myself to approach her again. What would she think of me after just leaving and never saying anything or explaining myself? Shy I wasn't, but reluctant to try and engage her company I was. I finally let go of it by thinking she probably had a serious boyfriend by now anyway. I really didn't want to know. I felt totally unworthy of her but still kept her in high esteem, as I fought the constant urge to drop by her house. It was as if there was this massive magnet between our houses, but was blocked by an invisible shield that I could not penetrate.

The one thing I felt I had to address when home was my twelve-year-old sister, Janet. Janet had a very high intellect like Judy and had just won a special award for a story she had done for *Look* magazine.

But I saw trouble ahead for her and her girlfriend as I found pot roaches in an ashtray in her totally messy destroyed bedroom. I told Mom and she just shined it on, claiming it must just be cigarettes. I told her, "Mom, I just came back from Vietnam and I know what pot looks and smells like. It is unmistakable."

"Oh, don't be silly, Jon, you are imagining things." Dad was basically unapproachable on these things, always protecting his girls, and was in no condition to deal with it, so it all went by the wayside. I did help Jan clean her room and take down what I thought were obscene rocker pictures and talked to her on the marijuana thing. She listened while I was there, but it would only be the start of years of drug abuse. I felt so bad because it was out of my control, her being my little sister. Janet was also a tremendously talented singer as I would find out by chance years later. She had all these incredible talents and never could capitalize on them. I felt somewhat guilty years later for harping on her so much, but tried to explain it was just the Marine in me trying to get her squared away.

During that leave, it became an incredible array of profound realizations. First, upon coming home from Vietnam, seeing how much the country had changed. The Beatles toured the country with their longer hair and expressive personalities the year I graduated in '64, and now that look and attitude had expanded. The country had progressed light-years ahead of the two years since the evasion took place.

The first response I had received from a family member regarding Vietnam and the war was, "I guess it was really hot over there." Hot, I thought, yeah hot. My mom had served up my first pizza, a pie from Totinos, which was headquartered in Minneapolis and was going national by local company, Pillsbury. She played her favorite two albums for me, over and over, including Tiny Tim's "Tip Toe Through the Tulips," and Perry Como's "It's Impossible." The latter became one of my favorite songs of all time.

Most other people I met were supportive of serving in Vietnam; some were first-class assholes who exhibited no human dignity whatsoever. Sometimes it could be real challenging. The thought that your own countrymen didn't support you certainly could get in your crawl, especially knowing all the sacrifice all those young men made. Minnesota, however, would turn out to be the lesser negative of many other parts of the country. You felt a definite difference in the country. It was like the top of a monster's head emerging from the confused, undefined, descending depths of America's core, the very belly of its soul. It was impossible to clearly recognize or define; it was just felt.

Dad was on the road to a full recovery by now, Gary was thick as molasses with Sue, and I had paid my respects to all my family members and friends. I had some great visits with my uncle Dick, who survived WWII, and talking with him now had special meaning after returning from a war zone myself. But now it was time to drive my Corvette to Camp Lejeune. I plotted my driving course and left, feeling I had life by the tail. I was nearly twenty-one, a corporal, owned a Vette convertible, had only two years left in the Corps, money in my pocket, and felt footloose and fancy-free, a butterfly on the loose.

Chapter Thirty

When I got to Lejeune and checked into my duty station, Second Am Tracks, a division of tanks, I took my sea-bags to the old WWII wood barracks and was the very first Marine to report into my company, an amphibious landing outfit, far removed from the engineers. But having numerous engineers like welders and mechanics was part of the terrain. I quickly picked a rack and flung my gear on top. Just then, the swinging doors to the barracks swung open, revealing the second Marine to emerge.

When I looked up, I was shocked and in total disbelief.

It was my old foxhole partner from Nam and the Chu Lai airstrip defense perimeter who gave me my worst Christmas Eve ever by killing that other Marine. We immediately locked eyes. His were strangely the same as that night—wild, crazy, and expanded beyond their sockets. Maybe they instantly returned that way when he saw mine. He was as surprised as I was, but then acted distant and disengaged. I greeted him, totally forgetting his name, but trying to break the tension somewhat, and I got nothing back but a distant garble and his continued stare. He just occupied space. You could have cut the tension with a bulldozer. We both went our separate ways, with him taking a rack way down on the opposite side of the barracks in a corner. I'm sure we both felt that the likelihood of something like this happening was impossible to calculate. The ironies of this reunion defied description. I wondered now about this "luck" of mine.

But my good luck was extended to other areas. Within several weeks of joining my squad and platoon, my gunny sergeant promised me a promotion to sergeant within just one to two months, as he seemed to appreciate my work ethic and willingness to engage in projects. I had also aced this personal inspection we had, and it shone back well on him.

Camp Lejeune was an old base but beautiful, with full mature trees everywhere. Since Am Tracks was located at the very rear of the base, no doubt for training purposes, it had a giant water tower perched right in front of our barracks. Rumor had it that actor Steve

McQueen was in tracks or tanks and had been stationed right where I was.

Another rumor had it that McQueen had scaled that water tower one day and painted his name somewhere toward the top base of the tower walk-around. For whatever reasons, it wasn't discovered until years later when McQueen was a major star so they kept it there for an unspecified period of time. McQueen's antics were still lingering behind his mid-to-late-fifties service in the Corps, where he spent his two years at Lejeune. The other scuttlebutt said that he had a few too many beers and painted a tank pink or some obnoxious color like that before driving it into a parade. He was busted for that and spent time in the Marine brig, which was no place for sissies.

Marine hero Chesty Puller always used to say after battalion inspections, "Okay, fine, now take me to the brig where the real Marines are." What he was referring to was the grit and guts of those Marines serving time in the brig. He felt, and I feel justifiably so, that the heart and passion of any warrior would always be reflected by those ranks. So in Chesty's mind, McQueen probably would have made a great combat Marine and won many medals. But because McQueen's service was just after Korea, he would never be challenged. But then, while probably reaching hero status, he may not have made it back, denying the entertainment world one of its great actors.

Practically right away, I ran into Fat Tony, the weapons armor we had at our company in Vietnam. He was in some other unit, and I met him at the PX. He was just closing a deal on buying a brand-new 442 Oldsmobile and immediately offered to drive us to Myrtle Beach in South Carolina for a weekend. While there, we met two southern belles that really rang our chimes. Both were college students and readying to graduate. Since they lived in the same area of Greer, South Carolina, we arranged to drive up there, me spending my weekend with Susan Clark and her family, and Tony with his new girlfriend and her family. Both families apparently trusted their daughters in picking the right boys for such a visit, and when the weekend came, we both drove our own cars behind each other up to their general areas then bade each goodbye at this major road junction and went our separate ways.

Susan was about as sweet and charming as a girl could possibly be, and she looked pretty fine, too. Her father was a big-time university basketball coach, and her mother a housewife and about the best cook in the South. I had my own room, of course, and her parents insisted we use their second car while I was visiting. Maybe they didn't trust that sporty Corvette in their driveway. Every meal was like a banquet, with steaks, chops, ham, corn on the cob, and a complete turkey dinner made especially for this occasion, followed by killer homemade desserts. I was in a hog heaven. Susan told me her parents really liked me and put their stamp of approval on this Yankee boy their daughter met and invited. Her younger brother also approved, loving my Vette.

Her father and mother were so gracious, giving, and warm like I was already part of the family. They asked a few things about Vietnam but were very considerate and mindful of where they took it. One thing for sure, they totally supported me; and with all the adversity turmoil brewing in the country at the time, it was so refreshing. It made me proud to think the war effort and that all the incredible sacrifice could possibly be symbolically protecting them. Susan and I meshed right off and made plans on seeing each other more in the future. But that future never arrived.

We exchanged a few letters and talked on the phone, but I still didn't really want to commit to anyone, even though she wasn't just anyone. We made some contact after we both got married to others and talked about regrets, but that was it. She was another quality woman and person that I guess fell victim to my immaturity. Fat Tony, who wasn't really fat but husky, ended up getting married to his lady friend. Life is sometimes like finding your way in the dark without a flashlight. Oftentimes, you end up doing things you just bump into. Other times, you trip and falter and never do reach a planned destination. Destinies aren't a given; you must search until you find yours. And if you don't, you simply make it, creating it from the hand that's been given you.

I had never been in the South—except Scott Air Force base in Saint Louis, Missouri—or the eastern seaboard, so I wanted to take in as much as I could. Another buddy and I planned a long weekend trip to Washington DC. He said he would pay for all my gas as he wanted to visit his sister in Georgetown sometime during our trip. It was about a six-hour drive, and we took it with the Vette's top down the whole way. When we arrived, we immediately got a room for three days virtually right outside of the capital, but definitely not a five-star hotel as it took all we could do just to afford our two-star with a military discount. The first day and night, I dropped my buddy off to visit his sister, leaving me alone for a thirty-six-hour period.

That day, I visited Arlington National Cemetery. I took a few pictures, most notably the Iwo Jima Marine Corps Monument and President John F. Kennedy's grave, including the eternal flame. Both these photos turned out incredibly well while some others were destroyed. Back then, mid-1967, Kennedy's flat gravestone with the extended flame protruding from the top was all by itself. There were very few visitors so I had no problem setting up some shots and getting quality photos.

I probably stood there one foot from the front edge of the gravestone for a good half hour, just contemplating his presidency and legacy. I greatly admired Kennedy for many things, among them his service to the nation and his wartime exploits on PT-109. I saw him as an accomplished regular guy with an irregular life and notoriety. I also saw it as a great loss for the Kennedy family, the nation, and the world.

After I left the cemetery, I couldn't help but draw a parting analogy between Kennedy and the Marines, being ashamed that Kennedy's assassin, Lee Harvey Oswald, was a former Marine. I went back to our hotel area to regroup, planning the remainder of the day and night. I drove all around Washington taking in the sights and finally parked outside this convention-hall-type place. Being adventurous, I virtually stumbled into a sit-down black-tie formal-dress affair. I was just wearing a nice pair of trousers and a dress shirt. But as I looked through the door and was ready to immediately leave, some guy looked at me and said, "You must be a Marine, young man. Your haircut is a dead giveaway. C'mon in and join the festivities. Just grab a seat somewhere and dig in." I couldn't believe it, but who was I to turn down such an offer? And wouldn't you know it, I just happened to see a seat next to a drop-dead diva and quickly sat down.

I had no idea who she was, but she immediately introduced herself and grabbed a waiter and told him to bring me whatever drink I wanted. Rum and Coke was a GI favorite, as well as mine. I wasn't quite twenty-one, so my drinking worried me somewhat; but when it came, I quickly let go. To say that drink wasn't strong would be like saying Coke didn't fizzle. I felt it right away, not that I needed that to loosen up and socialize. Sitting right across from her was her girlfriend, another drop-dead diva. Both were, shall we say, ten sheets to the wind, but still very controlled and dignified for the most part. I would have settled for either one in a Washington heartbeat, but things didn't go as I would have liked. The one next to me was rubbing my arm and thigh while the one across from me was running her toes up my leg. I couldn't believe this. They were great teases, that's for sure. This was like any Marine's dream touring the nation's capital, a free dinner and drinks, and being sandwiched between two babes. My only dilemma besides trying to eat my fillet mignon and lobster was trying to establish a beachhead of some kind, like trying to take the offensive between your front flank or your side flank. But I didn't have to decide after all because they made the decision for me.

They both winked at me, got up—with the one next to me still rubbing my arm—and left with their boyfriends or husbands. Based on the looks I got, I assumed they were husbands. Oh well, I just stayed there and ate steak and drank until the place broke up. What a night. I carefully drove back to our room and crashed for the night. Washington was all right in my book.

After nursing a slight hangover, I picked up my buddy. We drove around and saw two girls that appeared lost. I pulled over. They were German tourists and had no clue what they were doing. So they joined us, and we all had no clue what we were doing, except us picking up two very pretty young ladies who spoke good but broken English. We did, however, speak the universal language of having drinks and a good time. We walked everywhere as four people could not fit in a two-seat Corvette.

We had a great time together, sprang for a cheap dinner where they understood us being in the military, and later continued the party at a dance club, where they treated. Before we knew it—and boy, could those German girls drink beer—we were all tanked to the gills and ready for some serious fun.

Since they refused to go to our room—smart girls—we all got in the Vette. Mysteriously, we all fit and I still don't know how other than the booze factor. We had purchased a large bottle of vodka and orange juice as they apparently loved screwdrivers, every pun intended.

I then just drove around in a liquored-up daze until we hit the Lincoln Memorial. It was closed as it was late. I stopped at the gate, which was open. I looked in and saw all these inviting parking places right in front. I couldn't resist and drove in. I parked right in front of the memorial at the foot of massive steps overlooking Washington. We got out, walked down the steps a little, and sat down and started pouring our drinks, positioning the vodka and orange juice right there on the top step.

Before we knew it, we were separated and engaged in international relations, right there on the steps, all the while being gazed upon by Lincoln himself who could no doubt see my bum. Sorry, Abe. But doing anything successfully on those steps was even more challenging than putting four people in a Corvette. Here the girls were being very romantic, but they wouldn't go near our room? Maybe they were from the Black Forest of Germany or something and loved the outdoors. I suspect it was more the screwdrivers doing their part.

Before I knew it, I felt a hard tap on my back, then shoulder. I looked up and saw a uniformed security guard with a nightstick. He was not in the least bit threatening as he said, "Looks like the Marines have landed. I saw your bumper sticker for Camp Lejeune, but this is off limits. You are also parking in a no-parking zone. You'll have to take your bottles and leave."

We were soon gone even though I tried to win some favor with him to stay a little longer, but he graciously wouldn't have it. He then said we were breaking numerous laws like public intoxication and obscenity and should leave without delay. I bet those German tourists really brought back some great memories to their university, as we wrapped up our Washington trip with laughs all around.

Chapter Thirty-One

After another month or so at Lejeune, outside of Jacksonville, a town a couple of us proved had women—my gunny told me he saw an opening and was ready to put in my promotion. I was ecstatic as I really wanted sergeant. He told me it was as good as done. Meanwhile, back at the barracks, I couldn't stop my mind from thinking about those eyes of that foxhole partner. At night, sometimes in my sleep, I could feel the cold, rounded muzzle of that M-14 against my forehead. We avoided each other like the plague. He was like hidden in the barracks and I can't remember ever seeing him. Maybe that is what bothered me the most.

One day, when looking at the bulletin board for the week's activities, my eyes fell upon a request for one Marine volunteer, the request coming from headquarters Marine Corps, Washington, to fill a billet in California at a Marine Barracks on a naval base. I couldn't tear my eyes from that bulletin board. It was as if it was beckoning me to volunteer. It was for just *one* Marine and seemed so odd. Very seldom does a Marine get an opportunity to volunteer for a stateside duty station. The Corps is famous for putting you where they want. I also kept seeing in my mind this Vietnam Marine's eyes drilled on me, big and not blinking. I also thought of California, soon turning twenty-one, and owning a Vette. It was all enticing. I actually walked away only to return a short time later.

I put in for the transfer, never figuring to actually get it. I did it more as a lark. After all, I was a shoe-in for sergeant. Within twenty-four hours, I heard the position was mine and transfer papers were being drawn up. I couldn't believe it; neither could my gunny, who tried to talk me out of it, saying he could see about stopping the transfer and having the orders reversed. I was quite flattered by the adulation the gunny bestowed upon me, but I told him I had to go.

He tried everything to convince me otherwise, even a special liberty pass of seventy-two hours, but I turned it down and another stripe to sergeant. Part of me thought of southern belle Susan, the opportunity for rank and greater position in the Corps, but the other part—just one—pushed me to pack my seabags again and take the fresh cash in my pocket for travel expenses. I already had made some good friends but was saying goodbye again. They saw me off from the barracks parking lot, and I was off to the Sunshine State.

I chartered my trip from North Carolina to California primarily by using the original Route 66, for the most part. I put my foot to the floorboards for most of the trip, especially going through the panhandle of Texas. Most of my driving was done during the day so the highway was fairly clear. At one point in the panhandle, I wanted to see how fast the Corvette would go. I got it up to 144 miles per hour, and my front wheels nearly left the roadway. Just then, I looked to the right and saw a Texas patrol officer hiding behind this hill. I thought for sure I was a goner. To my utter amazement, he flashed his big red light once and turned onto the highway—the opposite way.

I took my foot off the gas somewhat and cruised at about 80 miles per hour. Before I left the panhandle, I again got up to 110 and passed yet another patrolman. This one just stayed there, not turning away but not following me. Just after he was out of my rearview mirror, I got the Vette up to 110 again, but this time I blew a front tire, with parts of rubber flying all over the highway as I fought to keep it under control. I finally stopped and saw that the tire was totally ripped from its wheel, but it didn't yet impact the rim. I was so lucky, I thought, in all ways. Could those patrolmen actually have seen my Marine Corps emblem and Lejeune sticker on my bumper? I changed the tire and resumed my driving, but this time keeping the speed within *fairly* normal limits.

For the rest of the trip, I just enjoyed the scenery and made stops for eating and sleeping. It went smooth sailing except for hitting the lower southwestern states where they were expanding Route 66 into new Freeway 40. My next big stop was coming up, and I was really looking forward to it. I had just turned twenty-one, and Las Vegas was in my viewfinder. I had purposely been very frugal on this trip just so I'd have more money for Vegas. When I pulled onto the famous strip with my top already down, I felt like I owned the place, and that would turn out to be not far from the truth. In those days, Las Vegas was still relatively new, certainly still a novelty. For the most part, the casinos were far apart from one another, with nothing between them but dirt and tumbleweeds, until you got to the downtown area.

Those casinos sprang up from the desert like huge neon-powered mushrooms, each one seemingly trying to out sparkle the other.

I pulled into the Sands Hotel and parked right in front. I was saturated with sweat from the drive and heat as it was mid-August. My clothes were messy and terribly wrinkled, so I felt I had no choice but to wear my uniform as I had no other civilian clothes. I got my perfectly pressed uniform from my trunk and went inside to find a men's room to change. When I emerged, I was a Marine again, fully ready to tackle any challenge before me.

As I left that men's room, this big spender from the Midwest stopped at a nickel machine and was just about to drop the last of his budgeted $2, when someone tapped him on the shoulder, then quickly again quite hard. I turned around and saw this large bald man with a little mustache. "Would you like to see a show, Marine?"

"I can't afford something like that," I said.

He bent down a little and looked very serious. "Now, do you think I would ask you to see a show if you had to pay for it? C'mon, what do ya take me for, a chump?" His accent was very New York, and he looked pretty damn tough.

"Yeah, I guess. What show?" I said, totally baffled.

I was right outside the Copa Room, so he made a gesture with one hand for direction and pulled back the curtain, had me wait there inside for a moment while he went over to this showgirl and whispered something. He came back and said, "Have a nice day, Marine, and enjoy yourself." I felt like a lost person at a bus stop who was wondering which route to take. Soon, that same showgirl—a breathtaking brunette with a face and body that a person like me could only dream about—greeted me with a huge smile and directed me to this huge booth area right there in the front side. The seat virtually still felt warm.

"Well, young man, you are sitting where Frank Sinatra just sat with his party, and I am to give you whatever you want, food or drink, on the house." My luck, it seemed, kept following me, and now I wouldn't deny it for anything. She came back with two strong rum Cokes. If I was silly enough, I would have pinched myself to see if this was really happening. Just then, Frank Sinatra Jr. came onto the stage and started singing after an apparent break in the program, probably when Sinatra Sr. left. There was probably one-half of the show left, and

I naturally enjoyed it, thinking Frank Jr. was certainly a chip off the older singer's block. Just after he left the stage, the entire entourage of showgirls who were standing in the wings jumped up on the stage and performed their number, with that one showgirl who led me to the table leading their performance.

After they came down and some comedian wrapped up the evening, that lead showgirl introduced herself as Marilyn Marx and then introduced me to every showgirl there, every one of them showing me an unbelievably warm welcome. She sat down with me, and we did a lot of small talk, including my drive to central California and that naval air station. Then she said, "Well, Jon, I am having this party at my house tomorrow night and I want you to come, and I won't take no for an answer."

I slowly responded, "Wow, I really appreciate that, Marilyn, but honestly, I only have enough money for a one night's stay in Vegas and then I have to go up to my next duty station."

"How much more time before you have to check in?"

"Three days altogether—" I barely got out my response.

"Okay, you have plenty of time, you have to stay. You have to come to my party. I'll make you my guest of honor. And don't worry, I'll put you up, so don't worry about money. I'll take care of you."

I just really heard all this, right? I was thinking my good luck seemed to have no boundaries. I felt very humbled and undeserving. I kind of stumbled around with my words. "I really appreciate it and everything, but I don't know, I don't want to be any burden or anything, and I don't really have anything to offer—" She cut me off again.

"Jon, Jon, Jon, you have YOU, that's all you have to worry about. C'mon, you really have to stay. I know you will love it and fit right in and meet all my friends. You must stay."

I couldn't stop blushing. "Okay, Marilyn. Gee, you're even more persistent than I am."

"All the more reason for you to stay," she said as she made a quick gesture to rest her head on my shoulder. I thought to myself, *I don't care about this party, but staying with her I do.* It seemed too good to be true.

And it was. "I'll arrange for you to stay with a good friend of mine. He's a singer and entertainer, and he's got extra room so it'll work fine." My heightened anticipation of staying with her in her house, in her bed, fizzled as quickly as a needle in a balloon. She gave me the plans. "Come to my house at this address tomorrow at twelve noon sharp. There's a few things you can help me with to prepare for this party, then we can just lounge around the pool. Don't worry about a thing, Jon, please, just get yourself there, okay?"

I was a few minutes early, and she greeted me like a long-lost friend and hugged me. Oh, she felt so good. She lived in an upper-middle-class track Vegas neighborhood, had an elaborately furnished house, later telling me all of it was outfitted by singer/entertainer Dean Martin, who gave it to her as a birthday gift. There was a big sparkling pool in the backyard, and frankly, I thought I had just landed in some pleasure planet. I helped her around the house a little, and then she insisted I go out to the pool, put on the trunks she gave me, and lie down on a large rubber raft with cup holders.

She made me a whiskey sour and told me to yell when I needed another drink. The raft also had a little shade cover, providing me with all the comforts of some elaborate dream vacation. Soon, another woman showed up, introduced herself as Marilyn's roommate, and told me she worked on the strip too in some adagio act. She was petite and athletically built, but not even on the same plane as Marilyn, looks-wise. She joined me in the pool and asked if while I was in town I could help her a little do arm-length holds to rehearse for her act, as she noted my build and said it was hard to find a partner strong enough.

Marilyn waited on me hand and foot, bringing several more drinks to the pool. After her roommate went in to help her, I fell asleep for several hours while lying on that shaded water. When I finally awoke, she called me in for a snack since the pool dinner wasn't until much later. While we sat and had a sandwich and chips, she told me the itinerary. We would have the party in front of the pool at 8:00 p.m., and after the party was over, I would be starting my two-night stay at this male singer's house, who she said was gay but had a boyfriend. Oh, that was nice and reassuring. And then every day—it was over the weekend—I would come back to her place where she would make me breakfast and plan the day. Talk about a lady in charge. But she treated me like royalty, and I was still trying to figure out why.

That night for the party, all of her showgirl friends attended, plus some other Vegas show people, including a female headline singer that was performing on *Ed Sullivan* while taping a Vegas show. She wanted me to wear my uniform, which I did but without a cover or tie. I would also be meeting my house host, a very handsome male singer who had been in movie musicals and Broadway. I knew his name for years after, but eventually forgot it. First, we all mingled around the pool and drank exotic mixed drinks she had a special bartender make. Then we sat down at the base of the pool, Japanese-style, while the food started coming out, and it was all very hard to believe what they were serving: big plates of steaks, shrimp, lobster tail, and every trimming you could think of, including salads and soups and foods I couldn't even identify. I was sitting two seats down from Marilyn with beautiful showgirls on each side of me. We were now drinking wine, and the bottles just kept coming. Who was I to refuse any of this lavish care and service given me?

Marilyn had hired several chefs—possibly friends—and the food was incredible. Toward the end of the evening and after dessert, my host singer brought out a microphone and sang three to four songs and dedicated them to the special guest of the evening—me. I was actually embarrassed; I couldn't believe this treatment. And while I was sitting there, these showgirls next to me kept cutting my steak for me and fork-feeding the lobster right into my mouth, napkin wiping and all. As he was singing, one of the showgirls exchanged places with that *Sullivan* singer, and the special attention just kept on coming.

One of the showgirls, it turned out, had her boyfriend there sitting on her other side; and when he observed all this attention bestowed upon me, he got mad—jealous—and left. She just shrugged her shoulders and said he was a bummer anyway. We all laughed. For a moment, I wished any Marine buddy I had could share this moment with me. I felt guilty that this level of luck was benefiting only me. Still, I forged forward and savored every second, thanks to the incredible generosity of one woman and all of her friends.

The *Sullivan* singer seemed to be spending all of her attention lavished on me; then suddenly she said she had to leave as she had to go to rehearsal first thing in the morning. She abruptly got up and started walking away. Marilyn quickly came over to me and whispered, "Jon, she really likes you. Go after her and stop her." I just looked back at Marilyn and quickly turned and followed the singer, running through the house and into the roadway. It was about 11:00 p.m. I caught up to her and didn't know exactly what to do, so I grabbed her like Clark Gable and bent her down and kissed her. It was not a pleasant kiss because she had horribly dry and chapped lips. We talked for a moment while trying to get her to stay or go somewhere private and cozy for a drink, but she wasn't having any part of it, complimenting me as she did and claiming any other night that she'd love to, but she had to get up at 5:00 a.m. or so to get ready to rehearse for her performance Sunday late afternoon. There's a reason why someone like that is so successful, and it isn't because they don't rehearse so I said I understood and left it at that. I ran back to Marilyn's house and assumed my rightful place on my throne, but by then, everything was breaking up. Weekends in Vegas are very active, and the shows must go on, even though I didn't want to turn it off.

Marilyn told me to come back to her place again at noon and we'd spend the whole day and evening together. Meanwhile, I followed my male singer host to his house in a slightly upscale area, and he quickly introduced me to his housemaid and said his house was my house and said anything I wanted would be provided by the maid. He then left, never to return all the while I was there. Perfect.

Chapter Thirty-Two

The next day, Sunday, it was basically the same as the day before, only Marilyn's roommate took care of my needs while she ran errands. Before I left the male singer's place, the maid made me this incredibly large breakfast. At Marilyn's, the roommate asked me to help her rehearse for her adagio act coming up later that day at a casino. All I had to do was lie on my back with my knees up and extend my arms up in the air in front of me and anchor them strongly in place while she did all her aerial moves on my hands.

It was a lot harder to hold that position than I would have ever imagined. It was a very hard workout, and at one point, my arms gave out and she came crashing down flat upon me and my arms naturally came down and wrapped around her. Suddenly, she seemed a lot more attractive and felt like she melted right into my body. We maintained that position for a moment until she said, "You know, this feels really good, but I must continue." We both smiled, and she got up. Another one bites the dust for a Vegas performance. She may have been only five feet five inches and 125 pounds or so, but she was solid as a thickly twined rope.

After about an hour of this challenging, torturous rehearsal, especially for me, she said she had her moves down and was confident for the show. She thanked me profusely for having the strength to hold the positions—seems her regular partner couldn't make it—and got me all set up for another stint in the pool, complete with snacks and a stiff drink. I would need it because I could feel my arms, even my wrists and shoulders, throbbing with pain. I knew enough from years of working out and even the Marines that I would be sore for days. My male ego wouldn't allow me to admit it, but for the remainder of my Vegas stay, I would feel like Frankenstein walked—rigid and in agony.

Marilyn, with her day for me all planned out, would make me forget the pain and have the time of my life. She was like this unabridged whirlwind of energy and activity, seemingly all geared around doing things for me. First, she came up with a nice sport jacket from her closet that fit nicely. Then we went to a clothing store where she bought me a shirt and pants. She was more like a mother or sister.

Next, we drove around in her car, stopping here, there, and everywhere at stores and casinos; and she introduced me to everyone. It seemed like she was a celebrity in her own right. Everyone seemed to know her and light up when they saw her. She showed me local places for this and that, and then we drove back to her home, where she told me to shower up and get ready for a big night out on the town.

It appeared that this dream wasn't about to end yet. Once, when something brought up the topic of Vietnam, she quickly skimmed over it and changed the subject. I thought nothing of it. She told me we would be driving in my Vette for our date out, as she called it, but somehow I sensed it would not be a date, date in the typical fashion. Just as we left the house, she looked deep into my eyes and said, "Jon, tonight is all about having fun and teaching you a few things on how to treat a woman, okay?" What could I say? She was probably eight to ten years older than me and clearly the boss. But I loved it as she was the sweetest, most giving boss in the world.

She emerged in a micro-mini short skirt that was mind-boggling. She had the kind of womanly figure that did perfect justice to that new rage, and boy, did she know how to work it. The rest of her outfit was equally sexy and alluring. She was so breathtaking I wondered if I would have to defend her honor that night. How could any man with blood pumping through his veins—young, old, crippled, married— not lose his eyeballs over this woman? Since she didn't have to teach me how to have manners and be a gentleman, I escorted her to my Corvette and then put the top down. Off we went.

Our first stop was the highest building in Vegas at the time, the downtown Mint. It overlooked the Strip and had a restaurant at the very top. She helped me act like the perfect manly escort as I seated her then myself. I opened the menu, and my sport coat nearly dropped off. Before I said a word, Marilyn came to my rescue. "I know you can't afford these prices, Jon, but I want you to learn a few things about taking a woman out to a nice place for dinner." I was able to stop my tongue from falling out. "Look at the hors d'oeuvres, can you afford a couple of those and maybe a glass of wine? Be honest, now."

"Yeah," I said real quietly. "I can afford that, I guess, plus maybe one glass of wine—for you. I'll drink water. It's fine, really."

She leaned over close to me and whispered, "Don't worry, you won't have any more expenses for the rest of the evening." I swallowed hard, not trying to show my relief, and she just smiled broadly. She told me many things about Vegas over dinner, such as secrets she knew about Frank Sinatra and the Rat Pack—which she would not share to any revealing degree—and the entertainment world in Vegas.

She had been an original Follies showgirl, the first of its kind in Vegas at the Tropicana, and she worked at the Frontier Hotel Casino and others besides the Sands, her favorite. She was also some kind of showgirl liaison or something. Not only was she absolutely beautiful, but she also had a magnetic personality.

Before we left the Mint—but not before instructing me on proper tipping—Marilyn told me something that was a little hard to fathom. She told me everyone at the party last night had remarked how much they liked—loved—me and that I could do no wrong as far as they were concerned, and I would be welcomed in Vegas anytime and they would all help me get a good job. She said they said I came across as myself, real and genuine with no pretensions. Also, they apparently greatly respected the fact that I didn't kiss up to them or get all silly. I guess even the maid gave compliments to the male singer about my stay because I made my bed and left the place as I came. She said with all those recommendations, I could figuratively "own" the town. I was humbled into complete silence and only said, "Thanks." She then said it went double for her. We left with me feeling like I was walking on air, with clouds as cushions.

When we got to my car, I again put the top down and nearly felt like making a pass, but I just didn't feel it was right or appropriate. She sensed it and quickly said something about her brother, or someone like that, being lost in Vietnam. When I asked her to repeat what she said because it was so quietly conveyed, she wouldn't. I then understood these days and the reasoning behind everything since I arrived in Las Vegas. I felt so incredibly sorry for her, but because of the immediate situation, I didn't know exactly what to say, so we just drove off. She told me to go to the Sahara, where she had a surprise for me. I could not guess what might be next.

The next thing I knew, Marilyn was directing me to this side door of a back portion of the big Sahara showroom. We then walked through this curtain and were greeted by a host who obviously knew Marilyn. She directed us to a table right on the side front of the stage. The place was already filled so the entire house was looking at us as we entered like we were celebrities. I felt like melting into the posh carpeting. We quickly had drinks in front of us as headline singer Nancy Wilson came out on the stage, immediately saw Marilyn, and dedicated her first song to us, seemingly right to me. Now, I wasn't just melting into the carpet, I was through the carpet and into the pad. Wilson was an incredible singer and a strikingly pretty black entertainer. I also happen to love many of her songs as she was very popular at the time.

The rest of the evening was a blur after we went backstage to meet Nancy. We drank more here and there, met more of her friends and acquaintances, and had a great time. I went back to the Broadway singer's house that night and slept like a baby, still not believing everything that had taken place. In the morning, I had a departing breakfast made by the maid, thanked her, and left to say my goodbyes to Marilyn and her roommate. It wasn't easy to leave.

I felt I knew Marilyn about as well as I knew anyone. I could not thank her enough as we hugged closely. She told me to remember everything she told me and to remember to come back to Vegas when I got out and she and the others would help me get settled. I was at a loss, really. She gave me her address and phone number and insisted we stay in touch. I reciprocated by saying I'd write after I knew my new address at the base. I left according to her directions, and before long, I was on the freeway and leaving Vegas behind. It was like a mirage as it quickly disappeared into the desert.

Chapter Thirty-Three

I arrived at Lemoore Naval Air Station in Lemoore, California, about thirty miles south of Fresno in central Cal. It was an isolated base right in the middle of endless farm country. I checked in and learned that Marine Barracks was a spit-and-polish outfit that did partial security for the base, and many duties related to Marine Corps pomp and circumstance. Since there was a roster of under seventy-five Marines, the imagery thing was ultra important here on a Navy base. Other duties would soon surface related to all this, making the duty very demanding.

All the duties were pivoted around base gate security, which Marine Barracks was totally responsible for. I also soon learned that the barracks had earned a very distinct reputation as being both respected and despised. Seems it ruled the base with an iron fist and was literally feared in some circles. There was a huge trophy case in the lobby filled with trophies Marine Barracks earned year after year for the base softball championships. But with that came many stories of fights and mayhem caused by the Marines to win at any cost, led by the barracks commander, an infantry officer, who had just retired.

After standing guard at the gates and doing a few P & C details, I earned the right to be corporal of the guard. It was a leadership billet, and I took personal pride in it. Since this naval base was unique in that it was the only one of its kind in the country that allowed wives—often called West Pac widows—and families to stay on the base while their husbands were abroad, most Navy pilots being in Vietnam, it also created unique challenges. In a huge base that had over seven thousand Navy personnel, our job was cut out for us, and the Marine Corps in this venue cut it to the bone. It was a zero tolerance base for certain military protocol that we controlled. First and foremost, we were military police (MPs), but that was just the tip of the bayonet. Our duties were ever expanding and sometimes coming at us spontaneously.

The main challenge came from the fact that there were many security breaches within the housing areas, enlisted and officer, and the base had a reputation of being like the TV show, *Peyton Place*, where everyone is fooling around and sometimes seems like one big orgy. I did my best to conform to the environment. Considering this was considered a high security base because of the specialized jet fighter training and cutting-edge aircraft being tested and utilized, the Marine Barracks had specific tasks and took them very seriously, sometimes too much so. There were numerous stories I heard transferring in about beatings of Sailors for base and security infractions, including one where a Marine on the back gate, a Vietnam combat Veteran, felt the Sailor wasn't respecting the base or him enough, so he hauled him through his car window and proceeded to test his nightstick out on his person. There was an investigation, but the naval captain of the base dismissed it, as he would nearly always do, giving the Marines the benefit of the doubt and unbridled freedoms.

This Marine in question was still there when I came aboard, and he was not only a great Marine but also a nice guy. But he had been through enough hell in Nam where he didn't take any crap from anyone, much less a Sailor, like he said. Sometimes, as the story went, if some Sailors knew this particular Marine was on a certain gate, they would drive around to another one for access. He somewhat struck fear into the fearful. On the plus side, his gates would never be compromised, not that any of the rest were either; but in his case, the passion of defense was much higher. I would guess that 70–75 percent of all Marine personnel on that base were Vietnam Veterans, many highly decorated. Marine Barracks around the country were notorious for the esprit de corps and hardcore Marine Corps imagery. Most seemed like a garrison outpost for infantry Marines, coming back from and going to war. I felt privileged to be in their ranks.

Early on, I had received my first letter from Marilyn in Las Vegas. It was quite long and brought me up to date on herself and all the people I had met, plus more news on the Vegas front. She reminded me to write and tell her all about the base and how things were going. I waited and waited before I responded, sending her a rather short letter, doing the typical guy thing. My excuse was I was so busy and tired, resulting from the demands of duties at Lemoore.

What I also heard about any Marine Barracks was their near-zero allocation of promotions because of their low profile and the very lean ranks and numbers. Thinking back to Lejeune and sergeant promised to me, I now wondered if I would ever make it despite having just over one and a half years left in the Corps. Moreover, I thought the volunteering was coming back to haunt me, but at the same token, I felt I did what was necessary despite not understanding it.

My duties as corporal of the guard went in two-and-a-half-day cycles. There were three of us and as many sergeants of the guard. I would be responsible for five Marines in my squad, and my men would rotate four-hour shifts within twenty-four hours. During the nighttime shifts, I would wake them and make sure they were ready for guard departure around the base. I drove them around in a large cab truck and dropped them off after their checking out magazines full of .45 caliber ammunition. The uniform of the day was always semi-dress greens, with white cover, white cartridge belt, holster/pistol and occasionally a sword at the hip during the day on the main gate. At the end of the shift, the oncoming corporal of the guard would take his men, pick mine up, and return them to the barracks, where they would check in, clear their weapons and return the ammo, and be off for another four hours. It could be rough because we'd all be getting up and going back to sleep over and over again. The sergeant of the guard would be in our guard office overseeing everything.

The three sergeants of the guard were all characters in their own right. My favorite was Sergeant Black, who had several Purple Hearts and a Bronze Star with Combat V. He had a long scar going from his eye to his chin. I naturally always assumed it was from combat, as in war, Vietnam, but instead it was from combat with his wife. Seems the sergeant told his wife he was going on overnight guerrilla training, but he forgot his pack with entrenching tool (small shovel) on the kitchen table. When he came home and gave his wife a big kiss, she returned the gesture by hitting him in the head with the entrenching tool, catching his face with a sharp edge and opening up a large wound.

He was hospitalized and this time he received no Purple Heart. He also had two teeth knocked out in the front and kept saying he'd have to go to the dentist one of these years and get a bridge. He was from somewhere in the South, had this incredible biting sense of humor, and liked to say he was just another cracker from the bottom of the barrel and country.

He would sometimes start laughing about something and have a hard time stopping. He had more colorful jokes than he had people to share them with. When we were together in the guard office, he would rattle them off like small-caliber rounds. One that he repeated constantly, especially when referring to himself was, "I'm 190 pounds of Marine Corps hell, take dope, chew rope, and fuck kinfolk." And let me tell you, Marine Corps hell was sometimes an understatement. When we went together with my men for the flag detail—raising or lowering Old Glory—he was an absolute beast when it came to perfect protocol of respect during colors. The guidelines for the base, which were outlined more by the Marines, said that when colors played, all people and cars must stop—completely.

Well, when Sergeant Black was overseeing me and my men do our job, his eyes were glued within his vision, at 360 degrees. He had a reputation of citing more cars and walking Sailors than anyone else.

One time in particular in this setting, I could hear Sergeant Black breathing hard behind me as I watched two Sailors continue walking while the music for colors started. I knew that someone was in for some surprises, shocking surprises. As soon as colors music stopped and we were gathering the flag together, Sergeant Black jumped in his MP pickup truck and peeled out in front of the administration building and took chase after these violators of colors. He came to a screeching halt and jumped out and started railing on these Sailors, giving them a lesson in base protocol and even a little American history.

He told them to stand at attention and not move a muscle. I bet they never even thought of having to do this in their Navy career. He then had them get in the back bed of the truck, and when he took off, the two Sailors nearly flew out of the back. He took them to naval security and put them on report, filing charges at the maximum degree. That was Sergeant Black. He became so notorious that when he was on duty, if anyone was walking, he would literally expect them to freeze their legs in place until the final note of music was played.

You'd also hear car brakes screeching to a halt if that first note of colors started playing. The thing was, he would expect you, the corporal of the guard, to be just as vigilant or he might write you up. When Black was on duty, the whole base was on alert. He joked about it, but was dead serious too. "These turds and their stinkin' cars are going to stop on a dime or else. I'll have their chicken asses in the brig." He wrote me up one time during the night watch just because I didn't jump out of the rack when he shook me, but the officer of the day dismissed it, knowing the both of us. I still held a high regard for Sergeant Black because I felt I understood him, at least as best as I could.

Waking guys up during the night was always quite risky. The Vietnam Veterans nearly always reacted in fear or worse, sometimes going for their rifles. I learned I had to shake them on their toes from a good distance. Sometimes they'd jump up and want to engage and I had to yell loud and quick.

One time I woke up another corporal of the guard—Corporal Martinez—in this fashion, but he still jumped up, looked at me with crazed eyes (I saw that look before), and wanted to fight until I finally got him to settle down and wake up. Marty, as we called him, was this little guy with a fierce temper and always ready to fight. He had won the Vietnamese Cross of Gallantry and some other heroic medals. I loved the guy. You could trust him with anything. You always knew where you stood with him because his eyes would go wild, his face would redden, and his jaw would start grinding. A great Marine.

Another sergeant of the guard was a Marine with Scandinavian roots who liked me because of my own Scandinavian background. He was a lot looser than Black was, and he had a Purple Heart as well. His claim to fame was his incredible artwork. It all came from his stint in Vietnam and was very vivid. His favorite were drawings showing a Marine holding a large bamboo stick with a Viet Cong head on the end. Also, he used rifle bayonets to illustrate the beheadings too. They also came in intricate detail and plenty of blood. Eventually, the barracks brass told him it wasn't the best idea to show such things around because young Marines who hadn't gone to Vietnam yet may be unnecessarily apprehensive about their own upcoming tour. He continued his artwork but put it under lock and key.

Yet another sergeant of the guard was Sergeant Gee, who was one of the only office-type pokes in our barracks. He had a background in accounting and was pretty smart, but didn't have a lick of common sense and did not fit into our large den of hungry wolves. He was nearly eaten alive as a Marine by everyone. No one could believe he would have ever made sergeant. Yet here he was leading grunt Marines that he couldn't even carry their jockstraps for. It was a joke, and everyone knew it. He said he got his promotion in headquarters

Marine Corps, Washington. Everyone thought and said that was the only feasible way someone like that could ever make sergeant, in the confines of a politically charged white-collar environment. It was always hard for anyone to look at him without laughing. Despite the office duty he came from, he was a mess, as we would call a "shitbird" in the Marines. His uniform was always out of order and in disarray. And it looked like he shined his shoes—we had to still shine our leather shoes back then from scratch—with a Hershey bar. He did not exemplify what a Marine should look like, and we all knew it, including the brass.

He tried to act like a sergeant, especially in this security duty, but came across as a stumbling, muddled, confused, screwed-up little boy. And when he tried to be tough, his Teflon demeanor went over like a frustrated Cub Scout leader. But he did cause numerous Marines some grief, and for that, he was held in ridicule and disrespect. And the harder he tried, the worse he got.

One night, during a whiteout of thick fog, we set him up for a little lesson. We about had it with his shenanigans to try and be gung-ho, which affected so many others. Marty and I plus another sergeant of the guard haphazardly orchestrated the ploy. Normally on a blinding night like this, we wouldn't make gate checks unless there was an emergency, like this night. As Sergeant Gee was coming in for his stint on duty, we told him there was a suspicious vehicle off the road en route to the high-security operations gate. We also knew that there was this blind turn going to the area and would be virtually impossible to see in fog, as it was hard enough under perfect conditions. We knew exactly what to say to the sergeant to make him leave in full panic.

After quite some time it seemed, he finally called us on the radio. We could barely make out his words as they were so low and near inaudible. But we did hear, "I'm 10-9 out on Operations Road, please send help." That could only mean one thing, and that was our plan worked. What we didn't fully realize yet was how well. I assumed my post as corporal of the guard as Marty called dispatch at the base naval security headquarters and requested a tow truck and went out with the driver. I soon received a call from Marty on the radio, stating Sergeant Gee had driven off the road at the blind turn and was about twenty feet off the road, tire-top deep in mud. He kept fairly calm and told me he would fill me in later.

As the tow truck driver was hooking up the sergeant's truck so he could pull it out, Marty called me on the radio inside the tow truck. He could hardly stop laughing to get the words out. "Meade, you wouldn't believe it, Gee was going so fast he flew off the (raised) road—his damn wheels musta left the pavement—and he sailed through the air like a rocket two to three car lengths away. The front end nose-dived into the mud clear up to the hood." I joined in the laughter, and it took us several minutes to recover. Marty continued, "To hell with coming in the barracks to sleep, I'm going to stay right here and see this thing go down."

Marty went on. "Damn, Meade, you should have seen the look on Gee's face when we had him in our headlights. About the only thing you could see were the whites of his eyes. Everything else was covered in mud. And his uniform was solid mud, like he went for a swim in the stuff. He looked like the creature from the black lagoon." The Sailor driving the tow truck was dying; he was dying laughing. He probably thought, "And this is supposed to be a tough-ass Marine?"

When it was all over and Marty and Gee returned to the barracks, the mud had dried on Gee's entire body and uniform. His normally very dark features—he was Hispanic—were coated in light-brown, nearly white mud. His hair was splattered in a mess atop his head, and his teeth were barely visible. It ended up taking not one but two tow trucks to get the sergeant out. Marty said Gee was the laughingstock of naval security and anyone who heard or saw the fiasco, including some Marines in the barracks who woke up.

The person who took it the best, eventually joining in on the laughter, was Sergeant Gee himself. He got to laughing so hard that he said he peed his pants. It would have been well hidden, that's for sure. Not only did he turn out to be an incredibly good sport, but the man changed his appearance and behavior dramatically. He must have gotten the hint, especially after we told him we set him up. He became the most squared-away sergeant we had, always keeping himself perfectly groomed and squared away. In my entire time as a Marine, and in my whole life, I had never witnessed such an incredible transformation. Marty and I sometimes joked that we missed the old

Gee, and from that point on, even referred to him as Sergeant Gee between us.

Besides all the West Pac widows on the base waiting for their flyboys to return from the war, there were quite a few wives of MIAs (missing in action) and POWs (prisoners of war). One time, while checking posts, I stopped this car that was driving erratically and speeding. When I approached the window, the lady driver seemed quite upset. I asked her for her military ID and driver's license. As she gave it to me, she started sobbing, trying hard to contain it. As she spoke of her husband being MIA, her sobs broke up her speech like a little girl. Nothing is more touching than a woman or kid trying to stop their sobbing but not succeeding.

It has always turned me to mush, especially in this case with her husband's situation. I gave her credentials back, and we just looked at each other. I finally said I was sorry. I said I was sorry two to three times in succession while her tears continued rolling down her cheeks. I asked her very soft questions about her husband, and she said he'd been missing for eighteen months and they were having their anniversary coming up. I wanted her to calm down and lift her spirits, so I complimented her on some incidental thing and she had no response. I just looked at her officer's sticker, saluted, and waved her on, saying, "Ma'am, please be careful and have a nice day and week." I thought about this woman for many weeks, months, accented by the fact that I kept running into her. Meeting these MIA and POW wives would happen more often than it should have.

Chapter Thirty-Four

Early in this duty station, word went out that the barracks needed a seven-man military escort detail for a deceased Marine close by in Fresno. I volunteered my squad as we were readying for guard duty anyway, and it would give us a little break. We drove a car pool Navy van to the mortuary. Then we lifted the draped remains into the hearse. Next, we followed the hearse to the church and brought it inside and placed it on the altar, followed by attending a two-hour high Latin mass. After, we carried the casket to the hearse again for the subsequent funeral procession. At the cemetery, we took the casket out and walked it to the burial site, where family and friends congregated. Then I presented the folded flag of the casket to the mother, sitting next to the father. We had arranged earlier for a military bugler who played taps. I then formally dismissed the team, and we went back to the van and base. Every single escort participant was a Vietnam Veteran, minimally half of them Purple Heart recipients. I told them they did a great job; they meagerly nodded, and not a word more was murmured. It was nearly mum for the remaining thirty minutes to the base.

That night, we had a call out for an emergency security breach down at operations where all the jets and training equipment was. Because my squad skipped a guard rotation, we were on call and I got all the guys up. We grabbed our pistols, ammo, helmets, and rifles and raced down to the gate area. I hit 115 miles per hour in that van as we were all poised to get out and attack the situation. When I finally stopped and the Marines quickly got out and created a flank toward the operations area, our company mustanger, first lieutenant was there with a stopwatch. He quickly yelled out that we could have been quicker and said the call was just for training. He was so drunk he could barely stand straight. We were all pissed but couldn't show it. This Marine who had been promoted through the ranks had never been to Vietnam, much less in combat or a war zone. And he was a short-timer with only nine months left in the Corps.

We got virtually no sleep that night and had to assume guard duties first thing in the morning. This same scenario would happen several more times, always unluckily hitting my squad, but others got it too. We all talked about the fact that we could have been killed driving down there at that speed, half asleep, and flipped over, all because of some egomaniac, alcoholic, phony-ass jarhead. Marty and I insisted on logging these "training runs" into the books, which were supposed to document every detail.

After a long weekend of duty once, when I was corporal of the guard with sergeant of the guard Sergeant Black, we went together to Hanford, a city just out of the base, next to Lemoore. For a reason I can't recall, Black said he wanted to get drunk. We went to this fairly swanky place that catered to the officer crowd and started drinking. We sat at the bar; the sergeant had his uniform on and I didn't. Black was shooting down boilermakers while I was content slugging on a beer or two. Quicker than the shots went down, the sergeant slammed his last glass on the bar and turned to the crowd, which was pretty sparse for a weeknight. He went over to the closest table where there were three obvious officers' wives, picked up each one of their drinks—one at a time with deliberate drama— drank them down, and slammed the empty glasses on the table. Even though it was very entertaining, as he went around to every table, about three of them with some men seated there as well, and he did the same, there were some gasps and ahhhhs, but no words came from their mouths.

I tried to go behind him and say sorry, but it went over like a twenty-pound weight. I then saw the bartender on the phone and sensed we were in trouble. While Black was still pulling his shenanigans, I went to the bartender and explained that the sergeant had been through a lot of combat and didn't realize the extent of his actions. He said he didn't care and it was too late and he already called the NSP (Navy Shore Patrol). He said he was calling the police next. I apologized to the bartender and a few more patrons as I grabbed Black's arm and left. Lucky for us, I was driving that night and the sarge just jumped over the door and landed in his seat, top already down. Just then, the Shore patrol pulled up, but we knew them since they were from the base and they especially knew Sergeant Black.

They told us to lie on the pedal and quickly leave, which we did. I heard the siren from a distance and felt like we slipped away from a major public artillery round. Had he been caught and charged, Sergeant Black, because he outranked me and the nuisance he made, would have been surely busted and probably served brig time, maybe worse. He thanked me later and felt quite sheepish so I just told him I was happy we got out of there, and it was forgotten. I would bet my next two weeks' pay though that the bar, bartender, and every patron there would never forget that crazy Marine with rows of ribbons and missing front teeth. Neither would I.

My reputation within the barracks as an alleged womanizer was pretty cemented in early on, but just by chance and circumstances in my view. One weekend night, I drove back into the base with a blonde and left after several hours out the rear gate with a brunette. The guys exchanged that information through the gate phones, and that was that. What happened was I took a date into the enlisted men's club and we danced and had fun, but she met an old girlfriend while I met this other girl. I slipped out with the brunette and told the blonde to not worry and have fun with her girlfriend. I never really got an answer, but figured it was a fair trade-off. I had the Vette's top down, naturally, and me and my new squeeze left out the back. It was all innocent, and I can't even remember the rest of the evening.

After this observation by other Marines occurred, everyone seemed to believe my story now about Vegas that granted for any service member was very hard to conceive. I would have a lot more stories before my barracks stint was over. It was hard to find another Marine to share my exploits with, so I usually was always a loner on liberty. Enter one Corporal Lopez, short-timer with several months left, who approached me one day in confidence.

I never met a Lopez in the Marines I didn't like, and this one was no exception. He was a great Marine, a strict, humble, quiet Catholic, and a very nice guy. At twenty-two, he also shared that he was a virgin and asked for my help, as he was set to get married right out of the Corps.

"Jon, sorry to ask, but . . . I was wondering, with your reputation and all, is there any girl you can set me up with that can show me the ropes about sex and break me in? I can't enter into this marriage and be a total dummy, because my wife-to-be is also a virgin."

"I'll give it some thought, and if I can, I will, yes."

I had a part-time West Pac widow girlfriend, and I went to her and thoughtfully explained the situation and asked her as a personal favor if she would do some charitable work for the United States Marine

Corps. I also threw in that Lopez was a Purple Heart recipient from Vietnam and deserved this special request. I told her that I was mainly asking her because I thought she would be the most perfect and considerate teacher. I was asking her out of respect. She agreed. What were friends for?

"Oh, by the way, sweetheart, would you show him all the ropes? Everything, don't be shy."

Well, before his discharge, my buddy Lopez was indoctrinated into the world of sensual love, and I cannot convey fully how appreciative and grateful he was toward me. He even got in some extra homework sessions with her. I don't know about her, but I gave him an A. I had his back; Marines stand up for other Marines, and teamwork and devotion to the objective. This was clearly a "mission accomplished."

One weekend, I wanted to visit my cousins up in Oakland and took along with me Private Rios, who needed a ride to visit someone up in the same area. Rios and I had become pretty close friends. He won several awards in Nam for valor and was wounded twice. I soon found out he brought his pot habit back with him. He had been busted previously from corporal or sergeant and had a record with the Corps. He took out his stash from his pocket and smoked several joints on the way up to Oakland. I wasn't crazy about it, but I knew he went through hell so I wasn't about to criticize him. I even took several stokes. I dropped him off and would pick him up in several days, or so I thought.

First, I dropped by my cousin Jeanie's house. A divorced lady, very attractive with two kids, across the street wanted to meet me, so after a while I met her. She apparently had a plan and the kids were not included, just me. She made scorpions, the drink with a bite, and I got sloshed real quick. She kidded that she made triple-strength drinks. But I was running late to visit my aunt Mabel, so I left saying I'd be back later that night. The drive was only three to four miles away, but I never made it. I gunned it only one thousand feet away from Mabel's place at the last light and went head-on into a light pole, just outside of Safeway.

I hit it so hard the front end went about five feet up the pole, completely demolishing the grill area and front engine of the car. I was in uniform and crawled out. The Safeway manager from inside heard the noise and came running out. He was also a former Marine. He asked me where I was going and literally pointed to the house as he helped me push the car off the pole and told me to quickly leave before the cops came. I drove to Mabel's and parked in the driveway. Both Rios and I ended up taking a bus back to the base. The insurance company had the car picked up, and I was told it would take three weeks for completion. That ruined the night with that divorcee, but she ruined my night, day, week, and month. Jeanie would disown her as a friend, but I told her it was just as much my fault.

Another weekend I spent with Private Hansen, another hell-raiser from Texas. He was married, lived in a town rental, had one boy. I brought my girlfriend along, Diane, who was the secretary to the Navy captain of our base. She was only nineteen to twenty, and we spent the evening with the Hansens having fun and drinking beer. Hansen and his wife were regular pot smokers and had their stuff for our get-together. Diane was this super straight ravishing blonde and had a rep to uphold so she only had one Coors with me, but later succumbed to a couple of drags of weed like me, which made her gitty high, saying her hand kept going out from her body. We laughed for hours. This evening out would come back to haunt me as surely as a ghost out of the woodwork.

Just before Diane, I had been dating Barb in Sierra Madre, Harry's uncle and aunt's neighbor from across the street. She had just started a flying career with United Airlines, and I drove my Vette down through the famous long, winding Grapevine to the Los Angeles area. Harry was now stationed in Japan, having gone there straight from Vietnam. He gave me his blessing as they dated a few times before. I would go down there and stay at her parents' house and just have innocent fun.

Although we dated for months, Barb's family was old-school and she was just an extension of that, so any affection was limited, which was fine with me. I needed no problems. We broke it off one weekend when we got into a verbal debate about her trying to make me jealous through this former boyfriend we had met. Halfway home from the night out, I stopped the car, opened the door, and told her she was a prima donna and told her to walk home. She summoned that same guy to pick her up, and as a result of all that, we broke it off. It hurt neither one of us, really, and we even remained distant friends.

Chapter Thirty-Five

But hurting other women back then was not something I was alien to. Yet another weekend, while bringing my buddy Moushart with me down to LA, we were driving down Hollywood Boulevard. I spotted this blonde at a stop sign, impeccably dressed, strolling down the sidewalk and gazing at the windows. She bore a striking resemblance to that cheerleader back around high school. After making a few sweeps of her stroll, I stopped. Mouse waited in the car. She was so pretty and sweet and had a heavy accent but spoke fluent English. She was shy and totally complacent at first. I had to work all my charms and humor to make any headway. I finally gained a semblance of trust. She was without doubt the biggest womanly challenge I had ever encountered. I brought her over to the car and introduced her to Mouse. Mouse and I agreed he would go back to our hotel room and watch TV for the night.

I met her at a local coffee joint, and we just talked. Turned out she was highly educated, formerly married, and had a child back in Czechoslovakia, whom she was sick with worry about and missed. She also said she fled her country because of communism and something she had done. It seemed to be a highly sensitive area so I respectfully steered clear. Although this lady was super sophisticated, she was also a sweetheart and was definitely not your ordinary girl. I would have sworn she was a dignitary of some kind. We spent hours at that coffee place, and I was totally wired by all the caffeine. Part of her was glowing like she enjoyed my company, but the other part seemed unduly stressed and secretive. We ended up staying together at this cheap Hollywood hotel, which she was very uncomfortable about; so I did my best to soften the situation and explain it was beneath me too, but with my budget and cost of the other room, my options were limited. She offered to help, but I declined, just treating her royally.

Next time I went down to Hollywood, which was clean and respectful back then, I stayed at her apartment, which was relatively small but elegant. Besides her, everything was perfect, and she treated me like a king. She was a 10 on the scale of womanly, feminine women, and the same as a person. I tried to find out more about her personal life back in Czechoslovakia but to no avail. She was highly protective of that life, but she did say she was somewhat worried about her stay in America. She added that I made her feel not only wanted as a woman but protected from harm. When we went out, her arm clung to me like a magnet. I was very touched by this and told her I cared for her and was her protector.

Before I left that weekend, she seemed desperate for me to stay, and I told her I was a Marine and didn't have options like that. She pushed for when I'd be back, and I told her as soon as I could, probably in another two weeks. But when she pushed further, I started backing away like she was a potential block to my bachelor freedom.

I drove us to a Malibu beach in the early evening to watch the sunset. She brought out this full, elaborate woman's off-white sweater, very heavy with incredibly thick sewing. She said her grandmother made it and gave it to her when she left Czechoslovakia, as a good luck charm. She insisted I take it with me because she felt that would ensure I would return to her. We went back and forth on this sweater until the tears came streaming down her cheeks and she tried to contain her sobbing. Not this, I couldn't handle this kind of emotion, so I wiped her tears with my hankie and promised I would return and bring it back with me. We hugged.

I broke my promise and didn't return her letters for quite some time. I was just too busy being a cad.

And being a cad wasn't too bad. Sometimes I didn't even have to make an effort. One day, I got called up to the major's office, and usually that was always a bad sign. On the walk up there, I wondered if this was anything about being picked up in Da Nang by the MPs in the whorehouse and being charged. I was quite scared as I reported in to the Old Man. He told me to be at ease as he took out a piece of paper. They were notes that he personally took from a high-ranking commander's wife on the base. He said I was at the PX that morning and had come to this lady's help when her shopping cart escaped her and fell over and spilled all her groceries and I picked everything up and helped her with everything to her car. She identified me by being the Marine with the Corvette. She said a Marine like me with such manners was a credit to the barracks and the Marine Corps. At first, I had no idea what he was talking about, and both of us seemed perplexed together. Then suddenly, I remembered the incident, but was shocked she would compliment me like this. The major thanked me and agreed with the commander's wife. I left scratching my head.

As I was walking through the hall back to my area, the phone in the booth rang. I was right there, so I answered it. The caller asked if I was Jon Meade. I said yes, puzzled. She then said she timed it just right as she wanted to catch me walking back from the major's office. She introduced herself as Bernadette, the commander's wife and said she did this whole thing because she wanted to meet me. And I thought, I was assertive? We talked for a while, and she was another West Pac widow whose husband was a pilot in Nam and wanted company. Since her husband outranked me, I did the dishonorable thing and accommodated her wishes. This happened numerous times as she told me I was the talk of this inner officers' group at the club—the Marine with the white Corvette. I was shocked and actually embarrassed a little. But I quickly got over it.

There would be other Bernadettes and many other indiscretions. Lust knew no bounds for them and me. Most didn't just bare their bodies to me, but their hearts and souls, which had much more meaning. They shared things coming from trust in me, and I would never betray that. Strange connections they were, especially from that base. But there were others related to some of the Marine funerals that defied description, but tied to human loss and the ties to someone similar to that loss, whether a husband, brother, or fiancée. I felt their loss through them. The tears and emotions were like volcanoes of loving, sharing, and giving. Why it happened to me so much I couldn't figure out, but it did.

The funerals were ever present, and since my squad and detail did such a commendable escort, we seemed to be the first to be called. The funeral detail covered central California and the lower south of northern Cal, plus the upper portion of Los Angeles county. Most were all the same except for the occasional request for rifle follies and jet flyovers. They were all Marines with one exception—a Navy pilot and 75 percent Hispanic, practically every one Catholic whose family wanted a full Latin mass.

All of these funerals encompassing every aspect of the funeral and burial from B to Z (A being the original officer contact delivering the bad news to the parents) caused a near indifference to death and all the surrounding pathos. You simply had to separate yourself from it all. At first it was hard, then it became like any job. You just did it, and forgot it. One time while maneuvering the draped casket over the six-foot-deep burial hole, the Marine opposite me, on the feet end, slipped his foot through the boards along the hole, nearly letting the entire casket fall. We recovered only later to find ourselves fighting giggles as the priest was sprinkling the holy water over the casket and was flinging gobs of water over our faces and bodies.

Taps always brought you back to reality. The crying and flailing sometimes went nearly out of control and naturally affected us all, but nothing, nothing like the family and friends were affected.

Being in charge meant I had to go the extra thousand miles and face the parents and give them the flag. It got so I did it as if I were going by the numbers. Usually, I had no more than a passing thought, like a tiny pebble in my shoe from the long walk. This death detail, as we sometimes called it, would also spring forward my guilt feelings from Nam of not doing enough. Here I was this "lucky" Marine escorting dead bodies home. And I was very much alive and living life to the hilt. Sometimes a parent or sister or someone else would be looking at me all over then say, practically the same thing every time. "Why?" they would ask. Or "Why my son?" Or "Why him?" Why? Why? Why? It was as if they wanted an answer from me, like I could answer such a question? I don't remember ever answering? But I do remember my feelings of guilt. I remember profound guilt from my "luck." I would think back to that hospital in Chu Lai. I would think of my boot camp buddy Clute who first identified my "luck."

During all those funerals, my "luck" was a dirty four-letter word. I often felt I was standing there before the parent with the flag in my hand, naked, fully exposed for them to see. But I was alive. I was alive. I had my limbs. I had my body intact. I had my life. I had my guilt. It gave me many nightmares.

Without really realizing it, I occupied every minute of my free time keeping busy, especially physically, spending much energy. I joined the Marine softball team and led in batting average, home runs, and runs batted in. I also lead in fielding errors as I was often so tired and stressed I couldn't focus very well except in batting, swinging that stick as hard as I could. I would be famous for hitting a grand-slam homer then turning around and giving away half of those runs with outfield errors although sometimes I would throw out the Sailor at home plate with a perfectly executed rocket from center field. I wasn't just throwing out a runner; I was also throwing out guilt, anger, demons, and inner turmoil.

One day, during an NCO (noncommissioned officer) meeting, I couldn't stand looking at that mustanger first louie that always called us out for bogus security runs, fueled by his drinking. I stood up, faced the major, and while not specifically using his name, laid out the drunken scenario that was affecting our sleep and duties so much. The lieutenant who had been standing against the wall in charge of the meeting became livid inside; you could see it and feel it. It was a real risk what I did, but I felt I had to since his behavior was so wrong. I sensed that the major and this other lieutenant got the point and knew who I was referring to. A couple of other Marines stood up after me and also supported my revelations. Within days, the board in the admin office that contained the softball stats, including my batting records, were all deleted. When some of us asked the mustanger why, he claimed he didn't think the team should have any inner rivalry. Inner rivalry? The Corps thrived on that. It was the only way that short-timing lieutenant could get back at me, as my duties couldn't be questioned. Before we knew it, the liquor-guzzling lieutenant was gone, discharged early. A disgrace.

A full-blown pot scandal had now taken over the barracks like a hungry whale opening wide to engulf all within its jaws. There were apparently fourteen investigations pending, and I was number 14. I could not believe and conceive what was happening. Shortly after these investigations started going on with the CID, the military's equivalent to the CIA, Private Rios went AWOL and stole a .45 pistol along with his hasty departure. Since Rios was such a natural leader and so cool and well respected, this was a total shock for the barracks. I was his buddy, and I had no clue. Also, we had a surprise locker inspection as these CID interviews were starting and our barracks captain found a bag of pills in my locker. He acted like I was somehow nailed and I would be paying the price. But I didn't hear anything for the longest time until I stopped the captain in the hall one day and asked.

"Sir, did the results ever come back on those pills you found?"

He barely looked at me as he left, looking back over his shoulder. "They were protein pills, and you knew that, Corporal Meade."

"Yes, sir, I did, but if you remember, sir, I told you that when you found them." I received no reply.

One day early on in the CID investigation and interrogation process, I gathered about a half of the Marines charged behind one of the cubicles as I was getting ready for guard duties. I told them to keep their mouths shut. To not rat on any one of the other Marines no matter what the CID may tell them about proof and other testimonies. I also told them that they didn't deserve this, that the use and habits were kicked off in Vietnam and was undeserving of undue punishment or a bad discharge. I repeated this to them over and over again, saying to keep our talks mum. "Listen, if they had enough proof to take serious action, do you think they would need any more from you? They want your confession so they can nail you. I don't care if you are guilty or not, the punishment doesn't fit the crime. Wake up, man, wake up. This talk never happened." I did all this with no disrespect to the military or the Corps, but with total respect to my fellow Marines, most combat survivors and heroes. I felt they would not nail these hard chargers on my watch. I vowed inside to help them help themselves. It was a mission.

I was determined to save myself and to save as many Marines as I possibly could. To think these brave souls to a man had gone through hell and back, only to face a country that didn't support them and then the Marine Corps itself would be willing to kick them out for infractions like this, absolutely sickened me. The tension in the barracks with clearly one-fourth of the troops under investigation for marijuana could be cut with a bayonet. And I had to keep my composure and duties as corporal of the guard at the highest possible level, as I was the only one in this leadership billet under investigation.

The CID seemed to stop at nothing to nail as many Marines as possible. Even when I went on liberty in the surrounding towns of Lemoore and Hanford, I was followed in my Corvette. When I fully realized what was going on, I played chicken with them, always two guys in a plain white car. I would purposely lead them on a wild-goose chase, stopping at shops and bars and quickly leaving again or peeling around buildings. They stuck on my car like towing a distant trailer, but I would always end up losing them and laughing while doing so. I had no idea if they knew I knew. They probably just assumed I was high on weed, was crazy, or both. I was as crazy as a fox in a chicken coop.

One by one, they were called into the CID office set up at the naval security headquarters. It was a little, tiny room with no windows. Everyone who came back would share with the rest what the procedure entailed. They would sit them down while staring them down, asking questions and taking notes. Often, they had basic accusations; and as the process evolved, they would gather statements some gave to apply against the others. In a sense, they were like paid interviewers by the government to gain evidence for prosecution. At any means. All the guys would come back and say while they had some hearsay, and snippets of truth, most were highly exaggerated and some out-and-out lies. I would continue my little talks behind walls to shut up, to not put the nails in their own coffins. I pounded over and over again the fact that they were playing two sides to the center. Most of the guys were down at the mouth. The whole ordeal was such a pathetic display of military justice, with the Marine Corps leading the charge. The pressure was building from every angle and, as grunts would say, every flank.

One time, one of the charged Marines asserted that he thought there was a plant in our barracks. No one believed him at first, including me, but we were proven wrong. There was this new Marine who recently checked in and was immediately put on mess duty over at the chow hall right next door. He seemed a little older than us all and carried a lot of excess weight. We figured out that he never went out on runs and PT with us and stood for no inspections, field days, or anything. Also, no Marine before was assigned to mess duty until him. Odd, for sure. After our suspicions were growing, we noticed that he often was leaning over the exposed wall from the top bunk, listening to us. We tested him on some casual Marine Corps topics, which he knew, but when we got deeper, his answers never came or made sense. This virtually outraged us all. Some of the guys wanted to deal with him one-on-one, but I told them, "Don't you realize how that would bury us or whoever was involved?"

I explained that since he was a setup, we would turn the tables and set him up. "Let's purposely lead him astray by feeding him misinformation," I asserted. "We would gather around and make sure he was up on his perch and spoon-feed him info we got back from the charges, and just mess with his mind."

It was a lot easier said than done when implementing this strategy, but we had fun with it and felt it was working. Before long, the "Marine" was suddenly transferred out. Yeah right, just like this lug was a Marine.

Chapter Thirty-Six

The pot scandal, West Pac widows, guard duty, and funeral details were broken up by other symbolic pageantry assignments. The best one ever was given to me and my small squad. It was considered to be a very big deal representing the country and the Marine Corps at the Tulare County Fair. It was a highly anticipated semi-dress blues event, complete with rifles and swords. We didn't know until we arrived what the exact detail entailed. First, we were to bring in and present colors at the end of this special presentation and dedication by then congressman Bob Mathias, former two-time Olympic decathlon champion and Marine aviator. After which Mathias would mingle in the crowd somewhat and come to our ranks and shake our hands. It was one of, if not the biggest, honor of my military service and life. What followed next was a coronation of various beauty queens and an incredible buffet. We joined in the line toward the end, on the heels of the beauty queens.

Ironically, I found myself right next to Miss California, a ravishing brunette. We introduced ourselves, and while we were waiting, she looked up at me with these big brown adoring eyes and put her hand firmly on my shoulder, giving it a slight squeeze. "I've always had Navy and Air Force escorts for different events, never a Marine. I am really thrilled. I always thought Marines were seven feet tall!"

I thanked her and assured her I wasn't anywhere close to seven feet tall. But inside, I suddenly felt seven feet tall, maybe taller. I found out she lived in Orange County and quietly asked her for a date. She immediately said yes and inconspicuously slipped me her phone number. We set a tentative time and parted company as she was grabbed away for something. I hadn't gotten much food yet so I dropped back in the line. When I looked to my immediate left, the next person in line was this very pretty blonde, Miss Disneyland. She wasn't quite as adulating as Miss California, but we too hit it off. I made a date with her and got her phone number. She also lived in Orange County. I didn't really think anything more of it; I was too busy feeding my seven-foot frame.

After the food and my height increasing by the minute, these other female fair officials and a couple of my squad members told me there was this blonde girl sitting over on the bench, Miss Cow Bell of Tulare County, the big shot landowner and cattle rancher's daughter, who wanted to meet me. Virtually everyone was trying to drag me over to meet her. I really didn't know how to handle this diplomatically without hurting her or exposing myself to the other beauty queens. She was so genuinely sweet and cute. I couldn't believe it, but she already found out about Marine Barracks at Lemoore and how far it was from Tulare. She really wanted to hook up. But I ended up shining her on. Mr. Marine Fancy-Pants was too busy trying to contain his ego and couldn't see the most obvious glorious flower in the bigger flower bed.

Meanwhile, a month or so later, I made the date with Miss California since she was first, in all ways, in my thinking. Feeling all of my seven feet tall again, I forced my huge body into my little Corvette and drove south. When I arrived in Orange County, I immediately called the breathtaking brunette. Just as immediately, she told me she knew about my tentative date with Miss Disneyland, her best friend, and she was breaking everything off. I was at a total loss. She said she was so disappointed in me and felt hurt by my double-timing. I felt seven inches tall. I was chopped down like a mini redwood. I apologized over and over again and said I would call Miss Disneyland to apologize to her. She told me that was unnecessary since she wouldn't want to talk to me. "Sorry, Jon, too bad, you blew it. Goodbye." On the drive back to the base, I felt like a little snot-nosed kid in my huge Corvette.

I felt bad about it for a few days then recovered. More women—including the blond Red Cross base officer—more West Pac widows, more burials, more P & C details, more rifle volleys, more taps, more investigations, more guard, more guilt. More. More. More. In one of my more illustrious weekend liberties, I went with a couple of Marines and a corpsman to a huge local dance hall outside of Lemoore. We got drunk and thought we'd act tough by taking bites out of the cocktail glasses we were holding, seeing who could draw the least blood. We figured we had a corpsman right there so chewed away. Before we could finish our ego-alcohol-driven insanity, a huge fight broke out and quickly turned into a riot and brawl. I responded by quickly going to what I saw as the center of activity and the main culprit—a big guy swinging and yelling. I got him into a full nelson from behind and cranked his neck down hard, totally incapacitating him. Soon, I heard yells and screams behind me as I was being hit by some lady with a large purse over the head.

"Let go of him, you goon, that's my husband! He's the owner of this place and he's trying to break things up." I quickly let him go, and she finally stopped beating me. Miraculously, it stopped the fighting and the mayhem. I explained myself and profusely apologized, which he accepted although his wife wasn't as gracious, and we left out the side door just as the police were entering the front. Another liberty down, no major blood drawn.

As a break from it all, I arranged to take Diane on a camping trip to Yosemite. Seemed like the whole base knew about it, probably because of Diane's stature with the base captain. She was a Navy Wave, with her blonde hair and height, struck quite an imposing picture. I checked out a camper/trailer, hitch, sleeping bags, and cots from special services, as well as a large food storage and freezer container. I got steaks, hamburger, hot dogs, and all complimentary goodies from the PX and went to the barracks to pack it all. I had to pull in close to the front door to the barracks for packing. My plans were as obvious as a pistol in a holster.

The sergeant of the guard that day was this black Marine who was always jiving around. He was another decorated leatherneck who seemed to get the biggest kick out of me. He came out and checked everything out, rifling through all the gear and food. He also helped me organize everything better.

He called over some other brothers, and the sergeant would lead them, slapping their hands together, laughing and just about falling over themselves. "Look at this hard charger," he said, raising his voice to a high pitch. "He knows how to do it right, man. He's no fool. Meade's workin' it, he's workin' it."

The brothers were just going crazy, jumping all around the rig, chuckin' and jiving, as they called it.

The sergeant yelled out, "Steaks, beer, you name it, this white brother has it covered. He's going to cover more than that in about four hours from now, ya understand, and she's blonde and a looker."

I couldn't have had a better send-off. The brothers waved me off like I was royalty. We had a great weekend, but Diane wanted to keep her virtue for marriage—and I had no reason to take a girl's virginity just for my ego's sake—so I respected that since I had no shortage of willing partners, like the one loony bird that flew her way into our barracks after visiting the enlisted men's club. Marty or another corporal of the guard told me there was a drunk girl in my rack that wouldn't leave. I knew her from town. If caught, this would be like court-martial time. I actually chased her as quietly as possible around the cubicles and racks as she jumped all over the place, finally settling on a back rack with her hands and feet glued to the head and end. Suddenly, her girlfriend was there trying to help get her out. Who the hell let her in? Why me? Together, we finally got her unglued and out of the barracks and into the car.

She was sitting in her passenger seat now, all pissy and pouty. I told her girlfriend, "Take this whack job off this base quickly, and when she wants to listen, tell her I never want to see her sorry ass again."

Whew, that was a close call, and while it was the end of that one, I had another one quite similar.

And it involved Diane—who when I heard from her that she was being investigated too and told the CID everything about our little party at Hansen's house—I broke up with her. Shortly after, while fulfilling my duties as corporal of the guard one night, I got an emergency call from the rear Capehart Gate, telling me I had to get out there right away as Diane was there. I rushed out there and found Diane stone drunk, sitting on the inside of the guard shack in the corner, motionless. I let Private Baretta take the truck and make the long drive to use the head while I took care of business.

The back gate, especially at this late hour, had very little traffic so I felt I could somehow defuse this problem. It was hard to reason with her though since her mind was muddled by liquor. I tried to reach her innocent and pure nature by saying she could get me in serious trouble, getting brig time and a bad discharge. She cared more about blaming me for getting her started drinking at nineteen (one and a half beers at Hansen's), and involving her in the pot investigation. She then said she couldn't believe I broke up with her and she was being too much of a prude and was crying and crying. We were both standing in the waist-high glass guard shack when I saw some car lights approaching. I told her to kneel down and be quiet while I waved this car through. When the car finally came, I waved the enlisted man through. But he wouldn't move. He was just laughing. I then made a motion to go outside and turned to find Diane standing directly behind me nearly naked, upper body exposed with ample boobs showing.

My heart dropped to my feet, and my feet turned to mush. I pushed her down and made gestures of regret and apologies to the Sailor, smiled, and waved him through. He left with the biggest shit-eating grin on his face you could ever imagine. Diane told me to take her right then. I told her no, that I would not take advantage of her, especially now, and would not be the one who would break her declaration of celibacy before marriage. I had to forcibly help dress her, and by that time, Baretta returned with the truck. I pushed Diane inside and drove back to the main base area, calling Diane's girlfriend in the process and eventually dropping her off at the Waves barracks. I wished her luck and quickly took off.

Later, I would find out how this scary situation with Diane would return to serve me positively.

I was getting more and more frequent flu-like symptoms and went to sick bay for ABCs (aspirin) quite often. Prior to Marine Barracks, I never even had a sniffle. I just wrote it off as being run-down from stress. I also got a nice card of a big hotel from Marilyn. She told me that she took an offer to go help open the showgirl assembly at the new Americana Hotel in Puerto Rico. She said she'd no doubt be returning to Vegas and was looking forward to seeing me again. "Please write," she said. I never did again. I was just too busy with P & C duties, funerals, West Pac widows, other local women, and the ensuing Mary Jane investigations.

I also finally stopped getting letters from the Czech girl in LA. Every time I opened my personal locker, I saw that incredible sweater she gave me and remembered her words. One weekend, my guilt overtook me and I made the drive to Hollywood. I found her apartment, but I couldn't get in because it was a security building. I went to the manager, and he said he never had anyone like that in his place. I told him that was impossible since I spent several weekends with her just months before. He went dumb. I asked a few neighbors and they too claimed indifference, except for one woman's response, which was a dead giveaway that she knew something. I actually spent the night nearby and went back there the next day. The whole scenario played out the same. I had to wrap it up and return to the base with my tail, broken and hairless, between my rubbery legs.

Chapter Thirty-Seven

I renewed my high level of dedication to my duties, which unfortunately included having another Marine busted. When I took out a formation for a run and PT, we stopped at the ropes to climb and wrap up the session. This one Marine, who had gained weight and was acting like he didn't care anymore, said he wouldn't climb. I told him he had to, everyone else was done. He refused. I told him I would climb the rope twice more just so I could get *one* out of him. He belligerently wouldn't oblige so we all ran back to the barracks.

When there, I reported the occurrence to the sergeant of the guard, Sergeant Black, and he told me what only I had to do—write him up. I did, attended a summary court-martial with the major, and this Marine was busted and had pay deducted. He had not been to Vietnam and never exhibited much heart. I still hated to do it. If he had been a war Veteran, I probably would have found some way around the situation. But that simply wouldn't have been the MO of a Vietnam Vet, especially a combat warrior. They always did their duties as a Marine although sometimes begrudgingly. Combat Marines-- in my opinion, were a cut above Garrison Marines—those stateside having never been in war or action. Grunts just bore down, faced the task no matter what, and did it.

This was immediately followed by an IG (inspector general) inspection. It had been planned for numerous months ahead of time and included many aspects of Marine training. Because of our constant conflicting schedules, the barracks brass had to ask for volunteers. Knowing I was under the gun for the pot scandal and wanted to reflect good on myself, I volunteered for two areas: an extensive written test on general military subjects, guerrilla warfare, and Marine Corps history and personal rifle of arms and inspection.

I studied for that test every day, hard as it was, and scored the highest mark ever recorded with an 88, which was only a high B in school; but it was that hard. In the rifle inspection—the general, a WWII, Korea, and Vietnam Vet infantry officer—told me when he returned my weapon that it was the cleanest rifle he had ever inspected in his career. He passed along a personal commendation to the major.

I was not only proud of that, but even more so, I felt I did something that would bolster my good reputation. I figured I needed everything I could get, or do, to help my chances of beating these charges looming. I knew my head was on the investigational chopping block, and I wanted to dull any blade that came my way.

I felt it was time to get away so I took a twenty-day leave. I left on the last flight of the day on Able Airlines out of San Francisco for Minneapolis. There were under ten people on that late flight, so the gate agents took it upon themselves to sit me right next to this attractive young lady, who turned out to be the daughter of an Air Force general. I was in my Marine uniform for the military freebie, and we made a connection. Well into the flight, the girl fell asleep on my shoulder. One of the stewardesses went by us numerous times and smiled at me. She was a ravishingly beautiful brunette with a dimpled smile that lit up the entire cabin. Before my passenger partner dozed off, the general's daughter invited me to come visit her and meet her parents, claiming if she liked me, they would too. It was a plan that was short-lived, however.

After the plane landed, the stewardess and I were feverishly talking, kicked off by her being charmed by the fact that a total stranger like this pretty girl would feel secure enough to lean on me and fall asleep. As the girl woke up, the stewardess and I kept talking; and the general's daughter apparently saw our mutual attraction, got somewhat agitated, and walked quickly off. The brunette asked me if I wanted to join her and the rest of the crew on the tram to downtown Minneapolis since she knew this was my hometown. We spent the rest of the night down in the lobby of the Sheraton Hotel, talking and laughing. She turned out to be a strict Roman Catholic, old-fashioned wholesome girl from Iowa, and one I deemed to be in a special category so I placed her on a reserved pedestal. Our meeting was one of those instant deep attractions.

During my leave, she flew back to Minneapolis several more times, and we would meet each time, furthering our attraction. She lived in Burlingame, a quaint city just outside of San Francisco Airport, where she was stationed, which turned out to be a four-to-five-hour drive from my base down south. We exchanged addresses and started a frequent letter relationship. Before long, I was making the drive up north from Lemoore to Burlingame to spend a weekend and sleep on the couch. She had a black stewardess roommate she had befriended at a time when they were far and few in between in the airlines.

She did not only stand up and by her, but they also became best friends. She was a very tall, trim, statuesque lady with flawless skin whose name was Janice Walters. Later, she would get some modeling gigs and much later became quite successful and dated Howard Bingham, Muhammad Ali's friend and photographer, whom I met. My Lady made me great candlelight dinners, and we ran around town in my Vette and had nonstop fun. When I was there, I was able to escape, if just for that short weekend, all the shenanigans of our barracks, stray women, burials, pomp and circumstance pageantry, and the ongoing pot investigation. It was like a couple of days of breathing pure oxygen amidst a sky full of thick smog and mist, the same stuff I often had to fight in my late-night drive back on the five-freeway to the base on Sunday night.

Those numerous one to two trips a month to go to the San Francisco Bay Area visiting My Lady nearly saved my soul, but I still had to return to the barracks reality and fall back into step. I was the last of all those Marines who were under investigation to be interviewed and had already seen casualties along the way, those Marines already getting bad discharges. It was like another form of escorting dead Marines to their parents and family, seeing one after another bite the dust and go home.

These young Marines had served so honorably—at least 50 percent with Purple Hearts and other combat awards—only to have the Marine Corps turn their backs on them and kick them out. In the Corps, it just proved that no matter what your pedigree, if you messed up, your head would be on the chopping block. It seemed so ironic that while we were trained to watch each other's backs, even with our lives, the Corps didn't have ours. While I was a dedicated hard-charger to the end myself, I could not get over this. We talked about this very fact among us, especially those getting the ax. They survived Vietnam, but not the Marines.

I was called to the naval security building and into the infamous windowless small room. As soon as I sat down, this CID guy shuffled some papers and said, without a shred of emotion, "Corporal Meade, you'll be facing a bad conduct discharge or worse and be leaving out the main gate anyway, so you might as well sign this admittance of guilt now. We might be able to be a little lenient with you because of your exemplary Marine record."

This little four-eyed Gila monster, I thought. I could have flicked my index finger on his temple and knocked him out. "Sorry, sir, but I ain't signing anything because I haven't done anything wrong."

He quickly shoved the papers in my face and told me to read them: "Sworn Statement of Diane ———."

I thumbed through it, not believing my eyes, as he kept tapping his fingers on the desk. It was three long pages of mostly facts that Diane admitted to from Hansen's little home party. It was amazingly accurate as Diane totally spilled her guts. I shoved it back to the interrogator. "Sorry, but most of that is totally untrue."

"Oh, is it now? So why don't you tell me, Mr. Meade—and you will be a mister again real soon, I assure you—what part is true, in your opinion?"

I quickly read the situation and dropped my head, as if ashamed. "I did make a mistake and I will admit that to you."

The wimpy little troll came forward in his chair, eyes widened and appearing so anxious he was about to wet his panties. "What, Corporal Meade, what, just tell me now and get that horrible burden off your shoulders? Your superiors have high praise for you, and this confession may lighten your discharge severity."

I sat there in a long drawn-out purposeful pause. "Okay . . . I gave beer to Diane and she is underage and I know that was wrong, so for that, I am sorry." He looked beside himself. He flung his pen across the table.

"And that's it! We are not concerned about Diane and beer in a private residence. Listen, Meade, the Marine Corps takes these drug charges much more seriously than the other services and wants to stop this marijuana problem in its tracks, especially with those returning from Vietnam. This is not to mention your security responsibilities on this base, so you may as well fess up and tell the truth. We know you know a lot about everything, especially Hansen who we think is dealing."

"Listen, *mister*, I don't even smoke cigarettes. I hate them. I'm into fitness above and beyond the Marines, and I don't believe in drugs of any kind. And that crap in that statement about Diane getting high on pot is false. She was a little high from some beer. She said Hansen was rolling them, but she didn't identify 'them' as pot. Hansen is a cowboy from Texas and rolls his own cigarettes. And he stuffs his pipe with tobacco. If I would have known that Hansen and his wife—who have a little boy—did any kind of drugs, I wouldn't have anything to do with them.

"And I'll tell you something else. I broke up with Diane, and she couldn't handle it, coming out to the back gate and creating a scene—and I have proof—so I see this as revenge. I think this statement is all lies and part of that revenge. Hansen is not a dealer nor is any other Marine. You're on a witch hunt, and I won't be part of it."

Sometimes in life one must stretch the truth a little, white lie if you will. After all, even the CID did it. They were masters of deception, exaggeration, and fabrication, sometimes advancing contrived statements and bits and pieces of what they did know or supposed. It was more than evident in all the alleged proof they presented, much of which came from the Marines themselves, who were told their fellow Marine admitted this and that, when it was a lie. They staged an adversarial game of bogus statements to uncover enough facts to trip the Marines up and make them think they were had when they weren't. Most signed their own bad discharge papers without realizing it. I wasn't about to, especially for just taking a few drags and knowing a little about other Marines, who also did, for the most part, the bare minimum. Never once did I smell it on any dutiful Marine nor witness any behavior related to it. If I did, I may have felt differently.

"So, Corporal Meade, this is your final statement today, huh?" He rocked back on his chair. "Okay, let me tell you this. In the court of military justice, if we have three sworn statements from others of someone's guilt, they will be as good as guilty. And, Meade, you now have two, with Diane's and Private Thompson's (Thompson was this young surfer turned Garrison Marine whom I gave a ride into town once and he started to light up a joint against my wishes only to turn around and claim I smoked with him). The third statement could come from Private Rios, who will probably be apprehended anytime now."

Upon doing some private due diligence talking to attorneys in both Fresno and San Francisco, they told me charges like these in a civilian court would never stand up and be dismissed. But this was the

CID acting on behalf of the Marine Corps. There was no such thing in the Corps as leniency. Inside, I was dying each time another Marine was kicked out. What an utter disgrace, I thought. Along with my regular duties, which could never be compromised, I had an interior of raw emotions and pure stress. I constantly worried, especially as the time wore on, that my third statement, Private Rios, would be caught and walk through the door.

As another way of escape from the barracks, Private Jolly and Lance Corporal Minor—both combat Veterans but also devoted Christians—got me a part-time job under the table driving a big tractor plowing fields that were adjacent to the base. It helped me pay for my trips to the Bay Area, but more than that, it allowed me to just sit on that big tractor seat for many hours and be alone with myself and my thoughts, which were always reeling in my head. These two Marines were always trying to get me to go to church with them, but I never did. They said they saw genuine goodness in me. I always thanked them and appreciated what they did, particularly their thoughtful concern—my only outlet, as I can't recall sharing my barracks ordeal with My Lady.

To add more misery to the mix, my Vette's engine was acting up, probably the result of all my trips and hard driving. We had this sergeant, another Garrison Marine, in our barracks who was new and claimed to be some car aficionado. He offered to give my car a top-end overhaul for only $250, half down to start, the rest upon completion. I quizzed him unmercifully on his qualifications, and he assured me he had done many overhauls in the past and that he would give me this big price break because I was a fellow Marine. Well, as it turned out, this jarhead couldn't screw the lid on and off his brain and I had to have my precious Vette towed away to a Chevy dealership in Fresno after waiting two months to realize he couldn't match a bolt to a screw. This clown had the top of the engine off and in my backseat. I was now in a real jam as I waited for the quote for Chevy to fix the mess. I had a savings account, but making only $190 a month wasn't exactly giving me much breathing room. To finish the botched job, the bill from Chevy was another $250. It virtually cleaned out my savings, but I was relieved as I drove away.

Chevy had told me they just finished the top-end overhaul job but could not guarantee to what extent the former mechanic may have messed up the pistons. I found out in about five miles as the Vette smoked like a rocket and had no power whatsoever. I barely made it back to the dealership. I felt like crying but was too conditioned to denying myself any tears, so I sat dejected at the dealership, with no more money, nowhere to garage the car, and no options. The sales manager felt somewhat bad and asked me if my dad would cosign for a loan. I shook my head and said I wouldn't even want to consider that because I valued what was left of my eardrums. The manager said he would call and explain my situation, insisting we had nothing to lose—easy for him to say.

Within a short time, the manager threw a sales agreement in front of me and said, "Great dad you have, he offered to cosign for a new car, and I have just the right one for you, Jon." *Wait a New York minute, you mean MY dad, John Meade, agreed to cosign for a NEW car—for me,* I thought? After the shock wore off, I drove away with a brand-new upscale Camaro that was on predominate display in the showroom with its special paint job of glistening silver and thin red pinstripes, touted for being the pace car in some big NASCAR event. It had four-on-the-floor and only forty-some miles on it, and I was elated.

They used my Corvette as the down payment—only a $500 credit, which sickened me—and gave me a supposed wholesale deal, making my monthly payment just $96, including insurance. As happy and proud of that showpiece Camaro that I was, leaving my Vette behind was like putting another dead Marine in the ground. My guts churned, and my head spun. That car was so symbolic of my return home from Vietnam, the visit to Washington DC, the drive to Camp Lejeune from Minnesota, the long drive across the bottom of the country from North Carolina to Las Vegas and my adventures there, and then on to Lemoore Naval Air Station and all my fun and trips out of there.

But I wasn't done with my Vette. I checked to make sure I wasn't going against an aspect of Marine protocol and filed a small-claims lawsuit against the shitbird sergeant. I gave him the chance to pay me back for the cost of his alleged overhaul, and of course, he didn't, just displaying an avoidance of any guilt. Finally, when we left the Fresno County courtroom, the judge gave me the nod and two-thirds of the cost of the monies paid to Mr. Mechanic, saying he wanted me to learn from this transaction for my mistake of trusting someone "who obviously had no ethics or decency." The judge was hardcore and slammed his gavel down very hard. Within a month, the sergeant paid me off, mustering a meager apology. My actions were really unheard of for one Marine to sue another, especially a superior, and I was the talk of the barracks—again—but even the major and adjacent officer smiled.

Chapter Thirty-Eight

The Marine Corps is all about high performance, perfection, and excellence in all aspects of duties. There is the Marine Corps way, and any other way. Marines don't have a choice, nor would they accept one. Begrudgingly or otherwise, the Corps always wins.

Major Tunget was a real commanding taskmaster and demanded that we all take extension courses out of Washington DC headquarters Marine Corps besides our demanding local duties. Two of them that he actually help teach included "Individual Protective Measures" and "Operations against Guerrilla Units." These went into your military record; but on my own, again, to add some luster to my name, I took an academic one—"Spelling." That one was a *slight* departure from the other combat-readiness ones. As a corporal of the guard, I was also required to give a few classes of my own, one being "Hand-to-Hand Combat." Maybe the brass saw "Golden Gloves Boxing" in my civilian record, but this one was strictly Marine Corps and combat style. The heat from the pot scandal was getting increasingly turned up, so I wanted to shine in front of the brass so I studied and prepared extensively.

When the day came to give the class to around twenty Marines each, in two to three time groups, I took the class outside and formed a circle. I wanted to have a hands-on interactive approach by first instructing them on all the basic moves and strikes, then have them attack me in the middle and apply what I showed them. A famous Marine officer had used this same technique preparing Marines to go into combat prior to World War II, with incredible success. I added two to three of my own martial arts moves I learned as a teen at the gym. Overlooking the fact that Marines are trained to attack and be very aggressive, I had my hands full, to say the least.

Although I could defend myself enough, I still took some lumps; and before I knew it, we had moans and groans in the circle, plus my own. It was a great concept in theory, but in reality, it seemed to create generalized mayhem. Our lieutenant finally stepped in and stopped the proceedings, saying it wasn't a wise idea to go on. So I just wrapped it all up with hands-off instruction. I would not have bet that the "Hand-to-Hand Combat" scored many points for me with the brass, but I know it did with at least some of the Marines.

I distinctly remember when my last class concluded and I was walking through the main hallway of the barracks to the front office to check the duty roster. Up on the board was a handwritten letter from the parents of this Marine, informing us of his death in Vietnam, thanking all the friends and fellow Marines of their son. I was shocked! This Marine, who had already served a tour of Nam, was killed in an ambush just two weeks after arriving in-country. He had volunteered to go back to Vietnam after he got a "Dear John" letter from his girlfriend just months before.

If there was such a thing as a "sweet" guy, it was him. I remember him getting that letter and being destroyed mentally by it. I tried to lift him up, and I took him to town a time or two where he told me he was going to volunteer to return to Nam. I tried to talk him out of it, tried to bolster his ego and well-being, and thought I had helped. Then one day, I literally turned around and he was gone, back to Vietnam. I quickly put it and him out of my mind, only to be painfully reminded of him in the worst way by this letter. It hit me like a mortar round.

There never seemed to be a dull moment in the Marine Barracks. We had our internal struggles once in a while with race and alleged prejudice. One issue arose from a couple of Hispanic Marines speaking out loud for lengthy periods in front of their Caucasian counterparts, with the latter taking offense by it by thinking they were talking derogatorily against them. But the issue was pretty much tempered and then forgotten. The bigger issue was this one black Marine who was always getting in trouble—late, no-show behavior unbecoming of a Marine NCO; you name it, and he either did it or didn't do it, whichever the case dictated. He would be charged with an infraction and be called up to the major's office for office hours. Every time he went marching up there, we thought he would be badly discharged or sent to the brig—because these were all very serious charges—but he always came away unscathed.

No one could figure it out except to say he got off free and clear. While the rest of us had to be model Marines in all ways, this guy was given special treatment and it started causing rife in the ranks and disbelief. The office-pogue Marine up in the administrative offices eventually told us the major had to cut him loose each time because the accused yelled race prejudice and the major was afraid of reprisals so he cut him loose. One other black Marine got in trouble too over being UA (unauthorized absence), went to the major, used the same tactic of prejudice, and was not charged. It was getting out of hand when suddenly the major was able to cut orders to release this Marine early from his normal upcoming discharge date. When he left, the problem left with him. You could feel the long sigh of relief throughout the barracks, especially the admin offices. Nothing is worse than the feeling of unfairness no matter what or who it involves, no matter what the skin color or nationality or situation.

One day in early November 1967, I was called up to the first sergeant's office who we respectfully called "Top." Top was a salt who was a grunt in World War II, Korea, and Vietnam. He had so many ribbons on his chest, including many for heroism, including numerous Purple Hearts, that he couldn't stand straight. He was nearly retired, and at about forty-seven years old, he looked eighty-seven and moved like it. His exterior was very gruff, but if you had the good fortune to talk to him at length and under certain circumstances, he was a softy inside and patient and understanding. This call to his office fell under those circumstances. But on the walk up there, I was nearly crapping in my pants as I thought this was something to do with the pot investigation. I stood tall before him at his desk in respect, and he quickly told me to stand at ease.

He looked at me long and seemed to have the beginning of tears in his eyes. "Corporal Meade, I have special orders for you straight from Washington DC and Headquarters Marine Corps." This was it. I was toast. They wanted me out so bad the highest brass even buttered the toast. "Through your family in Minneapolis, you have been requested to be the special escort for the remains of Lance Corporal Dana A. Pitts, who was just killed in Vietnam. I know you've done more than your share of these here, son, but this one is for home. I'm sorry. Pack your bags, and at 1000 hours, you will be brought to Fresno, where you will fly to San Francisco, be picked up at the terminal, and routed to Treasure Island where you will be further advised on picking up and handling said remains. You are dismissed, Corporal Meade, and I wish you well."

I didn't know a Dana Pitts, and while relieved, it was not about the pot scandal. I was equally mystified as to who this was, what my family had to do with it, and the entire incident. Just as I walked down the hallway, I came to the end and the phone booth, which had rings bellowing from it. This had happened to me before under different circumstances, and here I was answering the phone, and it was for me. The ironies. It was my grandmother Hilda, and she asked me if I got the request yet for Dana.

She explained he was the son of her friend Vivian, and Gram worked for them as a sewer in their company. She said Dana had just talked to his mother via shortwave radio while on a junket to the Philippines, and when he returned to Nam, he was scheduled to board a plane for home. Instead, that night prior to leaving, his camp was attacked and he manned a bunker in the corner of the base and was hit by a direct round of artillery, shattering his body in pieces.

When I checked into Treasure Island on the peninsula of the San Francisco Bay, I was waiting in the mail room for further orders that were being wired in. They had these see-through mail slots, and looking through there, I noticed this female Hispanic Marine sergeant who was jaw-dropping gorgeous. Naturally, I couldn't resist, so we exchanged numbers and addresses and would get together sometime after I returned. Dana now was just another escort, and I didn't give it another thought. Until the remainder of the orders came through. It was a closed casket, meaning bodily damage was substantial. In this case, the only thing in the casket was Dana's foot within his named boot. I still took it with a grain of salt. I was so used to death and burials and bodies, this was just another number.

When I was overseeing the loading of Dana's casket at the San Francisco airport from a military hearse, I recalled the order to make sure the head of the casket was loaded toward the front of the plane, so if there was turbulence and the casket moved backward, the head would be more protected.

Then I realized it made no difference because there wasn't a head. That hit me a little harder for a moment. I wore a black arm patch on my full green uniform and was seated in first class. Once at flying altitude, an attractive stewardess brought me a rum and Coke, and we made personal conversation, which continued throughout the flight along with the doctored Cokes. When we landed, I made a date with her at her hotel in downtown Minneapolis. A mortuary hearse was there at the plane, and I escorted the remains back to the mortuary, just outside of downtown. I then called my mom and told her I had some business to do and would come home much later.

When I met the stewardess at her hotel, we went downstairs, made out, drank, and danced. We both were tipsy, and she wanted to go to the top floor of the hotel and show me something. I thought for sure we'd make a beeline to her room and make love and top off the evening. How wrong was this naive jarhead? When we got up there, there was this side exit door that went out to a steel balcony. From there, there were other balconies and rooftops. I'll call her Ms. Weirdo. She said it really turned her on to have someone chase her from rooftop to rooftop. Turned her on, huh? Okay, I thought I'd play. I was now Mr. Weirdo.

We chased around a little and made the leap of a couple of feet from rooftop to rooftop. I followed her crazy lead thinking if we survived this exercise in creative sexual arousal, I would surely score a major feminine conquest. Well, not quite. After several hours of this cat-stewardess-and-mouse-Marine game, she said she was very hungry and wanted to take me to this late-night breakfast place. Okay, I thought, what's a little more delay en route to getting what we both knew was coming?

A double order of breakfast later—she was a chowhound after all that exercise—and about six cups of strong coffee, plus a piece of lemon pie, it was five in the morning; and Ms. Weirdo was suddenly anxious to go back to the hotel, saying she was ready to bring me to her room. Strangely, I had it. I was disgusted with her and myself. I really didn't trust what might come next. Who knows, maybe she had small parachutes in her room and she would want to jump off the rooftops next? I couldn't believe I was doing this, but I excused myself graciously and said I had to get home and get ready for a big day standing guard over the casket. *Now*, she displayed some displeasure and frustration and I loved it.

When I finally got home sometime that morning, I tried to grab a little catnap but couldn't. I shaved and made sure I was presentable and went to the mortuary to prepare for the daylong viewing. I met with the mortician about the viewing and talked about it being a closed casket. He said he was aware that there was only a foot in the casket and asked me if we should view it together. My mind goes totally blank from that time until the casket was placed on its platform in the main viewing room of the mortuary, with perhaps several dozen chairs and flowers everywhere. My mind only gives me brief snippets of opening the casket and seeing the foot. I can't recall it with any measure of validity or accuracy.

The Pitts family and members of my family, led by Grandma Hilda, visited that day as I stood at attention and at ease for many hours at the head of the casket. I remember several attempts by both Vivian and her other son to open the casket, but I was able to talk them out of it per my instructions by the Marine Corps to do everything possible to avoid showing the body part to the mother and family. I basically said it was a closed casket and it was best to remember Dana the way he was. Despite some close calls, they eventually gave up. I was also instructed to open the casket if I had to, but only if their demands became overly persistent. Thank God my persistence outranked theirs.

The funeral was the next day, led off by a hearse, with me and the mortician, and funeral procession from central Minneapolis to Fort Snelling in Saint Paul. We were directed to a new quadrant on the grounds where Dana would be the first to be buried there. In order to fulfill my proper burial execution, I had to recruit Marine reservists to make up the burial detail. Me and my team lifted the flag-draped casket from the hearse and brought it to the lift over the hole while mourners filled the seats around the casket, including most members of my family. Dana's mother, Vivian, was seated up front in the center, wearing a black veil. The minister was in position and addressed the flock, as me and my men stood at attention around the casket. Light sobs and cries rose from some onlookers. Taps were played during the funeral but no other military salutes.

After the minister finishing speaking, no family members advanced to give any words, and it was totally quiet. I directed the team to attention, and we proceeded to fold the flag over the casket until it reached me at the end, where it was properly folded together, only blue and white showing, with the stars illuminating against the background. I marched over to Vivian, squaring my corners and holding the folded flag mid-torso several inches away. All eyes were upon me as I looked down to Mrs. Pitts, huge tears blended with dark mascara rolling down her cheeks and into the corners of her mouth. Her eyes were dark, heavy, and stressed. I started to say my words upon giving her the flag and a salute.

"This flag is presented on behalf of a grateful nation"—I started breaking up—"in loving memory of your son, Lance Corporal Dana A. Pitts." I simply could not finish. My eyes locked into Vivian's; and suddenly, all my other burials—the other sad eyes, the families, the mothers, fathers, women, my detachment from emotion and reality, the whys and why nots—hit me. I maintained my composure despite feeling moist eyes, did an about-face, and returned to the head of the casket, where I briefly paused and vowed inside my shaking body to honor Marines for the rest of my life. I then directed our strict departure away from the burial site.

There was a reception afterward at Vivian's house. It was a very somber event. I hugged Vivian and told her I was sorry for not completely finishing my speech and told her to please remember her son for the best that he was. We continued embracing and talked a little more before we were interrupted by some loud wailing and screaming. It was Dana's older brother in the backyard, wrapped around the big trunk of an oak tree, yelling out and crying. It was such a traumatic scene that no one made any gesture toward him until I went out there. I knelt down next to him and said as many things as I could think of to try and soothe his pain, concentrating on remembering Dana as he was. He was also cursing the United States, the Marine Corps, and Vietnam. I basically just listened patiently and nodded. When he finally calmed down, I looked in his red wet eyes and told him I was so sorry and walked back inside.

Chapter Thirty-Nine

When I returned to Marine Barracks, I fit in a few visits with Tina, that pretty Marine sergeant, into my dating schedule, but found that my mind and heart was settled on my lady stewardess in Burlingame, where I continued my visits. My desire to run around and party were glitched by that Pitts escort and my guilty feelings of prior detachment from all the other burials. I felt now I was re-committed to any upcoming funerals. But the number of burials slowed down.

The only assignment out of the norm of MP duties on the gates and base was to re-qualify with weapons. I was slated to qualify again with the M-14, in addition to the M-1, the World War II and Korean War horse and the garrison weapon we used at Marine Barracks, and the M-60 machine gun. I qualified for sharpshooter with the M-14, missing expert by one point at 219. But I did shoot expert with the M-1 at 221, a rifle I actually preferred. We also did extensive firing of the M-60 machine gun and the A1-11 .45 cal. Pistol, but there was no formal qualifying, per se.

A nice break at the time was serving as best man for Terrible T's (Corporal Tyler's) wedding. We all wore semi-dress blues and carried swords for the military ceremonies at the base chapel. Tyler was yet another Purple Heart recipient and was nicknamed "Terrible T" because he didn't take any crap and was a fighter. I loved him. He married a pretty but lively and rascally Hispanic woman from Fresno.

We visited them a few times for some beers, and while they were all lovey-dovey, T's flashbacks from Nam were playing with his mind and causing a little division between them at times. He was discharged soon thereafter, and we gave him a send-off party and wished him well—he needed it.

Mid-1968, I took another short leave to Minnesota to escape some of the pressure I was under. It was nearly overwhelming so the departure was timely. While home, Democratic presidential candidate Robert F. Kennedy, brother of President John F. Kennedy and former attorney general, was assassinated, and it consumed the airwaves. It drowned out all other news and events. As bad as I felt for Kennedy's death, I thought the life of a dead Marine killed in war was every bit as important.

Escorting deceased Marines was both my great honor and my great sorrow. Sometimes it seemed like I was in a near constant state of mourning. If it wasn't for the immediacy around me, it was in my head from Vietnam.

The other constant that was still lingering around the barracks was the drug scandal, where Hansen and a few more of the original fourteen charged were being released with bad discharges. There was only four left: Rios, who was still AWOL; Lance Corporal Schroeder; PFC Archuleta; and me.

Right around the corner was the Marine Corps Ball, an annual event touting the Marine Corps annual birthday, with plenty of drinking and dancing. I had just met this Mexican beauty at a Fresno department store, where she was working the cosmetics counter. When I picked her up, I had to meet her parents, with emphasis on her father. The house was covered with statues of Mary and rosary beads.

She was only eighteen, and her father was justifiably concerned so I spent thirty minutes assuring him I was a decent guy and his daughter was in trusted hands. She had purchased a beautiful white formal gown for the event and was truly magazine-cover beautiful. I told them the latest I would return their daughter and drove off waving and smiling. Despite her age, any restrictions on liquor consumption was lifted for the Ball. I introduced her to my favorite of rum and Coke, and she quickly rose to the occasion, saying the only alcohol she drank previously was a few swigs of her father's beer. We listened to words from Major Tunget, toasted the Corps, and drank, danced, and had a ball.

When it was time to leave, we went out to the parking lot and couldn't find my car. I blamed it on the booze but quickly realized it was gone, as in stolen. My new Camaro—missing. On top of this, I realized that my date Maria was drunker than two skunks. I went inside and called Navy security and reported the loss. They sent a truck over and took us to the security office. As soon as we arrived, the entire security element was called out on some emergency. Only one Sailor manned the window in the front. Before I knew it, Maria had found the captain's office and was sitting back on his posh overstuffed leather chair. Could this really be happening to me? She kept complaining that she was still hungry and thirsty, so I rushed to the machines and got her a Coke and several chocolate candy bars. I tried to tell her she could get me in a lot of trouble for doing this, but she just dug into the goodies. Meanwhile, I had to go into another office and call the CHP (California Highway Patrol). I told Maria to just hold tight and finish her Coke and candy.

When I returned, I could hardly believe my eyes. She had her feet up on the captain's desk, her dress hiked up, revealing ripped nylons; and she was covered with chocolate all over her white dress, face, and hair. She looked like she had stuck her finger in an electric outlet, as matted candy had spiked up her hairdo in every direction. But she was the prettiest damn mess I had ever seen. She was smiling broadly so I said, "Looks like you're having fun, Maria."

"I am, Jon, and I wouldn't trade this for anything."

"Really," I said, "because I sure would."

Before we left to take her home with a Navy vehicle, I took her into the bathroom to try to clean her up. It was practically useless. There must have been more chocolate on her than in her. Trying to rub it out with water just made it worse. I didn't bother washing all the chocolate off her face because she had two small hickeys on her side chin, providing excellent camouflage. On the ride home, she was sobering up as I had her drink lots of coffee and water. I had her call her parents to tell them we would be late what with my car being stolen. I had no idea what my game plan would be, so I threw fate to the wind. I literally can't remember how it went when I took her into her home through the front door. My mind blanks out from that part. I can say I was more shocked by her father's response than he was by her appearance. He pulled a dad on me and was remarkably patient and understanding. At one point, he even appeared to be fighting back laughter as I told him the whole sorted tale. Maria's mother had whisked her daughter away. I apologized profusely and left. I wanted to get completely out before all that chocolate was washed off Maria's face.

Weeks passed after the Marine Corps Ball, and my car was still missing. I had maybe one to two more CID interviews, but they were quick and nondescript. I had heard through the grapevine that Schroeder and Archuleta were close to being discharged. I really cared for these individuals, and both had received Purple Hearts in Nam, so I decided to put myself on the line and fight for them with all I had. I went through the chain of command—a short one with so few Marines in our barracks—and requested mast to see the major. I rehearsed in my mind what I would say to him and stood tall in front of this John Wayne–like Marine.

"Sir, I would like to ask you if there is anything you can do to help save Lance Corporal Schroeder and PFC Archuleta from further investigation and a possible bad discharge."

"I can surely appreciate what you are saying, Corporal Meade, but as a commanding officer of a Marine Barracks and someone who has sworn to uphold whatever directives the Marine Corps hands down, I am bound by its rules, traditions, and military justice. But I have a career on the line here too."

"Yes, sir, is there anything I can do for them personally as an enlisted man and fellow Marine? Sir, you know they are great Marines and are highly decorated, and I am sure these charges against them are extreme and not warranted—"

"I think that's enough, Corporal Meade, and I respect you for standing up for them. But I've given this considerable thought already and there is nothing I can do, and certainly nothing you can do. But I understand. I do. Now, go back to the barracks. You are dismissed."

Within days, I saw Schroeder and Archuleta in full greens marching down to the admin offices. When they came back, they told me they both got undesirable discharges, one notch above the worst. We didn't say much but well wishes and goodbyes. I did tell them I tried to save them. That I had their backs. They gave me a sincere sign of thanks. I thought I could be next, but Rios was still at large and as long as he wasn't caught, I was safe. In my last statement, I repeated my outrage at my second negative witness, Private Thompson, and his out-and-out lies, even offering to take a lie detector test over his sworn statement, but then worried that they would then test other questions that would incriminate me. I never took the Fifth Amendment like some of the Marines did because it seemed like signing your own discharge warrant. When Thompson ever crossed paths with me during the guard rotations, I watched him like a hawk because if he made one wrong move, I would have written him up and brought him before the Man.

Soon, I got a call from the CHP. They had found my new Camaro, and it only had thirty-seven miles on it since it was stolen and the crook turned out to be a Sailor on the base. A whole month had passed, and for nearly that whole time, it was sitting in an inbound lot, wrongly identified. I was livid. Ironically, at this same exact time, I was ready to settle with my insurance company since the magic missing number was thirty days, which was exactly where we were, to the day. By this time, I was fed up with the whole mess and told them I would just go ahead and take the monetary settlement, which was only $500.

Back on the phone with the CHP, they asked me if I still wanted to press charges since this was a Sailor from the base. I not only told them I did, but got upset at the officer for even suggesting such a thing. "I believe in justice, and I've been in real short supply of that lately, so yes, I want charges filed within the full extent of the law and I'm going to check back later to make sure you did it." More than anything, I still missed my Corvette, my baby, my travel partner.

As the rest of 1968 closed out and Tet over in Vietnam was now history, I went to the naval hospital to see about a couple of old injuries I got—one was a ruptured testicle I got in Nam playing a rough game of football with a small sandbag and the other was a ganglion on my wrist from repetitive exercise. Since my tour of duty was up in the first part of the next year, I wanted to see about getting them fixed. They examined them and scheduled me to go up to Oak Knoll Naval Hospital in Oakland, California, which was across the bay from My Lady, for surgical repair.

I took a bus up there and checked into the fourth floor. In my room was a nineteen-year-old Hispanic Marine with shrapnel wounds all over his face, neck, and chest right next to me. Across from me was a black Sailor who was having a circumcision (yikes!) before his discharge. Across on the other end was a twenty-year-old white Marine who carried an artificial stomach around in front of him. I introduced myself, and we all became fast friends. I had to wait a week for the surgery so during that time, My Lady visited a couple of times, but mostly I went around to the wards just to meet Marines and others. Oak Knoll was a brand-new medical facility primarily created to take care of the worst of the worse casualties from Nam. Most of the old vintage wooden World War II clapboard single-story structures were still there. Some, I was told, contained Marines and some Navy corpsman who had no limbs. There turned out to be three wards of them.

Many had no legs, hips, arms, or shoulders. Some of them were on little skateboard-like scooters and played soccer using the points of the scooters or a few with the stumps of their legs or arms. Others had just a body core and lay there, staring at the ceiling. I went down there quite often and would offer to get some of the guys something from the PX. One Marine who lost one arm and one leg told me that all the worst ones were in la-la land from drugs and didn't care if they lived or died. They joked about it. So I cared for them in just the smallest ways I could. It made no difference, but it made me feel good. But every time I went there, I felt my *"lucky guilt"* return.

At the end of the week, the hospital was desperately trying to find volunteers to do some PR for the hospital and Vets. Since I was admitted for next to nothing, I volunteered, having no idea what it was all about. There were only six of us that raised our hands, and we boarded a private bus that also had civilians on it. Our destination was Modesto, down and inland somewhat. We were told to wear our full-dress green uniforms. One of the Marines had no legs, so we got him onboard and stowed his wheelchair under the bus.

I knew the Marine I was sitting with had an artificial leg so I stood in the aisle to let him in next to the window. He was a very strong-looking husky guy, and while standing in front of the seats, he reached down and up under his leg and pulled it off and out while standing freely on his one leg. This older lady seemed like she was going to faint and even started sobbing. He put the leg in the overhead bin, winked at me, and sat down. I didn't know whether to laugh or cry myself. The only thing any of us knew was that it had something to do with some television show. But Modesto?

When we arrived at the Modesto bus terminal and got off, a big van was waiting there for us. I was the most able-bodied Marine so I pushed the Marine in the wheelchair. They told us we were the guests of the *Joey Bishop Show* and would be well taken care of. Joey Bishop was an extended member of the famous Frank Sinatra Rat Pack in Hollywood and had a popular daytime interview variety show. He was filming his show around California to support and promote the right for eighteen-year-olds to vote and drink.

His contention was if young men could go to war, get wounded, or die, then they should have the right to vote and drink. We were told we would be called up to the stage and interviewed by Bishop as the final segment of the show. Meanwhile, they sat us together in the third row. But as the show progressed, the time was running short, so our segment was cut down to Joey ending the program by having the camera follow him as he shook all of our hands until we heard "cut."

The producer said Joey had arranged for all his guests, especially the Marines, to have a big catered dinner on the premises of prime rib and lobster and all the booze we could drink. We dug in like there was no tomorrow and drank the same. For dessert, there was every imaginable thing, all first-tier stuff. When all the powdered sugar had settled and they called for the van to take us back to the hospital, we were stuffed and drunk. And on the ride back, we all barfed our guts out, opening the van windows and flinging bits of prime rib, lobster, and whatever else out the windows. When we arrived, there were still remnants of lobster stubbornly hanging from the windows. The crew driver from the Bishop show couldn't stop laughing, saying not to worry, that he would clean it all up with a big hose. So much for the PR for the hospital and Vets. Who at the medical facility ever said that?

Chapter Forty

My surgery—where just before while drugging up I had written my dad a scathing letter about his fathering and my upbringing—was a success, or so I thought. Seems my doctor set the cast with the wrist in the wrong (up) direction, restricting blood flow. My fingers had nearly lost all feeling and had no color. I had actually said something to my doctor, but my complaint went unheated. The chief physician discovered this while making his bed rounds, causing strife with my doctor bedside, subsequently dismissing him from my case. He had some kind of (painful) shot put into the wound area and reset the cast. My stay was immediately extended. They were falling all over themselves apologizing.

Just before Christmas, the American Red Cross was making the rounds and offering to help all able-bodied patients go home for the holidays. I had no intention of taking another leave, but this Red Cross lady easily got approval for me to get a freebie leave and insisted to give me $100 to boot, saying I only had to pay it back if I could or wanted to. I took a one-week leave, wrist cast on and all, and flew back to Minnesota. Before I left, however, I proposed marriage to My Lady; she accepted, and when home, she flew in and we went ring hunting in Minneapolis. I also brought her home and introduced her to my mother and family. This was a first. And they all loved her. I paid back the Red Cross lady before I was discharged.

When I returned to Marine Barracks, I was a short-timer with only slightly over two months left on my enlistment. There had been so much turnover that there were very few faces I recognized. But the time flew by quickly, and to top it off, the major put Marty (Corporal Martinez) and I up for an early release date since we were soon being discharged anyway. Suddenly, I had only two and a half weeks left. And just as suddenly, I got the shock and scare of my life.

I was acting corporal of the guard and sitting in the guard office upfront. About four Navy security guards burst through the front door holding someone in handcuffs. That someone was Private Pete Rios. They made him stand spread eagle against the wall right across from me. This couldn't be happening, I thought. I was nearly ready to walk out the very same door myself as an honorably discharged Marine, now this? After one and a half years, Pete was caught down in Texas, .45 caliber pistol and all. When no one was around, Rios turned his head away from the wall. "Jon, I am so sorry. I can't say it enough . . . I'm sorry."

It took me a while to answer him. "Pete, you have no idea the problems you've caused for everyone. So far, because of your busting ranks and opening the rat cage, twelve Marines were badly discharged. You and me are the only ones left."

I got no response but his dropping head. The sergeant of the guard appeared and told me there was no one else around so I would have to chase Rios across the parking lot to the brig. He threw me his rifle after thrusting a loaded magazine inside and handed me the orders for his lockup. "If this turd tries to escape, shoot his ass." I put Rios in front of me and marched him to the brig.

On the short trip, he turned his head. "Jon, I got married while I was gone and have a little boy with another on the way. I know I messed up and I deserve whatever they give me, but I'm so sorry."

"That's nice. Just think of the mess you've created for yourself and your family. Damn, Pete. You were Mr. Cool and my bud and then you turned on everyone. I only have a couple of weeks left in the Corps and now you show up. Are you going to blabber any more, or have you learned your lesson?"

"I have, Jon, I have. You have been a great friend, Jon. I would never say another word."

I checked Rios into the brig with his papers and left, giving him a slight smile and nod, thinking I would never see him again. I swore I saw his eyes rimmed with tears, but none fell.

Within days, I got another call to go up to the admin offices. My first impulse was that Rios opened his mouth and signed the third statement against me. Instead, I was introduced to a Navy lieutenant, who turned out to be Rios's military-appointed attorney. He insisted we sit down, eyeball-to-eyeball, in the back room.

"Corporal Meade, I am privy to the entire story about my client, Private Rios, and he has been charged with the most extreme level of UA, AWOL, stealing and possessing a weapon, among other things, and is facing the harshest penalties allowed by military law. He told me you are the only one left who could help us since this all started.

Would you be willing to attend his court-martial and be a character witness?"

I went through a litany list why I shouldn't help him and showed a lot of anger, but then said, "Okay, I'll be there, he can count on me."

"Fantastic. I'll quickly request they move the court-martial up to accommodate your upcoming discharge. We have a tremendously difficult uphill battle, but at least maybe we can get his sentence reduced a little."

I told the attorney of one other Marine that knew Rios and was here throughout the whole ordeal and, while being an outsider to the entire story, knew Rios as a fellow Hispanic and may offer help. His name was Corporal Albo, and the attorney added him to our defense team.

When the big day came for the summary court-martial, to my amazement, the barracks was all engaged, so I was ordered to once again chase the prisoner Rios to the main Navy administrative building on the base. Bearing semi-dress blues (no jacket), my cartridge belt with pistol and nightclub, plus holding an M-1 at port arms, I once again did my duties. We engaged in minor conversation as I chased (marched) Rios about three long blocks away to the building. Pete was dressed in full dress greens with all his medals, including the Purple Hearts, as per his attorney's instructions. When we arrived, we were met by the attorney and Corporal Albo. The attorney's face was ashen. We were down the hall from the big room where the proceedings would take place.

"We are going to have high-ranking Naval officers sitting around the big long table, and they are going to be tough. Unfortunately, the court-martial prosecuting officer is this female captain, who has a reputation for not liking Marines. She has been the lead attorney for forty-three court-martials and has never lost." Pete's head dropped, and all of us looked like the blood had just drained from our bodies.

We discussed the case, and the attorney ended our talks by telling us to try to not be intimidated by the woman as she was very intelligent and extremely tough. That was not too encouraging. I think we all felt we were leading Rios into the bullring to be slaughtered. As the door to the room came open and we filed in, I suddenly felt like this was a challenge of a lifetime and felt the hackles rise on my neck and the desire to fight. I had no idea how, but I had a few minutes to brainstorm inside my head.

Pete's attorney took one end of the table, with Pete by his side, and the infamous woman prosecutor took the other end. We joined Navy captains and commanders in the middle, with me on one end and Albo on the other. It was like a king's court table, only the king was a queen and she looked mean. The ranking captain opened the proceedings and passed to the prosecutor, who read the long list of charges in military and legal jargon. The table was then open for discussion of the charges with questions and answers. The prosecutor made sure she got her digs in and tried to control everything, once even interrupting the senior captain, who seemed a little agitated by her. The table seemed to be asking me most of the questions until it finally boiled down to one by the lead captain. He seemed to be formulating his question to me with measured consideration, as if it was *the* question of the day to answer. I sensed it was like a wrap-up of everything.

"Corporal Meade, you have already been sworn under oath here so this question is very important. I want you to listen carefully and think honestly before you answer. If Private Rios was in charge of you in combat, would you have total trust in him and obey and follow him?"

I couldn't believe this question. I nearly chuckled inside and instantaneously knew how I would answer, but took my time and slowly put the thread through the needle.

"Captain, I would not hesitate and be proud to follow him as a Marine in charge, in combat, out of combat, or in any other situation in the Marines." What a question, I thought. I was a Marine; of course, I would follow him if he was in charge or I would get in trouble, or worse.

"Even if your life was at stake?"

"Yes, sir, even if my life was at stake." I then paused, as did the whole table, and I spoke in the silence. "Sir, may I add something?"

"Yes, Corporal, you may, and let this also be for the record." I gazed down the table to the queen of the proceedings, and it seemed like steam was coming out of her ears. I purposely took my time, reaching deep inside for the perfect thing to say at this perfect time.

"Private Rios was a highly decorated combat Marine in Vietnam and was wounded several times. When he was recovering back in the States in the hospital, he got a 'dear John' from his fiancée, and he went off on the deep end, did some drinking, and got into trouble and was busted from sergeant all the way down to private." I hesitated and collected my thoughts. All eyes and ears were on me, especially the lone woman's.

"I know it is no excuse for his recent behavior and charges, but he was having girlfriend troubles again back home and felt he had to take action and went AWOL, and then he got married and had a little boy and his wife is due again. Rios never asked questions when he was called by his country and served in war with honors, nearly losing his life. Captain and sirs (I excluded the ma'am), I hope the United States and this court will stand by this once-troubled Marine like he stood by his new wife, his little boy, his country, and comrades. He was and is a great Marine and doesn't deserve harsh treatment. Please try to understand and forgive him."

There was an overwhelming collective silence in the room, finally broken by the captain asking Albo, "Would you concur with Corporal Meade's testimony, Corporal Albo, and also support Rios's leadership and whether or not you would follow him in combat?"

Albo also answered in the affirmative, adding some accolades to Rios's character and circumstances.

Soon, the prosecutor rattled off some things, and the captain dismissed the court-martial, telling Rios's attorney to stay in the room with Rios while Albo and I waited in the hall. Albo and I quietly laughed about the question by the captain about following Rios in combat. "Albo, this captain doesn't have a clue about what the Marine Corps is all about, does he? How else would any good Marine answer?"

In about fifteen minutes, Rios's attorney emerged, thanked us for what he thought were great answers and testimony, but wore a worried look.

"I did the best I could. The prosecutor is determined to get the worst verdict—a dishonorable discharge, six years in prison, and forfeiture of all pay and allowances for six years. I tried to argue the charges down to an undesirable or bad conduct discharge, but I don't know . . . she's never lost a case. Good job though, Corporal Meade and Albo." We waited. And waited.

Finally, one of the officers opened the door and told the attorney to come back in with Rios. "Well," he said, "this is it, boys. Wish us luck, we'll need it."

Very shortly, the door swung open, led by the attorney, who wore a grin, and Rios behind, also with a look of glee on his stressed face. "Well, men, our lady prosecutor has just lost her first case, and boy, did she lose. Rios was given a general discharge under medical conditions. This is a major, major victory. Frankly, I'm still in shock. Corporal Meade, your words really turned them on their ear, and your collaboration, Corporal Albo, just drove it all home. Incredible job!" We all shook hands and stood back as the door once again opened with the prosecutor storming out of the room with a look of utter disgust etched upon her face.

We broke up after our extensive congratulations, and again, I had to chase Rios with rifle in tow back to the brig. I handcuffed him and led him away, as Albo went his way. On the way back, we talked about how lucky Rios was, and I was thinking maybe some of my luck rubbed off on Pete and I surely welcomed it and was thankful. After telling him he had to go home and be a good husband and father and lead a good life without any more trouble, I could hear sniffles and light sobs.

"Jon, I don't know what to say, man. Yes, I will, thanks to you. Thank you for what you did. I'll never forget this. I'm sorry. I'm so, so sorry."

"I know, Pete, I know. I forgive you, man."

When I turned him over to the brig officer, I signed him over and we made our last deep eye contact and I left. The whole thing was surreal. Surreal!

Soon, I found myself along with Marty getting our discharge physicals. After that, we made the rounds to the different Navy and Marine Corps departments and stopped at a room at Navy admin to get a sign-off. Marty was losing his patience with this office-pogue behind the counter in front of the secretarial pool, where I spotted my old flame Diane (she must have gotten demoted from her captain's secretary job). We were waiting and waiting, seemingly for nothing, and suddenly Marty lurched forward over the counter and grabbed the Sailor by his top uniform flap and started dragging him over the counter. Diane came over and tried to pull him the other way while Marty was calling her every foul name in the book.

Finally, I intervened, "C'mon, Marty, stop, man, stop! That's Diane, show some respect."

Marty broke his grip as the whole area was in dead silence. As we got our sign-offs, I made my little farewell to Diane and tried to explain to everyone Marty's behavior. I explained it away as prolonged combat fatigue. They quietly seemed to understand as I grabbed Marty and we left. The last sign-off was at Marine Barracks for our pistols and rifles.

The other gear had already been turned in. And we had long before gotten our shipping over speeches. The corporal up in admin told me the major had given me the highest pro and con marks he had ever seen, and certainly the highest from the major. We were as good as gone, DD 214s in hand. As I got my clothes packed and put away, the last item was that Czech girl's sweater still hanging on a locker hook. I took it with me over my shoulder with my sea-bags, and along with Marty, we walked out the front door for the last time.

Marty offered to give me a ride into town, but I saw his small car full of kids and his wife so I declined, opting instead at that point to hand over the sweater to Marty so he could give it to his wife.

"Damn, Meade, this is beautiful. Are you sure you want to give it up?" I told him a little sweater history and insisted he give it to his wife. We shook hands, waved, and off we both went, Marty out the main gate, and I to security where I hitched a ride to town with Shore Patrol.

"So, getting out of the Corps, huh? How many years?"

"Four years going on forty-four!" I laughed, he grinned.

PART IV

(AM: After Marines)

*Great spirits have always encountered violent
opposition from mediocre minds.*
—Albert Einstein

Chapter Forty-One

We had already made arrangements for My Lady to pick me up at the Greyhound San Francisco bus stop. We relaxed, I shared my incredible feeling of freedom, and we went down to the heart of the city to the swank, historic St. Francis Hotel and sat down to have a cocktail. I felt I could never celebrate enough. Just as My Lady departed to the ladies' room, a couple of young Marines just out of boot camp walked by, and I learned they were 0311 grunts and were soon going to Vietnam. I searched their eyes and wondered if I could see death. One of the Marines had large eyes, reminiscent of that Marine on Christmas Eve in Nam who stuck his weapon between my eyes.

Strange thought, but I visualized him not ever having a heavy trigger finger. I was proud of those very young leathernecks. I shook their hands and hoped my *luck* would rub off on them. It made me so proud to have served. Images were going through my head like a flash hailstorm on a clear day: boot camp, Vietnam, Marine Barracks, pot scandal, investigations, pomp and circumstance, funerals, Dana Pitts, Rios court-martial, and standing tall at the end with a perfect record and an honorable release. This was another time when I so appreciated my *luck*, especially not being the fourteenth Marine to be tried and not honorably discharged. But I couldn't get Schroeder and Archuleta out of my mind. I still thought the Corps turned their backs on them and I carried some resentment.

I guess I was a survivor but felt more like an alien going on leave into the civilian world. I naively wondered if I could adapt all right. They would always tell you that in your re-up talk. It was like I was leaving one atmosphere and going into another one. The hotel doorman had to go outside to chase some hippies away who were carrying Stop-the-War signs and argue whether they were trespassing or not on public or private property. Ironically, it broke me out of my thoughts as My Lady returned. We had a special combined "discharged" and engagement dinner—spare no expense, for me anyway—and after we returned to Burlingame, where I slept on the couch again.

We had our plan in place; and after a few days, I would hop on a flight to Minneapolis, where I would secure a job, save money, and prepare for my future with my fiancée. She would fly in often, and we would chart our course in greater detail. From the Marine Corps' insistence on excellence and my own eventual desire to become a good husband, father, and provider, I thought I'd take advantage of the GI Bill and go to college in the Bay Area, where we would later get our first place. I liked the idea of helping Vets, so I planned on concentrating my studies in physical therapy. To solidify my thinking, I took a job as a physical therapy orderly at Abbott Hospital, a private facility. Within a short time, I also got a job at nights at a neighborhood greasy spoon, where I cleaned and locked up. After checking into my local Marine reserve unit as part of my six-year-total enlistment obligation—with them saying I could be called up (never happened)—I was set for the next few months.

I bought an old beater and resigned myself to being a miser by just working and saving money. My mother just told me to take up a bed in the basement. Within weeks, however, that caused a major rift with my dad as he didn't believe in a free ride for anyone, under any circumstances, even a returning son from the service. Despite explaining to him that it would just be a few months and would enable me to save money for the trip back to California and a honeymoon, he was pissed. One night at dinner, he blew up, I blew up, and my mom acted as referee.

We argued and discussed everything, and Dad was at his rapid dog best, snarling, eyes flashing, name-calling, near-insane behavior. He got up and stormed away as Mom started crying, saying she was sick of him treating me like this, especially returning from Vietnam and the Marines. She also threw out something like, "He needs some room, God knows you'll never give him any money." Mom told me that the doctor always told her that Dad's rare medical condition of porphyria greatly affected his behavior. It went right over my head. Dad remained in full-blown mad mode, looking at both of us like he wanted to kill us.

One late night just before I was ready to close the restaurant and was mopping, there was a knock at the back door. It was Mom, and I couldn't believe it. This was totally out of character for her to just casually drop in unannounced, especially at work. As soon as she walked in, I knew something was up.

She looked worried and concerned. "Jon, I have something to tell you, and it's not going to be easy." She stopped talking and seemed to be searching for what to say next, pausing many minutes.

I immediately knew it had to be something serious and finally responded, "Okay, Mom, what is it? C'mon, out with it, you started to tell me something and now you are pulling back." Her face was etched in worry, and she was frigid. "Mom, you came here to tell me something, now tell me." She still hesitated and told me she apologized and it wasn't important and I really didn't need to know. "Mom, you're not leaving here until you tell me."

"Okay, okay." Her voice and manner took on a soft and humble tone. "When you were born, your father was in prison. Your dad never met you until after he got out when you were nearly one and a half years old. He was so glad to see you he hoarded you off in another room by himself. I just had to tell you."

My head took a nosedive. I was in shock. "Dad, in prison? The same guy that wouldn't be caught dead breaking the speed limit or any traffic laws? For what, Mom, what was he in for, what did he do?"

"Well, I might as well tell you everything. He served about six years in Leavenworth for burglary and robbery and some more time for breaking probation, about eight years altogether. You know, when his father Claude was shot and killed over that horse race, your dad and Lester took it really rough and went bad. They became a couple of tough thugs in Minneapolis, drank a lot and got into fights, always getting in trouble. They were notorious in Minneapolis for all the wrong reasons."

I can't recall saying much as I was dumbfounded and all ears.

"Finally, John and Lester robbed a gas station and stole a car and, after a chase through Minneapolis, were caught. When they went to court, Dad apparently took some of the rap for his younger brother Les and was given the harshest sentence. The judge gave Lester an option, either go with your brother off to prison or join the military. He joined the service and became an Army paratrooper with 101st Airborne."

"Yeah, Mom, wasn't he a hero in World War II and won medals, including Purple Hearts? Wow, I guess that explains why Dad never went in the service. Three brothers, Wesley, who became a cop; Dad, who went to prison; and Lester, who went to war. Poor grandma Mabel, what she went through?"

"But, Jon, listen, you can't let Dad know I told you. You must keep this a secret. When you were a little boy, he told me he never wanted you to ever know about his prison past because he feared it may give you an excuse to go bad yourself. He was too fearful. He actually said he would kill me if I ever opened my mouth to anyone."

"Oh, but he didn't really mean it, did he?"

"Oh yeah, I think he did because he had that look he gets when he loses his temper, and he repeated the threat over and over. Anyway, he scared me enough where I didn't tell a soul."

"Did anyone else know?"

"Just Gram, Chris and Marilyn, probably Dick and Ellsworth. And a few, of course, on Dad's side."

"I'm still in shock, Ma. Geez, what you must have gone through, too. But this does answer a lot of questions I've always had growing up."

"Yeah, I suppose. That's why your father never held a job that long. If he felt that his boss was on to him and his background, he would move on ahead of time. Anytime he had to take a test of any kind for a promotion or another job, he'd always ace it. But he was continually afraid of being exposed so he kept moving. You know, through it all, John's never missed a day of work. I know he's impossible to understand, but he always wanted the best for you, and all the kids and family. He's just . . ."

I was shaking my head. "Gee, Mom, I actually feel proud of him. Just think of what he's done and how he's provided. And all this time holding in this secret. And to think I used to watch gangster movies with him. I wish I could tell him I know and what a great job he's done raising us, but I can't."

"Oh God, Jon, you can't ever tell him you know. Promise?" I nodded yes; we talked a little more about certain details, especially how his diagnosed disease of porphyria affected his mind and behavior; and Mom told me she had just gotten divorce papers and was thinking of going through with it this time. She said the recent blowout and his treatment of me was just the last straw.

"Mom, before you leave, remember that critical long letter I sent to Dad from the hospital before I got out? How did Dad take that 'cause it was really rough? Remember, I was going under slowly for surgery and really goofy."

She tipped her head a little. "He took it really hard, Jon. It was very rough on him."

When I got off work, I just spent hours driving around our immediate area, rehashing what Mom told me and my existence growing up before the Marines. It took weeks for me to recover from that news. Living at home with the tension between Mother and Father and me was a challenge to handle, more hard still, knowing Dad's secret and making it my own. Or close.

The next time My Lady came into town, I decided to tell her Dad's secret and about his porphyria, also known as the vampire's disease in Europe, with victims being King Henry VIII and Queen Elizabeth. I didn't have to, but I wanted her to know so she would have the option to pull out of the marriage.

During the several weeks of waiting for her final answer and what I thought was an engagement in limbo, I fell back into some old habits from the Marine Barracks and had several flings with hospital nurses. I also had an affair with the wife of the workaholic president of a major U.S. Corporation whom I had met while taking her to physical therapy. She was a natural blonde beauty, and I had complimented her. Apparently, I had garnished a reputation in the hospital for lifting the spirits of numerous patients. There was Mrs. Danielson who would not cooperate with any of the staff. She was all messed up, or so I thought. Then I found out she had no real diagnosed medical problems and was just a lonely widow who had a big bank account. She was a handful, but she oftentimes wouldn't let the nurses help her out of bed and into her wheelchair but only me. I then got her from the second floor to the first in record time. No one complained, especially her.

The other two of note included the mother of the hospital owner/administrator and John Berryman, one of the greatest poets of all time. I didn't know who either one was the first few times I picked them up for therapy. They were both up on the exclusive sixth floor. Mrs. Miller had a host of severe ambulatory problems and was in her eighties. She was another one who hated being there and would not cooperate with anyone about anything until she met me. From the second time and on, she had personal makeup artists and hairdo people come in and prepare her for my arrival. It was the buzz of the entire hospital. Mrs. Miller was a changed woman, all for that upstart orderly. I had no idea until many of the ward nurses and Mr. Miller, her son, told me personally. She would be all gussied up waiting for me with the private nurses at the ready; I'd come in, tell her how great she looked, smile, and make our way down to the first floor, buzzing around people and having a ball. Even the therapists remarked that Mrs. Miller had never done so well since she arrived and was getting stronger by the day.

Then one day, after wheeling quickly around and into her room to pick her up, she was not there. I noticed the bed had no blankets or pillows. The chief nurse came to me. "Jon, I'm sorry, but Mrs. Miller quietly passed away last night." I shared my condolences and told her to pass them along to Mr. Miller and left. On the way down, I had flashbacks to the First Marine Division hospital in Nam. The casualties. The mayhem. The Vietnamese woman who came apart. Then, Mrs. Miller.

Early on when I picked up John Berryman in his private suite, smoke always filled the room. He was a chain-smoker and was constantly going against the rules by smoking. He would always share his frustration with me, and we hit it off pretty well. He got the biggest bang out of me wheeling him down to therapy as if we were in a race. We both shook our heads over his smoking and my driving and laughed hard. I never knew who he was at first. Some years later, the famous poet, said by some to be as good or better than Robert Frost, jumped to his death off a bridge in Minneapolis. I knew him. I liked him. He was like a manly poetic version of Ernest Hemingway.

My Lady turned out to be rather fascinated by my admission about Dad and his past and was very understanding, so the marriage plans continued along without a hitch. She also shared with me a tragic secret of her own. Her serious boyfriend out of high school was killed in a car accident, and it put her into depression for a time. She still seemed to be affected by it. So, we both carried some emotional baggage. By the time I gave my notice at the hospital that I was leaving for sunny California, marriage, and college, I had determined that physical therapy was not something I could pursue and end up helping Vets. The course curriculum had far too much math, biology, and the sciences. Let's just say they weren't my strong suit.

I left a month and a half before my marriage and stayed with my aunt Mabel at her house in Oakland. I partied a little with her son, cousin Earl, and watched Neil Armstrong and crew land on the moon. But I was back where I nearly totaled my Vette, where Pete had left a roach in my car, where I was down five miles away at Oak Knoll Naval Hospital. It kicked off many memories and thoughts and had me just sitting in her living room moping and watching the tube. The Marine movie in my head played constantly: the good, bad, and ugly.

Prior to our Nevada wedding--with her family living in Carson City--arrangements were already being made. My Lady made her own adorable wedding dress from scratch. Her father, who had been an English teacher back in Iowa, was frugal and arranged to rent the original town hall for $20 and an old-time barber quartet for another twenty bucks. We would be married at the only church in town, Saint Mary's in the Mountains. The only real issue we had was My Lady was Catholic and I wasn't, so we couldn't have mass along with the wedding ceremonies.

This was the main reason why I had left early to spend time in Oakland before the marriage, so I could take rush Catechism lessons to become a Catholic. I took the private class from this old hard-liner, and just before I would finish, he asked me if I had any questions or concerns about the Catholic faith. I blurted out that I did. I told him that as a confirmed Lutheran, I had a hard time accepting praying through a rosary—and to the Virgin Mary—giving confessions to a mortal man, and some of the other ceremonial practices. To my amazement, this old-school priest totally understood and thanked me for my honesty and said he thought I should not convert to Catholicism. He said he would explain it to My Lady and Father Meinecke, who was to perform the ceremonies. My Lady later told me the priest had high praise for me and actually told her he thought she was lucky to have me as a husband and that I had a "spiritual spark" within me. But the faith conversion wasn't the only issue.

The other issue was my own shaky confidence and fear. The day before the wedding, I was in near total meltdown. Dad had loaded up the car with Mom and my young sisters, Janet and Joni, and drove all the way from Minnesota to Nevada. He secured a local motel for their stay, and one day, I approached him in private—not Mom, mind you, but Dad. Frankly, I was apprehensive. "Dad, I am really having second guesses about marrying My Lady. There are a few troubling things about her--and me--that scare me. I feel like I want to pack my bag and run over that hill from Carson City to Lake Tahoe and never look back. She's so beautiful and sweet, with so many great qualities, but . . . also, I don't know if I am really ready?"

He knew what happened about a week before. We were enjoying the new apartment in Mountain View, not far from the college I would be attending. My Lady had secured this one bedroom, outfitting it with a few basic furniture items. We stayed there several weeks prior to driving to Carson City. While there, we had a major blowout, and I was so upset I called my mom right in front of My Lady and told her the wedding was off. I then packed my two sea-bags and walked out. Before I got to the bottom of the steps, I heard this wailing, but I kept walking. It got louder. My heart got the best of me so I went back up to the apartment, saw My Lady through the window sitting at the kitchen table crying—screaming, really—and picked her up and hugged her, dried her eyes, and apologized. I didn't know what I was apologizing for, but I easily swallowed my pride and humbled myself. When a kid or woman, especially one I loved so much, cries to the extent she can't catch her breath, I am mush.

I quickly called Mom back and told her the wedding was on. Humiliation filled my head.

Dad again came through like a champ. He spoke softly and with great consideration and patience. He also used a little perfectly placed light humor. Basically he said I should go with my heart and do what I really thought was best for me. He said it would have to be my decision. "But, Dad, you have driven all the way out here and put out this money and took vacation time, I would feel really guilty."

"Don't, Jon, don't. I would just consider it a good vacation seeing country I never have seen before."

Chapter Forty-Two

My Lady and I were married August 18, 1969, in Virginia City, Nevada, by Father Meinecke. We were both twenty-three. Fellow stewardess Janice Walters was the bridesmaid and sisters Janet and Joni were in the ceremonies, too. After the wedding, we got in My Wife's brother's convertible and drove slowly down Main Street, which is about all that town had. The entire population, it seemed, lined the streets and celebrated our marriage. We spent our first honeymoon night at the Bucket O' Blood Hotel. Soon, we would be leaving for the Bahamas where My Wife had arranged airline passes. After a relaxing week-long honeymoon there where we divided our time between the beach and bed, we flew home, stopping in Las Vegas for a few days.

We stayed at the Sahara, where Rich Little was second banana on the headline venue. Out at the pool, every ten to fifteen minutes, the loudspeaker would come on and page Rich Little. It actually got annoying and was obviously done to keep his name in your ears and mind. I met him at the pool (friendly guy). I also met the famous Ed Sullivan (unfriendly guy), who treated me like a piece of pool furniture. We got back home to the Bay Area and were now comfortable as Mr. and Mrs. Jon Meade. My Wife was very old-fashioned and traditional so she loved being settled and married. Her grand aspiration in life was to be a good wife and be a mother, a devoted Catholic.

Five years after that, upon a visit to nearby Carson City to see her sister's family, we heard that Father Meinecke had committed suicide. We couldn't believe it. He was this bigger-than-life priest that seemed invincible. He was no-nonsense, crusty, and had conducted our wedding by the numbers, not displaying much emotion; but he was a devoted priest. We visited St. Mary's in the Mountains again and the new replacement priest brought all the way in from France in some priestly international exchange. He took us downstairs to where Meinecke's very modest quarters were, displaying a single bed, a little wooden nightstand, and dresser. The ceilings were ten feet high, and he showed us the bullet hole that remained embedded high toward the ceiling. He then explained how the Father shot himself in the head and died in that same very bed. Nothing was changed.

After looking at the bullet hole, I lay down in the bed and tried to reenact the fatal scene, my best investigative instincts coming out. I tried various different positions on the bed, and no matter what I did, I could not come to the conclusion that he would have been lying there as the police reported and just picked up the pistol on his nightstand and shot himself. I asked the French priest, who was incredibly cooperative, many questions and posed various scenarios. None even made the remotest sense. Finally, he said, "I don't believe Father Meinecke took his own life, and most of the old-timers in town don't either." He went on to explain that shortly before his death, he had been left money in a will—hundreds of thousands of dollars—and was up on Main Street sharing every detail with townspeople. He even told them he didn't believe in banks and hid the money in the old furnace ducts, in the boiler room right across from his room, which I inspected also myself.

He went on to say that when the death was reported and investigated, there was no money recovered in those ducts. The priest said that there was a wayward son of a very predominant politician, business leader in Reno, who was in Virginia City around that time and acting drunk and boisterous. It was allegedly thought by many in the know on Main Street that this known troubled individual, who also had a drug problem, was the culprit. It was thought that he shot and killed the Father, made it look like a suicide, and stole all the money. The cops and subsequent investigative team were allegedly told to back off from the whole scene by the archdiocese in Reno, making the entire matter highly suspect.

I thought I had fallen across a huge story and scandal and wanted to break it wide open, but without living there and not having resources to cover everything, it became an impossibility.

Years after, and to this day, the tour of Virginia City that includes nonstop reports of hearing Father Meinecke's footsteps above on the old creaky floor from his wooden prosthetic leg perpetuates his story. However, his name now is only associated with his influence of initiating the town's center for the arts and his proposed uncovering of the town's most famous prostitute's secret graveside from the gold rush days. Julia Buelette was as famous for her big heart and philanthropy as she was for her commercial womanly ways. Otherwise, his name and history seems to be buried with him. There is no reference whatsoever to any allegations or facts related to his death. Truly, an American and Nevada injustice, in my critical opinion.

I started school at Foothill Junior College in Los Altos Hills, an exclusive wooded area, for the fall quarter. After exams, I determined I would major in liberal arts and go for an associate of arts degree first, just in case I never went on. I thought back to my dad who firmly told me he thought that going to college was a waste of time, that I should just get a regular job. My first pick and concentration would be physical education but quickly realized that required too much science, so I switched to journalism with a minor in speech communication (speaking). During the biology class I dropped out of, I saw a human fetus in a jar of formaldehyde. I studied it more than anyone else, I'm sure. I saw life and death in that little innocent thing. My strong belief in pro-life was cemented in my mind at that time, never to waver. When life is so precious, how could it ever be denied when so many fight for its survival?

I quickly got on the campus newspaper, the *Foothill Sentinel*, and was a sports and special assignment writer. Back then, the most advanced thing we had was electric typewriters, among the predominate manuals. It was light-years before PCs and cell phones, so everything was done by dial phone or in person, the old-fashioned way.

I also took all the major English classes from James Fetler, who was a published author in the *New Yorker* and *Atlantic Monthly* magazines, among others. We talked about writing after class quite often. He gave me the ultimate compliment by telling me my stories and writing reminded him of John Steinbeck. Fetler inspired me to aim high and become a novelist but to get all the experience I could.

Nowhere in the nation was there more civil unrest and anti-war protests as in the San Francisco Bay Area. With Berkeley on the north end and San Jose State University on the south and Stanford and many others in between, it was a constant hotbed of social activism, most related to Vietnam. It set the pace for the rest of the country. The pulse of the anti-establishment and subsequent demonstrations started in California and moved all points east. All the *isms*—communism, Marxism, fascism, pacifism—entered into the consciousness of the fringe vocal college crowd and hippie movement and usually got media attention and coverage.

And here I was starting college right in the heart and heat of it. I wasn't one as a Vet to wear a utility jacket with patches on it or a hat with some slogan. And I definitely wasn't joining in with those Vets who turned into hippies and joined the movement. I just considered myself a student who was trying to put things behind me and get an education. It wasn't easy sometimes because of stand-ins, sit-downs, protests, and demonstrations; but I did my best, nearly always avoiding trouble, yet maintaining my personal integrity.

I did write a scathing article on how disruptive and troublesome the campus demonstrators were and some in the journalism department worried it would cause repercussions, but no one approached me. I did hear some rumblings from Mr. Fetler, who was obviously a left-leaning liberal, but while voicing displeasure with my topic matter, he complimented me on the delivery. It was always his English class where we had the liveliest debates and discourse.

I was nearly always alone in my defense of Vietnam, but more for the troops and Vets who went through it or were fighting it. There were two other journalism students who supported me. One was Lucy Hillestad, the wife of a wealthy businessman, and the other Jack Dickinson, who served stateside in the Air Force. We all became fast friends. In my sophomore year, Lucy, from neighboring Wisconsin and Norwegian, got me a part-time job as staff writer with her husband's nutritional manufacturing firm while Jack and I became buddies.

Meanwhile, I told off my pseudo-intellectual philosophy professor in front of the class, and he ended up giving me a D—for "dope." Good thing I got enough As in big-unit classes like English and astrology to counterbalance that. I also took a small unit credit in Operation Share where you hooked up with some local troubled kid and tried to help. But with a divorced mother who was even more troubled and their teenage babysitter who had a crush on me, I had to bail after one quarter. I also entered a speech competition in Sacramento. Believe it or not, one speech was "the legalization of pot: pro and con." The other was "hatha yoga and its benefits." It had to be an original speech written by us as well. I forgot my papers at home and had to give my presentations extemporaneously and wing it. I did manage an honorable mention, but the competition numbers were rather light.

I really wanted to participate in numerous collegiate sports, but because I didn't have enough state residency built-up, I could only participate in intramural sports. One was powerlifting, where I was heavyweight runner-up two years running, and the other was winning the shot put in track and field. I vowed to myself in honor of all fallen Vets, that I would do as much and as well as I could in college.

In my sophomore year, some students at Kent State were shot and killed by the National Guard. Certainly a totally preventable tragedy where a few knuckleheads in uniform had spastic trigger fingers. It gave me flashbacks to Vietnam and my foxhole partner. I could still feel that cold muzzle on my forehead. The Kent State fiasco pissed me off but certainly not enough to join in any demonstrations on campus. One day when the whole campus was shut down and speakers were gathered around the flagpole with many students in attendance, I was standing next to my psychology professor, Mr. Atchison, who had served in the Air Force during Korea but had become quite a campus intellectual. I told him that if anyone started to burn the flag, I was going to intervene. To my surprise, he said he would probably join me. To both of our surprise, it never happened. But there were plenty of other flag-burning issues around the Bay Area campuses, especially at UC Berkeley.

For vacation, after school dismissal in 1970, My Wife and I used passes to go to the World's Fair in Kyoto, Japan. My Wife wore her bell-bottom pants a lot, and with her good looks, most of the Japanese women there thought she was a movie star. One of the hotel gals kept gushing over her while we had our pictures taken next to the staff. It was hilarious because this one kimono-clad lady would not stop. She had this cute little giggle and flashed this innocent little-girl smile and humble-head drop, as she kept patting My Wife on her backside.

On the flight back to America, I felt I was getting these flu symptoms again, like I had intermittently since coming back from Vietnam. But this time it seemed much more severe. When we got home, I was in bed for three straight days. When school resumed, and I had another heavy bout with it, I went to the campus nurse. She had been an army nurse captain in Vietnam. After an extensive physical and write-up, she said I probably had malaria, as she worked with that a lot in-country, and explained the many different strains of it. "Did you take your malaria pills every day?" I replied *no* because I was detached from my parent unit for many months and lived in the field. She didn't want to hear it; she said I had it.

"Well, Marine, the only way to treat malaria is to properly diagnose it, but it can't be properly diagnosed unless it is isolated during an attack. And friend, the VA does not make house calls." She then told me that if I wanted to treat it—and it was treatable—I would have to find a way to get to the VA during an attack. For the remainder of my college years, I was so sick I could never make it. At first, I thought this was my fate and it would kill me. I eventually called it my 3-3-3 illness.

About every three months, for three days, and three-plus active years, I was deathly sick with it. It started with flu-like symptoms and multiplied tenfold. My Wife would tuck me in bed and pile on numerous heavy blankets. Underneath, despite feeling cold, I was profusely sweating and shivering. I got a very high fever, sometimes scary high, and got terrible headaches. I couldn't eat or even get myself to drink water. She had to feed me ice slivers. If I did visit the bathroom, I crawled. Actually, there were times when I didn't care if I died. The absolute worst thing about it was when it struck. It could be during midterms or just before a paper or worse, before or at finals. I can't recall how exactly I handled it; I just know it was hell. But to really complain about it to anyone made me feel guilty. After all, who was I to be negative about my experiences in Vietnam when others were killed or maimed? I just sucked it up and tried to be normal.

Positive things that happen always lifted my spirits. Like the day I went to Stanford University to attend Muhammad Ali's speech during his exile from the ring after he was stripped of his title. He called his presentation "the intoxication of life." He wore a conservative suit and had the Nation of Islam watch his back. The speech was actually very good about how life can lure a person into lifestyles and habits that can undermine their existence and productivity. And he was a good speaker.

The event was staged outside, and afterward, he said he would field any questions. Students and others from around the Bay Area came to the presentation, especially many blacks, particularly black journalists. I had positioned myself right up front, virtually in front of him. The podium was slightly elevated on a knoll while we were at ground level. Question after question was flung his way, and he seemed to be doing his best to ignore my flapping, raised hand. But most of the questions were lame or political or appeasing in silly ways. Every hand he called belonged to minorities, especially blacks. But I would not be denied. He finally picked me.

"Champ, what would really happen if you fought basketball giant, Wilt Chamberlain?"

Suddenly, Ali came alive and threw a few imaginary punches in the air. "Watch out now . . . TIM-BER!" He made some faces with his lips, raised both hands, and turned to the closely awaiting limousine. I had my little piece for our campus paper, and I was very happy.

When I got home, I wanted to just relax and write my little article for the paper the next day. But music was blaring from the apartment above. I went up there and knocked on the door. Mr. Tough Guy who always wore a hunting knife on his belt, usually covered by his shirt, answered. I asked him politely to please turn down his music; he said he would, and I returned home. But nothing changed. It was now louder than ever. I ran back up there, and he was practically waiting for me. He stepped forward onto the threshold of the door and exposed his knife on his hip.

"You know, usually, if someone were to talk to me the way you have, they would end up down there on the cement next to the pool."

I walked forward, nearly in his face. "Well, I'm not just someone. Why don't you try it?" There was an impasse, and he stepped back and into his apartment. I went home again. The music was gone. And he gave his notice to vacate the next week. Everyone was in disbelief because this guy seemed to be dangerous and the management already had complaints. Maybe he saw me hit the heavy bag in my carport? Or maybe he was just a bully who needed to be called out? Life is full of them.

That incident got me all fired up to try boxing again. I looked up a local fight club in Mountain View and right away had a brief tryout with one James Ortiz. We hit it off immediately. I told him of my brief boxing past and said I was serious now and wanted to get a manager and train first for the Golden Gloves and then go on. He said he was a pro and fought as a welterweight. He liked that I was in school and had a brain and could talk well. Even more, he loved that

I was a heavyweight. He looked me over like a slab of beef. "Got the build, kid, maybe we can make you the next Great White Hope?" We laughed, especially me.

I trained a little, but with school and malaria, it was very limited. I did virtually no cardio. One day, Ortiz approached me and said he had a big tryout for me at Babe Griffin's Boxing Club in downtown San Jose, just outside of the university campus I would soon be attending. This gym was old-school and famous around the country as was Griffin, who had also been a top pro in his day. Since I already had my boxing license, the stage was set. When we got into the locker room, there was this Mexican heavyweight working the over-and-under bag. He looked tough and in great shape. He manhandled that beanbag, as we sometimes called it. I thought I wasn't even in one-eighth the shape he was. That was my opponent!

"You said you were serious, Jon, so you need to be tested." I wondered if I was being set up to be his punching bag. The thought made me mad so I put the trunks on, was wrapped, and had the gloves tied up. There would be no headgear. I didn't question it. I was ready. And crazy.

Ortiz said it was just a small trial and would last no more than two rounds. Despite not being in shape whatsoever, I thought because of my past in Minneapolis as a kid and never been hit or losing, I would use my power and bang out a quick victory. And fairies would be soon dancing in my head as he boxed me around silly—at will—and I had no idea where I was; I was out on my feet, seeing stars and galaxies and all the cosmos. But I didn't go down.

During the minute rest, Ortiz said he had never seen a first round like that in his life. I had *no* idea what he was talking about. But I was shaking away the cobwebs. In a second, he probably got arm weary and I landed some big shots and sent him through the bottom ropes. We just stopped the fight then. It looked like his nose on both sides had separated from his face. Later, in the locker room, James told me the guy I just beat was the favorite for that year's Heavyweight Golden Gloves in San Francisco. Before we left, Griffin called Ortiz into his office. He came out with a big grin on his face.

"They asked me if you would be willing to fight George Foreman in an upcoming boxing exhibition. They need a good man to lace 'em up with Big George."

I couldn't believe what I just heard. Maybe my brain was still floating around in my skull, and I had not recovered yet.

"Jim, you mean the same George Foreman who won the Gold Medal at the Olympics and hasn't lost a fight as a pro and is the number-one contender?"

Still wearing a grin, "Yeah, Jon, that George."

Boxing in those days still did the old-fashioned boxing exhibitions, where the top contender would tour the country showing off his skills against a local boy. They wanted to showcase the contender and to a much lesser extent, the local stiff, yet not take it too seriously.

Again, being thrust into challenges with no preparation, my ego and pride drove me, so I said, "Yes."

I just hoped I wouldn't be called when I was in a bout with malaria.

When I returned home, My Wife was there. She let out a scream when she saw me. She asked me what happened because my face was all black-and-blue. I saw it in the mirror, and I had many bruises all over from my forehead to my chin. They just took a while to darken. I had never been tagged like that, ever, so I was pretty shocked. I told My Wife the story, and she laid me down and put ice packs on my face and lovingly nursed me. There was no swelling or cuts, just bruises. I had to skip the next day of school and then had the weekend to recover. Monday, I still had to wear sunglasses, but my face was still covered. I was the bad boy on campus for the next few days.

Chapter Forty-Three

Months passed and while I hadn't had much time to train, I felt better prepared for another fight. At least I thought I'd be able to walk in and out of the ring under my own feet. Ortiz finally informed me that George's exhibition fight for San Jose had been diverted elsewhere and was called off.

It was a good thing George didn't show up. Good thing. I would have had to sue him for attempted manslaughter.

Gary flew out on a pass as he was a jet mechanic for a regional carrier and visited us from Minnesota. He was still going through a divorce and reeling from it. We got him a date with our pretty Jewish neighbor who worked for Stanford, but they ended up getting in a big argument over Vietnam, as Millie was a flaming liberal and Gary wasn't. Gary and I topped off his trip by going to San Francisco, seeing the hit movie *Mash*, visiting a few watering holes and getting skunked.

I continued my training with Ortiz. He told me the Mountain View Police Department expressed an interest in sponsoring me in the Golden Gloves when I was ready. I have no idea why or how that happened. But someone through the grapevine told me they thought Ortiz was training me wrong. I was shocked. Why? They said he was training me more like a smaller fighter, like in his old weight class, not like a heavyweight, and was focusing too much on the Mexican style of hooking. Since my strong suit was my long arms—77.5 inch reach—and my straight left jab and right cross, they thought it was a big mistake. Left hooks weren't my forte, true, but I simply couldn't bring it up to James at that point as I liked him too much.

One night when studying for an exam, I needed to rush to the campus library and do some research.

As I was going on this side street, this car ahead of me was driving all over the place, so I went to pass him and rolled down my window and said he was going to cause an accident. He pulled up next to me while we stopped at a busy intersection at El Camino. He was yelling at me, so I looked over and saw him and three other guys in the car. He was a rough-looking Mexican and was telling me to mind my own business and some other choice things. I rolled my window up and locked my door as he got out of his car like a madman and ran over to mine, pounding on the window. It was the longest red light in the history of slow red lights.

Soon, he was kicking my door—hard. And that did it. I scooted over to the passenger side, opened the door and got out. He quickly pulled my windbreaker over my head and bent me over. He had every advantage over me. I reached up and threw a right hook, hitting him squarely on the side of the head, and he went down. I got him in a full nelson and was going to ram his face into the asphalt, but I stopped. I looked over to his car as his buddies left him and drove away. Real tough guys. I got back in my car and drove through the light and noticed that his car was parked across the street, waiting at this closed gas station. Being upset now that he jumped me and ripped my jacket, I pulled in across from them on the other side. Talk about stupid. Revenge drives a lot of empty results.

My nemesis was now walking toward me so I got out of my car. His three buddies were also coming at me from the sides. With street thugs, you have to become one. I did. I pointed to both sides and yelled for them to stop or else. They froze, cowards they had already proven themselves to be. Then my attacker walked up to me within twenty feet, and I told him to stop. He pointed to his eye and said he wanted revenge. His eye was totally closed and swollen with a huge mouse, blue and bleeding, on the side. I told him I spared him the worst by hitting him on the side of the head and made a disgusted mocking sound. "And you want revenge? I won't hold back next time."

Just then, a cop car pulled in, gave a quick siren and light, and from a loudspeaker told us to disperse and leave. It was the Mountain View Police, and I was fairly certain they did not recognize me.

But it made no difference as I hurt my thumb quite badly— hairline fracture—and my doctor wrapped my hand and thumb for nearly a month. My boxing ambitions were thwarted, or at least put on the back burner.

After getting my AA from junior college—my final paper for Fetler's English IB class was "Why a Bunker?"—he gave me an A plus, and I was elated. I started my junior year at San Jose State University. I took a 3.1 GPA into the university and continued journalism school at SJSU, one of the top schools in the nation. I was assigned the sports, features, and general assignment posts on the *Spartan Daily*. I added the military beat to my duties and covered the ROTC on campus and a front-page feature on the first female cadet in the country to graduate ROTC. In the body of the piece and in her quote, she said that she "didn't feel any different than any other male cadet." Part of that was also in the headline.

Herb Caen, the longtime revered *San Francisco Chronicle* columnist, picked up on this from one of his Bay Area stringers and featured me and my story in his extremely popular column, giving me an entire graph, some in bold. He actually chided me a little, relating my headline to some recent figures about male and female cadets, and ended his remarks by saying, "Well, Meade?" I had no problem with it and was honored to make his column, but as a newspaperman, he knew full well that a reporter's article would always go to the headline desk, where another journalist would write the headline. In other words, the headline was not mine; it was condensed from my article by another.

While I got accolades from friends and acquaintances as far away as Minnesota and Nevada, I received the cold shoulder from the newspaper staff for the most part. I had never murmured a word of Caen's piece to anyone, but it was obvious as Caen was considered as the journalism god of California. The jealousy was evident, especially from the class elites, but more so I think because of all the large articles I had published about the military. The antiwar sentiment was very much alive and thriving. I was the only student even remotely taking a stand in their defense, yet I was just doing my job objectively covering my beats.

The only exceptions were my buddy Jack Dickinson and fellow journalist Laura Dayton, who had become a friend and someone I confided in and had many laughs with. Many years later, Laura would become a huge success with her own publishing company and books, a player in the fitness industry, not to mention being instrumental in the burgeoning women's gym arena.

In my first semester at San Jose, I had my first fitness/ bodybuilding magazine article published about a local businessman, James Pollock, who was also the world light heavyweight wrist wrestling champion, as seen on ABC's *Wide World of Sports* held annually in Petaluma, California. This would be the first in my series spanning the next eight years. One of those years, my grandmother Hilda was showing my magazine article in *Muscular Development* around to her friends. There were a lot of bodybuilders within the pages, and I heard many gasps and sighs. But when she mistakenly called the magazine *Muscular Dystrophy* and I corrected her when everyone picked up on it, I started laughing uncontrollably, soon being joined by others. Her "mistake" probably made more sense as a title for all those humongous bodies than *Muscular Development*. Perception lies in the eyes of the beholder.

A Hispanic Vietnam Marine Veteran, appreciated my work on the campus paper, and got me a VA grant doing public relations for Veterans needing benefit help, where I did this primarily during my junior year. I also took literature and creative writing classes. Besides my duties as campus journalist, I also followed Ernest Hemingway, John Steinbeck, James Joyce, and all the famous authors, thinking that I too wanted to be an author. I had notebooks filled with book ideas, outlines, and characters, all fiction. I had over twenty-five briefs on many topics, but always with strong characters, plots, and with a common theme of fight over flight, intricate pathos, underdogs, intertwined humor with sorrow, never-say-die, and positive ends. To that end, I earnestly started my first novel, which I titled, *U-S-M-C*, with the subtitle *Uncle Sam's Misguided Children*. It was a tale of a Marine in Vietnam based on a *little* of my own service.

Just as finals were upon me, Grandma Meade died at eighty-six. I could not attend her funeral because of my college obligations. What that woman went through in her life with Claude's murder during the Depression, left with three strapping boys, Dad included, could only be recalled superficially. I felt bad I couldn't talk to her about it all when she was alive and give her my respects. I'll always remember "Kool-Aid" Mabel for her incredible giving (she loved to feed the "bums" on skid row), her cooking, and her infectious smile.

When I entered my senior year, we bought our first house in the upscale neighborhood of Los Altos. Despite My Wife having a good job with the airlines, they would only consider me and my income to qualify. Even though I had one-third of the house's value saved in the bank from us working and the GI Bill, I still had to have Don Hillestad, my boss at Hilcoa, come in to give the bank a nod of support. He knew the banker anyway, and I got the loan of $27,500 on a house worth $31,500. Our lady realtor was a real crackerjack and tried to convince me to buy another house for the same amount by leveraging collateral from the first house. Two mistakes were then made. The first was listening to my mom freak out that we even bought a house for us. The second was not taking Georgie's advice. My Wife also thought it was a good idea. Within twenty-two years, that one move would have made us millionaires. Eventually, that house we bought, with a small addition, sold for over 1.2 million dollars. Double that for two. But what-ifs don't count in life. They are regretful afterthoughts.

We became very close with the Hillestads as I was helping with my writing introduce sports nutrition and supplementation into pro teams, including the San Francisco 49ers' locker room. The company made superior-quality cutting-edge nutritional and protein bulking and recovery powders. Niners quarterback John Brodie and lineman Charlie Krueger endorsed the line. Charlie's hands were like sides of beef ribs that were run over by a Mack Truck. Shaking his hand was an unforgettable experience as arthritis set in and his massive fingers were bent up in every position. He would end up as the first NFLer to sue the league for bodily damages. Just imagine playing fifteen seasons without missing a game. Talk about old-school and tough. They don't make men like that Charlie anymore.

One time, the whole Hillestad family and My Wife and I went to Yosemite for the weekend. First class all the way with shrimp and steaks. When we returned to the Hillestads' mansion in Los Altos Hills, it was 4:00 a.m. and Don was walking ahead of me down their massive hallway. As we passed the chandelier, I noticed that several of the bulbs were burned out. "Well, I guess you got a few lights you'll have to change out soon."

Don turned around. "No, Jon, when bulbs go out, you don't wait. You change them right away." He got a ladder from the garage, hauled it inside, and changed out both bulbs as I held the ladder. That lesson coming from a successful and wealthy man took some time to totally sink in, but when it did, I always thought back to it. When something needs to be done, why wait? Do it right away while it is on your mind and available to do. You never know when and if you will have the same chance again. That was the basic thinking Don was conveying. And he made these points while looking directly in my eyes. I saw no exceptions, hesitations, or doubts. He followed that with the strong suggestion that he was grooming me for a vice president's role down the road. It was like a huge hint of what he expected.

One day, upon a visit to the company from Lucy, she visited my office and I was telling her that I was acting as a guinea pig of sorts for the sports line, especially the protein gainers. I said I had gained about eight pounds in the past few weeks, but most was muscle since I also worked out at the Palo Alto Health Club right across the way from Stanford. I then said I didn't want to get any bigger and would turn right around and peel off the little fat I gained. She made some unusual comment about Don being big and asking me if he carried too much fat. I've always been one of these "tell-it-like-it-is" people, especially since the Marines; so I told her I did think Don, about sixteen years my elder, could "probably lose some fat and weight." She then stormed away.

The next day, Don called me in his office and said he understood that me and Lucy got into a little spat. He related that Lucy told him I thought he was fat. I told him exactly what was said, and he quickly excused his wife's behavior by saying it was that time of the month. He followed that by saying how highly Lucy thought of me and really his whole family. We shook hands and I assumed that was the end of it, but for the next few months, My Wife and I had nothing to do on a personal level with the Hillestads. And that carried over to my writing position, where I had earned my college journalism internship and was forever grateful. For my final senior semester, I couldn't juggle my company staff writing position as much as they needed with my school paper position, so I transferred down to the shipping department, where I stayed until college graduation.

I was still toying with the boxing dreams, but they slowly faded away. There were too many obstacles, and I didn't have enough hunger anymore. I did take solace in the fact that Ortiz told me he ran into the manager of the guy I fought that day in San Jose and he told him his fighter not only didn't go on to the Golden Gloves that year, but never fought again. James said I really made an impact and could have gone on much bigger things, but it just wasn't in the cards. Part of me always regretted it, but things in your life usually boil down to priorities. I was a little older than most, after the Marines and college, and did not have that burning desire anymore. Maybe too many things still played in my mind, and the malaria certainly didn't help; but without your heart being totally into something as grueling as boxing and with my fighting style being balls-to-the-walls, do-or-die, I decided against it. I never did like the look of a pug with eye scars and a smashed-in nose, anyway.

Chapter Forty-Four

The most significant lesson I learned in journalism school was how different and unique the profession was compared to most of the world, especially communist countries. In my journalism history class, the professor showed us examples of *Pravda*, the state newspaper of Russia. We went over all the articles and news and were told that the communist paper was the perfect example and direct opposite of America's free press, as opposed to Russia's controlled government-run press. The other huge example was pointing out that America's journalism was primarily—from the straight-news perspective—objective, unbiased, compared to Russia's that was subjective and biased.

Russia's paper was nothing but state-controlled propaganda while the *San Jose Mercury* and *San Francisco Chronicle*, which we studied, were examples of freedom of the press, covering all areas of life. The differences were not only obvious and striking but also reflected to me the freedom and liberty that was America, including all of her endless possibilities and opportunities. The bottom line: capitalism versus communism in all its comparative venues. I was happy and proud to know and understand the difference and totally embraced its underlying principles. Even though they were utilizing the university in journalism, I don't know if my exact sentiments were shared by all, based on some of the faces and murmurs—nothing extreme but subtle.

To me, I was of the persuasion that the press—more than any other American entity—best reflected the society and culture of the United States, as it would in other cultures and countries with their press.

In my law and journalism class, we were required to cover court cases around the Bay Area. Since I couldn't secure any dates in San Jose, I went to Berkeley where there was an abundance. The one I picked, solely on my available time, turned out to be a trial so bizarre in freakish nature, I cannot repeat it. It involved male prostitution and a revered judge or politician. The facts presented to the jury were so difficult to comprehend and listen to that we were all cringing and gasping in our seats. There wasn't any drugs involved or anything, just sick, demented behavior. I couldn't wait to get out of that courtroom, along with everyone else. What was even more incredible to see and understand was the fact that some of those jurors never flinched or displayed any response when hearing the case. I wonder if that said something about Berkeley's citizenry at the time.

When we handed in our paper, we had to also bring in a newspaper report of the case—if there was one—and compare it to our own, with ours having a whole new slant to the story. This was in addition to proof that we were in court that day. The news story in the Berkeley paper was greatly watered-down, not revealing most of the sordid details. My account, however, while being very blunt and revealing, was much more colorful and descriptive.

After shocking the class with most but not all the facts, the professor went over legalities and truth in journalism and to what extent a reporter would detail the news. He used my story and approach as an example of a journalist who took risks and pushed the envelope. The defense to libel, we learned, was the truth. While not saying so, and being rather shocked himself, he seemed to support me, and it showed in my final grade.

I was not so fortunate with another journalism professor. He was one of those holier-than-thou lions of highfalutin academia and always showed favoritism to this small group of self-proclaimed elite members of our class and paper. Most were females, and everything they ever wanted to cover was dealing with racism, male dominance and alleged chauvinism, counterculture, women's rights and antiwar and establishment. Certainly there were some valid slants within that subject area, but not to the all-consuming extent they thought it should be carried, which was virtually always.

One day when we were to give the class our final verbal presentation on public relations and the press, a couple of these class elites gave excuses why they couldn't give theirs. These same whiners who got out of so many assignments and requirements because of urgent deadlines (we all had deadlines!) asked for extensions—and got them. I had it. When I gave my preso, I also brought up how wrong it was in any environment to show favoritism or cronyism. I insisted that most everyone was required to meet certain criteria and make deadlines, but a select few. When I got to the podium, I slammed my fist on the top, demanded quiet, and gave my speech. It was stone-cold quiet, but eyes were drilled through me, especially the preppy professor. Afterward, I took the argument outside the classroom and into his office. He gave me a "D." Nothing in my assignments or tests reflected that grade.

Meanwhile, back in Minnesota, Gary was requesting me to attend a final divorce court date and be a character witness (where did I hear that request before?). I absolutely could not make it as it conflicted with my upcoming finals and graduation, so I asked and arranged for my mom to fill in for me. Apparently, Mom did a good job as it helped Gary's case and its complications and results. Right on the heels of that came a request from Mom to come and stay with us, as she was leaving Dad again and this time wanted to get far away and start a new life. We agreed and she was soon living with us and in no time got an assembly job in Palo Alto. She shared with us the recent story about our family doctor, finally convincing Dad to go get tests for porphyria so he could be treated properly.

They sent him down to the Mayo Clinic in Rochester to be tested by the world expert on porphyria, Dr. Watson (no relation to Sherlock Holmes). His stay and everything related to porphyria was free as they wanted to use Dad as a test subject. Well, apparently he didn't like being experimented on and stuck with a lot of needles, so one day he just ripped them all out and left. The nurses told him he couldn't leave, but he told them, "Watch me, I'm not going to be some guinea pig." That was the end of that, but just the beginning of extreme discourse between my folks. Dad was back to being Dad.

Mom's tenure with us became very inconvenient for her, us, and her job; and within several months, she was back in Minnesota. They made up, at least as much as they could, and life for them resumed.

Just before graduation, I had a sit-down with the dean of journalism school. I complained of this unfair professor and said I challenged my grade of D and I could prove it. I also shared the special perks he gave to a small segment of the class. He agreed with me but said that since I was already published and doing so well as a writer, why rock the boat at this late date, that it could delay my graduation. So I relented and received my BA in journalism, reporting, and editing in the fall of 1973. In the last week of school, our department had various newspaper reps from around the state come in to interview us for newspaper jobs. I had two to three offers, but none were local, which would mean we would have to sell our house and move, possibly jeopardizing My Wife's flying career. The pay for a beginning reporter was also pathetic.

Just when I was ready to give up on a position with a newspaper, there came some openings across town on the *San Jose Mercury*. I brought all my writing samples plus my résumé. My interview was with the editor of the paper. His office was a working mess, and over in the corner was a four-foot-high stack of papers. We shook hands, I sat down, and he immediately started going over my materials. Suddenly, he stopped, put everything down, and said, "Impressive, very impressive." I thought the job was mine. Then he pointed to the stack of papers in the corner.

"See that stack of résumés there?"

"Oh, they are résumés, huh?" I replied.

"Résumés and cover letters, yes. Your stuff is going to go on the very bottom. I don't want to take the risk of a Vietnam Veteran going crazy on me and shooting up the place. I just won't have it."

"Me?" I said. "I don't even own a gun. Besides, I would never do something like that." There was a long pause. "I might punch someone out, but that's about it."

"I think you better leave the premises."

I scooped up my papers and left. I wasn't about to give him the pleasure of putting my stuff at the bottom of his pile of prejudice. His words and manner made me feel like I wasn't even worthy of being human. The only regret I had was stubbornly clinging to the notion of putting my military service on my résumé, along with *Vietnam* in parentheses. Preceding that was "Military: Enlisted United States Marine Corps, four years." Despite it being one of the hardest things I had ever done, I dropped the military reference and never used it again. It was like I had to deny a part of me that I was proud of, a part of my existence that I had to virtually strike from my life. The status of all Veterans flashed before me. I thought that in order to land a job in my own country, the very country I served, I had to erase that portion of my life. It was hard to fight the urge not to be bitter. Very bitter. It accentuated my thoughts.

An acquaintance offered me a job as a bartender at his little restaurant, "the Station House Brochette," housed in old train cars close to home. That was just not me, so I soon left.

My buddy Jack, however, landed a sports editorship at a small paper in Woodland Hills, California. His position was even over before my bartender job. Seems Jack was at a local party and the party was busted by the police for drugs. Poor Jack was just at the wrong place at the wrong time, made his own paper's front-page news as sports editor being busted, and was quickly released. We both ended up in different fields, Jack going his way and me landing a position under a federal grant at Saratoga Community College as communications specialist. I was assigned a post with career education, ending up spearheading public relations and communications with International Work Experience. The director of career education was another Vet, Clyde Reyes, a highly decorated Army Vietnam Vet. Clyde was a great leader, very articulate, and he always got a kick out of my "fearless frankness," as he called it. I was able to accomplish some noteworthy milestones with the IWE program, receiving many accolades, but if Clyde would not have given me room and freedom to be creative and myself, it would have never been possible. He always had my back, and me his.

Chapter Forty-Five

During my tenure at Saratoga, My Wife and I had our first formal split. We agreed to live apart, with me staying in our house closer to my job, and her getting an apartment halfway to the airport. It only lasted two and a half months, but since we agreed to live as though we were both single, I took advantage of the situation. Since I had so many contacts through International Work Experience, I had outside flings with French, German, Swedish, Chilean, Spanish, and Arab women, not to mention the campus librarian and a school administrator. I guess you could say I was like a serial romanticist.

I could have personally renamed the program International Sex Experience Plus. I also had liaisons with an ABC executive's wife I had met while doing my magazine article in Petaluma and a competitor's wife. I think I fell back into my lifestyle while at Marine Barracks with a vengeance. Funny, but during that time, I had many flashbacks to Vietnam and burials. It was like a feeding frenzy of sex mixed with remorse, guilt, sorrow, and pain. Not a proud time, for sure. My Wife was more honorable than me, choosing not to even date.

It was at this same time that Billie Jean King started her new highly publicized magazine, *Women's Sports*, following her victory over tennis hustler Bobby Riggs. She established offices for the launch in San Mateo, on the way to San Francisco. I knew that the first annual women's national wrist wrestling championships were coming up in Las Vegas, so I pitched the new editor on covering it. I used my two-year experience covering the Petaluma event on ABC's *Wide World* as my credentials. She agreed, paid me up front for expenses and initial work, and I soon went to the 1974 event. Supposedly, I was the first male to be given an assignment by the predominantly female magazine. After I checked into my hotel room at the MGM Grand, I spent hours trying to find Marilyn Marx, the showgirl that befriended me years before. I made phone calls, visited the Sands, Frontier, and Tropicana, but had no luck. My intention was to surprise her and treat her to a nice dinner, rehashing my stop in Vegas as a Marine and our time together. It was as if she disappeared. It was a major disappointment.

But I had an assignment to do and got busy drumming up character copy, finding the most colorful ones I could find. That day, the *Las Vegas Sun* came out with an article about a competitor challenging Bobby Riggs to a wrist-wrestling match, calling him a "chicken liver." Riggs was a chill for the Tropicana, enticing high rollers to come in and drop their wads on the baccarat table. He responded in kind to the woman's challenge, but apparently didn't show up or something. Through my persistence, I was able to get a personal interview with Riggs about the whole challenge thing, knowing it would make great copy, especially following his previous loss to Billie Jean. He was a trip to talk to, rattling off more quotes and information than I could ever use. His demeanor and delivery was like a machine gun. I got it, put it in the can as they say, and was off to add to my character pool.

I thought it would be a good idea to follow one of the competitors, so I picked the lady who came from a woman's Ivy League school on the East Coast. She was said to be undefeated and had also never lost to a man. She came off pretty hard, but the promoter's wife highly recommended her so I agreed. I walked around the MGM Grand with her and basically interviewed her, assuming she would be the one who would live up to her hype and win the event in her middleweight class. As the day progressed, we had an early dinner together and a few drinks, which she said she seldom ever did. She was a champion rower in college and very competitive, but she was getting nervous and wanted to relax. She knew that I had trained with world champion James Pollock sometimes, so she wanted to go to her room and practice with me. She said she wanted me to give her no quarter.

We got down on the floor and turned wrists. She was tough, but I beat her every time. She couldn't believe it because she said I was the first guy to ever beat her. I wasn't proud though and felt her confidence wane. I felt bad and wished I could have taken those victories back. Suddenly, her sweet, feminine side emerged, and we were kissing and carried it over to the bed, where I ended up staying most of the night. Before I left very early that next morning, I gave her as many tips as I could, bolstered up her confidence, and wished her luck. I also told her during and after the event I couldn't be lovey-dovey because it might show favoritism and apologized ahead of time. What an ass I was.

Besides the buzz in town about the Riggs challenge that never came to fruition, there was a showgirl who was signed up to compete. What made her unique was her breasts that measured seventy-four inches. I was given a press photo of her, and she had a movie star face to go along with her boobs that hung to her knees. Reports had it that she had a growth mutation as a teen, and it was concentrated in her breasts.

Appropriately, her stage name was Chesty. No one knew if this was just a publicity gimmick or the real deal. The woman's event, sandwiched in between all the men's classes, was the main marquee and received national press, along with emphasis from ABC's *Wide World of Sports* and emcee, football great Frank Gifford.

Two big things resulted from the women's event. Number one: Chesty couldn't compete because her boobs were so big; she couldn't get them out of the way to put her elbows in the table cups to wrist-wrestle. Even though they got tons of footage, ABC decided not to use it as it was practically obscene. Number two: The big favorite to steal the woman's middleweight event—the lady I wrestled with both on the floor and in bed—lost the championship and came in runner-up. She seemed to have lost her hardened edge and wasn't the same Hellcat I had first met and was rumored to be. I felt so bad from the night before. I personally shouldered the blame, but no one knew. I left Vegas with an incredible story, and after panicking because I couldn't find the photographer *Women's Sports* assigned, I was finally assured he was there and secured many photos.

Back in the Bay Area, I took a week to finalize the article, making it a long text-intense exposé, much like *Sports Illustrated* did. The editor was excited for all the copy and colorful coverage. They also had great accompanying photos. But it didn't make that first premier issue with Billie Jean on the cover. The only thing that survived was a little blurb and a great quote I came up with, partially given to me by a competitor: "Behind every curve in a woman, there is a muscle." I subsequently found out that there was an internal editorial shake-up and that the editor and her staff were released, replaced by new blood. They shelved everything she had in the hamper, no matter what the circumstances.

Ironically, a few years later covering the wrist championships again in Petaluma, Billie Jean King was the ABC commentator. I introduced myself and educated her on some of the sport's history while mentioning my gig with her magazine in Vegas and what happened. She seemed totally oblivious to the entire event, but admitted the shake-up they had. Billie Jean was both incredibly warm and friendly, and cold and indifferent. Her thermostat went on and off very quickly.

Chapter Forty-Six

Just as I was getting back together with My Wife, the opportunity of a lifetime materialized within my grasp. It was a job opening right there at the campus for chief information officer. Because of Clyde's influence, my direct involvement with existing program journalism and PR and positive accomplishments, I thought I was a shoe-in for the job. Clyde told me there were hundreds of applicants already but thought my chances were high. After weeks of résumés and interviews and out of a record 450 applicants, I made the final three.

I assumed it was a foregone conclusion. It was between me and two other females, one working under the same federal grant as me. Soon, I was told it was down to two, me and some anonymous lady. The next day, I was called into the communication director's office. I was so glad to be going in there to get my congratulations for the position. I felt elevated to be able to get out from under the temporary federal grant and into a permanent campus position.

As soon as I entered his office, he closed the door behind me and wasn't wearing the kind of congratulatory face I would have expected. "I'm very sorry, Jon, but you didn't get the position. It went to the other candidate."

I sat there in shock. How could this be? I was upset and started picking the director's brain, trying to maintain my decorum and temper. He told me he had to be honest with me, that I deserved the truth and the lady they hired over me wasn't nearly as qualified as I was. She hadn't worked in over five years, had never published anything, and had no knowledge or experience in the programs and specialties of the college. She was also much older being closer to retirement age. So what could it be, I asked?

"Jon, I would have to deny all this if it ever left the room, but we had to hire her over you because of minority quotas handed down from the state to hire more females in professional positions within the community college system. My hands were tied. I realize how you must feel, but I had no choice."

"Okay, but how about the extra points as a Veteran I get according to federal law? That's five whole points, surely that would bring me up even higher? What good is getting five extra hiring points as a Veteran if the system doesn't recognize or honor it?"

"I know, I know, I gave you those points, but still couldn't give you the job. Her priority trumps over yours. As a white man myself, and one who feels that the best candidate no matter who they are should always get the job, I am sorry. If I could change the system, I would, but I can't. This is like a carefully crafted and quietly executed directive. It is more hidden than it is disclosed."

I continued my disbelief and questions, often repeating myself, but I could see I exasperated all avenues of fight. Since when did one alleged injustice deserve another? I left seething inside. I went back to Clyde and expressed my frustrations and sorrow. He understood and cut me loose early from work. I went to a restaurant close to home and quietly got drunk. I ate Mexican and washed it down with beers and tequila, staying out until the place closed.

I sulked in my beers and felt I didn't belong, like an alien of society, culture, and life. Then I thought maybe I denied my destiny of dying in Vietnam. Maybe I was supposed to be among the ranks of all those poor souls who were killed. But it wasn't my fault; I tried everything to get deeper in the shit, but my "luck" wouldn't allow it. I was very confused. Why would I have this "luck" in Vietnam and the Marines, only to come away from it all as a survivor, do all the apple pie things as a perfect citizen, only to be denied a job in my field of study, education, and abilities? It made no sense. I thought, why did I get out of the Marines? I should have stayed in and went back to Nam. I was perplexed and sad.

What did I do wrong? I served honorably, got married to a wonderful woman, went to college, never got into any trouble, worked hard, accomplished some unique things, and just wanted to start a family. I always thought I could fight hard and win in most situations, but in this one, it was like fighting an invisible foe.

The foe was an unjust system and a life that seemed to circumvent my best efforts. The term may have not been born yet, but *political correctness* was anchored solidly in the times and was the driving force behind much of America's burgeoning liberal mind-set, particularly mainstream academia, government, and certain factions of corporate America. But push comes to shove, as a nation, especially in dire circumstances, we *generally* still had the unity and commonality of all being Americans despite politics and there being societal discourse. The manifestation of change had a foothold and was digging in for the long term. But when it came to jobs and being a white man, I was on the shit end of the stick. And it stunk! Being a Veteran was like a cruel act of futility. To me, the point system to help give Veterans the benefit of the doubt was like the points in a rigged poker game.

During this frustrated time, my nightmare with Marines Minor and Jolly returned often. They got shot in the foxholes, but the enemy let me be unhurt, like I wasn't good enough and qualified to die with them as a Marine. My *luck* kept me out of harm's way and alive in Vietnam, yet *luck* failed me as a civilian just trying to get a job and be productive.

Sometime later, our staff was constantly complaining of these double doors jamming in our old house on campus. A few maintenance workers tried their hand at fixing it, but it was given zero priority and remained a problem. The primary problem was the big thick post that was slightly warped and divided and held the doors in place. One day, frustrated by the lack of results, I yelled out to Clyde and the staff that I would fix it, once and for all. I took a running leap, went high in the air with my leading right foot, and performed a perfect dropkick upon the top of the post, knocking it completely off and away. There was a lot of anger and disappointment in that kick. I then took a hard fall on my side on the wood floor, but wasn't really hurt, just bruised a little. It didn't bother me. I felt damn good.

The job was done, but my reputation, for whatever that was worth, took a hit when some visiting ladies to our center didn't take kindly to my "roughhouse shenanigans" and reported the incident to the college president. Clyde was called in on the carpet, with him in turn discussing the action with me, for protocol's sake. He couldn't stop laughing, said he was formally reprimanding me, and quickly dropped the issue. Clyde would never totally discuss his Vietnam experiences with me, but I could see, feel, and understand why Clyde would have been a hero. He had that something within him: heart!

In 1976, we planned a European excursion throughout the Scandinavian countries, including my grandmother's Norwegian roots in Bergen, Norway. We also hit Germany, Italy, Greece, and Switzerland. The two things that stood out were having a German lady lift her skirt and show us her scars from World War II and the

"American bombers" (I, of course, defended America and told her we were the saviors of Europe) and a six-hour hike from Zermatt all the way up to the first and last major plateau to the Matterhorn in Switzerland. My Wife showed no signs of quit and was a first-class trooper all the way. We had to brave an incoming snowstorm on the way down, and it was a bit hairy. Our feet were covered in blisters as we did it with no special shoes or gear. I made an 8mm movie with my new Bolex camera, and the jaunt gave us a tremendous sense of personal accomplishment. At the plateau, we had a cup of soup at the cabin and sat on the thick rock fence, staring at the magnificent Matterhorn.

Its incredible size stretched into the heavens. I immediately thought of all those Marines and other GIs killed in Vietnam and all the world wars and Korea. I said a silent prayer and dedicated the hike in their honor.

Since we had flown into Rome to start our tour, that was where we wrapped things up. I was determined to find a statue of Hercules sitting in repose after battle that I had seen so often in art history books. But I could only find cheap composite replicas so we went to Florence and I searched everywhere, coming up empty. The composite ones, mainly made for tourists, were made from marble dust and other elements compacted together. The details of Hercules were greatly muddled and not close to the quality I was looking for.

This one older shopkeeper told me that the originals that were genuine pieces of art and in real Carrara marble used by Michelangelo were out there but in very short supply, nearly impossible to find. He said the key was to be able to clearly see the finely crafted facial features and the entire bodily form. He added to make sure to look for any seams, especially dividing the piece in half. Those would be the phonies, even if they had finer artwork. It must be one solid piece. He told me not to worry because if I found one, the quality of the pure marble and incredible details would jump out at me like Pinocchio's nose.

I finally found one in the back of this very old shop as I was walking out and giving up. Funny how that works. It was a one-foot-high masterpiece sitting on a small slab of shiny granite. The shopkeeper told me I could have it for only $26 since I was an American and had looked so hard for the "Hercules of original quality," as he called it. It was three times the cost of the fakes, but priceless in my book, undoubtedly worth far more. Along with *Hercules* that he expertly packed for me and would ship home, I previously had a two-foot-high Greek vase, specially made for us depicting Greek mythology, shipped home. We wrapped our trip with vino, bread, and cheese in Rome to a perfect ending.

As it was getting closer to the time we wanted to start a family, we both wanted a more rural place to hang our hats and raise children, so we decided to sell our house and move to Colorado, where we had purchased two and a half acres on the edge of a mountain overlooking beautiful Mount Evans, outside the city limits of Evergreen, thirty minutes north of Denver. We had just paid off the final payment on a purchase price of $13,500, which was a pretty good chunk for barren land back then. We quickly sold the house, with me doing everything without a realtor, and more than doubled our investment. I gave my notice to Clyde—several months shy of the federal grant ending, anyway—of leaving, and the department gave me a big lunch and cake.

I sold my second beater car and my rare all-chrome 305cc Honda motorcycle (what a mistake) and recruited Jack and another friend to help us empty the house and pack the furnishings in a twenty-seven-foot U-Haul. I actually drove our Volkswagen Bug up into the cargo area of the truck and packed all our basic furniture around it. Crazy, but it worked. Just before this, My Wife informed me she was pregnant. I wondered in what foreign country did the conception occur. It wasn't necessarily planned at this exact time, but I was very happy to hear the news. We had been married nearly seven years and had our challenges, but both of us felt this was a new exciting chapter.

Chapter Forty-Seven

To help solidify a better future, my sister's then so-called big-shot boyfriend from the East Coast told me he was expanding his credit card machines into major chains in the west and promised me a marketing and public relations position in Denver. At the twilight hour, My Wife and I purchased a ten-acre mini estate in the country, twelve miles from Evergreen in Conifer. It was a small house but had a pond, a gazebo at the edge of the pond, a little dock, and a nice guest cottage. Simply, it was an incredible setting, with meadows, rocks, trees, and views. Judy's boyfriend, whom I knew was all about impressing Judy, confirmed to the local financing bank that I was under new employment with his company. My Wife had taken her maternity leave with Able Airlines and maintained her medical insurance. We settled into what seemed like a secure situation, and I was anxious to start my new position.

My new employer said he was still setting up all the logistics to start up in Denver and that the kickoff would be forthcoming. Weeks passed, then a month. I kept pressuring him for answers on what was happening, and he assured me it was just normal problems in setup. Soon I would receive a call from him saying the whole thing fell through. If my body would have fit, I would have crawled through that phone line and strangled him. Instead, I told my sister what a piece of human excrement I thought her all-blow, no-good boyfriend was, and she basically concurred as their relationship was on shaky ground.

I conducted a massive job search and came across an ad for a temporary public relations person with the Denver campaign for Democratic candidate for president, Jimmy Carter. I had a phone interview with campaign director, Wellington Webb, and follow-up résumés and letters. All went well, and I was ready to come aboard when Webb said the campaign's budget was exceeded and he couldn't get extra funds to bring me on. Even though I didn't get the job, I still voted for Carter over Ford, as did My Wife. What a mistake that turned out to be.

Rather than panic, I decided to work on the house and property. We had new storm windows put in, and I made a new kitchen pantry and started the tedious task of assembling all this wood that the seller said was like a corral. They were large sections of fence-like walls that turned out to be six feet tall and were incredibly high-quality intricately cut and formed wood that all weaved together. As I assembled it, I couldn't believe how big an area it covered. It was as big when I finished as the entire backyard of our house in California. It also ended up having a two-story tower that had stairs and a roof. It was like putting together a massive Lincoln Log set we used to have as kids. I was finally told by a neighbor that it was an elaborate horse-training setup. To me, it was a perfect fort and playground for our upcoming kids.

But I had more concerns than assembling that fort. My Wife's delivery date was getting closer, and she was having blood pressure problems. I told her not to worry, to just relax, and I would make most of the meals and handle the housework. Meanwhile, we attended Lamaze classes and shared with other expecting parents. The winter up there at 8,800 feet elevation left our property nearly buried. And soon the due date of early February was approaching. We had a hospital picked out, but it was way down in Denver, the closest we could secure, with insurance dictates. We rehearsed the directions and felt we were ready, at least as ready as people could be way up in the mountains in the winter without a four-wheel drive.

The delivery time came and left. My Wife's blood pressure was a concern as the weeks passed by, and at the third overdue week, the doctor told us to come down and he would induce delivery. It had been lightly snowing, but as we packed her bags, it was now a full-blown blizzard. Perfect timing for a disaster. I knew we were in for a grueling trip because it was hard just getting out of our long driveway.

We took our planned route and braved the elements the best we could. My Wife was having major contractions, and the timing indicated we may be facing our own delivery, at least that was my worry.

She was moaning and groaning, but the trip went without a hitch. As soon as we arrived, a nurse was waiting, took her blood pressure, and we wheeled her in to maternity. Her face was red so I know her blood pressure was very high, an indication of toxemia, not a good sign at this late date and hour.

It took many hours for her water to break and eighteen long hours for the baby's head to finally be seen. But the delivery was still being stubborn, and My Wife was so tired she couldn't push anymore. Several extra doctors came in so I knew there was some threat of danger. The doctor used a forceps to help the baby's head, but clipped a corner of the child's eye, later causing a somewhat serious infection. It was a boy. It was over. And we were delighted. As the father, being there throughout the birth and then seeing a newborn was emotional and touching. It creates a special bond.

Because of the eye infection, they had to put our son in an incubator as they quickly sought to bring My Wife's blood pressure under control. The doctor later admitted it was dangerously high and they were genuinely concerned. They were also just as concerned over the little boy's infection, plus they had to ingest so many last-minute drugs into My Wife to lower her blood pressure from the toxemia and save her, that all those toxic chemicals went straight into the baby. They had to pump them all out. It was a touchy situation all around.

When I was assured everything was currently stable, I went out and found a little old Catholic church right around the corner and, for maybe the second time in my life, got down on my knees in a pew and prayed. I prayed for their life and their recovery and normalcy. I stayed down on my knees for a good half hour. A priest finally came to my side as he probably heard some sobs. When I returned, My Wife's blood pressure had finally dropped and she was asleep, heavily sedated. I went to visit the boy and was told the nick was in a delicate area in the corner of the eye, but that it showed good signs of recovery. They had done most of the critical extraction of the drugs from the baby, but were still closely monitoring his condition. He was in the infant IC unit. I felt I shouldn't put it off anymore, so I made all the calls to our family members and friends. I then fell asleep myself in a chair next to My Wife. This was an aspect of my *luck* that I would always cherish. I somehow knew before I dozed off that all would be fine.

When mother and son were safely home, we decided to give him the strong name of "Alexander."

My Wife was a great first-time mother and breast-fed him. She also started an elaborate baby scrapbook. But she was having the post baby blues and greatly missed not having some family around. She was crying a lot, and I felt her pain. I was impulsive as usual and suggested that since we couldn't move to Carson City where her family was because of the airlines, would she feel better if we moved to Minnesota, where Able Airlines had a base? Then she would have all my family to support her. Oh God, I couldn't believe I was saying this as when I joined the Marines and left home and Minnesota, I thought I would never return.

It was early 1977, and the real estate market was tightening. I went back to our realtor that found us our present house, and she said if she could sell it, after everything, we would take a loss. So again, I acted as my own realtor. I put up little cards down in Evergreen on bulletin boards and ran one little ad in the local paper. I sold the house in several weeks, and we made about $10,000 profit after living there less than eleven months. At the last moment, however, the purchaser who had used a VA loan had a snag in the paperwork. We had already made a contingent purchase of a house in Minnesota and any delays would cause a major rift with the seller, so I took action in my own hands.

I found out that the runner for the VA in Denver didn't deliver the paperwork to a different department in time and would have to wait until the next week, after a holiday. I called a manager at the VA and found out that the *other* department was right across the street. I debated about their protocol and then asked if there would be anything wrong with me coming down there, picking up the papers, and delivering them myself. He said it had never really come up. I told him I was coming down and would pick them up. I did just that, with this surprised look from everyone, and made the deadline.

We moved into our big new house in Plymouth on two and a half prime acres, close to Lake Minnetonka, about twenty-five minutes outside downtown Minneapolis. I felt good about it because it was totally away from my family who all resided in the north suburbs, "across the railroad tracks" as they always said. I started working for my sister's new husband Kerry in cement construction until I found something in my field. In the absence of not finding a writing or PR job right away, I took a position as a claims adjuster and investigator for a major insurance company in the Midwest. The position came with a new car and an expense account.

Before the job formally started, we had a big family reunion at our new house, and Gary and I decided to make a trip to New York so I could push my book, *USMC*. We got a hotel right in the heart of Manhattan and decided we would party in the area at night and I would pound the long blocks of New York during the day to meet editors and publishers. That in itself was a lofty goal and very difficult to get past the gatekeepers, but I did meet with two editors, one Doubleday and one Random House, who both liked my writing but said the topic matter of Vietnam was still touchy and for the time, they had to pass. The Random House editor asked me to stay in touch. Close to the end of our short week there, after visiting the Statue of Liberty and the World Trade Center, we went to Maxwell's Plum in Midtown Manhattan and drank manhattans for the occasions, getting quite tanked. We also visited the disco right next door, where Donna Summer and the Bee Gees music rumbled the walls.

While there, we met this black guy who ended up inviting us to a private party in Harlem. His beautiful black girlfriend was a bartender there. But bars don't close until 4:00 a.m. there so we had a long night of drinking and dancing ahead of us. Toward the bewitching hour, who should walk in but Joe Frazier, former heavyweight champion of the world. I went right up to him and introduced myself, and we briefly talked about boxing, Ali, and Foreman. He didn't have much affection for either one, especially Ali, whom he still called Clay. I went and got Gary and dragged him over to shake hands with Frazier. He was very friendly and cordial, but it soon stopped when his entourage was calling his name.

Our new friend who invited us was telling us that he picked up that Frazier had his eye on his woman and wanted to invite her to his own party. He told us, "I don't care if he is big-shot Frazier or not, my lady would never go with him. She's mine." The bar was closing, and his beauty came around the bar to leave. "Watch now, she'll come straight to me and into my arms. There won't even be a hesitation." She walked toward us as we were standing there waiting, and just then made an abrupt beeline right to Frazier and his awaiting entourage and limousine. The night was over, as well as the trip, with any publishing dreams put on hold.

Within weeks of starting my new insurance job, I was solving cases that had sat dormant for lengthy periods. I was then doing investigations directly for the legal department. The chief attorney told management that my investigations were so thorough and conclusive that his legal team seldom had to do anything, but cross a few Ts. And when I dropped off my belt transcripts of interviews and investigations to the massive secretarial pool, I learned they would argue over who would get mine to type up. Seems they said I articulated my material slowly and enunciated everything clearly. They were able to do three of mine to one of the others despite mine being more in-depth. It served to gain me respect and to elevate me very quickly in the company.

My manager gave me a raise and took My Wife and I out to dinner. During dinner, My Wife made a derogatory remark out of the blue to him in front of his wife. It was something to the effect that who was he to assign so much work and then drop by our house occasionally and check up on me and my home office? His demeanor changed quicker than the Minnesota weather, and it was all downhill after that. Meanwhile, My Wife was flying again and we had to secure child care, usually at this facility but sometimes with the teenage girl she had found that was from a disadvantaged home and family. I asked My Wife over and over again if she came with references and a perfect record, and she assured me she did. I still felt uncomfortable about it. One day when I came home early to do some office work, I noticed that Alex was in his crib. He was red in the face and sobbing. I sensed something was wrong. He was still too young to talk coherently.

I picked him up, and he hugged me tightly. I kept quizzing the girl on why he was upset and if anything happened. She kept saying no with a straight face. After I paid her and took her home, I went home to change Alex's diaper. I immediately saw a huge seven-inch square black-and-blue bruise. I called her mother and told her I demanded an explanation. Her response was that he was crying and she didn't know what else to do, so she kicked him repeatedly. I told her mother I would be reporting her to family and child services in Hennepin County. I spoke extra tenderly to Alex and said I was taking him out to eat and have treats. I was fit to be tied. I took photos of the bruises to show the officials later. But that later never came.

When My Wife returned from a trip, I filled her in and she wanted to forgive the girl and not cause problems for her. I couldn't believe it. For her to go unpunished was even worse than the abusive act.

My logic that going unabated and not officially recorded could result in another child being victimized went by the wayside in favor of forgiveness. Even though I had already initiated papers on a formal complaint with the county, I dropped it midcourse in lieu of making a complaint with the child-care company and mother, saying I had left an open and pending complaint about her for the records.

Right on the heels of that came another incident involving *our* son. One day after a long trip, My Wife returned home and wanted to spend some undivided time with Alex. So I figured that while she had this special one-on-one time with him, I would go shopping. When I returned, I saw My Wife slumped over in the overstuffed chair, sleeping. I looked around but could find no Alex. I checked the entire house. I noticed the door was not latched fully when I opened it. It was cold outside with a light snow falling.

I was now in a panic mode. I checked the garage and outbuildings and entire property. I then applied what I learned in the Marines as a radius search. I left our property and went to the distant neighbor across the street. I went around the back of the house and there was Alex, sitting there against the house in his wet diaper, crying his eyes out. He had his little Ford hat on, and his eyes were red and his cheeks rosy. I picked him up, and he was so glad to see me he was nearly choking me with his arms around my neck. I ran home and rushed to put him to bed, with layers of blankets. My Wife was now awake, and we both attended to his needs, which were to warm his body up as quickly as possible. I made him hot chocolate with marshmallows, and we both rubbed his limbs and changed his diaper. My Wife had tears in her eyes. I was outraged, but I contained my anger enough so I could just explain to My Wife what happened and how I found him. I simply could say no more because I knew I would lose it. I concentrated on Alex only, and he soon recovered.

Chapter Forty-Eight

While we lived in Minnesota, I wanted to reach out to my dad more. I bought tickets to go see Ken Norton fight Scott Ledoux at the auditorium and treated him to a hot dog, peanuts, and beers. He loved it. I would want to tell him I knew his secret, but with my promise to Mom, I couldn't. We also got in an ice-fishing trip together, but at forty-eight degrees below zero and sixty-four degrees windchill, we made a bad call to go and nearly ended up freezing, barely making back to his car. We spent the next forty-five minutes in the car waiting for it to heat up.

We could barely move and didn't share a word, just agony, moans, and groans. Even with the gloves, our fingers were nearly frozen as we had to expose them earlier to the freezing water from the ice hole. As they thawed out, the pain was excruciating. But my mind was racing thinking it would be the perfect time to tell Dad I knew his secret. We were suffering, and I thought it would be a great buffer to offset my words. But I didn't because I knew there would never be a perfect time. And I didn't want to betray my mother. But I still relished the time we had together, pain and all.

Later one day, Dad took me to a local tavern in New Brighton, where they lived. We had a few beers and a great greasy hamburger and fries. While there, the local town drunk came in and was stumbling all over, dropped by our table, and promptly fell on the floor, hitting his face. The husky bartender rushed over, apologized to us, and picked him up and started to drag him out the door. Dad stopped him, raised his voice very seriously, looked at the bartender with his steely blues, and told him he would take care of him. "But, John," the bartender started.

"No buts, I said I would handle him." The bartender, a big rough-looking guy himself, backed off as if a *bar god* had spoken. Dad's soft, giving, nurturing side came out, and he sat the drunk down, brushed him off, gave him his handkerchief for the little bit of blood, and bought him a coffee. I was so tempted just then to tell my father I knew his deep-down secret, but I couldn't. This was the dad I was most proud of. The fighter, the helpmate, the giver, the unconditional compassionate human being.

My sister Judy, who was divorcing her second husband, was acting as the subcontractor for the building of her own home in Minnetonka. Judy was very attractive and many guys had their eyes on her. One day, Dad called me and was in an absolute huff. He said that Judy had called him, all upset over one of the older construction workers saying lewd things to her, and it wasn't the first time. He told me he was going to pay a visit to her house and have a word with the guy. I talked him out of it, which was not easy. I told him I would go over there instead since I lived nearby. He insisted over and over again that I take care of business. "Jon, you have to promise me, without a doubt, that you will take care of this guy. I don't want to hear this from your sister again." I assured him that I would.

When I went over to Judy's unfinished house, I found the guy working by himself on the cement finishing of the front steps. I asked him if he was So-and-So and told him I was Judy's brother. Right away, tension filled the air. "Judy has told us that you have been making sexual remarks to her and making her very uncomfortable." I told him to look into my eyes. He did. "You must stop right away, or I will personally stop you. I will make you wish you never said a word to her. Stop immediately and it will all be over." It was. I reported back to Dad, and he too was relieved and thanked me. It was probably the first time I felt a wave of respect come my way. But with Dad, feelings and emotions were like waves as they washed up to shore and back to the ocean again.

After Christmas, Dad called My Wife when I wasn't around and called me many four-letter names, including an asshole, just because he thought my present to my niece wasn't good enough. It upset My Wife so much she said she never wanted anything to do with him again and didn't want his negative influence around our house or child. It caused My Wife to schedule marriage counseling for us. After a few sessions and the PhD hearing all about Dad, including porphyria and the whole story, he came right out and told me, "I really don't know how you survived all that or your mother for that matter. You must have some constitution!" The room went silent.

"I have some homework for you, Jon. And you must do it for our next session. Ready?"

"Ready."

"I want you to approach your father and tell him—don't ask, tell him—you want him to tell you he loves you. Say it exactly that way, nothing less, nothing more."

His instructions sounded so strange. And so impossibly difficult to say, especially to my dad. I questioned the good doctor over and over again and finally gave in. But I fought his demands like a fish out of water. Doing this, I thought, would be harder than pulling eye teeth out of a giraffe. Within the week, I called Dad. I made some idle chitchat and then took a deep breath and said, "Dad, I want you to tell me you love me." There was a long pause and silence.

Then with an avalanche of emotion and sobs, he replied, "Jon, I do. I do love you very much. And I always have, I'm proud of you. I know I have never expressed it, but believe me, I do." I was so utterly shocked I can't recall what else was said except I thanked him. In a way though, it was confusing because that statement didn't match the past. But nonetheless, I gleefully accepted it. I shared the results with our counselor and My Wife, and it softened her attitude toward him somewhat.

But many negative factors in our relationship soon clashed, and we were talking of moving out of Minnesota and separating. Alex was just two and a half years old, but I sold our house myself, as before, and three other homes we had purchased as rentals. Of both my parents, my dad took it the worst, asking me if there was any way to work it out. I replied that there didn't seem to be, and he appeared very dejected. Sad. We made another hefty profit on our real estate and were moving back to California, Orange County, to be exact. We agreed to split our money fifty-fifty and start a trial separation. Another trip on U-Haul, going back west across many states.

My Wife took her money portion and bought a nice but simple house in a middle-class neighborhood of Yorba Linda. I went to Hollywood and got an entire second floor over an old house. I wanted the space for Alex when I had him. Right away, the separation from my boy was horribly painful. And I missed My Wife as well—but not nearly as much as the deep anguish a father feels when detached from his son. I thought of him every minute of the day, especially how he was doing when My Wife was away on a trip. I had picked Hollywood because I was set to meet this guy in Beverly Hills that wanted an editor for a new newspaper.

He gave me his address on Doheny Drive in Beverly Hills, a block up from Santa Monica Boulevard. It was a two-level building that most people used as condos or condo business offices. It was right behind Hughes Market. One of my first times in Hughes to get my favorite Famous Amos Chocolate Cookies, I stopped to use the payphone up near the door. Who comes in right behind me to wait for the phone but Charlton Heston, the big-screen Moses himself. I gave him a nod; he politely smiled back and just stood there and waited. He had a tennis outfit on and a strong Ben-Hur-like body odor. As I hung up the phone and he said thanks, I looked outside in the parking lot for his chariot but only saw a Rolls Royce, obviously his. That same tennis outfit of Heston's would be pictured in the first and only issue of our joint venture newspaper, the *National Family Gazette*.

Only using his first name, Joe, we hit it off immediately. He was from New York, was full-blooded Sicilian, a former pro wrestler who at five feet ten and 270 pounds posed a pretty intimidating appearance. But he was such a nice, educated, intelligent, highly experienced man in publishing, writing, advertising, and even the arts. What started as an interview for a writer and editor ended as a partnership in the tabloid paper he had planned. Joe drafted up paperwork; we shared our ideas and formulated a publishing plan and agreed that we would be fifty-fifty in all things, including initial up-front costs, totaling thousands of dollars.

We worked out of his condo office, and both went our separate ways drumming up advertising and articles. He supposedly got commitments for the Beverly Wilshire Hotel and LearJet, where we would combine ads within informative text called advertorials. I arranged an upcoming interview with Erik Estrada of CHIPS TV fame and a few other celebrities from the B-list. Things seemed to be going great, and with all the interfacing I was doing in and around Beverly Hills, Los Angeles, and the Valley, I felt like I was just fitting in, that this business and publishing venture was custom-made for me. Joe and I got along like long-lost brothers, and I was confident I could make a go of this and build a fantastic paper and future. I loved the concept of an alternative paper that covered entertainment, sports, cuisine, nutrition, the arts and family, and was upbeat, positive, and free of scandal. Joe touted it as the perfect alternative to the *National Enquirer*, only on a local and regional level.

I was always out and about meeting people in (mainly) Beverly Hills and building a network of contacts in every arena. I even went back to Minnesota to visit with my old acquaintance Verne Gagne and do a big feature on his wrestling career in our first issue. I also visited my grandma Hilda who was living up in Seattle and did an exposé on her as a human interest story. During all this running around, I became a regular at two hot Beverly Hills watering holes. Both were on Santa Monica Boulevard. One was the Salon and the other the Rangoon Racquet Club. I met many entertainers there, like Academy Award winner Jack Lemmon (loved martinis), black comedians Scoey Mitchell and Slappy White (Redd Foxx's sidekick), and numerous others. The Racquet Club had free hors d'oeuvres and made their own killer scotch eggs every day for happy hour. I virtually lived on these incredible eggs, once eating eighteen of them during a bartender's challenge, and mixed nuts, garlic toast, celery, carrots, dip, and beer. I think Slappy had the same game plan as we bumped into each other quite often, always sharing jokes and laughs. I made numerous hookups there with ladies, but also met this Italian doctor (MD) visiting the States and doing research.

His name was Luigi, and despite having movie star good looks, being very tall at six feet five inches and trim--plus highly educated and accomplished--he was without doubt the shyest, most introverted man I had ever met. We hit it off as he spoke perfect English and I immediately took him under my wing. I started by starting a conversation with a few ladies and building up his confidence. But it was short-lived as they thought I was doing all the talking for both of us. And I was. Luigi introduced me to a hot spot in Beverly Hills that turned out to be a fabulous pickup spot called the Ginger Man, a restaurant and bar owned by actor Carroll O'Connor (Archie Bunker). We fared better there, but I really had to coax my Italian buddy to loosen up, relax, and have fun. He did, for the most part. But I was on him constantly.

One night, I took him to my favorite hangout, the Salon. After a bit of no action, we decided to leave and walk down to the Racquet Club. As we were leaving, actor Robert Culp (*I Spy*) and his wife or girl was entering. Culp's lady stopped dead in her tracks and was spellbound by Luigi. I thought we were going to have a ruckus right there as Culp gave him this incredible snarling look, showing his teeth; and as he pushed his lady in, I pushed Luigi out. Now, why couldn't Luigi have this connection with someone else during our hunts instead of an unavailable one? But I thought Culp acted like a genuine jerk.

As it turned out, years before, Luigi had befriended this famous singer/entertainer and her husband, in Italy and helped them in some unusual tight spot. So when he came to Los Angeles to do his study and research, he contacted them and they gave him their Mercedes convertible to use and put him up over their garage in this ultra-elaborate apartment. Because I had this old beat-up green Plymouth Scamp that fit in Beverly Hills and the surrounding area like a bum at the Ritz, we always took the Mercedes. And always came back to the apartment. I met this famous singer several times in our comings and goings—once being treated to lunch made by her in their house—but I will keep her name anonymous because I am not sure I have her accurate name. They lived off Wilshire Boulevard going out of Beverly Hills toward downtown Los Angeles. She had several smaller children, and she couldn't have been more cordial and accommodating. Her husband was some entertainment executive. Although we were very respectful and quiet and did it relatively little, that apartment acted as our hunt and party central.

Downtown Beverly Hills had some incredible body shops, as we used to call them. And if Luigi wasn't able to rumble, I went out on my own. It was my way and excuse for not thinking and worrying about my son. I would drink, dance, sing at a piano bar, party with others, and just have a grand old time. I also was constantly trying to make contacts for stories or advertising. That's when I met this incredibly stunning Mexican lady at Tony Roma's, where I learned that her wealthy family had owned all the major vegetable and food distribution channels in the LA area. She was estranged from her husband and, after years of loneliness, decided to go out on the town.

Although I wanted to write up a story on her family's incredible success for our paper, I was more interested in her. The feeling was mutual. We both got drunk after sharing our sob stories about our breakups and kids. We never made it to a bed. We made passionate love in the doorway of an exclusive shop on Rodeo Drive. After that, she disappeared like a brisk wind. As hard as I tried to reach her, I never could. Rodeo was the fitting place for her body and beauty. It was one of those unforgettable fledgling experiences you can never forget.

During my time in Hollywood, I also had a steady date in the pretty form of Greta, a natural blonde B-grade actress from Germany. Once, she insisted I dress up and escort her to a big shot fund-raiser in Brentwood. I debated that a fund-raiser was an event that solicited funds for an event or charity, and I was not in any position, especially at that level, to fork out any cash. She insisted that wasn't necessarily true and she was invited by friends and they would understand that I was just another struggling artist. I dug my suit out of the mothballs and picked her up in my green beater and parked blocks away so no one would see me with her in that jalopy.

The party was an elaborate affair with roving music, tables of expensive food—which I consumed like a culinary fiend—and abounded with *beautiful* people, as they are called in those circles. My girl was really down-to-earth and, to me, didn't fit in with the phoniness that filled the air. But she really put on an act and paraded around with me like she owned the place. We greatly enjoyed the festivities, and I had Greta just introduce me as a writer who was starting his own newspaper. I could sense that was a mistake right away as they seem to see me with deep pockets. After dessert was served and the music was waning, they started opening bids for the charity items. What? I felt the pressure already.

Based on the numbers that were thrown around for these bids, I started sweating bullets and had no idea how I was going to handle this as it wasn't that huge of a group.

The actual charity was for some animal rights organization protecting some indigenous reptile from extinction up in the Los Angeles National Forest. It sounded to me more like something that should have been BB'd for the main entry plates that evening. With all the beautiful people and environment we were in, plus the gifts for winning bids, and the cause, there were times I had to fight back laughter.

I whispered to Greta, "Shouldn't this be a fund-raiser for poor kids or something more worthwhile?" She smiled and we kept mingling in the crowd, with me sensing this was her way of avoiding being pinned down. I heard bids for hundreds and thousands of dollars, like they were all trying to impress each other. At one point, she asked me if I had anything to bid. I said I had ten bucks in my wallet but needed that. She let out a loud giggle. I responded, "And how may I ask, can I pay? Money order, bank draft, or as a debit from my invisible international monetary fund?" She nearly fell over, but I thought it was more from the big fountain of endless champagne.

We finally ran into one of her girlfriends whose date looked like a male mannequin. I just about wanted to reach out and touch his face and skin to see if it was real. I felt looking around his back to see if he had a string or something to pull because he didn't speak. When we were introduced, I understood why. His voice was like some weaselly character in a cartoon. He fit right in. Soon, the guy conducting the bidding was going around and getting personal, asking for commitments. What could I say if he asked me to bid on something? "Sorry, sir, but I already own a *gold* pencil sharpener." If I had a diaper on, I would have used it.

Since we were now hooked up with Greta's girlfriend and Mr. Mannequin, I had to find a way out of this. So I excused myself to the restroom and never came back. I slipped out like the reptile they were honoring. Greta was great, but over.

One day, just before our first issue was being printed, Joe and I had a meeting. First, he showed me a notarized document stating that if anything happened to him, I would share fifty-fifty in his estate with the rest of his family. He proceeded to go on and explain to me how the Cosa Nostra (the underworld and mob) started on the steps of a church in Sicily. And how a Sicilian bride was snatched up by intruders and raped and murdered. There was much tension in Sicily then with the local Sicilians and outsiders and other foreigners to their land. The townsmen got sick and tired of the continual invasions and vowed to form an underground counsel to deal with it outside of the law. Hence its roots, and as the Sicilians immigrated to America, their secret, insider culture came with them and expanded into the underworld and crime families. Interesting stuff, but why was he telling me all this?

That entire next week was filled with situations that didn't even seem real. It was one unbelievable thing after another. First, our editorial model was not being met, especially in a timely fashion, and Joe suddenly was not sharing things with me. He seemed much more distant, detached. And the first edition was delayed. I was getting uncomfortable and started pressuring him for answers. He then told me about when someone doesn't meet their promises and obligations, they might get "bent over a car hood." He then suggested I come with him while he ran an errand. We jumped in his pink Cadillac, and he drove to the next block over, stopped at the end of this driveway with a car in it, and walked up to the house. He seemed to be talking to the man sternly. Was this childish stunt supposed to scare me? And why?

The craziest day, however, came when he told me to meet him at his office at a certain time. As I walked in, I noticed a big Rolls Royce parked in front at the curb. The back California blue license plate read, JAGGER. I asked Joe if that was Mick Jagger's car. He said it was and to walk down several doors and go inside. Sitting inside was Bianca Jagger, Mick's estranged wife, bookended by two huge goons. We talked small talk and the goons said Joe wanted me to meet them. Bianca never said a word; she just stared at me. I found all this so strange I didn't have a response. I was utterly speechless.

I went back to Joe and asked him what this was all about. His response was about as bizarre as the experience and totally forgettable. Next in this charade was this woman strolling her baby in a very expensive European buggy. She had darker skin and looked very Italian. I noticed she was crying and Joe gave her a hankie. Joe had fancied himself, card and all, as a consigliere, or an adviser to Italian people. He said it came in handy when he needed favors. And he said he always expected his paybacks.

Chapter Forty-Nine

On the same day that our first issue came out, Joe was off the charts weird. It was printed on cheap paper like the *Enquirer* but only had eight pages. I didn't even know what articles Joe was going to contribute until I saw the issue. The cover story was called, "Why Me God?" an as-told-to-Joe piece.

It was an incredible story of a Polish couple who were aerial acrobats but had an accident, with the husband being killed and the wife landing on her head after a twenty-five-foot fall. She had written an autobiography and was in the works to have a film made. It seemed Joe was helping to push and publicize that fact. He also had a story on the "World's Fastest Growing Church"—the Mormons. My stuff was in there, and large advertisements for secondary actors, the biggest one pictured with many big names like George C. Scott and Charlton Heston. Not much of it made sense to me because it seemed like a hodgepodge. I saw it as a flimsy attempt and not something I was very proud of.

Within that week, Joe also told me that a certain building on Hollywood Boulevard was going to burn and the Cafe Monet, a trendy French restaurant just a block or so away. Sometime thereafter, both buildings were burned, with the Cafe Monet being burned right down to the ground. He told me these things like a modified tongue-in-cheek psychic premonition. I found it strange and took it like a grain of pepper.

When we discussed the Mormon article, which I found a little odd to include, Joe told me there was a secret project underway by the LDS Church to make a major motion picture about their history and that it had been in the works for quite some time. He told me a little of its history and said he thought I would be perfect cast in the role of Sidney Rigdon, one of the early Mormon heroes that was later tarred and feathered. He said I looked like his pictures and that he could pull some strings and get me in there.

"Joe, I'm not an actor, I have no experience doing such things and I am not in the least interested."

"Well, Jon, you have a great look and I think you would be perfect for the part."

"No, Joe, not me, I'm afraid. I'm not the type."

"But, Jon, you are the type. We can have you professionally trained, you know. It'll be a great chance to get you in the movies. You're a hard worker, you can do it."

"Yeah, but that's not the point. It's not me."

"Okay then, just keep it in the back of your mind. And oh, don't mention this to anyone else."

When I left him that day and went to my car in the building's underground parking, I noticed eight pallets of the *National Family Gazette* stacked four feet high, totaling the 250,000-copy initial-print run. I certainly couldn't find fault with a quarter-million newspapers, just like he said we would have and I didn't believe. Now what? I already had enough stories and copy for the next issue. In my local travels, I ran into a woman and her sixteen-year-old daughter on Hollywood Boulevard. They were from Nebraska and terribly lost. They had a car but not much else.

I led them to Van Nuys where she had an interview to be an apartment manager, a desperate move just to get settled. They were near busted so I bought them lunch and learned they had left her husband because of drinking and abuse although I suspected it wasn't all that serious. I also found out that she was a holistic healer and trained in herbal plants and supplementation. She was also a born-again and very religious. A smart lady. I engaged her for a series of articles to be paid upon publication. I gave her some money to buy some groceries. Things seemed to be happy for her until her daughter crawled out of her bedroom window and ran away.

That night, when the cops were alerted and she didn't come back, we sat and drank wine—boy, could she knock them down, she must have taken a lot of communion—and she was scared to be alone, so I stayed and we made love. Between her husband, her daughter, her situation, and her guilt, she shed enough tears to fill a sink. The daughter returned herself early the next day. We stayed in touch.

Now, I wanted answers from Joe. And I wanted them now. I dropped by his office, and he immediately made us a large salad, seemingly very outgoing and jovial. I asked him what I deemed to be a perfectly logical question given a quarter-million newspaper copies sitting on pallets. "Joe, what's the distribution plan? How come all those newspapers are just sitting there? And how come we are not planning the second issue?"

At first, he came back with some puzzling comments about how the Sicilians work, saying we might be stepping on the wrong feet, trying to compete with the *National Enquirer* and the very Sicilian family, the same one he was highly praising before. But I reminded him that it was him who said we were the direct opposite in most ways—providing no real direct competition—and the grand idea was his in the first place. He was evasive, fidgety, and nearly desperate acting.

There was a counter between the kitchen and the living area where I sat waiting for an answer while Joe was leaning over the sink. He turned as I was taking a bite, walked to the counter and me, and quickly put a large butcher knife to my throat. He put one of his meat hooks on my shoulder, guided me to a standing position, and with the sharp point in the crevice of my throat, pushed me toward the door with his weight against mine. I flexed my neck muscles thinking that would create a better shield of protection from the knife plunging into my neck. My neck exercises for boxing helped.

Just then, I had an immediate flashback to Vietnam and that fellow Marine sticking his rifle onto my forehead. Joe's eyes were huge, with a craziness in them, just like that Marine. I became agitated and was waiting for the right second and opening to counter his action, but before I knew it, we were out the door, down the steps, and we parted with some verbal exchanges as he went inside. When that door slammed and was locked—as I soon confirmed—I knew it was all over. I felt my throat and a slight nick where the point had punctured my skin. While the Marine thing was a scary unfortunate incident, with Joe, I was seething mad inside, and I wasn't about to let him get away with this. I was entering a dark place and wanted revenge!

I spent the remainder of the day at the Salon, pondering what just happened and my fate. Seems like no amount of beer had any effect on me, as my system just soaked them up. I called the Nebraska lady and shared with her a little of what happened, mainly because I felt bad I wouldn't be using her material and expertise. We got together, and I was glad to hear her daughter was doing better and liking school. I treated her to Nate's Deli in Beverly Hills, and we spent hours there together as she picked my brain enough to get the full story. Several days later, we got together again when she said she had some urgent things to share with me.

It seems that behind my back, Nebraska took it upon herself to do some private investigating, meeting Joe at the Beverly Wilshire Hotel. She told me she pretended to be upset about me telling her the paper would not be continuing. Out of their conversation, in this convoluted way, she told me she feared for my life as well as her own. She told me Joe had some sinister connections and he saw me as a liability.

She pleaded with me to leave town and cover my tracks. She pounded over and over again that my very life was in jeopardy. The more she said these things, the more intense my sense of rage and revenge inside. I thought to myself, who does this fat *Godfather*-like figure think he is?

To my utter amazement, Nebraska called me over to her apartment, introduced me to her husband who had flown in from Nebraska, and told me she shared *everything* with her husband and that they were moving to Seattle the next day and advised me to move out of the Los Angeles area, even California.

She and her husband agreed that this brief association with Joe was not worth their safety or even their life. I argued that they were overreacting and thought the whole thing was unnecessary. But she told me there were many factors involved that were working against me and that I shouldn't take any of this lightly. We hugged, wished each other well, and parted ways. I left her with the thought I would watch myself and consider all her thoughts, concerns, and worries. Inside my mind and heart, however, was lurking my dark thoughts of payback, revenge, and offensive moves.

The only thing that calmed the murky fluids in my brain was my son Alex. I got him for the weekend and brought along his Ernie and Bert dolls from *Sesame Street* that he loved so much. We watched *Sesame Street* on TV and played for hours with the little matchbox cars. As I watched him play, I thought of his safety and thought that if anything ever happened to him, especially because of me, I would die a thousand deaths. I was thinking that LA was a horrible place and didn't represent mankind in a decent and positive way. I took my son with me to my gym on Santa Monica Boulevard. I parked right in front of the Sports Connection. I got out of my beat-up car with my son in my arms. He had his large ever-present Ford baseball hat on sideways, where he preferred it so he could see better, he said.

Pulling up right behind me was a big Rolls Royce, and the driver got out with this big smile on his face and we made small talk. He asked my son's name, obviously loved seeing Alex's cute hat and face, and we briefly visited. It was famous singer Herb Albert (Tijuana Brass). With his outgoing manner and extreme warmth and friendliness, he temporarily gave me hope in mankind again and LA. But it was short-lived. I determined right then that when this wonderful weekend concluded, I was going to take some action against Joe. I figured I'd show him a good dose of Norwegian Viking power.

The first of the next week, I dug the aluminum baseball bat out of my trunk. As soon as it got dark that night, I drove to Joe's complex and parked underneath. I could never figure it out, but no one was ever around that place, maybe one car besides mine in the good-sized structure. The lighting wasn't the best so I figured that was to my advantage. As I walked up the stairway and passed all the pallets on the garage floor with our newspapers, I overrode any doubts I had of doing the right thing, which was stopping this nemesis and getting revenge.

When I got up to Joe's place, a light was on, so I figured he was in as he was a night owl and got most of his *work* done then. Perfect, I thought. Right next to his place was a small alcove, where I positioned myself. My plan was to knock on the door, and when he answered it, I was going to break his legs, mob-style. I also wondered, if I lost my temper and control, could I hit him in the heart area or head and kill him? I did not have the covert intention of killing him, yet I knew the possibility and obviously accepted it. I knocked on the door with my bat ready on my shoulder. I'd teach this rotten SOB. No answer. I kept knocking and knocking. I listened with my head against the door and swore I heard noises. I resumed my knocking, with no answer. I finally gave up for fear of someone seeing me and went to the Salon to drown in my sorrows with beer. I always found a receptive audience there as I had made some friends, including the bartender, ironically another Sicilian. No one had any clue of my dark desires.

On Tuesday and Wednesday, I followed my same plot of revenge, with the same exact result. It was like a movie clip rewind. The only other thing that broke up the week was my meeting Arnold

Schwarzenegger at his office in Santa Monica. I was out and about trying to drum up business for the little company I had formed called "Creative Meadia," a writing and public relations service. I figured since I had been writing as a freelancer for several of the muscle and fitness magazines for eight years, I had an automatic door opener. While Arnold's secretary wasn't very accommodating, Arnold must have overheard my pitch and came out and invited me in. We shook hands and I sat down. While we had a nice little chat, he said he had no outside needs at that time but would keep my brochure, letter, and card. But with all my pending personal issues and a tremendous sense of loss over my son, I had zero confidence and absolutely no ability to focus and concentrate.

It didn't help at the time that I often thought of seeing Dana's foot and boot in his casket. I also was continually having that same nightmare of being left in the foxhole alone, without being shot and killed, but thinking, why was I spared, didn't I deserve to die like my fellow Marines? My sense of self-worth and unworthiness had my mind deep in the doldrums. Certain things, like this fiasco with Joe, kicked off many Vietnam and Marine experiences and thoughts. They were always on this shelf in my mind and subconscious, ready to be taken off.

When Friday came, I was determined to make good with my plan for Joe. I just felt in my bones this was the night, this was the time, do or die, as we said in the Corps. The movie clip was rewound, and I was up in my position, knocking on the door. I knew there was someone in there; I could clearly hear people talking like Joe and his woman. I didn't want to bust him up in front of her, but I thought it was one of the prices for revenge. The bat was ready. My mind was dark. My heart empty. I had already done the act in my mind. But I could not move forward. It was as if something was holding me back besides my own mind and thoughts. My hand could not knock on the door, and the bat wouldn't position on my shoulder. I simply lowered the bat and left.

I went to the Salon where it was happy hour, but I was anything but happy. Fridays there were always jam-packed, barely enough room to move. I pushed my way through the crowd, and right in the middle of the place, there was a vacant high table. I couldn't believe my good fortune and actually asked the surrounding people if the table belonged to anyone, and everyone just shook their heads and ignored me. I sat down and ordered a beer. If someone would have taken a picture from the ceiling, it would have revealed a packed house but a small vacant area right in the middle, with one person sitting down— me. I just found the setting nearly surreal. I slugged back a gulp of beer, and as my head returned to its frontal position, I thought I saw someone sitting across from me. His image was getting closer, and it was now becoming clear, like a slow focus. His image was as close as someone in fact sitting across from me at the table, crystal clear yet dimensions away. It was nearly eerie, but in a warm and welcoming way. I immediately felt a calm sweep over me.

It was Jesus Christ, just as his depictions conveyed him to be since I was a kid. My entire being was frozen, yet my mind, ears, eyes, and heart were clear and I could actually feel them. Me, of all people, could not murmur a word. I cannot exactly convey the immediate *circle* that seemed to be surrounding us, like we were the only two in the room.

Suddenly, through all the noise and incredible racket, He called my name and said with a distinct softness that broke through the existing environment like a supersonic jet going through the sound barrier, "*I love you.*" It just about embarrassed me because of the setting. I guess it seemed to be exactly what I needed at the time.

I was taken aback by those words, directly to me. It wasn't the words so much as it was the delivery and the circumstances. Jesus sitting across from me in a tavern? God seems like He gives the brightest of messages in the darkest of areas.

He then said I did the right thing with Joe and that he knew I could "forgive him," but that it was ultimately my choice. Then He said I didn't need a résumé or cover letter for a job with Him because he would hire me "anytime." The feeling of humility overwhelmed me. His words were so peaceful and unassuming. My very soul and spirit seemed uplifted, refreshed. But I was also baffled, confused, struggling with disbelief. I clearly heard it all but can't say I understood it.

I was in a stupor, but found myself saying the same thing that some loved ones of the dead Marines I escorted said to me, "Why? Why of all people, Jesus, are you visiting and talking with me? After everything I've done, I don't seem very worthy." He conveyed that it was told to me, and through me, as a simple message that all mankind could also hear—if they opened their heart and ears.

He said it was because I had conviction and couldn't be bought for any amount of money and that I had a "pure heart." He also said while I certainly had my shortcomings and long list of indiscretions as a human being, it didn't take away from the "good and pure part." It was that "part" and the fact He wanted to visit and support me. He added that he was presenting himself to me in a form, complete with language, that I could identify with and relate to. Perceptions aside, that is exactly what it was like—like talking to a buddy who had my back. It was as if I were talking to another Marine, a close buddy.

As quickly as He appeared, He disappeared, but left me with the thought that he would be around. I quickly felt his presence leave my table and the tavern, like a gust of wind was being sucked through the eye of a needle. I asked a few of the patrons around me if they saw Him, if they saw someone sitting there. They kind of looked around and replied, no one other than you. Why? Then they looked at me quite strangely. Who could blame them? Part of me could not believe what just happened. The other part of me knew it did, and I couldn't deny it—I only had one slug of beer and never did drugs! While I felt undeserving, I also felt extremely privileged.

Moreover, I felt that the urge to revisit Joe had dissipated, like a puff of smoke in a rainstorm. The entire weekend was like a surrender to serenity. I felt the feeling of forgiveness envelope and blanket me like being wrapped in a cocoon of comfort and relief. I played back the "visit" in my mind over and over again. Each time gave me more resolve to go on and do the right things. I thought about approaching My Wife to get back together and not to harbor any ill resentment toward Joe. Nothing much else mattered but those two things.

Despite the profound personal spiritual experience I had with God, through His Son Jesus, my dark feelings of resentment and revenge returned the next week. It was like a fire in a field of dry brush. One strike of a mental match in my head, and the flames were igniting. One night, again, I found myself getting my baseball bat ready and driving over to Joe's place. The closer I got to his front door, the more the rage flamed within me. I thought of him sticking that knife to my throat, all the promises, wasted time, and lost money. The pallets of newspapers still sitting in his garage fanned the flames. This time

I knew I could do it, feeling my hands wrapped around the bat like an anxious big leaguer, with the bases loaded. In my mind, I could feel the baseball bat penetrate his soft tissue and hit bones, breaking them like branches on a tree. I could feel the rabid distortions twist my face. But on the final steps of the stairwell, my grip became weak on the bat. I had no strength. I was suddenly sapped of desire and power as surely as being struck by quiet lightning. A wave of empathy and forgiveness came over me just thinking of hurting Joe. I returned to my car and went back to my Hollywood apartment. For the first time in a while, I slept like a tired newborn baby.

The next day, guilt about being told all about those fires by Joe caused me to call the Los Angeles Police Department. I basically told them about the predictions of the fires by Joe and his sticking the knife to my throat. They immediately funneled me to a special department within the LAPD that dealt with underworld issues and the mob. The detective I was dealing with was all ears about the fires and all related facts.

He also told me I was lucky to be alive. He explained that while I did nothing wrong myself, being in his condo, I could have been stabbed to death, and the excuse for the murder would have been self-defense and Joe probably would have gotten off free and clear. While the detective agreed with me, I couldn't believe the whole thing. When it was all over and they had their facts, the special unit released me, saying if I chose to press charges, I could later. However, the detective clearly suggested I cut my losses and move forward, hinting that Joe might even be a hitman for the mob. He said I had to weigh my priorities, and some things in life may not be worth pursuing. I reluctantly agreed.

Chapter Fifty

For the next several days, I was in some kind of stupor over mixed feelings and terrible depression.

One night while aimlessly driving around Beverly Hills and stopping between the Salon and the Rangoon Racquet Club, missing my son and Christmas season quickly approaching, I felt very down.

Just then, like being poured down through my car roof, sitting next to me, was the same figure of Jesus again. Same as before, clear enough to see so close, yet like dimensions away. It was certainly the most surreal experience, next to the first visit, that I ever had in my life. Virtually impossible to fully explain in a coherent way. We talked about many things, including me writing a memoir someday. He said he knew I was going to be shockingly honest and said some complimentary things related to it.

He then added that since I would be so frank and revealing in my book, I should also be honest and revealing about everything that would be in the memoir, like His visit to me. He said if I was being so honest about myself and everyone and everything else, I should cover the complete story in total honesty. After all, He said it was a memoir and it was my life. He made some supportive predictions and said a human life being revealed in its total honesty is comprised of good and bad and all the frailties of mankind. He said He knew how hard it would be to reveal His visit to me, but thought it was just as important to include it along with everything else, perhaps more so. But He also said it was my decision. He added, "Write it the way it happened to the best of your ability." He actually used levity by asking me, *"You're an unbiased, objective journalist, right? Just tell the truth."*

He also said that he knew I wasn't a Bible reader or churchgoer, but some of the things He said and that I said and thought could be traced to something in biblical history and the Bible, just like many things in life could. He said a Christian biblical scholar could find reference points. He said also remarkably that preachers and great talkers from the pulpit and the fanciest churches with the greatest material riches were not necessarily the answer. He said the real answer lay between Him and the individual—that there was no real necessity or requirement for a go-between or middleman.

While He admitted that churches and preachers may act as helpmates and provide people the resources to have and reach a personal relationship with God through Jesus, it is not necessary, but may be helpful for many for fellowship. He did actually name one preacher by name with a positive bent, and that was Billy Graham, one who was not infallible but genuine in his faith, beliefs and teachings. He mentioned the *pure* heart again. And again.

Now, I would never take it upon myself to try to quote God, except for those *three words* I revealed earlier because they were so short and simple; but two other things He said that I feel confident enough about to convey in paraphrasing related to having a personal relationship with Him. The first was, *I am the way and I am the answer.* The second was, *Seek your own path with a pure heart and you will find the way.* The other thing He said that was much more vague to me was there would be *end times* and the symbol would lie in the sun and everything related to it?

I just kept driving around Beverly Hills with Jesus taking up the passenger seat. I can't remember anything else taking place except our conversations, which were not constant but always picked up where we left off. Before He seemed to be signing off, He left me with some profound thoughts. He said the only way to know if my forgiveness with Joe was real and pure was the *walking test.* He said the only way to know without doubt that I forgave him was to be walking down a sidewalk toward him and to reach the pureness of heart to greet him, shake his hand, and hug him—all without one smidgen of hate or revenge. Only love and forgiveness. He said he had every confidence I could do this and do it with utter sincerity and pureness of heart. It made my senses silent when He said, *If I can forgive you, you can forgive Joe.* He also asked me a question that is the hardest possible thing to repeat.

He asked me, if He needed me someday, could He count on me? He actually asked me this, and I felt, and feel, so humbled by it. Could it have been a rhetorical question? I felt guilty, but I pondered the question at length and put forth a few questions of my own, which he was somewhat ambiguous about. He said it was a simple question that only required a simple answer. But My God, it was not so simple for me. I knew in my very being that his visit would soon be over. It was like the best movie you had ever seen in your life was about to end.

I finally answered *yes, that He could absolutely count on me no matter what. That I would be there for Him.* I can't say I saw it, but I sensed a smile. He then complimented me on my lifelong, steadfast faith in Him (since I was confirmed a Lutheran as a kid) and my continual belief—with never a doubt, no matter what the circumstances. The last thing I can remember is Him suggesting I would probably enjoy reading the Bible, especially Revelations, and that if and when I did go to church to only carry sincerity and a pure heart, just like in forgiving. The very last thought that He conveyed was that a visit like this may never happen again, but if it did, I must reach the ultimate, highest level of pureness of heart, which often came during times when it was mixed with life's pathos, humility, and surrender.

He was gone, as surely and quicker than my thoughts could follow. The first afterthought I had was, God sure does work in strange and mysterious ways if he thought me worthy of a personal visit for all the things—sins, if you will—I had ever done. If I qualified, then surely anyone else could. Nonetheless, I felt privileged, thankful, appreciative, *lucky,* and incredibly humble and surrendering.

Within a short period of time, I was taking the *walking test* in my mind and approaching Joe on the sidewalk. I was able to do everything I knew I had to, and when I cleared my mind and kept a pure heart, it was actually easy. And it made me feel incredible. It was a burden I was carrying, and it dissipated like magic. Moreover, in prayers, I admitted to everything from stealing neighbors' vegetables from their gardens as a kid to personal pleasures derived from an endless array of females.

I had called my friend wrestler/promoter Verne Gagne to give him an update on the newspaper I had featured him in. He couldn't believe the whole sorted story—naturally, I didn't reveal the spiritual experience—and said he was coming to Los Angeles anyway on business and suggested we get together. After we met, he brought me to a close friend of his who he had served with in the Marines, Paul Caruso. Caruso had an office on the edge of Beverly Hills and was one of the more successful attorneys in Los Angeles, representing various players from the LA Lakers and other celebrities. He was also Sicilian himself. He said he would take my case pro bono and file charges on my behalf as a favor for Verne.

When we later met at his office, he handed me the letter his secretary drafted up, and we went over it. It was addressed to Joe and which demanded my partnership investment back (despite having a quarter million papers printed), called him on his actions, and threatened criminal charges. Caruso signed the letter, *Disrespectfully Yours*, which got a good laugh out of me. But what he said after that was not laughable.

He told me not to worry. If something happened to me, the evidence would clearly point to Joe and appropriate actions could be taken. "Well, that's really reassuring, Paul, thanks for that vote of confidence . . . That will make me sleep better at night."

"We can just rip this letter up and forget the whole thing if you want."

I approved the letter, and it was sent certified mail that day. With it, I departed and went to my next planned stop, the Mormon Temple on Santa Monica Boulevard. I had contacted the temple office earlier and told them of the information I knew about their upcoming film project Joe had told me about. They seemed fascinated with what I was saying and told me to come to the temple side office and meet with the leading elder of their church. I brought a copy of our newspaper with the Mormon feature inside.

The man I met with had the warmth of a cold snail. He looked like he was risen from the dead with his incredibly pale sunken face and a suit that looked like it had been cut back in the thirties. At the conclusion of our meeting, he casually wrote down a man's name and address on the edge of Van Nuys to visit. He said that the individual was the appointed chief of church protocol in all things related to the movie and entertainment field and was a working director and producer of many of the church's projects.

I arranged an appointment time and went to his sixth-floor office suite overlooking the entire valley.

As I told him my whole story, he was virtually sitting on the edge of his chair, all ears. At the end of our meeting, he admitted that everything I had told him about this very private and protected Mormon movie project was true. He added that the information I was sharing with him proved to him that elements of the underworld were infiltrating the propitiatory project for sinister reasons, which included blackmail. The article in our *National Family Gazette* about the Mormon Church growing had particular interest to him since Joe apparently utilized contacts that were privy to church history and figures. I didn't propose to understand any of this story, but felt glad to pass it along,

The gentleman I met thanked me again and again for my information and suggested that maybe Joe saw me as a good guy who could infiltrate the project, which was a new take on the LAPD's and Caruso's that I was being used in some elaborate scheme as a pawn, even with the *National Enquirer*. All crazy and all confusing. If bullshit could only walk and talk! The truth was, Joe was a great writer and had extensive experience in all aspects of marketing and publishing. Why couldn't he just be honest with his skills and be a stand-up guy instead of a cheap hood with contacts, which is what I saw him as?

But I still passed the *walking test* with him in my heart and mind and gleefully went on.

However, I had to take care of some loose ends from our paper that I felt guilty about in the way of returning photos to people, including cherished family pictures from Verne Gagne. I didn't want my loss to be their loss no matter how small. So I took out a post office box at a private mail company, where I was able to include different options in the mailing address. I chose saying apartment. I then wrote and called Joe endlessly to have him return those photos. He finally said he would have them returned to me by courier, "just to be nice." Perfect, I thought, just what I wanted.

After a few days, I went back to my mail drop and was told they had a package for me. But the proprietor was somewhat taken aback as he described the courier. He said it was a menacing-looking black man who looked like a linebacker and acted very agitated when he found that my apartment was a mail drop. And when he tried to get my actual physical home address, he nearly blew his top and became threatening. The shopkeeper told me I should take this as a threat and very seriously. Hearing just some of my story, he thought the courier was out for blood, either murder or grave bodily injury. He said this was *Hollyweird* and stranger things had happened all the time.

The courier threw the package on the counter and left, leaving the shopkeeper thanking his lucky stars.

I knew right then I had to take every precaution to insulate myself and protect my wife and kid.

Just before Christmas, I got back together with my wife and son. As I assumed my position as husband and father, I made Alex an elaborate drag racing strip for matchbox cars out of wood, with starting gate and all. I received a letter from the *National Enquirer*; talk about ironies. Before my own newspaper launch, I had written them about being given any writing projects when I lived in Hollywood. One of their editors offered me a prime-time assignment digging up dirt on Hollywood icon Lucille Ball and her husband Gary Morton. Seems the couple were rumored to be on the marriage skids and had been heard arguing in public. They wanted me to dig up all the dirt I could shovel and also asked if I could get some photos of them in and around their home or anywhere in Beverly Hills. The pay was very high for the whole delivered package.

That writing and photo gig would have given me an open door to further and bigger projects and certainly big paydays, according to the editor. While he admitted it was a challenging and difficult assignment, he claimed getting it could seal my future.

I turned it down—flat. What an intrusion upon someone's life and privacy, I thought. If any of this were true, why would they want to publicize it in such a nasty way? I knew what the *Enquirer* was all about, and in most ways, I was okay with it. But to me, this far exceeded journalism with integrity, and I had no desire, despite promise of personal gain, to uncover a story that could be so personally damaging. Even if it met the *truth* standard of libel, I was disgusted by the whole thing.

Nineteen eighty would be a big year in every way. First, my family was back together, and My Wife was pregnant. I wanted to immediately cover my tracks, so we sold My Wife's house and bought a much nicer and bigger one across town. As soon as we moved in, I got a job as editor of a fitness and bodybuilding magazine, *Muscle Digest*. I felt I was in my element and was very happy. I made huge changes and improvements to the publication and revamped relationships with vendors, writers, photographers, and gym owners, mainly in the muscle-meat market of Santa Monica. During this year, I also secured a two-part interview/story with Lou Ferrigno, TV's Incredible Hulk, with a competing magazine I had previously contracted with. I became a recent visitor to the two main gyms there, the original Gold's Gym and the newer World Gym, both started by legendary Joe Gold.

Toward the end of the year, the coveted Mr. Olympia contest was being held in Sydney, Australia. Our contacts told us they suspected that despite denials, emerging action star Arnold Schwarzenegger was making the trip for alleged publicity purposes and would probably enter the event. I had personally seen Arnold training at World earlier that year, and it sure appeared he was getting in contest shape, but I didn't think much more of it.

Our insider tips turned out to be true as Arnold not only entered but won a very controversial decision. There was a near riot behind the scenes, most of which centered around the last-minute entry and shock of Arnold's victory, many of whom thought he won by cronyism through his mentor Joe Weider, contest promoter and publisher/editor of *Muscle & Fitness* magazine. Weider was, without doubt, the big cheese of the bodybuilding world, especially in his California headquarters. He was Arnold's right-hand man, the man responsible for bringing the Oak over from Austria. And some thought he wanted Arnold to win because of his burgeoning movie career and upcoming production of *Conan the Barbarian*. That in turn, certainly wouldn't hurt Weider's huge publishing empire, as they had a marriage of mutual benefits, so to speak. What-ifs abounded, but the facts were in short supply.

One fact became clear to me despite the controversy; I thought Arnold did win by a whisker of a race horse's snoot, but win he did. Even before the dust settled in Sydney, we had slides and photos overnighted to our magazine office by three to four different photographers, led by Australian Vince Basile. I spent the next two to three days studying the slides under special lighting equipment in our graphics department.

And eyeballed every photo. We had over a thousand of them. It was a tedious task, but I always reached the same conclusion: Arnold. The competition was fierce, with the top guys of the day, but it didn't change my mind. In the end, I felt Arnold won with help from his height and the balance and proportion of his muscularity related to his overall appearance. Sure, he had his flaws, but he prevailed.

I burned the midnight oil for days because I wanted to "scoop" the story and beat all the other muscle magazines to the newsstand, especially Weider's. I quickly called all the major competitors in the event and got exclusive quotes from them about Arnold's victory. They were all stablemates in the Weider camp, and I thought if I sparked their discontent enough right away, I could get their opinions.

It worked; I "scooped" Weider's own men right under his feet. One day just before press time, our office secretary handed me a note, along with a personal request: "Arnold called, Jon, and he wants you to call him back right away."

For the next three to four days, I must have easily gotten close to a dozen notes on my desk to call Arnold: Urgent! At one point, Debbie, the secretary, got a little upset with me, pleading with me to call Arnold back. "Don't worry, Deb, I know what I am doing. I'll call him back on my time. I am building my value and Arnold's anticipation."

Soon, I received a certified letter from Arnold's highfalutin Beverly Hills attorney. The letter basically demanded that I *cease* and *desist* any and all articles or reports concerning Arnold and his Olympia victory. First, I called the legal firm and informed the attorney that as he should well know, the defense to libel was truth and that I intended to follow the rule of law and refused to be intimidated. I added that unless there was flagrant malice, they wouldn't have a leg to stand on. I also said the attorney had no *just cause* to try and demand me to cease and desist anything.

Second, I called Arnold. Initially, he picked up on the heels of the attorney's letter. I repeated everything I told the attorney and added that he should know better to try to stop someone's First Amendment free speech and press rights before they are even published. I reminded him that I understood he got a college degree here in the States and was an intelligent person, but he should realize that he was wrong trying to get me to not write a story before the fact.

Although it was cordial, we went back and forth somewhat on what I would be writing. After some two-way bantering, I told Arnold that since I had all these quotes from other competitors and overall results of the contest; and since there was all this controversy all levied at him, I would agree to interview him and publish his response and defense along with the big report. I said I would call it "Arnold Answers."

Right away, Arnold agreed and then wanted to have full approval rights before it went to press. I told him absolutely not and that I had just interviewed Big Louie, "the Hulk" and he and his wife Carla wanted the same approval rights. Then I said I would tell him the same thing I told them. I show my copy and work to no one prior to publication. I added that I would promise accurate quotes and only print what he said. I said my article would be revealing and honest but fair and objective. We bantered a little more, but he relented.

He reminded me that his movie career was just getting in full gear with *Conan*, and he didn't want any slurs or bad publicity to undermine his career. Under my breath, I felt Arnold was giving me a lot more credit than necessary for my ability to damage his burgeoning stardom. Who was I? Simply, I guess I was someone he didn't really know; oh sure, we had met briefly the prior year in his office, but I was not a member of the muscle-meat market circle of influence peddlers. I was not in his hip pocket. Wherein lay my proposed personal power. I was just a bodybuilding industry upstart and nobody, but I represented the unknown. I loved it and I used it.

The very next day, I conducted a grueling three-and-a-half-hour taped phone interview with Arnold. I held nothing back, nor did he. I thought maybe I could catch him off balance or rattle him so he'd lose his temper and say things he didn't want to divulge, but it didn't happen. I'm convinced that based on our extensive conversation— including his admittance that if he could have his name synonymous with bodybuilding and fitness, including an equipment line, and have some success in the movies he would be happy—he had no idea just *how* successful he would ultimately become. At that point in his life and career, despite his positivism and persistence, he even underestimated himself. Arnold and I were both Leos—me older by a year—but polar opposites. He a smashing success, me a fledgling failure.

When the issue came out on the newsstands, I quickly heard through the grapevine that Arnold got hundreds of copies while filming in Spain and was quite satisfied with my coverage. According to reports, he even proudly handed out *Muscle Digest* to all cast and crew on the set of *Conan*. Case closed.

Chapter Fifty-One

As a nice break, a month before Christmas, My Wife gave birth to a bouncing baby boy—Adam James—who was delivered in twenty minutes and literally shot out like a vaginal torpedo, quite the departure from our first traumatic firstborn Alex. Born pure blonde like a little Viking, and at ten pounds, he looked like he wanted to kick my ass. I was there with My Wife as we used Lamaze again, and maybe he didn't like the idea of his father cutting his umbilical cord, which is a very squeamish thing to do.

The Arnold episode did not close the controversy or its effect on our editorial offices. John Williams, our magazine director, office Svengali and self-admitted tongue-in-cheek communist, was convinced that our offices were bugged during this time by Joe Weider. I argued that why would multimillionaire huge fitness publishing magnet Weider give a rat's ass about little old us over here in Whittier, across LA county from his world headquarters? Williams, an intellect who had an unusual sense of humor where you never really knew where seriousness started and ended, had our staff convinced of it, except for me, the pot-induced graphic artist, and perhaps the publisher, Dr. Donald Wong. John's son, society dropout with an attitude who hung around our offices screaming, *"sex, drugs and rock n' roll,"* was his father's greatest ally. Ironically, John's son would end up a Marine later.

With an atmosphere like that to work in, it was like being in a small sinking boat paddling with your hands across a lake on a stormy day. And that was on a good day! Williams was always wheeling and dealing trying to maintain some semblance of a financial bottom line—that had no bottom. But amidst all the mayhem and excitement, John was planning to take the whole staff and jump ship, leaving me alone with Clyde, the Canadian pothead, who was also planning his departure.

Needless to say, Dr. Wong, a renowned internal medicine surgeon with the Chinese community, got the notice from John and was desperate. He spent hours and days trying to get me to stay and sleep in his medical office so I could be close to him while we tried to keep the boat from sinking. Not that I blamed him, but as the days passed, it seemed he was losing his mind. I finally stuck my neck out and assured him I could keep the magazine operating full bore myself while living at home with only a part-time graphic artist and layout person. Both membership and subscriptions, as well as advertising and marketing—because we had numerous automatic advertisers—I knew I could do myself for at least one more issue, of which we published bimonthly. We agreed.

Before I knew it, Dr. Wong had hired a young upstart publishing consultant who was coming in and analyzing the entire operation. This was greatly upsetting as it showed me that while I had shown my loyalty to the magazine and the doctor, he showed no loyalty to me. I had an interview with Toastmasters International in Santa Ana, not far from our home in Fullerton, Orange County. I gave my notice at *Muscle Digest* and was hired by former Olympic gold medalist in wrestling, Terrence McCann, and subsequently terminated by him within four months. I came aboard as membership director and immediately discovered a major set of problems in the department, which had been buried by the ongoing director, great guy that he was.

I found that the department secretary was a major pothead and was virtually sabotaging nearly every function in the department, some possibly involving membership funds and credits. To prove my case to McCann and our management, I conducted an investigation for nearly two months, showing them proof of letters I had dictated, which came back for my signature with up to twenty errors in grammar, placement, spelling, and typos. I often had to correct her new errors, and this process took four to five drafts to compose a simple business letter. I also noted the times and dates, showing a terrible delinquency in meeting deadlines. I also kept a running track record of her constant breaks, long lunches, early departures, and skipped days, noting her demeanor, eyes, and her marijuana breath. I was tremendously patient and understanding with her at first, noting her alleged desire to improve, but it just got worse. I even spent hours teaching her business and communications protocol from scratch to help her. It was the most pathetic situation in a corporate environment I had ever witnessed. She was totally incompetent, had an attitude, and also affected the two other positions I had in our well-sized department, so vital to the operations of Toastmasters.

When I presented all my documents and proof to McCann and our management, it was very awkward because it was bound to reflect very negatively on the outgoing director I replaced who was elevated to vice president. He was as nice a guy as you could ever meet, and I believed that was the problem; he was too nice and could not, or would not, face the challenge honestly and resolve it. McCann and team could not believe my evidence and how bad it was. McCann looked at me and said, "Well, Jon, it's your department now, what should we do?" I didn't hesitate: "Fire her, immediately, with two weeks' pay but termination tomorrow."

"Okay," McCann said. "Do it." He dismissed the meeting and called the VP into his office.

Within a week, McCann called me into his office, cited my great work in uncovering the long-lasting problem and its negative impact, then gave me my marching papers, saying he had to do it because he feared the girl would come back and file a sexual discrimination suit. Seemed she fought being fired but couldn't argue her case, so when I let her go and shook her hand to leave, she said I touched her hand in a suggestive way. What!? With eyes that were drowning in drugs—I thought pot and cocaine—a huge and sloppy body, an unattractive face and demeanor, she was the absolute *last* female I would have *ever* been interested in, even being the horniest devil on a desert island with no women! Obscene.

Just before I left, however, I had hired her replacement, against all recommendations because she didn't necessarily fit the younger profile they wanted. She was this Jewish lady, fresh back into the job market after a bad divorce, leaving her hometown in New Jersey to start fresh. She hadn't worked since she had been an English teacher before she got married, had three kids, and was a housewife for nearly twenty-five years. She told me how hard it was to even get an interview and would appreciate it if I could give her a chance. I related to her, liked her greatly, and saw from her résumé and a little test I gave her that she was very bright. I called and hired her the next day. I could sense her tears over the phone and felt strongly that I made the right move for the department and Toastmasters despite some shock by who I picked. I defended my move, and many years later, I heard from an insider that the lady I hired was still there doing a great job and loved by everyone.

When I announced my termination to my two other staff members, both women and wholly nice and competent, they were sad and in disbelief. There was also a half-dozen Toastmasters members that got wind of it and were somewhat upset, citing all the outgoing strides I had made for improvements and open communications with the membership for input. The accolades were nice but didn't replace the job. I received a severance package and was out the door, again.

The best memory I took from that brief position with Toastmasters was attending the annual convention that year being held in Las Vegas. The keynote speaker for the event was acid-tongued comedian Joan Rivers. Our headquarters management team was seated high up on a long stage, with the podium in the middle. I was positioned next to the right side of the podium. With her husband Edgar off in the wings, Joan made her way to the podium within an arm's length away. I cringed and hoped she would not use me as a pawn of some kind in her comedy routine, which basically slammed certain celebrities, including actress Elizabeth Taylor and the other Elizabeth, the Queen of England.

Rivers was at her biting best and spent perhaps forty-five minutes throwing barb after barb. As much as she was enjoyed and brought the house down, I was extremely relieved when she departed the stage. Ugh!

Based on contacts I had made over the years by covering wrist-wrestling events, especially the ones covered by *ABC's Wide World of Sports* and other projects, I was contacted by a Jewish businessman in Beverly Hills who had been a competitor himself and had followed my writing over the years. He had a successful company manufacturing pools, many for celebrities, and had a healthy bank account.

He wanted me to head a new magazine for the sport, made me a tentative offer to be editor and partner, and said to me to go home, come up with some ideas, and that we would meet again soon. When we arranged to get together again, he was bringing in another partner, a Jewish attorney, and I insisted upon bringing in another partner on my side, John Williams, my associate from *Muscle Digest*.

Having these business offers and writing projects came to me quite often during the day. A couple of years before, another offer came from a Houston businessman who followed the *Wide World* event and my writing and wanted me to write a book for him, promising to pay

$1,000 a chapter for about ten to fifteen chapters. This offer came when I was living in Minnesota and having just lost my investigating job and needing the money. He promised me an up-front fee to cover expenses just to come down, which I did.

After he picked me up at the airport, he brought me directly to the strip club he apparently co-owned. We talked about this book covering the sport and related competition he wanted to do, with me as dual author or I would ghostwrite, with that being more money. I had brought my article that Billie Jean King's magazine didn't publish and said it was the equivalent of two to three chapters in a book. He said he would pay me his rate, sight unseen. I was seeing this guy in a light that didn't impress me, and as the weekend unfolded, it only got worse.

This businessman brought me to another big dance place, cowboy shit-kicking stuff, and we ran into several girls we took back to his condo. Even though I was in the separation mode again before My Wife and I left Minnesota, I was in no mood for any women as I felt guilty and missed my son. While there, we were drinking wine and this businessman was doing the best job he could to be a big asshole. I took him aside. I told him I didn't appreciate his disrespectful treatment of the girl he had and to stop. He stopped long enough to take her up to his bedroom.

Meanwhile, the girl I was with told me thanks for being a gentleman and asked me what I was doing with such an ass. I shared why I was there, and she said that I should have nothing to do with him, but rather her family would pay me the same amount to write their family history in book form. She said her family were land barons and had been wanting to hire someone for the task anyway. I agreed. We shook hands. Suddenly, screams came from upstairs and the girl came running downstairs and grabbed her friend while yelling, "Sicko, sicko!" They were gone and along with them my contact information.

Early the next day over breakfast, I told the businessman that I didn't want to continue the deal we had agreed to, and I wanted him to take me to the airport earlier. I got my bag, we got in the car, and were off. Houston's freeway system is massive with many lanes of traffic. When the businessman kept trying to obtain the writing I had brought and stop and withdraw cash to pay me for it, I refused. I told him he didn't understand that I didn't want him to have my piece and would not release it. He was livid. He stepped on the gas of the muscle car he had and quickly reached 120 miles per hour, zooming in and out of traffic. It was early in the day on Sunday so there wasn't much traffic. He lurched at my briefcase, but I prevented him from taking it. He gunned the car back up and was weaving erratically down the multiple-lane freeway, going from the extreme right to the extreme left, dodging cars in the process.

I yelled at him to stop and threatened to grab the steering wheel if he didn't, making the gesture to do so before he finally backed off. He pulled into the airport, and I got out and walked around to his opened window. I told him I wanted the money he promised for expenses up front, cash. He refused. I asked him if he was really ready to pay me the money for the manuscript, hinting I may have a change of heart. He opened his wallet and peeled out hundred-dollar bills. I took them and said, "Like I said, I want nothing to do with you." He laid rubber and left. Good riddance.

There were more than enough hangers-on and players surrounding the sport of wrist-wrestling, especially the big one aired on ABC. Because of my many years covering it, I guess I was considered somewhat of an expert or guru of the pastime, and because of that, many people approached me for many different reasons. This offer was, on the surface, the best. After we had our discussion between myself and John plus the pool man and the attorney, we agreed it would be a four-way partnership with them footing the entire bill for the publication of a bimonthly magazine, which would include salaries for both John and I, with me heading up all editorial and graphics and John advertising and marketing. Our next meeting was set for the following week.

When we got together again, John and I were shocked to see a mock magazine cover in full color, with a simple and ridiculous masthead title, plus a Playboy bunny posed on the cover with a good old boy from Georgia and world heavyweight champion. It was truly the most ridiculous thing I could have ever imagined, making no sense. Along with a rolling-out PR campaign in several cities, our partners had shelled out $ 50,000 already. Also, we were introduced to another "partner" from New Jersey, a real thug-looking kind of guy. Here we go again!

I delivered my mock magazine, which was totally different from theirs. Mine was titled *Sportstyle*, and it incorporated *Arm-Sports*, my coined term, including arm and wrist-wrestling, sports fashion, and active lifestyles. I had it all departmentalized and broken down for advertising tie-ins. I explained that since there were major beer companies already endorsing the sport because they saw the value in a quick event that could deliver entertainment in a half minute's time, I thought my venue would get other big-name mainstream advertisers. Williams loved my concept; the others hated it, thinking it was totally inappropriate for wrist-wrestling. The pool guy also said there was one more "silent" partner in New York. We all agreed to meet again soon after further deliberation, shook hands, and John and I left. I also left them with my mock issue *Sportstyle*.

Within several weeks, I sent my partners my total formal withdrawal from the project, saying I wished them well but we weren't on the same wavelength and I was canceling my partnership. In reality, as I also shared with Williams, I wanted nothing to do with this new arrangement and their business plan. Ironically, in the next year, a big glossy *Look*-magazine-like publication came out of New York called *Sportstyle*. I only saw the one issue and bought one for old times' sake.

Right after that, in Century City, two more big-shot Jewish entrepreneurs contacted me for similar projects. There was big-money potential in arm and wrist-wrestling because of the sports entertainment value in only a few seconds, perfect for advertisers. One of these guys made a half million dollars a year pure net profit by tapping into the malls around the country, staging local boy contests and utilizing the mall budgets allocated for publicity and entertainment. Nothing materialized. The second one was a real wheeler-dealer who had this fancy high-rise office and had ideas that I just couldn't fathom. As I sat across from him in his huge overstuffed chair, he was listening very intently to everything I had been saying. And we talked extensively.

Finally, he said, "You know, Jon, I don't think I have ever met anyone as gifted as you are. You have more talent in one finger than I do in all of mine, yet I have amassed a small fortune while you are just struggling by. Why? You are a nice guy?"

I literally didn't have an answer. He added, "I just don't understand it, Jon, I really don't." I certainly didn't have an explanation and thought his analysis was a huge *pro*, trumped by a bigger *con*. We shook and I left. The quicker I could get out of the Beverly Hills area and go back home to Orange County, the better. Every time in that Beverly Hills area, I thought of the Salon and Jesus's visit.

In a couple of weeks, I got the nod to come aboard Orange County Transit District (OCTD) as information officer. The position was vacated so the woman who was in the position previously could be moved up over this one, making sense only in the government sector. The newsletter I was in charge of was dull, boring, and underutilized. I revamped it almost completely and worked quickly to open lines of cooperative communication between the drivers and the rest of the organization.

One day, when I had to take My Wife to LAX because of my wife's car problems and then pick her up again, I was waiting in my car across from arrivals. In those days, there was a place to park at meters right across from the doors. That's where I was when who should come walking across the roadway toward me but Muhammad Ali. He was wearing a dark conservative suit and carried a briefcase. His head was down slightly and looked like the saddest man on the planet. He was obviously headed for the bigger parking structure beyond me as he approached my hood. "Champ, champ," I said, "can I get your autograph?"

I quickly reached down and got an OCTD newsletter, handed it to him, as he broke a very small smile and said, "Sure." I told him my name didn't have an *h* in "John." He nodded and signed. I told him I had asked him an interview question as a college journalist at Stanford, said I liked his speech on "the intoxication of life" and that I knew Howard Bingham through My Wife's best friend, Janice Walters. He responded with a brief "really" and grinned slightly. Since I was a huge boxing fan, it made my day and more even though I felt a little bad that I couldn't lift his spirits.

In less than a year, I was terminated from OCTD. First they said it was for budgetary reasons as the PR, communications, and marketing departments were always the first to go. I knew my tenure there was very productive except for one minor altercation, I thought, with a female department head in the printing division. I had corrected her on misguided assumptions she had made on printing the newsletter, and she only stubbornly obliged. The incompetency, disorganization, and cronyism in government is beyond belief. The waste and layers of needless bureaucracy defies logic and reason, but it thrives in its own cesspool of misdirection and self and management adulation and overindulgence.

There are so many babies in the environment it was like going to work in a big child-care center. In a way, I fit in like a bent-up cat in a docile birdhouse. That was certainly part of my termination. But to ensure my departure, the woman over me made up this scathing report, suggesting I didn't do a good job, citing I was more suited as a creative writer than a straight-news and technical one. While I could not argue that point, I always did my job and easily made deadlines. She also provided an example of my last newsletter that had a photo bleed—a photo going off the page—which I had done purposely, related to the story direction. She said that she had been in the transportation industry for years and that the concept was never used. She also cited the local newspaper reporter who complained about me because of my lack of cooperation. These two were friends, and before when she needed quotes, she was spoon-fed by them without any work on her part. With me, she had to do a little due diligence, and I would not kiss her little liberal ass. Even our department director came to my defense and couldn't believe these allegations, saying I did a quick and thorough job and went to great lengths to do my duties, never having to be reminded of anything. But he didn't fight for me with the brass and didn't have my back, which I hate.

When I had my exit interview with human resources, I pulled no punches and laid it on the interviewer. He went to shut his door. Where had I seen this before? He told me he had to be honest with me by saying I was released so the department could fill the position with another female. He explained that OCTD had gotten directives down from Sacramento that they needed to fill more staff and management positions with minorities, particularly women. He even admitted that it didn't matter if they were fully qualified or not, it was a matter of equal opportunity and the political scene. He, too, thought it was terribly unfair. I got a little upset and cried out, "Yeah, unequal opportunity." I told him I had done a bang-up job and had two kids and a big house mortgage. The guy nearly cried and at least I left feeling some solace from him. This news for My Wife was devastating, and I couldn't blame her.

Chapter Fifty-Two

Less than two years later, I decided to file a wrongful termination suit based partly on reverse discrimination. I had an entire large box full of work and newsletter proof for a case, including every newsletter in the transportation industry and the use of creative layouts and "bleeds." The attorney thought I had a pretty foolproof case but said, unfortunately for me, California had just revamped the statute of limitations law from two years to eighteen months. I was just over that and out of luck.

Later, a friend from OCTD told me they filled my position with a woman, supposedly a friend of my fearless female supervisor. I couldn't help but wonder if it was that newspaper reporter.

So I served as a Mr. Mom while My Wife flew, picking up more trips and income. It was a little unusual for the woman to be the breadwinner back then, but what could we do as I was burned out. Our third child was born, Jeanette "Jenny" Ann, and was about the prettiest baby I had ever seen. It was like God took the best of babies he could find and put them all together to make this beautiful baby girl.

One day, when Jenny was about four months old, we took the kids to Knotts Berry Farm, the large amusement park close to Disneyland. I dropped My Wife off at the outside ticket counter while I went to park the car. Suddenly, before I had a chance to leave, absolute mayhem broke out as this car was driving back and forth through the crowd, finally running over this little boy. I panicked and jumped out of my car, only to see the car go back and forth over the lying boy. My God, no, this wasn't one of my boys, was it? I couldn't see my wife and the kids and assumed the worst. The runaway car, driven by a woman, finally stopped amidst screaming, yelling, and crying. Just then, I saw this small pickup truck and My Wife standing in the truck bed with all the kids. That woman had the wherewithal and quick-thinking action to see this danger and take her and the kids to safety. She well could have saved a life. Any indiscretions on her mothering instincts back in Minnesota had dissipated with these actions. I was not only happy for their safety but also very proud of My Wife and told her over and over again. She had the kids' backs and was a heroine in my book.

As it turned out, an older woman who had a bum leg got her foot stuck in the gas pedal and panicked. Miraculously, the little boy that was run over twice survived with no life-threatening injuries. I had offered myself as a witness to the mother for insurance purposes and keep abreast of his recovery.

Not long after that, Orange County had a rash of child molestations and murders; and along with plans to escape the rat race and live in a more rural environment, we decided to sell the house and move completely out of the area. Again, I sold the house myself without a realtor, making another great profit. Before we loaded up the U-Haul again to move ourselves, I brought the Wife with me to visit my old Marine buddy Harry Parmer and his wife and my old girlfriend Barbara, also living in Orange County.

Harry was now an officer in the Marine Corps, going through OCS after college. I had thought of doing that myself, but never went through with it. From the church we were attending close to home, we heard that some parishioners had left the rat race as well and moved to Arkansas and were very happy. So we chartered our course for the South. My wife took a leave of absence from Able Airlines. Our intention was to start a new life by me finding a business to buy while My Wife would be a housewife. I prepared extensively for this plan by studying the Internal Revenue Service (IRS) formula for buying and selling businesses, utilizing the tax code. It was foolproof, and I knew the formula inside and out, chapter-in-verse. I also took courses in Los Angeles on the subject from an expert in the field. Along with our extensive bank account from real estate investing, we felt prepared.

Somewhere along the way, when I had Alex asleep on my lap, a car from the right-hand shoulder of the road drove across the road right in front of me. As I swerved to avoid him, truck contents swaying from the erratic turns, I grabbed Alex with one arm with all my might and held him down, not having put a seat belt on him because he was sleeping. With a twenty-seven-foot truck and a heavy load, the brakes were not equipped to handle such a demand and only slowed me down. Fortunately, there was no traffic on the freeway, and I was able to barely avoid disaster. The car had stopped in the medium, and I pulled over there as well, ready to tear into him.

I started to yell at the old man, but seeing how shook up he was, I backed off. They were German tourists and were totally disoriented. The husband driver made a rash decision in frustration to drive across the lanes and particular to the traffic. He couldn't speak, but his wife apologized profoundly as I yelled that her husband's actions could have easily gotten us killed. Despite the ruckus, my son nearly slept through the whole thing, incredible as that was. My Wife was in our car behind me with our two other children, and she had the good sense and survival instincts again to follow my tracks exactly as I swerved all over the freeway.

When we arrived in Arkansas, we stayed a few nights with our church friends, and I unloaded the truck in a rental house we got on ten acres in Springdale. While My Wife stayed home, I started the search for a business to buy. The immediate trouble I faced was that all the businesses I looked at were grossly overpriced, according to the IRS formula. I did find a few that weren't, but I couldn't picture myself in them, and their ledger sheets were greatly askew. I spent two months doing this while checking everything else out. With the weather and humidity, the huge bug problem, and a place that didn't necessarily accept northerners and outsiders with open arms, we decided Arkansas wasn't for us. So I rented a car for a week myself and drove across the South, hitting Tennessee, Kentucky, North and South Carolina, Georgia, Alabama, Louisiana, Texas, and Oklahoma, before coming home. I looked at many businesses and found the same challenge in the brief amount of time I had. The one thing I shared with My Wife was of all the states I went through, looking at businesses and houses for sale, I picked one—Asheville, North Carolina.

But after extensive soul-searching and analysis, we decided the South wasn't for us and decided to check out the Bitterroot Mountain Range in western Montana. We gave our notice and got another twenty-seven-foot U-Haul and were off and running. It was the same scenario, me in the truck with Alex and My Wife in the rear car with the kids. We got a hotel for several nights when we arrived and found a house to rent. The neighbors—all Mormons—helped me unload the truck, which was very nice, but they also pushed hard for us to visit their local church, which I politely declined.

Once again, after checking out local businesses for sale, from a chemistry lab to a trailer-making outfit and everything in between, coming up blank, I rented another car and went to Idaho, Washington, Oregon, Nevada, and back home. Many businesses I found were highly leveraged and overpriced mainly due to displaced Californians who bought these places at greatly inflated prices, couldn't make a go of it, and tried to sell the same way they bought— like desperate, unrealistic idiots.

I returned home to My Wife and the kids bone tired and totally burned out and discouraged. Maybe I learned too much and reality didn't match the hypothetical. But to err on the side of unnecessary risk and other people's mistakes, I wasn't about to get caught up in it. One day, after hearing that a place called Grandpa's Pizza in Hamilton was for sale, we got a sitter and I took My Wife down there to check it out. I wanted to prove a point about how hard this process had been. And I wanted to see if she may have a different way of looking at things than me. Amazingly, after discovering a great recipe made by the realtor selling it, a new building, great parking, room for more menu items, a great location right on the highway going into town, charming decor, and a reasonable asking price along with every point being met by the IRS formula, I found out two major snags just before wanting to buy: (1) the realtor forgot to put in a furnace and vent system, only having a big potbelly stove; (2) a new Mormon Church was proposed to go in across the street; (3) and the city council rejected Grandpa's a beer and wine license.

We had a delicious pizza there, which the realtor had done extensive research on, arriving at the best pie he could find after a one-year search, using secrets from the others to come up with his own. We sat there for hours, checking out the customers, asking questions, and splitting the proverbial atom. I shared the highlights of my learned experience with My Wife, and as we drove home, she said she couldn't believe everything I had gone through to find a business, a home, and the perfect area, and felt it was time for me to stop, that she didn't want anything to do with it anymore. She said, "If you chose to go on, you will be on your own." I agreed and took a breath of fresh mountain air although we found out that the valley we were in had a terrible pollution problem because of the inversion problem and so many wood stoves. If you were outside in the winter, which was when we were there, after ten to fifteen minutes, you could wipe black soot off your face.

We decided to leave again and move down to Salt Lake City, Utah, where Able Airlines had a base. My Wife said she would resume her career and that it would be her final move. But eventually, it wouldn't be mine. Another twenty-seven-foot U-Haul and another packing job, this time with not one single hand of help. I probably deserved this. Even though I dreaded moving again, when the time came, in every single instance, I embraced the thought knowing I would be moving to a better place, a safer place. And every time, I had flashbacks to Vietnam, the Marine Barracks, and burials. Seems I was always running and couldn't keep still.

I thought, why not Salt Lake? Singers and entertainers Donnie and Marie Osmond were Mormons and seemed wholesome, decent, and likable. Couldn't be that bad? I thought. I thought wrong!

We settled on a five-thousand-square-foot three-level cedar house in the country, thirty minutes from Salt Lake and Provo, both sandwiched in between. Highland, Utah, next to Alpine, in what was referred to as "Happy Valley," was on the other side of the mountain from actor director, Robert Redford, who had a resort there named Sundance. We were on two acres with the most incredible valley and mountain views you could imagine. It was in an exclusive, private development that claimed some of the most famous artists in America—Gary Smith, painter; Dennis Smith, metal and bronze sculptor; and Neil Hadlock, another metal sculptor. Our neighbors were few and far between, and the locals claimed our house was sitting on a former Indian burial ground.

But before closing on the house, which took two more U-Hauls to get to after renting interim house in Salt Lake, I pleaded with My Wife to go back to California, saying it was a learning experience and we still had plenty of money to buy a house in Orange County. She wouldn't hear of it. Down in our rental, I spent a great deal of effort trying to convince her otherwise. I pleaded that I didn't have good vibes about Utah and wanted to get out while the getting was good. But she liked the casual hub base there and would not consider it. I didn't blame her since I sensed she was totally fed up with my roaming spirit.

After we moved in and attended our first homeowners meeting, my feelings were magnified despite primarily the artists being great people. I once again felt like an alien, as we were the only people that weren't baptized Mormons, including one homeowner that claimed to be a "Zen Buddhist Mormon," which only would make sense to another *Zen Buddhist Mormon*. Perfect, dead Indians and Mormons, what more could I ask for? I fit in like a clubfoot in a moccasin. Anyway, the environment was natural, with creek running through it and our kids loved it, making close friends right away with the Gardner family, the most down-to-earth folks around. Along with our family dog Highness, whom I named, the family was content.

At the same time, I was doing my business and job search, checking into a Vets center in Salt Lake to feel some camaraderie and being a "Mr. Mom" while My Wife flew. I started planting evergreen trees on our total barren lot during which time I saw very unusual, distinct deep ax marks in the side of the house cedar, about four feet from the ground. With the exception of a half dozen, I personally planted over forty-five trees, all from four to ten feet high. It landed me in the hospital twice as the venomous sap from the blowing pine needles pricked my corneas. The pain was incredible. As soon as that pain subsided, I got kidney stones, man's closest companion to childbirth. This was my second (kidney) child as I had them before in California. I was like a camel and thought I didn't need much water.

We found out more things about the house we purchased. We had gotten an incredible deal on the beautifully designed house, and it seemed almost too good to believe. Seems the former owners had five kids and they went through foreclosure when the husband lost his business and everything they held dear. Stories had it that they became so broke they had to put up mattresses against the sliding back doors to keep the snow and wind out as their heat was turned off. It was truly sad. With the desirable benefit of having nothing behind us but only open land and a small mountain, it came with a dear price—the most relentless, persistent, strong wind I had ever witnessed. It blew two to three days a week and was often gale force or more.

We had moved in around wintertime, and after going to Salt Lake for family pizza, we returned down the Alpine Highway, the only way to get to our area. We were caught in this incredible, blinding snowstorm that was so powerful it blew down and over six straight telephone poles, wires and all. We just had a regular-drive car, and after making three attempts to get up the hill to our house, we finally made it only to face our private road totally gone, snow drifts four to five feet high. I took a run at it with gas pedal to the floorboards, but fell short of making the driveway by a thousand meters. The wind was so strong it was blowing totally parallel to the road, taking away virtually all visibility. It was ice cold and truly scary. I would go first with Adam, return to the car to get Alex, and help My Wife and little Jenny. It was a battle of wills between man and nature, with man barely prevailing. Again, My Wife was a trooper. We found out later just before we moved in that five people were killed on the Alpine Highway in similar conditions.

During the winter, I spent many nights outside on my knees in snow storms and wind, bailing water out of the basement window wells that were flooding water into the lowest level. Sometimes I'd be out there for several hours braving the pounding conditions, with my hands feeling numb with cold and my knees on fire, kneecaps later removed of their skin. I become to see it as a battle, a challenge I wasn't about to lose, so I just kept fighting it, swearing enough to disturb the buried Indians and the Mormon community that thankfully couldn't hear me. Sometimes I would take a minute break and stand back while screaming to the skies just in case someone was listening. I didn't have time to pray. During the course of the years and winters we were there, I imagined I did this a half-dozen times each season. Barriers I tried to implement had no to little effect, as the wind would blow them away.

The winds also blew off our TV antenna three times, the last one anchored to the roof with double steel cables. Besides that, the winds also blew apart parts of the back deck, the sliding glass doors in the back and side, and broke nearly all the seals in the double-pane windows throughout. Maybe we just weren't welcomed, as I had those feelings inside trying to make light of the situation. One day, early on in the summer, My Wife took the kids shopping while I stayed at home upstairs organizing my storage.

Soon, I thought they were home as I heard the floors creak—terrible noises with the poor job done on the floor joists—and I heard other loud noises.

I finally got up and went to the stairway, looking out of the huge seven-foot picture windows to see the car—it wasn't there. I returned to the room, only to quickly return to the foyer as I heard many footsteps on the stairway again and what I thought were distant screams. I ran downstairs thinking to find trouble with the kids. Still weren't home. Then I heard those floor joist noises going down the stairway to the basement. I quickly ran down there thinking I would catch an intruder. No one. Then from the basement, I heard the steps going upstairs again. They were unmistakable because the floors were never properly secured with nails and adhesive, and I hated that yet, it certainly let you know if someone was coming.

When the Wife and the kids finally came home, they made less noise than the noise I heard while they were gone. I just shrugged it off. There must have been some explanation although I had no idea what? Humorously, I thought maybe I should have a little powwow with the deceased Indians and apologize for assuming their land and make peace. I followed by subliminal speaking that I may even have some Indian blood in me, as my grandmother, Dad's mother, used to claim that Claude, her husband and my never-seen grandfather, was the son of a Cherokee Squaw. It just gave me a chuckle and that was that.

Chapter Fifty-Three

I finally nailed down two major job opportunities, both in the nutrition field at local herbal firms, which were growing like crazy at the time, one with many promises and holding time; the company changed hands, totally revamping their organization and my writing, PR position. The other was more convoluted and upsetting. I dressed up in my three-piece suit, put my then-pregnant wife in the car along with the kids, and with the feeling of a family support mechanism, I went to the company in Springville, outside of Provo. I parked the car full right in front of the total glass facade. An older dressed-up gentleman greeted me, all smiles. He took my résumé, cover letter, and writing samples and looked at me, citing how qualified I was and a perfect fit; noticed my car full of family out front; smiled broadly; and noticed by my credentials that we were new to the area.

"Oh, I noticed you now live in Highland. Do you know So-and-So?"

"No," I replied.

"Well, do you know, So-and-So?" Again I replied in the negative. Suddenly, his smile turned upside down as he said, "I'm sorry, but this job is filled."

I was dumbfounded from being a perfect fit to being rejected in minutes. I questioned his process and thinking, quickly realizing it was futile. He dumped me on the spot, qualified or not, because if I didn't know one of those two people in my area—in the *wards* or *stakes* as they call them—that would only mean to him that I was either a fallen-away Jack Mormon or a gentile, non-Mormon, either of which sent me to the door. I was both devastated and mad. Disqualified again for reasons aside from being more than highly qualified. For a second, I felt I could have thrown the four-eyed monster in his perfect suit right down the open stairway. But I may have broken a step, and I certainly didn't want that. I shared with my wife quietly my thoughts, and she felt incredibly bad but understood my feelings.

Since I couldn't seem to secure a job nor find a business to buy, which I quickly gave up on anyway, I assumed my role as frustrated Mr. Mom although I loved being home and overseeing my kids, as they meant everything to me. I took care of them well, fed them three squares a day, went out for treats, let all their friends come over, had video parties and other fun, and knew exactly where they were at all times. When My Wife was gone, I would play matchbox cars and Legos with Adam for hours, practice boxing with Alex endlessly, and watch Jenny and Chrissy play house with their dolls in between. I also kept the house clean, did all the dishes, but admittedly seldom washed clothes.

Because my eldest son Alex had taken karate locally and earned a purple belt, I took him downstairs quite often to teach him boxing, especially the standard one-two, left-jab, and right-cross combination.

He was a great student and, as a test, once went ten straight rounds of hitting my heavy bag just like a pro with three-minute rounds and a one-minute rest. I cheated though and made each round twenty seconds longer and the rest ten seconds shorter. But that kid never flinched. Incredibly, he did that at ten years old, so I always told people and referred to Alex's *ten and ten*. I told him he did way more than me when I was training as a teen for the Golden Gloves.

Adam, meanwhile, was a young but gifted artist who won an award for his bird drawing at our yearly association picnic, selected by, of all people, our own artists, the two Smiths and Hadlock. They were truly decent guys, always willing to help someone. Jenny and Chrissy just continued being darling little girls. They were always making little forts inside for themselves and their entourage of dolls.

Early on upon visiting the Vets Center, an independent and outside subsidiary of the VA, I was getting counseling from a decorated Army paratrooper who served in Vietnam. He was a great support liaison on my total frustration with Utah, jobs, and the Mormons. He was also a major real estate investor and hated the prejudice shown to Veterans when he came back despite *then* being a Mormon.

He also had absolute disdain for the Mormon hierarchy that he witnessed get many young Mormons out of the draft and out of serving in the war, many of whom were in his school. He was half Indian and openly joked about how he was on the warpath with them ever since, working hard to legally and lawfully beat Mormons at their own real estate game.

For whatever that was worth, he was the best helpmate, fighter, and counselor ever. He tried numerous times to file a claim with the VA for me for PTS (post traumatic stress), but I thought I was undeserving, and who was I to make a claim with the government when I was alive and well? I could not justify any such thing in my mind or heart and always would cut our talk short and leave. He said I had all the classic symptoms, centering on various forms of guilt; but from those early eighties to mid to late eighties in SLC, I would have no part of it. I refused to allow him to initiate the paperwork. It was so far from my mind, I even forgot the term PTS.

Our fourth child, Christina Rene, born a perfect little brunette like her mother, came without trouble and I once again cut the umbilical—ugh!—cord after utilizing Lamaze, being right there during childbirth and lending my support. Seeing your child born makes it real hard for a man not to cry. I tried.

During my tenure as house husband, I heard some pretty strong tales from my kids about "visitors" to their rooms. While being patient and nonjudgmental, I found ways to dismiss the allegations. Years later, Kerry Gardner, who often took care of the kids, conveyed a story from a time once when she was sleeping over in Adam's room. She said she was abruptly awakened by a man standing next to the bed, but of course, there was no man there, at least in the flesh. It freaked her out so much she would never stay overnight again. Considering Kerry didn't drink or do drugs and was totally honest, reliable, and down-to-earth, it confirmed certain things to me, at least by thinking that one had to keep an open mind in life.

During those days, we belonged to this little Christian church in American Fork, an adjacent town. A new family was introduced into the congregation that were waiting to break their ties to the Mormon Church, going back numerous generations. Because this family wanted to "officially" disavow their beliefs and desire to cut all formal ties to the Church. They arranged through their ward bishop to go to church one day and go before the congregation and say they no longer wanted to be Mormons and wanted their names removed from the records. Being new Christians and being sincere, the whole family obliged the formal process and showed up with suits and dresses to stand in front of the entire church.

But instead of what they were told would happen, the bishop read "charges" against the parents of not tithing and not following beliefs and church protocol. Well, since they gave their notice months before this day, naturally that occurred because they chose it to be. The couple told our church that while the Mormon bishop read off the litany list of infractions, the wife and kids were standing there crying, feeling ashamed. Strength. Fortitude. Pure guts. That's what I call a family with convictions, belief, and faith. As terribly sad as that story was, it won the hearts and support of everyone. But it didn't end there. Right after being formally excommunicated, the former friends of the family's kids were not allowed to play with them anymore, calling them names and devil worshipers.

Our own kids had numerous accounts of being ridiculed in school by their Mormon counterparts, causing some unfortunate times of awkwardness and tensions. It pissed me off to no end, just confirming to me we didn't belong there. One time, when having an off-record neighborhood meeting, the artists, all fallen-away Jack and Jill Mormons, told me some incredible stories of their church that went on behind-the-scenes, validated by the fact that they sat on management boards of the church headquarters in downtown Salt Lake. Often, I would argue with My Wife that we should move out of the state. It went over like a non-Mormon in Utah. I argued on behalf of our entire family and for my job/career situation. My folks visited us once, with Dad buying groceries and remarkably giving me some cash. Dad totally agreed with my frustrations and understood. At least I had that. We had lengthy talks while going shopping alone, and I was once again tempted to talk with him about his *secret*, only again to decide against it.

I finally got a job for a national sales, marketing, and motivational trainer who had moved his entire operation to Alpine from the South. This businessman had trained many successful people over the years, including some big names, but he was very unorthodox in his approach, bordering questionable.

I was brought aboard as a writer and public relations man although I quickly became an idea man for traditional concepts that were foreign to him, by choice or otherwise. He gave me the task of formulating titles and slogans for the training and company in which I produced many dozens of bankable ones, somewhat shocking him. Based on the word *success*, which was the benchmark of his business, I was to produce a plan that would be incorporated into his presentations for success and personal and business improvements, covering all major aspects of life. This would be for both his employees and trainers, plus his customers and clients.

The unveiling of my business and marketing plan centered around the concept of new training materials, using more time-tested traditional techniques, but with his own twist and signature, plus a monthly newsletter that I titled *Prosperity Plus.* The subtitle was *The Positive Way to Financial and Personal Success.* Days later, although many others loved my approach, the training guru shot down my idea, saying it was too traditional and wanted instead for me to find negative ways to success.

What? At this same time, I had a deep sense that he was in severe financial straits himself and I sincerely questioned his motives, company, and honesty. Right away, he had real trouble paying me and hinted that if I was really sincere, I'd work for free for a while. I quickly found out that many of his loyal staff were paid practically nothing or nothing. I would not join them on some dog and pony show.

Up in Park City, the beautiful ski area, the guru held a huge weekend event to train people on his principles and to teach how to sell his *huge* very expensive course to others. I saw this entire operation as a last-ditch desperate attempt to save his ass and salvage his company. He was making the argument that if their hearts and heads were really into success, they would do anything to finance their venture, even if it meant selling their house or taking out a second mortgage. I was outraged and personally seething inside. During the last day and a long lunch break, many people were contemplating how to come up with enough money. I went around to their hotel rooms and discussed options with them, mainly ways to not proceed. I had it. I refused to be party to this charade any longer. I talked two ladies out of tapping into their bank accounts, one young newlywed couple to not get a loan from their parents, and the last, a husband and wife team with three children, to not mortgage their home at the tune of some obscene amount. This last couple was a real battle, taking me nearly an hour.

With their entire life in hock, debts up to their ears following this guru, I told them in no uncertain terms that if they didn't leave out the back of the hotel right then, I was going to kidnap them and haul them away personally. The wife broke down in tears and agreed with me, sobbing uncontrollably. The husband finally relented as well, tears welling in his eyes. And with their departure, I left out the back as well, telling his primary secretary—a great gal—that I was quitting and would not be back.

After the dust settled on that fiasco, I applied for a PR position at a large downtown Salt Lake Hospital, which I was more than qualified for. I never even got a call for an interview. Then I saw the ad again in the paper just two months later, suggesting to me that the hire didn't work out. I applied again, dressing up in a suit and personally delivered my résumé and papers. No interview. I couldn't believe it, so one day, I dressed up again, went down to human resources of the hospital, and asked for clarification of their hiring practices and this position. They were fairly indifferent and borderline belligerent, saying they hired the right person. Despite wearing my three-piece suit, I didn't come across as a Mormon, and it was obvious I'm sure. I didn't have that docile, subservient look and manner. I was much too strong, confident, and in-your-face. I stood out like a bold little cabin perched by itself on the side of a mountain.

I demanded to see the highest-ranking management authority at the hospital. After much delayed discussion behind doors, they directed me to the vice president of the hospital high up overlooking the downtown temple. When I went through the gatekeepers and got to his posh offices, I was cordially welcomed and told to sit down across from his desk and huge office chair that was raised on an elevated level. I grabbed a cushion from another chair and added to mine, raising me up. This move took away his speech for several minutes.

I told him the whole story, showed him my résumé and papers, and basically argued my case, stating primarily that with my level of direct experience exceeding every perimeter, how could I not even be called for an interview. He turned around to the walled desk behind him and called the PR department, asking for particulars on the hiring and why it took two attempts to fill the position when they had other qualified people like me who never even had a chance for an interview. He turned back and told me they hired the most qualified person for the job. We politely debated briefly until I said, "I'll tell you why I wasn't hired."

I took him by surprise. "Okay, Jon, I'm all ears. Please tell me."

"Because I am *not* a Mormon. I was not even qualified enough to get an interview when they ascertained that I was not one of *them*."

His response was incredible disbelief and aloofness. "And just what makes you think such a thing? I assure you this hospital is a great mixture of Mormons and non-Mormons alike. We employ all the standard hiring practices, I assure you."

"That may well be, but your PR department, I am sure, is a highly sought-after level of hire, and I bet that despite the claim that Salt Lake City now has more non-Mormons than Mormons, every one of the nine member staff down there is a Mormon."

The VP rocked back in his big leather chair and told me how years before he left his Methodist roots, moved to Utah, was baptized a Mormon, he had great success going to college and becoming a doctor and had never looked back.

I couldn't help myself. "That's unfortunate that you left your Christian roots and faith to become a Mormon."

He was beside himself as he spun back around and called downstairs again, only to turn back to me and claim there were five staff members that were non-Mormons and four that were Mormons.

"Doctor, call back downstairs again please and honestly ask them, how many are actually baptized Mormons, non-practicing Mormons, or not?"

He was now visibly upset and thought it was a "waste of time and another call." But he reluctantly made the call. I could hear every word he was saying before he slammed the phone down. "Okay, Mr. Meade, all of the nine are baptized Mormons. Are you satisfied?"

"Besides the job itself and how they handled it, I believe there is an unwritten, silent, subliminal policy that by nature of how Mormons believe they are the one and only true church, and that they are trained to think they are in a higher echelon than the rest of mankind, I just didn't make muster."

"So what are you saying exactly, Jon?"

"I am saying—I think proving—that I was discriminated against in the hiring practice, never had a chance to begin with because of who I am, and this is against equal opportunity and federal discrimination laws. There was not a single reason why I shouldn't have been called in, at least for an interview. Add this to the fact that

I apparently was not even given my five points' advantage for being a Veteran."

We bantered back and forth until he pulled out a little piece of paper and wrote on it. "Jon, I think you have some real issues here, being a Veteran and all, so I am going to advise our psychiatrists at our facility to provide you with free counseling for three months."

Right then, I envisioned myself reaching over his desk, grabbing him by his suit lapels, dragging him about ten steps over, and flinging him through the wall-to-wall window and down upon the sidewalk chewing gum. Rather, I crumpled up the note in front of him, said "thanks," and left.

I went back to being a house husband and Mr. Mom, totally disenchanted with everything but my wife and kids. I hated Utah and everything it stood for, but the worst was yet to come.

My Wife was somehow introduced to some organization that indoctrinated its members on how to harness all the inner beauty and talent within them to make them a better person. She ran it by me, and it seemed good so I approved. The name was Lifestrive, and they charged a hefty fee for their training over one weekend in downtown Salt Lake, which was facilitated by non-professionals. When she returned, she was somehow "enlightened" and I was somehow unimpressed. But I still supported her. My Wife was now fully embracing all that she learned, acting as though she had all the answers to life, but not making much sense. In her muddled mind she probably thought she was doing the right thing, but as it played out, her thinking became deeply flawed. The more training, the more confusion.

One day, all the disappointments, pressures, and failures made me lose it momentarily, ripping out the phone and throwing it down the long hallway, nearly missing Adam. I quickly went to him and hugged him, feeling bad. My Wife and I had an argument in front of the kids, and we finally took it to our bedroom, where I remarkably found myself saying I wanted a divorce. My Wife was shocked and tried to understand my frustrations, but ended with telling me I should attend Lifestrive too and learn.

The very next day, she asked me to please come and get counseling with her with this well-respected local marriage counselor, PhD, who was also a local Christian pastor. I said *no*, my mind was made up, and that I wanted a divorce. She pleaded with me. I refused to listen, thinking of no one but myself. Within several weeks, My Wife had a change of heart and said she agreed with a divorce, citing that we were on different paths and didn't have the same goals in life anymore. Just hearing her say that knocked sense into me. Now, I had a change of heart—not believing what I had said about wanting a divorce—and told her I was willing, more than willing, to attend marriage counseling. I told her I couldn't believe I said those things and couldn't conceive the idea of a divorce and breaking up the family. But she again said it was the best idea to get the divorce. She was now into another related psychological group called *The Future*, with the same format as the first, and said she was made to realize that I was only looking out for myself and was using her as a gravy train. And that I was holding her back from realizing her true inner potential as a person and a woman. Her support group of mainly like-minded females told her I was nothing more than a typical user and abuser.

Coming from her now in this demeaning way, I thought back to our entire marriage and recalled how she'd rave about me as a man and husband to other stewardesses, friends, and anyone who would listen, almost to the point of embarrassment. She would always compliment me on my natural instincts as a parent and father, oftentimes admitting she wished she were better. And now this. I was at a loss, confused, with no sense of direction. *It was raining, I was tired, and I felt the cold steel of a barrel again upon my forehead, as surely as if I was back in that foxhole in Vietnam.*

Just weeks before, My Wife had written a glowing love letter to me, so to be blindsided like this was a shock that reverberated through my body like an earthquake. But even in that short period of time, she was overcome with self-pity and victimhood. I thought to myself, how could I have even contemplated a divorce with my own self-pity? But mine lasted a few days, and I totally realized the error of my thinking and reversed course. My Wife, however, was pointed on course to discover the real *her* within, and nothing was going to stop her, especially me.

The psychology of success was written for her in the cards of her newfangled training, which took precedence over me, the kids, and the family. She actually expressed this to anyone who would listen, including those in the last day we attended church together. This one ex-Mormon lady with eight kids, who was going through a divorce herself, took me aside, said she thought My Wife had gone crazy and was wrong, understood, and wished me well. The minister tried to counsel with My Wife many times to no avail. From My Wife's switch from Catholicism to claim of being *born again* when we lived in Orange County, she was now entering into her own form of *new age* wackoism, where she was the centerpiece of her own life. The PhD counselor My Wife had raved about wanting to use before she had a change of heart had also tried to reach her with common sense and logic. He told her the story of his own secretary that had over twenty years of work experience before moving to Utah but couldn't secure a job for nearly three years until he hired her. He did this to support my struggle with employment there and try to reach her thinking with reason instead of her training using personal self-realization and pure emotion. It failed.

As a last-ditch effort to reach My Wife, I found out where one of her meetings was in this big auditorium and brought little Chrissy with me. I saw My Wife sitting up front, so we sat toward the back, listening to much of what I thought was pure BS. When the crowd was dismissed, I humbly approached My Wife while holding Chrissy and tried to talk to her. She totally shined me on, with some of the other women around her looking at me with total disdain. She all but ignored Chrissy in my arms. It was as if we were both total strangers. It hurt.

Chapter Fifty-Four

$\mathbf{M}$y Wife filed divorce papers, and I suddenly had two weeks to move out. When I realized there was no hope of salvage, I resigned myself to it and agreed to an uncontested divorce through My Wife's attorney, solely based upon the best person I knew her to be and saving the family untold money, loss and grief. It was a huge mistake. As I was moving my stuff out from the basement, I found that all my service and Vietnam photos were lying in water. Seems My Wife flooded the basement bedroom with a hose through the window well while watering something, claiming it was a mistake.

I picked up the huge pile of wet, blackened, ruined photos and went upstairs and dropped them heavily on the floor, saying I couldn't believe what she did. I was very upset and certainly raised my voice. The kids were there so I quit. My Wife then threatened to call the police if I didn't pick up my photos and leave immediately. I did, just to avert a scene. But the move caught me off guard as it was before the scheduled departure.

I went from living in a five-thousand-square-foot house to being homeless in hours. In the divorce settlement, I signed off on all the house equity in exchange for child support for a few years. I took all the credit card debt we had racked up recently with major home repairs and upgrades. We split our savings account with a solid advantage to her because of the kids. She got all the furniture, except a few little pieces and souvenirs from Europe. We split the cars. My Wife naturally had her job, income, and benefits while I had nothing. But my biggest mistake by far was bequeathing sole custody of the kids to My Wife. My second biggest mistake in my humble opinion was assuming she would be decent, maintaining the same qualities of the person I had married.

Artist Gary Smith heard of our divorce and called me. I basically told him that the pressures of not finding work undermined our marriage. He immediately offered to lend me money, even giving me thousands of dollars, but I refused knowing that was not the driving force behind our union collapse. Gary's very thoughtful gesture, however, helped give me *some* semblance of humanity and personal hope, as I readied to depart the house and marriage. But I loved being a hands-on father, and now it was fading away. Gary had my back and it felt good, but my front was collapsing.

Saying goodbye to the kids was another blur, blinded by hurt and utter devastation. I do remember that as hard as I tried to explain a divorce, they could not conceive me not coming back home to live. I felt I had to keep a strong face and demeanor, but inside I was dying, just simply not believing this was happening. The youngest child was barely three, and the eldest was ten and a half. All so terribly young. I even had a hard time saying goodbye to our dog who was with us all through the birth of our kids. I was usually the one who fed and played with her.

So this was what divorce was all about, especially with kids? I already hated it. What a totally immature and selfish act, I thought. While I could certainly understand divorce in some extreme spousal and child abuse cases, I couldn't understand how couples could fall in love, have children as an extension of that love, and allow it to all fall apart at the expense of young and innocent children. I had learned about forgiveness through my spiritual experience in Beverly Hills, but apparently, despite her claims of previously being *born again*, My Wife didn't. It seemed like she was *dead again*.

The first several nights I spent in my car despite winter starting. I felt that any discomfort was a small punishment, and I had no complaints. I drove down Alpine Highway at one point and saw our big house from the road with the lights on. I wondered what the kids were doing and had to shake off moist eyes. For some days thereafter, I lied and said I was a recovering alcoholic so I could get a room in a halfway house in Provo. It was disgustingly filthy, with enough big bugs to pick up the bed, but again, I was in the self-sacrifice mode to save money for an apartment for the kids' sake. After several weeks of staying with a friend—Jimmy Hughes, who had been following the guru I briefly worked for—and his small family, I secured an apartment toward Salt Lake.

I was so excited to have the kids over for the first time despite it being so awkward. After I got them settled in, Alex, my eldest and we always shared a special bond, grabbed me in the kitchen and hugged me with all his might. "Dad, I hate this divorce, why can't you cancel it and come home?" He was crying, and I tried not to join him. I couldn't hug and be with those kids enough. I tried many times, in many ways, respectfully, to be with my kids more; but My Wife usually circumvented my efforts unless occasionally it served her convenience.

Her favorite sayings from her weirdo training were "Does it add quality to my life?" and "Does it serve my higher well-being?" It was all about her. She used it while overseeing the kids, and it was making them frustrated and upset because she verbalized those drumbeats all the time, word for word. One time, in a rare moment of humanity and me returning the kids after a weekend, she shared that she now believed in reincarnation. Respectfully, I asked her what she felt she would be reincarnated to and she said a *horse*. I responded quickly, "Yeah, maybe a horse's ass." She slammed the door in my face.

For the holidays, we agreed that I would take the kids early for Christmas while she went back to Nevada to visit her family. I had gotten a Christmas tree and three to four presents for each child, plus tons of food and treats, even making a complete turkey dinner all from scratch, just like I had done for them on Thanksgiving. On the night My Wife, not yet officially divorced, dropped off the kids, we were having a record-setting severe and cold snowstorm.

She dropped them off with barely a word murmured. I made a quick transfer with the kids from her car to mine, as I planned a mall visit to see Santa and play video games. I asked her to wait just a moment while I started my car and warmed it up. It didn't start. I asked My Wife if I could pop her hood real quick and jump-start my car with my jumper cables. She said no, saying it *didn't add quality to her life*. I said, "Can you imagine Jesus saying that to anyone?" I argued my case, citing the storm and the kids, but she said *no* again and drove off. Maybe I should have called it a night because of the conditions, but I had promised them and hated to make promises I couldn't keep. I asked this old lady for a jump in the parking area and got it.

While we were at the Crossroads Mall in downtown Salt Lake across from the temple, we were on the escalator on the second level fighting the crowds. Suddenly, the kid right in front of me, who was too cool to tie his tennis shoes, was screaming and panicking. His shoelaces were caught in the elevator, and they were being sucked into the machinery. I yelled at the kid to curl his toes, and I pulled him up and out of the shoe. The entire shoe was sucked into the elevator with just a hint of the end. The whole system shut down. The kid, around Alex's age of ten, was pretty shook up. His mother nearby couldn't believe it all happened so quick and was very appreciative, couldn't stop saying *thank you*. Between Alex saying it was a good thing I was there and the mother's nice words, it helped erase what My Wife had said. Later, I found out that the mall elevator was totally down, setting a record for "out of service."

After Christmas Eve passed and it was early Christmas Day, I agreed to return the kids home. When I was back in my apartment and calling my folks for holiday wishes, I laid down to relax and turned on the radio, which was a big mistake. The first song I heard was "White Christmas" by Bing Crosby. It softened me up. Soon, I heard "I'll Be Home for Christmas," with words that curled me up in a fetal position and made me cry: "You can depend on me . . . I'll be home for Christmas, if only in my dreams." Even there alone, I tried not to cry; but the more I did, the more I cried.

My entire face was wet, full of tears. I couldn't uncurl my legs. Just as I was drying up, Tony Bennett's incredibly touching "Smile" played. The lyrics were heartrending: "Smile, when your heart is breaking, smile when you know it's breaking" and on. I had a new round of tears. I missed my kids so intensely I thought I was having an emotional breakdown. I turned off the radio, went to the kitchen to eat, but couldn't. But I slugged down some vodka—it took a lot—and finally crashed.

During that time, I had met a lady at a dance sponsored by the Mormon Church. She greatly sympathized with my divorce and the sense of losing my kids. She said she belonged to the polygamy colony and said that if I first became a Mormon then transitioned into the polygamy group, she could be my main wife and she would help me get young wives to add to the clan. Then I could start a large extended family with many kids and never feel loss again.

While finding the whole thing hard to conceive, the offer was temping—for about two days. I loved the idea of never losing kids again, but that emotion was driven by my own profound sense of loss. The lady had come from a long line of family practitioners of polygamy, and they justified their beliefs by a verse in the first page of the book of Mormon, saying, paraphrasing, that having "plural" wives and multiplying, they would be in the highest graces of God. Naturally, the Mormon Church itself distanced themselves from such beliefs when they took statehood status in Utah—they had to.

This lady was only slightly attractive, but quite intelligent, thinking that I had something "special" for the colony and she would introduce me to the right people. After thinking, "Why me? How do these things happen to me?" the inner journalist came out and my interest was greatly piqued. I knew there was nothing Christian about any of this whatsoever, but at the same time, I was fascinated. First, through her contacts, I was asked to clean up these bricks that had been knocked down from a very old building. The pay that was offered was quite impressive, but the job was way too big for me alone. So I got the approval through this polygamist contractor in charge and brought in my buddy and the guy who helped me, Jimmy Hughes, who was big, strong—college ballplayer, having gotten a pro offer with the New England Patriots before getting injured—because he wasn't working.

I shared the story with Jimmy, and with his sense of humor, we spent our time joking around about the polygamist thing besides busting our buns cleaning and chipping bricks. We were there all week, calculating our time and money earned. In the end, before the job was totally done, they pulled us from the site and told us thanks for all the help. We asked about the pay, and they dismissed it, saying this was committed to by a prior arrangement with So-and-So. The guy pulled me aside, asking if I was Jon and told me in so many words that this was a test for my commitment and patience. I told Jimmy, and he just laughed it off, great guy that he was, saying it was a worthy workout anyway. My tests weren't over, however; they were just beginning. I kept an open mind just to see where it would take me.

While Jimmy was out of the picture, I was given the address of a polygamist family and was to join them for dinner. Bluffdale is a town on the Salt Lake side of the point of the mountain and is where the primary polygamy community resides. The family lived in a very modest house, considering they had five children from several years old to a teenager. They simply could not have been more gracious, humble, decent people. We shared a huge dinner, with the mother and eldest daughter making everything from scratch, including the best apple pie I had ever had. Even the bread was homemade and such a treat for a vagabond like me. The father was in the financial field, working primarily in the polygamist area. I spend the night there, and the plan was to take me to the polygamist church the next day. Apparently, my visit was also being coordinated with some big family transition the same day.

The church itself was a large all-cement structure with no visible windows and could be faintly seen from the 15 freeway. I was told I was the first ever non-Mormon, non-polygamist to step through the threshold of that church. Add to that the fact they knew from my background disclosures that I was also a journalist and writer. I was told by some church elders that it was virtually unheard of. They seemed mystified by my admittance. I was taken aside by a lead elder and was told that Mr. Allen, leader and president of the polygamist colony, said I may be a special messenger from God and someone he wanted to welcome and embrace. I was dumbfounded. I wasn't even a basic Mormon. But the lady that initiated the whole polygamy thing in the first place got me to open up about my divorce and kids, and with the outpouring of emotion, I told her most of the story of my *visit* from Jesus. This, no doubt, was all conveyed to the polygamist leader.

The church was jammed to the rafters, with a row of church elders up on the stage, half of them nodding off. I noticed quite a few girls and young women checking me out, giving me a sweet and innocent look. I later learned that it was usually the women who picked the men to form the extended polygamist family, with some certain exceptions. There was this one pretty young lady, natural blonde and very wholesome looking, who never took her eyes off me the entire three hours I was in that church.

If ever a man were tempted, it would be under these circumstances. But surely she must have heard about this unusual guest, in the form of me, the church was welcoming in, as everyone knew everyone. It was said that how these women picked or put a request in for a possible meeting with a man was by seeing how they acted with their present wife and children in church.

Besides the seven-member family I sat with in the pews, there was another lady, Hispanic, who joined us. The whole service was based upon some general church protocol, then a series of members from all age groups who would go up to the podium and give their testimony of belief, with personal slants. I found it incredibly long and boring because there was little to no emotion showed and this low-key level of humility that caused their voices to barely project outward.

As the service ended and we were leaving the building, the husband kissed his wife and kids and went off with the Hispanic lady. The eldest daughter told me to come with the rest of the family. I was floored. What was going on? The wife and kids were trying to hold back their tears but weren't too successful. The wife finally told me as we left that her husband had gotten a spiritual revelation that it was time to take a second wife and produce more children. And that they would all reunite later after they had their "time alone," normally called a honeymoon. The wife was devastated. The kids were walking like zombies. Whatever else made me feel uncomfortable, this situation was the ultimate sad and nonsensical. The wife was attractive, feminine, and as sweet as that apple pie she made. She nearly gave me diabetes. That five-hundred-meter walk to their car was like they were dragging the weight of the world upon their perfectly dressed-up shoulders.

No matter what else I thought about Mormonism and polygamy, I knew that these women, for the most part, were about the most self-sacrificing, underappreciated, fiercely devoted, loving mothers and pure sweethearts in the world. I also thought it was a male-dominated dictatorship for the husband and father and very unfair, abusive actually. When we got home, the wife told me through wet eyes, this had been coming, and her husband, in this case, had picked the lady, who came from Mexico City and was a nurse. She said the lady would get a nursing job in Utah and would buy a small house, where they would make their home and start a family. He would then divide his time between his original and first wife and family and his new one.

The wife then told me how polygamist living arrangements usually worked, with the different scenarios. They could all live under one roof, wives in different bedrooms or parts of a big house, or they could just use the same bedroom and rotate nights, or weeks, or whatever. It seemed like a big religious cult brothel to me, with the spiritual, sexual benefactor being the husband. It was like an adult version of adolescent musical chairs, only using houses, rooms, beds, and wives. I wanted to just take the wife in my arms, hug her tight, and hold her, telling her it would (somehow) be all right. But I couldn't or wouldn't.

Later that early evening, the wife told me we were going back to the church for another three-hour session, but there were various classes and learning options. The family spread out when we arrived. I was encouraged to sit in on the class in the auditorium by the almighty polygamist prophet himself, Mr. Allen, whom I had been properly introduced to earlier being told I was among the privileged few to have a personal audience with him. He seemed like a regular joe to me, very likable, but he had seven wives and over fifty children. Just the thought of it made me gag, but for the devoted, it is the highest and oldest true calling of a polygamist Mormon, who chooses to take the plural (multiple) marriage and family plunge.

They are going against the mainstream Mormon Church and against the alleged state and federal laws. They do it anyway and seem to enjoy the challenge—and just *maybe*, the multiple wives and bedmates. I had even overheard several of the teenage polygamist boys joking about it, like they couldn't wait—of course, their testosterone was running on overdrive.

Chapter Fifty-Five

I'll never forget the title of the presentation given by the polygamist prophet: "How to please all of your wives all the time." I simply couldn't believe it, but I heard it and was now listening. He was sitting up on a stage, seated with all his wives, his main, original bride next to him. About twenty feet away from me was that same young blonde, staring at me and sometimes smiling. It was just about as if she was teasing me, and doing a great job, I might add. I was too busy exchanging glances with this pretty lady—just checking if she was still looking—to remember any of the presentation, which was no doubt a good thing.

After we returned to the family house and had another incredible meal, with me being waited on hand and foot, I was told that the next step in my conversion process was to first become a Mormon then become a polygamist, after which everything else would fall into place. The lady told me they had their eye on me as a potential leader and I would be given preferential treatment. The whole thing seemed like a book of fiction and I knew I had nothing stronger to drink than homemade lemonade, but I knew I was as far away from Mormonism and polygamy as man is from the moon. But I just couldn't bring myself to say so to the wife.

This was very obviously *not* Christian in any sense of the term, but considered a cult, with the extreme of polygamy pushing the envelope even further. I could speak to this now, firsthand. And *my* testimony would be out-and-out disbelief and utter rejection. I met some nice people, but nice doesn't mean right. The wife seemed to be clinging on to me as we said our goodbyes. I saw the pain in her eyes, and she had even shared a few of the frustrations she had with sharing her husband and life with a strange woman she had only met briefly at church. When I profusely thanked her for her hospitality, complimented her on her wifely and motherly skills, she seemed close to screaming out; but she merely waved at me through the glass door, crestfallen. Pathetic!

Any calls I would get thereafter, I did not answer. No one knew where I lived outside of my kids but Jimmy Hughes, and they didn't know where he lived so I was safe from being contacted. I left it at that. This whole experience gave me tremendous desire to somehow reach out to my wife, try to salvage the marriage, and reunite with the kids. One day, I just decided to drive back home from Salt Lake, be close to the family, and call. I couldn't have picked a worse day as a snowstorm was gathering as I began the drive. As I was approaching the Point of the Mountain, between Salt Lake City and Utah County—with an incredible history of highway havoc from the incredible winds and where they nationally tested hang gliders—the snow was suddenly blinding. The point had been hit much harder than Salt Lake, and the highway was fast becoming obliterated with snow.

Soon, I was driving in a near-complete whiteout, straining over my steering wheel to see the covered highway. I could not tell anymore if another car was right in front of me or on my tail. Headlights made the vision worse, as it was midday with the weird hint of sun blending into the heavy, thick snowflakes. As I got farther up, I started seeing cars off in the shoulder, with some turned over in the ditch and people actually out of their cars looking desperate. There was a huge four-wheeler completely turned over with people trying to assist the driver. I was praying like crazy, for me and everyone. I was just waiting any second for a big rig to hit me from behind or me to hit someone I couldn't see in front.

As I kept going up toward the apex of the point, I even said my last words and asked for forgiveness as I really didn't think I would make it, that I virtually didn't have a prayer. Then I sensed my car leveling, meaning I had reached the top. I couldn't believe it as I saw a hint of blue sky. I made it. A miracle! When I went down the freeway away from the snow and fog and impossible conditions, I was very thankful and pulled into the gas station at the bottom of the mountain and called My Wife and shared the ordeal with her and asked if I could see the kids since we hadn't entered into the formal visitation of the final divorce decree. She refused, so I went on to spend the rest of the day and early evening with Jimmy Hughes and his family.

As I was going through American Fork quite late to return to Salt Lake, with the remnants of the day's storm still lingering on the streets, a car was coming toward me on the opposite lane. Suddenly, the car swerved erratically in its lane and drove straight into a building on the side of the street. After it happened, I looked in my rearview mirror, thinking and hoping someone else would stop. No one did as there was not another car in sight. I was quite tired, but reluctantly did a U-turn and rushed back. The car's front end was embedded in the brick building, with the engine racing. I knew it was serious as I saw a woman at the wheel with her head tipped back. She was having labored breathing as a strapped-in little boy in the backseat was screaming loudly. I noticed that her tongue was going down her throat a little bit and blocking her air pipes, so I quickly pulled it out, unblocking her breathing. I also noticed that she was pregnant and very large. I turned off the car. I tried to console the little boy and was somewhat successful. The woman was still in a daze.

Soon, some people arrived on the scene as well as the police, and I told them what happened as they turned out to be family members and were quite shocked. After giving the police the basics, I backed away. The family members, obviously Mormon, looked at me in the strangest way, not knowing who I was, why I was there, and just looked so puzzled. One man looked deep in my eyes and repeatedly said thanks. An ambulance was summoned, the scene secure, so I just left. I may have not seen my kids that day as I hoped, but at least the day ended on a positive note.

With just a few days left in the year, I had a renewed sense of fight and wanted to see if I could put in for an appeal of the divorce. The night before was a tough one where I missed the kids so much it hurt. I had thought how with each one of the kids I always sang them the same three songs, "Old McDonald Had a Farm," "Twinkle, Twinkle Little Star," and "Rock-a-Bye Baby." Since these kids were so young, the absence from them was like having an extreme headache, high fever—well, really like my worst malaria attack. Without delays of phone calls, I headed back to Utah County and Provo, where the divorce decree was waiting to be signed and finalized the last day of the month and year. I found out I could file an appeal, but with the clock running out, I was facing an uphill battle. Some of the people in the court system didn't give me a chance at this late hour, but after approaching numerous people, I found this one lady, a Mormon mother of many, who, after hearing my story and plea and crying herself, agreed to help.

By the lady's relentless calls, politely pushed by me, we found out that the presiding judge on our divorce had already been on Christmas leave up at his mountain cabin. I kept pushing, and the lady kept trying. She got a number of players in the court system to agree that although he was said to cherish his annual holiday in the cabin without any calls or contact, they also knew he was a devoted family man and under these circumstances would probably understand. What we needed was his signature so the divorce appeal would be official and make deadline. Even though it was a heavy snow season in the mountains, I could either go up there to his place myself or have a courier do it for a hefty fee. I saw hope. But a major snowstorm was moving in, and it made things seem quite bleak.

Now, we just had to reach him by phone. The lady was persistent as the midday arrived. No answer. She tried every fifteen minutes. Then every five to ten minutes. The day was wearing thin. She told me that unless we reached him within minutes, we wouldn't have much of a chance because the paperwork with signature had to be postmarked and documented by the end of the business day. When the clock pushed the hands of time, she looked at me and said, "Pray, Jon, pray." I did; I probably even wore out my welcome-to-the-prayer line above. Then she said, "Oh, that's funny, I can't even get a dial tone now."

I knew in my heart it was over. Even the weather wasn't cooperating. She looked at me and with sad eyes said maybe the phone lines were down as he lived way up high in the Provo mountains. We tried. It was over.

The drive from Provo back to Salt Lake seemed like a lifetime, as my mind scrolled back to Vietnam, burials, marijuana scandal, marriage, kids, and now divorce. The sense of loss, guilt, and emotions were tearing at my insides like a jagged dagger. When I got back to Salt Lake, I found myself just aimlessly driving around the temple area. I once again saw this young mother with this beautiful child in hand walking down Main Street. The little girl was all bundled up, but they both looked a little scruffy, as if homeless. I had an idea that maybe could salvage the day. I would drive around the block and find them again and offer the mother to stay the weekend at my apartment. I still had many leftovers from the Christmas turkey and trimmings I made for kids so there was plenty of food. I figured that for their comfort, I would tell her I would be gone and return Sunday night or so. I could always go back south to Jimmy Hughes's place. I was excited now to find her, but didn't. I drove around for an hour looking—no mother and girl. Seems I just couldn't win on any front this day, the final day of 1988.

I went home and had company with the rest of the vodka bottle I had, shaking its hand and symbolically talking to it like a friend. The stress from the day had overwhelmed me. I turned on the TV to bring in the new year and close out my eighteen-year marriage. Neither one had any meaning.

A short time before, my mother had informed me that her sister, my aunt Marilyn, who had never had any kids, suddenly had one in the form of a lady named Natalie. Mom told me Marilyn had actually gotten pregnant at eighteen and adopted out the baby girl, who fortunately was adopted by a wealthy national trucking company family. In the terms of the adoption, Marilyn had requested a total severance of any future contact, with the promise that Marilyn's identity would never be revealed. But Natalie found out about the adoption before her adoptive parents passed and desired to find out who her biological mother was. I was always thought to be the eldest child in the surrounding family tree, but now I found out that Natalie was about four months older. Family secrets just bumped up a notch. Since Natalie said she felt closest to me, she felt compelled to talk to me.

Natalie introduced herself, and we updated each other on our lives. When she heard about the fresh-inked divorce, she invited me to come out to Burbank, California, where she lived and stay with her. She also said she would get me a job as a movie extra to help take my mind off all the agony, saying she had grown up babysitting occasionally for some celebrity families, including John Wayne, and had a lot of contacts. With such an offer and My Ex being nearly totally uncooperative with child visitation and zero rent or expenses, I agreed and gave my notice to vacate my apartment.

Now, I had to break my departure to the kids. I decided to do it as thoughtful as I could, so I decided to make a video for them covering everything in life and how much I loved them and would always be there for them. I also would tell them I would make small tapes to play in recorder, which I called the "Daddy Bear Love Tapes" for each child. The two-tape set I made had me sitting in front of a chalkboard, covering life A to Zebra over nearly four hours. My idea to call them bear tapes came from youngest daughter Chrissy, barely breaking three years old, who absolutely adored bears. With the help of Jimmy Hughes, we cut the tapes at his house as he had top-of-the-line equipment and knowledge. Along with those tapes, I promised the kids I would write several times a week and call regularly, plus have our summers together and other visitation dates. I felt like I was throwing them leaking life vests from a sinking ship. I was truly dying inside. But with a credit card balance to pay and no job prospects and a total collapse of my belief system, I had to grab at the only straw offered to me.

I gave a big party to my kids the weekend before, and after filling a large storage unit with my *stuff*, I bade my farewells and left for California. Upon arriving in Burbank, I met Natalie and discovered she had her daughter and her boyfriend living with her. It was a very large nice apartment, and Natalie insisted I take her bedroom as she slept on the couch, which she claimed she did usually anyway. Other than knowing the obvious about what a movie extra was, I had no idea what it entailed. Natalie took me around to these casting companies and helped sign me up, filling out profiles and taking photos.

Natalie's "friends" didn't seem to be around, but she was outgoing and friendly so I easily made some initial friendly contacts. The pay was like slave labor, but most extras didn't seem to complain much as they were happy to be in a movie and have the chance for exposure, which was something I would learn all about with great humor. I immediately didn't take Hollywood too seriously, but thought it was a great diversion away from my pain and loss through the fantasy of playing cops and robbers, being removed from reality. It was like the perfect prescription for me, and I had to thank Natalie for it all.

Chapter Fifty-Six

Ⅰt took only days of calling hotlines and tapping into the process before I got my first call. It turned out to be incredibly simple but incredibly boring, often waiting for many hours on the movie set, to finally be called to walk across a street in the background of a scene. As amazing as it was, some extras would actually mess it up, making some gesture or action that was out of character for their "part." After the scene, some extras would converse about how good they did their scene, walking in the background, doing some minor action, and walking back again. Many of these extras were like working professionals, having done it for many years. They liked to point out that nearly all the big stars also started as extras—from John Wayne to Kevin Costner—but failed to say those stars had major acting talent. Being an extra was a *little* less challenging as you didn't have to open your mouth or act; you just had to "be." It was sometimes hilarious, but even *being* for some was hard. I would always beg the question, how can you overact not acting? I never had more true belly laughs in all my life.

Some carried scrapbooks with them showing their years of work and pictures with the stars of movies and TV. Many of those were locals who had family they stayed with, so the money issue was secondary. They were absolutely dedicated to their craft, be that as it may. I saw extras more as barnacles on a ship. The ship was the movie or TV show, and when it came into production or in dry dock, the ship had to take on barnacles as it was just a side price they had to pay for the price of making a production. The extras were the barnacles they knew they had to take on during the dry dock of production. It was the cost of doing the movie business. Like it or not, Hollywood could not do its creative endeavors without extras, and extras could never otherwise have a shot of being discovered or getting an honest gig of acting, no matter how small, without taking on this important, but necessary evil.

One of my first gigs was for *Guts and Glory*, the Oliver North story, a made-for-TV movie. They used me so much for so many different scenes that the director and producer had a little rife over it. Once, for an outdoor scene involving the presentation of an award by President Ronald Reagan, they called me in at the last minute to be a Secret Service agent, sent me to wardrobe, and with no dressing room right there, I ran around this park building, stripped down to my underwear, and donned the dark suit. The whole set and scene was waiting for me. I even got a $20 *bump* for the hassle, but costing the movie thousands for the delay. That's showbiz. Most extras would have a schedule of all the gigs they had and watch themselves on TV when they were aired. I watched a few of mine but didn't like seeing myself, so I shelved that idea for the most part.

I was now working full-time, oftentimes twelve to sixteen hours a day, and establishing myself as "reliable," a hugely desirable thing in Hollywood circles. The food was usually fantastic, and no matter when the director or assistant director said he had to return to an active set, it virtually never happened and was a long lunch or dinner. In one gig downtown Los Angeles in some old federal building, while hiring me as a stand-in for the actor in this detective flick, I was sitting behind this desk while the crew framed me for the shot and the actor's position.

While the cameraman was blocking me, this very old and large hanging fluorescent light fixture, with large chains holding it in place, had the one end break. Just as that happened, I moved backward a tad for the cameraman, and the whole fixture came swinging down at this incredible speed, just missing my head. It could have nearly severed my head off or killed me because it had very sharp edges and tremendous weight behind it. All stopped for a moment, and the director and crew rushed to my side. I told them I was fine, and they cut me loose early with a special trip home and a $40 bump. I felt like royalty.

Into the active industry by only two weeks plus now, I was called to be an extra for the hit TV show, *Unsolved Mysteries*. It was a very small studio setting, and there were only fifteen people altogether with cast and crew to shoot the segment "The Dale." It was a true story of a transvestite who milked investors into a car-building scheme, only to be ultimately exposed as a fraud. In their casting call, they actually found a real transvestite to play the part. Both the real person and the actor were six feet five inches tall. The actor who played the part brought along his "partner" who cracked us up with jokes while waiting, but sent some of the female extras packing because he was also quite obscene. Now, the set was short and past deadline. The director was getting panicked, made worse by the fact that the person they hired to be the arresting sheriff continually blew his lines, causing delays. I was a nonspeaking deputy right behind the sheriff for the scene.

Finally, the director called at me. "You look more like the sheriff anyway, do you think you can do this part?"

"Sure," I said. "I've heard the lines now enough." I was also cognizant of the advice I got to never say no or turn down a part. I switched parts with the sheriff and felt really bad for the guy. He had been an extra for eight long years and finally nailed down this opportunity for a speaking part, but he blew it. I could tell it destroyed whatever ego he had left. I bolstered his spirits up and downplayed my sudden claim to fame. I nailed it in one attempt, but still the scene had to be repeated four times because once, the cameraman fell off a ladder and broke the camera and his kneecap and the other delay was that the transvestite didn't like the way the camera got his walk-off, as he said he didn't nail the sashay right. The director was fit to be tied, but we finally called a wrap at 2:00 a.m. after fifteen hours in that studio. But because of that speaking part, I was given a "Taft-Hartley," the highly sought-after union qualification for the Screen Actors Guild (SAG). What took that poor devil eight years to nail a speaking part, I luckily got in just two and a half weeks after arriving in Hollywood.

Later, when on another shoot, as it is usually called, I was an extra on the *Jessica McClure Story*, about the little girl who fell down a well in Texas and survived. One of the other extras yelled out my name. "Jon Meade, you are on a segment of *Unsolved Mysteries* after the commercials." Seems some extras that were waiting in the house noticed the show announcement. I was free so I went in to see myself for several minutes in an only-me close-up, making the arrest. I absolutely hated it, and despite all the talk and handshakes because it was on prime-time network NBC, I felt like crawling out of there. Part of it was due to the fact I was currently in a dispute with NBC over union pay for that gig, and as I watched this segment, I thought of how SAG was arguing my case in New York over it and what a bunch of BS it all was. While now being the hugely sought-after SAG-qualified, I could not afford the $700 to join so I kept my lowly status. I coined the term "Shaft-Hartley" to better define the "Taft-Hartley" speaking part union qualification process, and it drew a lot of laughs, catching on with some second-tier extras and bit players. It was humor towards my coping skills.

On one call, I was to be an extra on the set of *Postcards from the Edge* with Meryl Streep and Shirley MacLaine. Word had it that Shirley was notorious for checking out each and every extra that appeared with her in a movie. I was on that set for three days, and on the last day, when Shirley was due to act, she would also check us all out, which personally outraged me. Who was this "star" to think she could look us over like cold cuts in a deli? Other extras told me that she had a reputation for not "liking" someone and having them kicked right off the set. I told myself if that happened to me, I simply wouldn't take it and tell her off. But her scene was canceled that day so Shirley and I would not meet.

My meeting with Streep was much warmer. I was dressed with one other extra in this alien aluminum suit for the filming of this scene for the movie. I was simply supposed to walk across this street as Meryl walked past me, talking with someone. The suit was real tight, making my rear end like a drum. On the third and final take, upon the director saying "cut," Streep reached over with a big smile and giggled and goosed me, making me jump a little. Well, I guess she didn't "reject" me.

Anytime an extra would get a call directly from a casting director, rather than the extras casting, you knew it usually meant something more. One of the times this happened, it was for a wardrobe fitting—for the "Joker," Jack Nicholson's character in *Batman*. The cost of using Jack himself would be far too costly, so their plan was to fit me in the whole outfit, take photos of me from every angle, and then transpose Jack's head on my body. It would then be used in all advertising and marketing, including making a cast for the animated dolls for the character. They said it would not only be a good payday for the fitting and photos themselves, but it would provide me with very healthy residuals for years. They had said I should feel flattered because they had looked at hundreds of bodily profiles and ended up picking mine even though I was taller than Nicholson and a little trimmer, which is exactly what they wanted.

I put the entire Joker outfit on, hat and all, being only spared the makeup as they would be using Jack's head on my body for all stills and casts. I got paid for the day and never saw a dime thereafter. I tried to contact the production company but got a terrible runaround, soon giving up. I just wasn't up to another futile fight what with my stress levels away from the kids and divorce fallout. I saw *Batman* like everyone else, laughed at the Joker character, but for a little different reason than most viewers.

As was often the case, nonunion shoots took place and afforded many with opportunities they wouldn't otherwise get. The pay was usually less, but they were often more loose sets and fun. I was called to be on one titled, *Demon Wind*, a sci-fi zombie movie starring Lou Diamond Phillips, a very nice guy. I was picked to be a zombie who would attack with a large ax and be shot, squibbed as they called it. I was said to have the equivalent of the longest and most intense facial makeover to transform me into a hideous vampire. After four and a half hours in the makeup chair and only having the ability to eat all the delicious food they had through my fingers used like a shovel, I was set after they outfitted me in farmer's bib overalls and the crew jokingly calling me "Mr. Greenjeans."

For my big part, they put little pieces of wood with plastic vials inside my shirt around my stomach area and had wires running down my pant legs. The vials were filled with a combination of plain yogurt and raspberry jam, said to simulate demon or vampire blood. I had six of them planted on my person, ready to be exploded away from my body at the exact same time I was shot. The shoot was up in the beautiful and serene Santa Monica Mountains and was an all-night affair, to take advantage of the demon dark.

When the time came for the shooting, the director realized they didn't order the body pullback equipment to be positioned well behind me so when I was shot, it would abruptly jerk my body up and radically back. So they asked me if I was fairly athletic and could I jump up and back as I was shot, utilizing perfect timing. "Sure," I said, not wanting to test the "always say yes" mantra. The special effects man explained that I would feel a *tiny* explosion, but it would be *nothing*.

When the time came for the shooting, the hero Phillips was to shoot me from about twenty meters away with a shotgun shooting blanks. He aimed the weapon to the side of me, with the camera at his back, and fired six loud shots, as I was supposedly hit with vampire blood propelling out of the front of my shirt from the thinned material. The little charges actually exploded the fake blood through my chest and stomach shirt areas. I jumped up and back as the shots started, doing so well that I went backward down the side of the gently sloped mountaintop, rolling end over end in the dark, finally hitting some rock outcroppings. A few of the crew came running after me, but I assured them I was all right. As I joined the top and that special effects man, I said, "Damn, man, two of those charges really hurt and I have big red blotches on my stomach."

"Yeah, sorry, sometimes it happens as careful as we are to not overdue the charge. But it has to be a big enough charge to break the shirt material and thrust the blood through it and out. Suck it up, Marine, it's just part of the duty."

I knew the guy was also a Vietnam Vet Marine and was just kidding, but little did he know how it tapped into my Marine trust issues and tested my patience. But he felt a little bad and cleaned me up as we talked shop. I got a $40 bump for my scene, but paid for it for years in bodily pain from the fall. I got another $20 bump for wearing all that heavy makeup. When I returned back to Natalie's at 10:00 a.m., I was a mass of bumps and bruises, especially the ones on my stomach that were now heavily swollen, and still picking pieces of rubbery makeup out of my mouth and teeth.

Even though the movie sets had a tremendous amount of downtime, it was ideal for me to write letters to the kids. I often wrote four to five letters a week, sometimes a joint letter and more often individual ones to address each child on a personal level. In one letter I was writing to my oldest daughter Jenny, I had tears in my eyes, which was picked up on by some other extras. They were very sympathetic and supportive, especially the women, but I shook off the emotions and wrapped up my writing although inside, my nerves were in tatters. I had to force myself to stop thinking about them by joking around and picking out some woman to playfully hustle. I always greatly enjoyed talking to these retired Jewish women who had incredible wit and humor and pulled no punches.

They would always bring their soft portable chairs and joke about what being an extra really meant—nothing. Yet because so many crew, directors, and producers were Jewish, they supported them in a humorous backhanded way. These Jewish mothers and grandmothers gave me great comic relief from my inner turmoil. They also always had supportive things to say, even in a few words or sentences. One time, this crusty one—she was the greatest—took issue with the director about what she conceived as disrespect. They went at it, face-to-face, with the grandma holding her own until the director backed down, smiled, even laughed when she made reference to his leadership as "not being kosher enough, with pureness and quality." They hugged and even seemed to create a bond. The atmosphere changed.

At this time, I met another extra who had done stage work back in New York and had a few minor speaking parts under her belt. While she seemed a little *off,* she was quite attractive; and we started a brief relationship, which took unusual twists and turns. This woman, daughter of a prominent surgeon back east who didn't support her acting in Hollywood but still supported her financially, clung to the hope that she would still "make it." We sometimes read parts together from scripts she had, and while certainly having strong acting skills, her negative persona came through too much. I told her that once very tactfully and diplomatically, but I thought she would kill me, going into rants with flashing eyes. But then she would turn on a dime, flash this incredible smile, break into laughter, and want to get affectionate. Sometimes I wondered if she was playing me, but came to realize that it was her flippant personality.

Chapter Fifty-Seven

One day, a casting agent called me with an urgent message after seeing my photo and profile. She set an appointment to come to the old original MGM Studios, home of stars like Elizabeth Taylor, for an audition for a big upcoming movie. When I got there, I met the director and screenwriter, Rock O'Bannon, creator of the TV series *Alien Nation*. He had me parade around like a prized heifer, then asked me some questions, said I was perfect, then said I would be the stand-in and double, including minor stunt double, for the murderous star of *Fear*, a big-screen production, also starring Ally Sheedy, former runway model Lauren Hutton, Dina Merrill, and others. I was the non-talent side of Pruitt Taylor Vince, a character actor who was getting great attention and push in Hollywood.

The obligation was for at least two months and would provide a steady, miserable income. I was told in no uncertain terms was this gig would take my undivided attention because all framing and blocking of the star depended on my commitment. It was simple, but I had to be there or be ready for all the scenes at a second's notice, sometimes requiring me to freeze in place for hours. Me and the other stand-ins and doubles were referred to as the "second team," and you had to be ready to jump in the same demanding way as the Marine Corps.

The food was incredible, and when they needed me, they always treated me great. When they didn't, I was just another piece of set equipment. They often sent me home with candy and treats, which I saved. I gained about twelve pounds on that shoot. One day, out of nowhere, I received a call from my Ex-Wife, and she informed me she could not handle my eldest son Alex anymore and was putting him on a plane. I had no say in the matter but was given a day and time, and she hung up. Thankfully, I had that day off and picked Alex up at the Burbank Airport. He was eleven now. I had just gotten a guest house rental from this widowed Armenian woman in Glendale weeks before and would have to find a way to make it all work. I was on my own as my parents not only didn't support me much as their son going through a divorce and hard times, but they also never sent me a dollar.

It was okay though. My grandma Hilda insisted to send me a little bit here and there, and the thought alone was nice.

After that, I welcomed Alex with open arms, said we'd share a queen-sized bed, and had a special first night together with a movie and pizza. It was a very tough situation I was thrust into and had to balance going to the movie set, enrolling Alex in Glendale school, and mapping out a schedule and plan the best I could.

Aline, the homeowner in front, had a younger son and her sister living with her. She was an accountant and had long hours as well. I never asked for any favor from her but shared Alex's exact school and my sporadic movie schedules. From the get-go, Aline had said she was looking for a husband and used to say she wanted an American with blue eyes, just like her cousin's cop husband. There was a gate that I often had to open and pass as I went to leave for the set. Its opening was right by her kitchen window. I always had to pass it as I left, usually being stopped by her through the window as I opened the gate.

"Jon, Jon, you have such deep-blue beautiful eyes. I dream of a man like you, please come in for some Armenian (Turkish) coffee and pastry." The request was always the same, but my response wavered more. Sometimes I did and got to greatly enjoy our little coffee talks and thick, strong coffee.

She was so sweet and giving and the most persistent woman I had ever met, but I respected her. After Alex came, she of course wanted to include him too. One time she insisted we join them for dinner.

"Jon, before I give you main course, I make for you *rock* soup. It is a traditional soup made from love, and I do for you and Alex."

"Aline, what is rock soup? You mean soup made from rocks?"

I got an answer, but I couldn't repeat it if my life depended on it. So I accepted and we would have Armenian *rock* soup, plus other Armenian specialties made with meat and leaves, I guess. We were there at the table with Aline, me, Alex, and her sister, mustache and all, but nice. Then Aline placed the bowls of rock soup before us, bringing a certain smell with it. Alex and I exchanged coy looks.

"Jon, Alex, you dig into the *rock* soup, it's delicious and so good for you. I gave you big spoons to enjoy more, go ahead now." She was all smiles, along with her sister.

We both took our first spoonfuls and nearly gagged. It was the most incredibly terrible, unrecognizable taste I had ever put to my lips.

Alex's acting was so good I could have landed him a role in the movies. We swallowed another spoonful; then Aline's son called her from the living room to fix his Nintendo. She excused herself, leaving her sister to watch over us. We stalled. Then Aline called for her sister's help. As soon as her ample behind left that chair, I took the bowls of soup and poured them down the drain, feeling first for rocks but not finding any. I quickly realized there was no garbage disposal so I had to reach into the drain and force it down, nearly clogging the drain. Even the drain didn't like the stuff. I rushed back, and as Aline and her sister came back, Alex and I were running our spoons through the bowls as if it was delicious.

Aline's eyes lit up like a Christmas tree. "Ohhhh, Jon, you love the *rock* soup. I knew you would love it, here let me get you some more. He love the *rock* soup, he love the *rock* soup, Alex, too." She literally danced to the stove and came back with soup and filled up our bowls.

"Aline, that is the best *rock* soup I *never* had, but I can't, we can't have more 'cause it was so filling, hearty, and satisfying and you know we had a late lunch before dinner with you and we are both stuffed." I then played tag with her hands to try to get her to stop trying to stuff *rock* soup into my gullet. She really was a giving, generous sweetheart.

In the time there behind Aline's place, she would try everything to win me over to accept her as a potential mate, including pizzas with her son, ice cream parlor visits, a weekend trip to a rental cabin at Big Bear, and a seventy-pound weight loss. I always told her the same: I couldn't commit to anyone because I was still reeling from my divorce and didn't want to be serious with anyone.

One day, she came to me with a plan that beat all. She insisted we be alone in her living room as her sister took the boy to a relative's house. I knew I was in trouble—deep doo-doo. She was pouring me this potent Armenian liquor that hit you instantaneously. Before I could stop her, she got down on her knees and treated me royally. She was so incredibly persistent, like a salesperson about to close the biggest deal of her career. After that, how could anyone not give her your undivided attention?

"Jon, I have an idea for you to make lots and lots of money where you wouldn't have to work in Hollywood anymore and have a better life. You must listen to me, Jon. This could change your life."

"Okay, Aline, I am all ears."

She proceeded to lay out this elaborate plan where I would make numerous trips to Beirut, Lebanon; have meetings with clothing industry manufacturers, vendors, buyers, and sellers; and establish a network for an international fashion and clothing exchange. She said she had many inside contacts and had been waiting to do this for some time, but her husband's sudden death at thirty-eight years old changed everything. She added that she had a silent big money backer in Los Angeles, and would fly me over first-class, stay in five-star hotels, and eat the finest food. She ran some money numbers in front of me that made me gag even more than the *rock* soup. It was very tempting until I stopped to think for a moment.

Just weeks before, there were constant bombings and killings in Beirut, and some Americans were killed. I thought of Alex and my kids and the divorce. There was no way, no matter what the payoff. I told Aline as much, and despite her beat-it-to-death persistence, I told her once and for all I had to decline. It seemed to really make her upset, probably kicking off feelings of not only business rejection, but personal. Her demeanor became somewhat confrontational, and one night she sat outside my cottage with her whole extended family, drinking and making lots of noise until 3:00 a.m.

Within days, I found a big apartment and told Aline I was leaving. She took it well when I promised we'd keep in touch, and I did call her and drop by once just to keep my promise. Alex got in a little trouble at school, and mainly because he missed his brother and sisters so much, he was torn but decided to go back home after we conferred with My Ex. My heart was again heavy, but I knew it was the right decision for Alex because he was homesick, as close as we were. After he left, I just sat in my new living room, drinking a beer and looking out the window to nowhere.

By the time we wrapped on *Fear*, I had worked many ten-to-sixteen-hour days, learned more about human nature, come to greatly appreciate the art that is acting, especially by standing in and observing Pruitt as he was so absolutely dedicated to his craft. I also came to respect movie crews, especially camera and stunt people, directors and producers, and really the whole motion picture process. The planned and spontaneous creativity is mind-boggling. I was now seeing my Hollywood experience as a challenge. To really take it more seriously and go for more. I even saw myself as a little more than a dock-worthy movie barnacle.

As a member of the cast and crew because of my duties, and privy to nearly everything going on in the production, I witnessed some both funny and pathetic things. The first was the behavior of a diva, in Lauren Hutton. When we had a shoot at the LAX airport, Lauren's stand-in, a sweet and innocent girl, was standing in her blocking position next to a window looking out toward the runway. When the assistant director called for the first team, Lauren walked up to the girl and, with her hand on her coat, flung her away like a rag doll as she assumed her position. It was so embarrassing for all who witnessed it; most people had dropped their heads to the floor. No one could believe the actress's gall to treat someone with such total disdain. Lauren's other demanding behavior caused her to be basically very disliked by the crew.

When the time came to kill off her character by suffocation in the front seat of a car on top of the airport parking structure, the crew joked about how they would really like to see it happen for real. They held her in such disrespect. The suffocation took place with a large plastic bag over her face by Pruitt, the *Shadow Man*, as he was called. The crew handed out more plastic bags to jokingly simulate the murder and ending of Hutton's part. After the scene was complete, it had reached 4:00 a.m. and Lauren wanted to leave the set and go to her personal trailer next to the lower parking structure. No one would walk her there in the dark. She was scared to go alone, not that I blamed her, and we took the elevator down together so she asked me to walk her. I agreed.

She took my arm, and as we walked along the long sidewalk on the side of the parking structure, there was popping and crunching under our feet. Lauren screamed out, jumping and freaking out, as I noticed from a light peeking through the wall that we were walking over a bed of snails. It had rained heavily that day, and the snails had emerged from the brush along the sidewalk. When we finally got to her trailer and I bade her good night, she couldn't have been sweeter and more thankful. Too bad the crew couldn't see that side of her. The snails did, despite losing their lives.

Behind the scenes in movie production creates more memories than the near two-hour movie ever could. One of those was a problem the director and producer had when killing off Pruitt's dark psychic character. It was at the circus, and the *Shadow Man* was climbing up the Ferris wheel in a chase scene.

They thought of using me as the photo double and then the stunt double but realized they needed a close-up of the killer, so Pruitt himself was the only logical choice. But Pruitt was scared of heights, and it didn't help that he had a vision problem. They asked him. He refused over and over again, saying he wasn't hired to do his own stunts. For this all-night shoot, his agent wasn't around. Finally, the producer explained that this was an important scene for the entire movie, and because of the close-up needed, using Pruitt had become a must. There was a long impasse. The producer offered a bump in money. Then more. Pruitt said it had to be cash, on the spot.

They agreed on just under $1,500, and the producer sent his assistant to go fetch the money from his ATM. When the scene was shot, it all went like clockwork. Pruitt was a real trooper and performed under extreme pressure brilliantly. When his character fell from the structure, invisible cables and all, and met his fate, they rushed me in to lie down in the position on the ground where he supposedly landed. But they had some camera malfunction and delay so I had to lie there on the cold ground for two hours. They brought me coffee and made sure I was all right, but even my joints from the cold ground gave me pain. Meanwhile, Pruitt's part was over as well as the movie, as he counted his cash.

I didn't even get a twenty-dollar bump. Such is the pecking order.

While on that weeklong night circus shoot, they filmed a scene where a chair-whirling ride was filled with extras. They blocked the scene, and while doing so, the ride made many, many stints. At one point, the crew literally forgot the extras up there as they set up. As I was watching the whole thing, one of the riders bent forward and threw up, sending reams of vomit all over the riders behind him. The ride kept going. A few more extras got sick as the vomit moved in perfect unison to their ride direction.

Finally, they realized what was happening and stopped the ride, as many extras left the scene adorned in various food colors. In the movies, sometimes the creative process forgets they are dealing with human beings and not just props. To see all this though, and how the chain of events happened, it was very hard not to laugh. Behind some trees, I laughed with a few others so hard I cried.

When filming a movie, it doesn't necessarily coincide with the eventual outcome of the end product. Such was the case with the very last day of filming, which was a scene inside a prop plane involving the psychic star, Ally Sheedy. The director O'Bannon decided to use me as a clone of the killer walking on the plane, deceiving Sheedy into thinking I may be the bad psychic she had been talking to in her mind. After waiting for twelve hours for this scene, I was tired and missed my marks once I got in the plane, but a few takes later, it was successfully shot. As I approached, Rock didn't think it appropriate for me to just make eye contact with Sheedy, so he told me to say something. I decided to be surprised as I saw another passenger, said a few words, smiled, and left the eye-to-eye stare with Sheedy.

That was a *wrap* for *Fear*. The movie ended up having distribution problems as the company went under, so there was nearly a year-and-a-half delay, sending it straight to video. Since I had never gotten SAG minimum pay for that featured speaking part, I complained to SAG and they once again argued my case in New York. This one I lost because of the statute of limitations running out. When I got together with Rock O'Bannon several times in Studio·City later, I never brought it up because I liked him too much and his sister too, Kim, who was one of the assistant directors and one who I thought a lot of. So much for a missed really good payday.

Afterward, Pruitt asked me to train him at his home in Hollywood with his new Nordic trainer. I showed him all I knew, and besides him cracking me up with his incredible sense of humor—he missed his true calling to be a comedic actor—he simply wasn't into it, and that died a quick death as his acting parts kept growing.

A casting company called me and said they wanted me as a featured extra on the hit kids show *Saved by the Bell*. After I did a few shoots at the NBS Studios in Burbank, where they shared a sound stage directly across from the *Tonight Show* with Johnny Carson, I got the nod too for the continuous program. I was the "silent" coach at the school who walked around the halls and displayed my hanging whistle, usually just a blimp on the screen. But it was considered a prime gig for an extra, with many more build-in perks than normal. I was also told there was the possibility that myself and this "silent" female teacher extra could be groomed for possible minor roles on the series.

Chapter Fifty-Eight

NBC Studios was like one big city inside. Like anything in filming, there was a lot of downtime.

Just outside the *Tonight* sound stage, there was this shoe-shine stand, operated by this black man who had the gig for over twenty-five years. Bored one day, I jumped up on his stand and got a shoe shine and heard all the stories about the stars he had given shoe shines to.

While there, an NBC tour guide stopped in front of us with twenty-five to thirty onlookers. He was telling them all about the *Tonight Show* being taped behind the shoe stand and then made reference to the famous shoe shine stand. People were staring at me and whispering things like, "*Who is he, he looks familiar?*" or "*I know he is somebody famous?*" It was so uncomfortable being stared at and talked about that I dropped my head so they could continue their star fantasies while I humbled myself as they finally left. Little did they know I was a nobody in Hollywood circles, but it fascinated me as to how easily people could be let astray and plant beliefs in their head. I did play the role of *somebody* when I was a *nobody* quite well, but what else could I do?

One day, probably because I was reliable and Hollywood loves that, the director gave me a voice-over for Screech (Dustin Diamond), one of the child stars in the segment *Close Encounters of the Nerd Kind*. They used my voice as the *alien* inside the space helmet for Screech. The director took me to the recording studio right across the hall from the *Tonight Show*, where we took three takes to get the voice down as he wanted it. It was just a short one-liner. But it was a big payday as NBC had paid for my joining AFTRA, the union mainly for TV. I would end up getting residuals for many years thereafter, over sixty of them, but they graduated down in amounts until my final check was about fifty cents, which I just kept.

I had that gig for about four months straight, usually working anywhere from two to five days a week, with a few breaks. I used to hang around the halls quite a bit while waiting for scenes, often running into Johnny Carson himself as he walked into the studio and narrow hallway at three thirty every day. He always had his dry-cleaned suit hanging over his shoulder, and when I first saw him, he was not friendly. But it got to the point where we ran into each other so much he always said "hi" and sometimes said more, and always with a nice smile. After his live program was over, he would leave at five thirty and go out to either his white Corvette or his black Mercedes, parked right out the side doors. There was a steel post there holding his name, and when his guest host Jay Leno would be on board, they would take Johnny's sign out and replace it with Jay's. It was like musical hosts. Jay's cars were always different and very classic and elaborate. I met a number of "stars" at NBC so it made the hours less boring.

One day on the *Bell* set, I met guest star Carol Lawrence, former Broadway dancer and star, and former wife of singer Robert Goulet. She was quite attractive and had these killer dancer's legs, but she also was a sweetheart. We got to talking during downtimes, and she told me she had become a born-again Christian after her divorce. We shared our horrors about divorce, and before I knew it, I was opening up to her and sharing snippets of my Beverly Hills spiritual experience and visit with Jesus. She was so intrigued by my story, she would not let me stop. Later, she invited me to go to church with her at this fairly famous place called "Church on the Way."

I met her there in Van Nuys and saw this beautiful modern church outfitted with the finest sound and video equipment; sermons were sold nationally by renowned preacher, Pastor Jack Hayford. I joined her in what seemed to be an upfront special section. We greeted, kissed, and hugged. After, when everyone is shaking hands and hugging, we kissed and hugged again. After the service, she directed me to this official church individual who she said wanted to hear my story, and she left. The guy seemed very detached, cold, and indifferent and I decide not to share anything, but I took him up on his offer to join this singles group. The group did their rounds of introductions and talk, and at the end, the group leader asked for my opinion of the church and their message. He apparently knew a little of my experience.

I said, "Do you want my honest opinion?"

"Yes, Jon, of course, we would highly value it, especially as a special first-time visitor."

"After the service when the congregation was mingling around and hugging everyone, I noticed a lot of pain and suffering from those pews. This one woman had lost her daughter in some tragic accident, then her home, and was reeling. There were numerous other broken people. Yet with the obvious riches of this church, with many celebrities (including the director of *Bell*) bolstering the coffers, it takes money from people instead of giving money."

The group of a dozen people seemed stunned by my words. One nearly sarcastic woman demanded to know what I meant or was implying. The others were anxious to hear more. So I let them have it.

"You know when the church passes around the collection plates for people to give, I think once in a while it would be nice if they made an announcement that if anyone had a real genuine need, without any judgments whatsoever, they should take money from the plates."

"Where did you get this idea? It's preposterous," shot back one response.

"The idea just came to me when I was meeting these people in the pews. What would it hurt? Isn't God and Jesus about giving, being there, and helping in times of severe need? I would ask the church on those infrequent days to encourage people to be honest with themselves, put their guilt and ego on hold, and take from the plate. Everyone could close their eyes in prayer to help provide privacy and respect. It would also be a perfect time to discuss unconditional giving and loving."

The one sarcastic lady left. No one else said a word, just wearing blank faces. After we dismissed, I was given a cold shoulder by some, but a few of the women plus one guy loved the idea, conversing more about it, but voiced concern how the church would respond to it. As I left the group and church—never to return—I went to my car parked on the street, only to find a window broken and all my fresh-laundered clothes stolen. I was mad at first, I mean fuming, but then realized it was all about forgiveness and figured the person must have had a need far greater than mine. Replacing that window, however, nearly busted me as the door lock was jimmied too.

During the breaks away from *Bell*, I took gigs where I could, always having offers. One was a Coors Light commercial with comedy star Lesley Nielsen. I had some stupid part but loved that set as Nielsen was a pure cut up. He had everyone in stitches all the time, mainly due to his fascination with whoopee cushions, which he carried in his tote bag. One day, this tall, leggy model actress came to the set to be a bimbo in the commercial. She had the custom high "star" chair waiting for her. Lesley prepped everyone to pay attention as she came in to assume her seat before the scene. Nielsen had a cord pumper attached to his whoopee cushion and activated it just as she sat down, letting out this incredible simulated fart, catching the model by surprise and nearly causing her to fall from her chair in shock. She turned and defended herself, saying she couldn't believe that she did that, wearing five shades of colors going down the pink to purple scale. Nielsen wore the perfectly surprised but innocent look. He could have won an Emmy Award.

Over a period of an hour, Nielsen pulled his trick more, sometimes making the fart come out in spurts and dribbles. It was hilarious, and finally he broke the secret to the model, apologized, as she figured something wasn't kosher on that set. She took it in stride, joining the laughter. But that whoopee stint wasn't the only humorous thing on that near out-of-control set at times. We had Mexican food for lunch. Two of the extras had to adorn the inside of a horse for a scene, one in the front of the horse, one in the back. During the rehearsals for the scene, the guy in the front kept farting, and they weren't from Lesley either. The guy in the back would take off his hind end and yell at the guy in the front, telling him to stop farting as he was being gassed out. They finally got the scene shot but not before they had to break up a little fight once.

The director, this huge mustached Jewish guy, kept approaching me and asked me if I was Jewish.

He kept saying I was a good-looking Jew and should just admit it. He thought it was my mouth and lips that reminded him of singer Neil Diamond. I gave up convincing him otherwise, but he gave me a little upgrade and bump. I started thinking Hollywood was one big "somebody always looked like somebody" place. I got it all the time. I just found it amusing.

Another gig I took was for a Mexican film company making a movie in Van Nuys and the Valley.

I had no idea what it was for but soon found out it was to play a gigolo. When the Mexican director saw me, he immediately had a conference with his crew and expanded my part to my ultimate embarrassment. I was essentially this gigolo that sat in a king's chair and was adorned by Mexican beauties. The movie starred Mexico's biggest stars, the Rodriguezes, a husband and wife acting team.

They obviously had no idea who I was and asked me questions on how they should play their roles and scenes. I couldn't get out of my proposed celebrity, so I just winged it. Everyone treated me like the star on that set, and I sucked it up; after all, who was I to argue?

From my position on the throne, I was reduced to a mumbling, stumbling drunk out by the pool. I took a few drinks of tequila a cast member had and exaggerated my role, with them very happy with it.

Mexican movies are a strange mix of sex, violence, blood, mayhem, and over-the-top questionable acting. I fit right in. From that gig, I got a date with a relative of a relative of a relative, but she had a beautiful Hispanic face and features.

I had to pick her up at her house in East Los Angeles. When I arrived and parked on the street, I knew I was way out of my element. But as I walked up to the apartment, little kids called out my name.

When I entered her place, several Mexicans were sitting on the couch watching football. My date came out from the kitchen, looking ravishing, and introduced me to her brother and his friend. She excused herself while she had to calm down her little boy before she left. I just sat there with her brother and talked like he was a friend, fairly common for me. He told me not to worry about my car because the neighborhood knew better. My date came out, I made my farewell, shook her father's hand who spoke no English, her brothers and friends, and we were on the road.

I took her to a movie and an inexpensive dinner. We went back to my place, where I talked her into spending the night with me after we called her family. She said they trusted me. That was great since I couldn't trust myself. Within several weeks, she called me saying she feared she was pregnant. Normally, I never had to fear these things as I always took extreme precautions. But those precautions went out the window with this beauty. I sweat lead pinto beans for days. Then she called. "Jon, everything is fine, I had my period." I was so relieved I literally leaped off the floor. "My brother really liked you. You are the first gringo that he has ever had a nice thing to say about. I was shocked, because he's been a major gang member for years."

"Wow, I guess that's a compliment then. I'll remember that if I ever need a drive-by."

I suppose that was a very risky thing to say, but it busted her up laughing. However, we lived in different parts of LA and the world, for that matter, so I never saw her again.

Yet another extra gig involved the *Police Woman* TV star and longtime movie star, Angie Dickinson. I had been on other Angie segments, and we had talked some about divorce and her only child, Nikki, with music composer Burt Bacharach in between takes when I was just a lowly extra on her show. She was so incredibly nice and seemingly down-to-earth. She also exuded the most incredible amount of pure sex appeal that I had ever encountered. It just oozed from her beautiful pores. And boy did she know how to work it! On one shoot in the worst part of downtown LA, the set had extra police guards because of the area dangers, and we were there at night when the vermin came out.

In the front of the old building where we were filming, as I was walking out, a car came smashing through the police barriers with a cop car right behind. I thought it was part of the movie, but it wasn't.

It was real, and made a person realize the dangers of nighttime Los Angeles, even when on a movie set. The last day I was on the sequel to *Police Woman*, I was dressed to be a detective and was to oversee this murdered individual lying on the floor in a pool of blood. The scene called for me, another detective extra, a police costar, and Angie.

Earlier that night, baseball manager great, Tommy Lasorda, of the Los Angeles Dodgers, pulled up in front of the building in his limousine and came in to visit his obvious friend, Angie. During about eight takes it took to get that scene, in between, Tommy was shaking my hand, patting me on the back, and playfully shaking my shoulders. He was like a long-lost buddy, just enjoying overseeing our play acting and immediately calling me by my name. No wonder Tommy had such success as a manager, as his people skills were incredibly outgoing and warm. After the shoot was wrapped, Angie left with him in his limo, where they were talking about getting a bite to eat. Two stand-up people that had nothing but my respect.

One day, I got a call from some director in Hollywood who wanted me to try out for this rare musical theater production. He got my name and number from some casting person. I told him I was about as suited for a musical as a police dog would be for a uniform. I laughed and declined, saying I could sing well in the shower, but I doubted if they would be pouring water on the stage. He talked me into trying out for the part as one of the leads in the show and told me this kind of experience would be great for an acting career in TV and movies. He said big-shot Hollywood types always attended local plays, and it was a great place to be discovered. He also said that Hollywood was really a small town and that everyone knew each other and it was the kiss of death to say no to any offer.

I couldn't believe it, but I nailed the part, singing and all. He said I needed some formal training and polishing, but I would be fine. Now, I was dead set against me moving forward. After hours and days of phone calls back and forth, I finally convinced him that acting on a stage and singing was not something I was comfortable with and had to bow out. I felt flattered and appreciative but I panicked when I thought about being "discovered" and maybe having to sing again, or worse. I put it behind me.

During all my waiting on sets, my mind was constantly churning, mainly about the kids' welfare, past thoughts about the Marines and Vietnam, my future, and movie script and Hollywood ideas. One of those ideas was staging the first annual "Alley Awards," a mock version of the Academy Awards only for movie and TV extras. The presentations would be for *best walk across, best walk behind, best voice/lip-syncing, best look for the part, best nonexistence, best double-take, best foul-up that was kept, best stand-in, best stand-out, best acting without being noticed,* and the final biggie, *best performance in a featured extra role with a star without murmuring a word.* The awards would be the plastic Academy Award Statue that were sold all over Hollywood for a few bucks. Judging specifics to be sealed in an empty beer can high up on a windowsill in the alley, where I had found a large one right in the heart of Hollywood.

Dress code would be as is, and the guest menu would include Hostess Ho-Hos, Ding Dongs, soda, chips and chewing gum, which was always a no-no to have in your mouth as a professional extra. I was even going to try and get free lunches in town for all the winners. I checked with a local rag in North Hollywood, and they were willing to carry the event in their paper. I also checked with a nondescript local radio show in the area, and they were willing to carry the event live when I laid out how much attention the show would get for a quick good laugh. But with my own heavy schedule as an extra, I never had the time to launch it.

When it came to extras, as you could imagine, they came in all sizes and shapes. To find one that was normal or not a genuine character took some searching. But it was also amazing the number of folks that wanted to be a part of showbiz or hope for being discovered. It was equally amazing to realize that many of those extras who would have nearly killed for a chance to open their mouth and get a Taft-Hartley union qualification froze or backed off when they finally got the chance.

One of the extras I ran into a lot was Errol Tyrone (from idols Errol Flynn and Tyrone Power). He was the most dedicated extra I knew as he lived in his tiny car with all his earthly possessions. He was from back east and had quite an impressive résumé in local and regional theater. He was also formally trained and educated in acting and all levels of stage performance. He was quite overweight, but still filled extra roles in many categories. He seemed to be everywhere and was hard to forget.

One time after a late-night shoot and him previously telling me that many of the parking lots in Hollywood had kicked him out of their lots, I offered him to come and stay with me. What a mistake that was. After he left the shower, I looked around to see where the dead body was because it smelled like death, whatever gross smell that would be. He loaded up with cheap Bay Rum cologne, but it had about the same impact as putting it on a wild moose. I gave him clean sheets and blankets and a pillow, and he slept in the living room on the couch, asking me if I would mind if he watched TV. What could I say? I closed myself up in my bedroom and went to sleep or tried. I came out and asked him to turn down the volume, which he quickly did. The volume came right back and I was out again, being as nice as I could be, but finally shutting off the TV. As soon as my head hit the pillow, the TV was back on.

Later I got up to use the bathroom and went in there and turned the TV off. He was snoring like three lumberjacks on steroids. I just stood there looking at him, shaking my head. But *quiet*, finally. I went to bed, only soon to be awakened by a loud TV again. I couldn't believe it and gave up, getting at least a half night's sleep. Since I was into self-torture, I told him he could stay on a second night and catch up on his lost sleep.

The same exact scenario happened the second night. The bathroom now had a permanent stench to it as well as all the bedding and really entire apartment. Even after he departed, he left behind his mark, like a filthy stray dog leaving a clean holding kennel. But I would have given him a special *Alley Award* for being the most dedicated extra in Hollywood. To think, with some exceptions, that he lived out of his car with all his wardrobe and life and still wore a smile and never complained or gave up was truly amazing. I respect fighters and people who never give up, and he easily lead that parade, at least as an extra in Hollywood.

Back on the set of *Saved by the Bell*, I was the first to sign up in my downtime for the NBC *Writer's Workshop* and the first to attend with a handful of others. But for the time I was in Hollywood, the management of it faltered, and it never took off. I had come up with a couple of script ideas for *Bell*, and one was a psychological challenge for the program character of Slater, played by Mario Lopez, who was a varsity wrestler both in school and on the program. The fact that the AD and director even listened to a little of my ideas was encouraging.

But the adult extra characters of me as a coach and the lady as a teacher weren't progressing because they were still building and strengthening the characters of the kids. And I knew they never would; after all, the kids were the stars of that show, and with them, except for school principal Mr. Belding, no one else could possibly add to their incredible individual and collective talent. But there were some tense moments on that set occasionally, mainly driven by Diamond, who played Screech.

One time, Diamond was raising so much hell on the set and making chaos everywhere that producer Peter Engel, a longtime NBC executive, lost his temper. He said he was so disgusted with Dustin's unruly behavior that if he didn't change immediately he would shut the set down and maybe even cancel the show himself. Diamond's father, acting as his manager, was called in and they all managed to calm the waters and weather the storm. Every time I would be walking the halls outside the *Bell* set, I would pass the little room used by Diamond's father, and he would be working on the spreadsheet on his son's hours and earnings. Every time we talked, it was all about the money being generated by Dustin/Screech. Always interesting to me since Dustin was not even close to breaking the teen years yet.

Sometimes when I emerged from the *Bell* sound stage, there would be a familiar face standing in the hallway waiting for me. It was Jill. She claimed she knew many people at NBC and got through the security to get in. One time, I bawled her out because her unannounced visits were getting annoying. I never said anything again because I embarrassed her and brought tears to her eyes. Yet it was rather weird, I thought. She seemed to know what days I worked and when I got out. She used to always tell me the Hollywood dream was fading and that she realized her biological clock was running out. She came right out and told me she was desperate to get married and have a child, and she always batted her eyes when she told me that, which was fairly frequently. Several times at my apartment complex, I would go down to my car only to find Jill walking around. It always made me think—double guess—about her mental and emotional well-being. Like a scary movie, it was always a little discerning, mainly because her behavior was really offbeat when she explained herself. But I looked at her inner sweetness and overlooked it.

She wasn't the only odd female in and around that apartment at the time, which was quite nice and in a great Glendale location. The other was a divorced gal with four children and a claimed devoted Scientologist. She invited me over several times for home-cooked meals, and she was educated, sweet, and seemed to have so much going for her. She had the biggest and only four-bedroom in the complex, just ten doors down from mine. Her entire living room was a wall-to-wall library, all Scientology books. She caught me looking at some while she was in the other room. When she came in, she got quite excited by the fact that I seemed interested. Soon, she arranged for me to go to downtown Glendale for a reading at the Scientology local offices. I went, and after asking questions about their "faith," I refused to go further, telling the tester I thought it was psychological quackery and had nothing to do with Christianity, except for maybe on the dark side. They said I was wrong and should probably leave. I told him, "Thank you, you did me a favor." The lady never looked my way at the apartment again nor said a word, even when we shared the same sidewalk.

Chapter Fifty-Nine

Summer was around the corner, and My Ex agreed to send the kids for my visitation month. I made big plans for their stay, including going to Disneyland and stay the entire day and night, riding every ride we could. When they arrived, it was on a day I had to show up on the *Bell*, but they broke me free long enough to pick them up at the nearby Burbank Airport. My Ex always wanted the kids to be dressed up for air travel because they were traveling on passes, and she feared she'd be called out by the airlines if she didn't. The boys wore suits, and the girls were made up like Shirley Temple on dress-up day.

The cast and crew made a big deal out of my kids, especially the girls—Elizabeth, Tiffany, and Lark—and treated them like princesses. They loved meeting the cast, especially Screech, the show rascal, real and imagined. He flipped over the girls. The whole thing was really special for my kids—they watched the show at home too—and the powers on the set could not have been more gracious. My youngest, Chrissy, was dressed in this long white gown, and Screech—Dustin— called her Tinker Bell, the Disney character. He made the same fuss over my other daughter, Jenny. The boys, Alex and Adam, got the same attention, especially by the girls.

During one week, Jill had offered to watch over the kids while I went to the *Bell* set. She did a remarkably caring and loving job until the last day, when I left a paint coloring set with many scenes for the kids to color. When I returned home, there were paint drops all over the rug. It was just about like the kids used the carpet as their canvas. I lost my temper a little and pointed out all the damage to the rug, with Jill not knowing what to say. I was sure Jill made the offer to babysit not only to help, but also to show she could be a good mother. She seemed to sense she blew that as I was not very pleased. Later, I apologized, saying it was more my fault for leaving paints for kids than hers for not paying attention and being a ditz.

The week before we were set to go to Disneyland, I received a call from *Saved by the Bell*. The assistant director said they had a juicy speaking part for me as referee for Slater (Mario Lopez) in a wrestling match. I was excited until I heard of the day of the shooting, the same day of the Disneyland trip.

"Oh, I'm sorry, that's the same day I'm taking my kids to Disneyland, and they leave the next day. I can't break my promise. I just can't."

"Jon, I know you are a good father and we all appreciate that, but this is a great opportunity for you to get ahead. The coach and referee character will probably be expanded and given a regular slot on the show. You're perfect for the part and you were the first person the producer and director thought of."

I was at a complete loss and didn't know what else to say, so I broke the silence by saying, "Okay, I will give it some thought. I really have to sleep on it. But I really appreciate the offer. Thanks."

"Okay, Jon, but this episode was a last-minute decision, so we must have an answer tomorrow, first thing. I know how important your kids are, but think career too."

That night, I discussed Disneyland with the kids, talking to each one of them and getting a feel of how much they were looking forward to it. That night, I had a hard night's sleep, but knew I had to make the right decision for me and my future. The next day, before noon, the AD called me. "Jon, what have you decided? I need an answer right now."

"Yeah, I decided I have to pass on the part. I can't break my promise to my kids, it means too much to them, and it means too much to me. I am very sorry. Please tell Peter and Don I so appreciated the offer and thought, but I simply have to pass."

"Are you sure, Jon? Is this your final answer?"

"Yes, it is. No question, I'm taking my kids to Disneyland as planned."

The role was filled with another actor, and as the AD said, the coach part became a part-time but regular feature of the show. My last day on the set was a little uncomfortable for me, but only because I felt guilty and bad for turning down the part. As always, the *Bell* set was upbeat, positive, and fair. The two things I remember were outside of the *Bell* sound stage. The first was standing in the men's room urinal, between David Horowitz, the consumer advocate, and Alex Trebek, star of the game show *Jeopardy*.

The second was walking outside of the *Tonight Show* sound stage and suddenly having two very large Bulldogs lurched toward me from behind this hallway curtain. The dogs were literally pulling its owner right through the curtain and into the hallway—it was a smiling Doc Severinsen, the *Tonight Show* orchestra leader. He apologized profusely, but no harm done, and I joined in with his good-natured laughter.

We arrived at Disneyland by eight thirty in the morning. I had gotten a stroller for Chrissy and told the kids about safety issues of always staying right with me. We went nonstop all day, hitting virtually every ride, not that I went on all, but we stayed until 8:00 p.m., nearly twelve hours. I treated them to all I could afford and had an incredible day. I made it a point to compliment them on their behavior as they really were model kids.

There was only one thing that nearly ruined the day. I put the kids down across the way, with several older ladies looking after them, and took Chrissy to the girls' room. I waited outside, and waited, and waited. Finally, I asked a woman to check for my little girl. She came back empty-handed. I went crazy. I ran to the main gate right across from us and told them to shut down any departures because my little girl was missing. I told them I wanted Disneyland to close all gates. I was in full panic mode. I ran back to the bathroom and looked around and felt a tug on my shirt.

"Hi, Dad. Where were you?"

I nearly fainted. But I grabbed her and hugged her so tight she let out a squeal. "Chrissy, what happened to you? I was waiting for you in front, I don't understand, what happened?"

She took me by the hand and led me around the back of the bathroom and pointed to a door. "I went out the back door, Dad, so what?"

"Okay, Chris, Daddy thought you'd come back to me in the front, I didn't know they had a back door. Never mind, Dad loves you." I took Chrissy back to the main gate area and told them I found my daughter and showed her off. "This is my little munchkin here."

Within weeks of the kids returning home to Utah, my boys, Alex and Adam, called me in the middle of the night, crying. They said they missed me and didn't want to live with My Ex. They were very emotional and acted desperate. They had just started school again and were highly distraught over everything. I made a decision right at that moment. I told the boys I would finish the year out in Glendale, work hard, save my money, and come back to Utah and get an apartment, and figure things out as time went on. They seemed relieved, and I promised them I would return just like I said, saying Hollywood is not nearly as important as my kids. Their tears brought on my tears. When I hung up, I felt like I was dying inside.

I kept working, never at a loss to fill my schedule. Toward the end of the year and my departure, I took a stand-in job for Vegas star Robert Urich, a super nice guy, who was playing a bad guy role in a made-for-TV movie. He talked a lot about family, and I knew I was doing the right thing leaving Hollywood. But one AD lady that I had been with on set a number of times told me I might be making a mistake leaving Hollywood. She said the camera "liked" me and it was funny how the energy worked in Hollywood. That usually if a person left when they were on a *roll*—like she said I was on ever since I arrived in Hollywood—you could never really come back. It was like she said; once the genie was out of the bottle, it was near impossible to get it back in. But I made my decision and the kids got the nod, and I couldn't wait to leave and go back to Utah for their sake. I gave my notice to vacate by December 15 and would sell my clunker and fly back.

Out of pure luck, High Fly Airlines, My Ex-Wife's new assimilated airline from Able Airlines, put me in the last row of first class. After we reached our cruising altitude, this seven-to-ten-year-old girl came up to me and asked if I was a movie star. I said no, I wasn't. Then she said, "But I saw you on *Unsolved Mysteries* and you were the sheriff!"

"Yeah, honey, that was me but I'm no movie star, I'm just a regular person just like you."

"But you are in movies and TV, right? Don't you do acting and stuff?"

"Well, yeah, but really that's nothing. It's just the little tiny stuff. I'm no one important, believe me."

"You are to me, and I like your face. Can I please have your autograph?"

I persisted in downplaying myself, but she wouldn't have any of it. She threw a few more personal compliments my way as I noticed her mother looking on from nearby.

"Okay, sweetheart, okay, but only if I can have your autograph too."

"But I'm not famous," the girl said, puzzled.

"You are to me, sweetheart, you are to me."

We exchanged autographs, and she left with the broadest grin. Right behind her, a few other people approached me, asking me questions about acting and Hollywood. I was highly embarrassed and defused the situation that collected about six people my way, several also saying they saw me on TV. That little girl would never know what a shot of adrenaline and saving grace that gave me.

As soon as I realized I relinquished my transportation and would not have a car in Utah and no way to get around, certainly not having enough money to buy one, my dad told me he wanted a new car and decided to give me his. Talk about a coincidence. He never gave me anything so this was huge even though it was nearly a twenty-year-old car. I told the kids I would go straight to Minnesota first then see about getting them for an extended Christmas stay with my family. And that's exactly what happened; I got my kids, and we all stayed with my grandmother Hilda for ten days.

Despite the huge bullet holes of rust on the white body, the engine was tight and sound, Dad being a meticulous car owner. I ran scenarios through my mind about telling Dad I knew his secret over all the talk we had about his car, but once again, I dropped the idea to protect my mother. Dad and Mom, especially Mom, didn't want to discuss my divorce whatsoever so I didn't have a chance to be heard or supported. It was an aloofness I could never understand, and it deeply hurt. I tried concentrating on getting my kids and parents together more since they seldom saw them. I was happy for any time I could get.

All said, we had a great family Christmas and New Year. Afterward, I got together with Gary who now had two little boys with his new wife. I was so strapped for money that I took someone's tip to apply for job openings at Trans World Airlines (TWA) on the ramp, slinging luggage. The airline had an inside reputation for promoting from within, so I felt I could move up into corporate sales, marketing, or public relations. The only promotion I got was a ticket out the door by being laid off after just three months. But I kept my work status open as I got a good reputation as a hard worker, especially resulting from offering to clean the inside of a 747 myself along with one Dave Bergman. The management couldn't believe it because they usually allocated six people to clean it over one shift. TWA brass loved it, other ramp people hated it because the union always had them drag their feet and this made a bad prescient. Talk about counterproductivity. Unions! I gladly left Minnesota and went to Salt Lake to be close to the kids.

After I got an apartment and an offer by this doctor/MD investment group to be research analyst and chief operating officer for their project, I felt I had a future there in Salt Lake, as much as I hated the place, feeling I lost my entire life there. The project was the group's purchase of the W. Edwards Deming name in order to package and sell training to individuals and corporations. Deming, a PhD statistician, was famous for quantifying modern-day quality and customer service. He was held in great esteem the world over, especially in America and Japan, where he was the driving force behind the Toyota auto line. But while the lead doctor was a visionary, he was quite difficult to deal with so I left, not wanting my name to be associated with an inferior package and presentation to the public.

Despite sons Alex and Adam staying with me, where I made their school lunches every day and oversaw their schooling, I couldn't find a regular job, so I broke the news to my kids, added more stuff to my storage unit, and packed my car to leave for California. It was sad, but I couldn't deal with Utah.

Arriving in the valley area, I had to sleep in my car for weeks, trying to figure out how to get a life. I got some extra jobs in Hollywood and finally found another extra, a lady, who let me sleep in the back of her house, in the pool house. It had a shower, toilet, and sink. I had enough room, barely, to put an air mattress down on the floor. She charged me a token amount of $25 for a month where I stayed for two months, working and saving money. During that time, I went to a real estate seminar just to get motivated and met Catherine, a former Pan Am stewardess. She was very English and very proper, but very bright and pretty. We quickly became a twosome.

She shared a house in Studio City with a former actress and her husband. When they were out of town, I would go there and spend several weeks, leading what I saw as the good life. Catherine worked as a word transcriber and advertising and printing consultant. Although divorced, she had no kids, so being introduced to my flock of four was a bit shocking for her, but she was a trooper and very patient.

I got a cheap apartment to prepare for the summer with my kids, which I always had to have. Catherine helped me during that month long stay, and although flustered at times, she really helped. After they left, I kept working as an extra, including a month on the *Saved by the Bell* set, but the energy was gone, just like I was told it would be. I got a few good gigs and decent paydays, but it was far and few between and just different.

Many of my former helpmates and casting people hardly remembered me, and I couldn't believe it. I did a little help with a secondary casting agent, but he was soon busted for drugs and that ended. I also did some marketing and public relations for this other actors management group, providing fresh ideas and many new concepts of client and production applications, but it soon fizzled as they had major financial problems and I wasn't about to work for free anymore.

One time, in the Glendale area, I stopped at a light and this Rolls Royce pulled up next to me with the top down. I had my window down on the hot day. He smiled and said hi then casually said, "You know, you are creating an eyesore with that car of yours on the road, full of big circles of rust everywhere." Initially, I was outraged and wanted to get out of the car and teach this wiseguy a lesson, but instead thought I'd go along with him and have a laugh.

"Yeah, you are right, who am I to ruin your view as you drive and take away your driving pleasure? I'm sorry, I really am. I'll return this eyesore to the garage as soon as I pick up my Porsche." The guy gave me a disgusted look as he drove off, and I gave him a disgusting mouthful of spit on the road.

Christmas soon arrived, and I had the kids with me again, making my traditional full array of a turkey dinner, this time with some help from Catherine. Saying goodbye to the kids was always like pulling teeth without Novocaine.

My Ex had said as she sent the kids to me for the summer, that my "Daddy Bear" tapes I made for the kids—recommending that they could listen to them at night and feel closer to Dad in his absence—were sexual in nature, especially with the girls. It was such an outrageous thing to say I didn't bother to defend myself except for a few choice words. She had tried to throw them away, but the kids fished them out of the trash and hid them. I found out she had also thrown away many of the letters I had sent the kids, claiming the content was questionable. When I sent the kids home to her, I packed two large boxes to fly with them, of clothes, shoes, some new, some used, but all nice, found in a consignment shop in the upper end of Burbank. According to the kids, she ended up throwing most of it away as it "wasn't good enough" for *her* kids.

Divorce for me was a nightmare beyond description, in every way. Even when I tried to discuss the upbringing of the kids and their welfare, always saying it was a mutual communication we should be sharing for their benefit, she would not give me the time of day, usually hanging up. When I brought up some of these issues to my mother just to share and vent some, she got huffy and wouldn't listen. Sometimes I felt I couldn't win for losing. I had also written My Ex many letters suggesting we bury the hatchet and get back together, which normally just drew laughs when I called her to follow up. I wrote dozens and dozens of letters over those early years of divorce and never got a single response. I begged her not to create any divisions between me and the kids because besides the feeling of having the kids ripped away from me, it brought back memories of lost Marines and this profound feeling of loss. She just snickered.

Right after the holidays, my family back in Minnesota informed me TWA was trying to get ahold of me for a callback. I found myself packing up my car again for the return trip. I bade my farewell to Catherine and said I would probably return. After working on the ramp again for another three months, staying with Grandma Hilda again, they once again had a layoff, so I put in for a transfer to Los Angeles (LAX). I got it, to my disbelief. I packed up the car again to drive back, planning a one-week stop in Salt Lake.

Before I left, I was determined to talk with Dad and tell him I knew his secret. I wanted to find a way to just "suggest" to him certain elements of his secret, whether it be his brother Lester, WWII, prison, convicts, turning into model citizen, etc.; but when the deciding hour came, I couldn't do it. I couldn't betray my mom. Off to Utah I drove. There was a certain feeling of escape and relief that I always felt when I moved. It always kicked off memories from the Marines, especially the reoccurring dream of escaping from an enemy in a swamp, Viet Cong, and even the mortician for my escort of Dana Pitts. Every time I moved, no matter how close or far, I had that same exact dream.

Sometimes I would have the dream of being spared being shot in the foxhole by the Viet Cong even though my buds Minor and Jolly were killed on either side of me. It always made me yell out, "Hey, wait, I'm a Marine too, aren't I good enough to be shot?" The psychology of that one always drew self-analysis from me, and I always came to the same deduction of it coming from my experiences of wanting more action and feeling guilty. Before I left Minnesota, My Ex called and was very nice and sweet, at first. She wanted to bring the kids to visit personally herself and visit my family too. After she visited, I left the kids with Gram Hilda and drove My Ex back to the airport. She had asked Hilda before we left if she could have a small pan of water, some soap, and a rag. What? On the way, she asked to stop at this nearby lake and she came around to my side of the car, opened my door, and proceeded to wash my feet, telling me to just relax, enjoy, and not say anything. As she was drying my feet, she said she apologized for her behavior since the divorce, that I didn't deserve any of it, and told me this was a biblical gesture of asking for forgiveness, and she said she would never act like that again and was so very sorry.

She told me what an incredible father I was, what a decent man I was, and that the kids loved me so much. She was sincere, she really was, but I still couldn't believe her attitude and actions. She told me just to call in a few days and she would fly back to pick the kids up. I thanked her and was very appreciative. After four days of calling and endless messages, she finally answered and was back to her old self, as if what she did at the lake never happened. She was totally uncooperative, finally coming reluctantly and refusing to talk to me when I met her with the kids at the airport.

Upon my short stay in Salt Lake, where I stayed in a cheap dump, I was still so outraged by my Ex-Wife's behavior that I decided to find an attorney to file an appeal for child custody. Just before this, my daughter Jenny revealed that the babysitter's older son had violated her right in the house. My Ex-Wife said she never told me because she was afraid of what I might do and she was right, but I certainly wouldn't have killed him, just messed him up with my fists for life. To make this situation even worse, I had talked to My Ex about this particular babysitter over the phone, when the kids told me about her and her whole clan she brought over to babysit. I told her I was totally against her decision. It meant nothing.

I found a highly recommended female Mormon (mother) attorney and engaged her services. She was totally shocked by my story, actually bringing tears to her eyes. We agreed on a basic starting fee, and she filed the court papers to appeal the terms of the divorce, centering on joint custody or my full custody. She also filed for child support and the same basic rights a divorced woman would get, but I told her that was my least worry as I would find a way to make it myself. We conversed many times on the phone, and when I saw the bill, I was shocked. It was an amount way beyond my means and she defended it by saying all those telephone conferences were billed. I lost it somewhat in her office and picked up this huge beautiful leather chair I was sitting on and smashed it down on its ornate legs, breaking them all off, except one.

I immediately saw the error of my ways and profusely apologized. Terry was such a sweetheart and didn't deserve this from me, but she understood my frustrations, said to forget the chairs, and cut the bill in half, which I paid on the spot, nearly breaking me. Terry then revealed her arguments to the court for my custody and said the system was far less fair with fathers than mothers, and I would have to prove my ability to care for four children outside of any child support issuance. This would all include proper housing, schooling, and living.

She also threw another monkey wrench at me with the fact that it would all be made harder living away from Utah, out of state. As I left and told her my plans and that I would be in touch, I felt the weight of the world dump on me. I always prayed as I felt it was the only thing I had left, and they were always selfless prayers, and life went on. But I somehow knew it could always be worse, and for that I was thankful. I checked into the Salt Lake Vets Center and said my hellos and byes.

One day upon returning the kids home, I noticed that our longtime family dog, Highness, didn't run out to greet me. I asked the kids where she may be. They told me she usually walked across the street to a neighbor's house and hide under their porch. They said she became so depressed since I left and had just gotten worse. That dog was like my fifth child, and I was devastated. I remembered the time in California when I came home early from work as a quirk and Highness wasn't around to greet me, so I searched the house and yard and finally found her whining and convulsing behind the toilet. She had gotten into some snail bait, thinking it was dog food, and wolfed it down. I picked her up, which wasn't easy 'cause she was not cooperating, and carried her to the car and emergency Vet, where they were able to pump her stomach and save her although it was touch and go because of the poisons in her system.

I got out of the car, went to the street and called her name. After many calls, she finally came, with her head down, her tail tucked under her legs. I could hardly take it as I petted and then hugged her. I tried not to show my emotions to the kids, but I think they saw my tears and rasping voice. I hated divorce with every cell in my body. I also hated life right then the same. My kids, my dog, my life. Destroyed.

I took a chance and walked up to the front door and asked if I could talk to my Ex-Wife. She asked why, and I said I wondered about Highness and if she could fill me in. I asked the kids if they could go play while I had a little time with My Ex. After briefly addressing Highness, I told My Ex I wanted to tell her something sincerely and for whatever it was worth. I brought up all the shortcomings I may have had in our marriage like the could-haves of being more loving, more attentive, more sensitive, more understanding, more romantic, more stable, as in jobs and work, and more giving of myself. She seemed to ingest it all and said she appreciated it all and thanked me, but asked me what my motive was? I replied first and foremost, I just wanted to say it, and secondly, if she were receptive, I would like to try to get back together. She said it was too late and showed me the door. I left.

After assuming the TWA ramp position in LA, I slept in my car for a week, stayed with one ramp worker and his family for another week, then secured a little cottage to rent behind another worker's house. I reunited with Catherine, and we got together when we could. Out of nowhere, I got a call to go to New York for an offer to become an assistant editor of another bodybuilding and fitness magazine.

I made some work trades and vacation time and got an entire week off.

The publisher, who was a friend of this fitness player I had met years ago while editor of *Muscle Digest*, flew me first-class to New York and put me up in his penthouse, high up overlooking Manhattan.

He was another Chinese gentleman, just like my previous publisher, and was gracious with a capital *G*. But after meetings up on the very top floor of the Empire State Building, the current editor didn't seem anxious to bring on another voice and writer, so his opinion of not bringing me aboard prevailed. I also seriously questioned my ability to move to New York, what with the kids, which weighed in my decision.

On one day when I went to their incredible offices, with the most spectacular views of the Big Apple, they were shutting down the elevators and building because Iraq president Saddam Hussein had apparently made threats to blow it up. I was the last one, along with the publisher, to leave the building, which seemed somewhat fitting for my trip there. I went way up to the top floor, was exposed to the views and opportunity, only to go way down and get booted from the building. Nothing ever happened.

I flew back *coach* to Los Angeles.

Back on the ramp, I was cleaning a plane before takeoff and met eyes with an attractive stewardess named Elaine, who was also very sweet and unpretentious. I touched her shoulder in the hallway where they congregated before outgoing flights and handed her a complimentary note of romantic interest. She said she kind of had a new boyfriend but maybe we could talk. We did and immediately hit it off. She was divorced and had no kids. Perfect. We started dating shortly thereafter, but she lived in San Diego so it wasn't convenient. We talked a lot on the phone and remained friends.

Meanwhile, I found a nice big two-bedroom apartment in Sherman Oaks, right off busy Ventura Boulevard. I had made a deal where I got greatly reduced rent for simply overseeing the apartment. Practically right away, I got a call from Alex begging me to take him in and his buddy, Mike, whose parents were kicking him out. Alex said he couldn't take My Ex anymore and had to leave, even if I was unable to take him; naturally I did. I took Catherine in for a while because she had a big argument with her roommates, and I felt it was the least I could do. We slept together in the big master before Alex would show up a month down the road. When Alex arrived with Mike, Catherine decided to return to Heidi's since they had made up. Now, I had two teens in my midst, with Mike's parents sending a little money with him to ensure his care and safety.

Since Alex and Mike were both musicians and played in their own band in Utah, they wanted to check out the music scene in Hollywood. I dropped them off at Guitar World on Hollywood Boulevard. And told them to be outside at 8:00 p.m. When eight came, I was there waiting, and waiting, and waiting.

I took a final drive around the block, and when they still weren't there, I parked and started looking for them. I was freaked out with fear thinking something bad had happened. I did a recon search and found them a block away an hour later. I was quite upset but more happy that they were okay. I signed them up for school, and after a month, Mike was homesick and wanted to leave. I brought him to the airport and he was gone, leaving Alex alone with me. I was gone working a lot, and Alex got into trouble at school, lighting a small fire with something and dropping it in a locker.

The school called me in and was set to press criminal charges. I explained to the principal about the divorce and everything Alex had been through and pleaded for them to give him another chance. The fight was tough, and I had to confer with school board officials, plus ongoing discussions with the principal. I finally got the charges dropped, but he was on detention, probation, and I had to pay for locker damage, totaling slightly over $100. Soon, the rest of my kids were having their summer vacation with me. I took them to Disneyland once again.

One day, My Ex called and was all emotional and crying and said she "missed her babies." She said she was admitted as a patient at the John Bradshaw Center for depression in a Los Angeles suburb and asked me if I could bring the kids over for a visit, despite it being my limited visitation time and them only being with me at that point four to five days. She asked me to do it right then so she could take advantage of visitation times. Even though it was right in the beginning of the LA commute and I had to drive with the kids in a hot car all the way across town, I agreed.

When I was there, they let two of the kids visit her at a time in this semi covered outside yard. I was to wait there with the other two until they called. When they finally called for them, I waited and waited for a hospital person to come out and escort the kids back. So I finally got fed up and just opened the door and brought the kids back there. My Ex saw us coming and screamed and hid behind a tree. Two big white coats came out and told me I was trespassing and My Ex did not grant me permission to visit. They both grabbed my arms, but I flung them off and told them to get their filthy hands off me, telling them I was just escorting the kids safely in and had no intention of staying. I went back out in the waiting room, where a female doctor called me on the desk phone.

We talked about the entire incident, and I explained everything to her as well as our history after the divorce. She finally said that although she was breaking all hospital and ethical privacy codes, it wasn't my fault. "Mr. Meade, let me assure you, it has absolutely nothing to do with you, nor anything you may or may not have done. They are her personal issues." When the kids finally came out, I was so serene and relaxed from the doctor's comments, my patience seemed unlimited, so I stopped on the way home at an amusement ice cream parlor and bought them their heart's desire while I just observed them eating and talking and having fun. I just felt relieved, vindicated and cleansed.

When I took them once again to the Burbank Airport to leave, we said our tearful goodbyes, and Alex was going back with them. The other little trouble I found out later about Alex was he and a buddy attacked the gay pride parade floats with tomatoes and eggs on Ventura Boulevard. I heard about it from a few distant neighbors, one who was Alex's friend's mother and boyfriend. We all agreed, *boys will be boys*. Alex also told me later about the incident, and he admitted it was bad behavior and was sorry. Life goes on, gay parades and all.

Just after the summer with the kids, I suffered an injury on the ramp at TWA and was on disability, which I hated the idea of, as I didn't believe I was disabled at all. Because of insurance concerns and lawsuits and crybabies, this disability thing is something the system, for lack of a better term, nearly pushes a person into. TWA was super about the whole thing, and I was very uncomfortable about it from the get-go. I pushed for some lateral move in corporate sales or promotions, where I had an idea to launch a national campaign for more passengers and corporate accounts, related around incentives and contests plus unique forms of advertising, but it didn't go anywhere.

Considering that some of TWA management types loved some of my ideas, some others thought they were too radical and too outside the box. Outside the box is exactly what they needed, but complacency and comfort zones challenged too many people. Sometimes it is just a matter of plain old jealousy. Some weak ego-strong people become very uncomfortable around newer people with huge fresh ideas. It becomes a threat to their pathetic little existence that they project with much more importance than justified.

Then LA was hit with breaking news; the Rodney King riots broke out, dominating the air waves and turning into a near race war. It was truly disgusting how the rats and vermin came out of the woodwork to escalate the situation with looting, burning, and nonsensical hate. A little forgiveness, understanding, and patience would have gone a long way after Rodney King was beaten by the police much more than necessary under the circumstances. Human beings are fragile, sometimes too much so, especially if they are coddled and spoiled by a liberal media and factions of discourse. I blamed the media nearly exclusively for that terrible social and cultural fiasco that was over fabricated and fueled by constant coverage and extreme negative reporting. Even King himself, clearly not an educated or articulate person, toward the end, may have had the definitive thought: "Why can't we all just get along?"

Chapter Sixty

At another (free) success seminar I attended, I met this unusual wealthy couple whom I sat next to. After much talk about many of our mutual experiences, they asked me if I would write something for them about Unidentified Flying Objects (UFOs). I told them I had no background, experience, or knowledge in that area, but they said it didn't matter because I could learn as I go. They invited me to go with them to San Diego to attend the annual UFO convention, which I did. They paid for all expenses and said I would learn everything I needed to know to have a foundation for this story. I wasn't working and had this extreme inquisitive nature, so why not? It was an entire weekend affair and provided me with an experience I would never forget.

The "Men in Black" controversy was very well and alive during the convention. I was wearing a pair of black pants and a jet-black windbreaker, plus a black baseball hat. My attire selection couldn't have been more ineptly selected. Someone started the rumor that I resembled this well-documented "Men in Black" character. Someone even showed me a picture, and we did look alike, but I thought the comparison was ridiculous. I was no more a man in black than a man in white. The more I ignored it and tried to distance myself from it, the more it followed me. The seeds that some people can plant.

Suffice to say, that there is some incredible evidence out there about UFOs, both factual and bogus, but all fascinating. By the time it was over, I thought I would be taken away in a spaceship, maybe even commandeered by my Ex-Wife. Seriously, this story could easily take another book, so I will stop here. Just know that we may not be alone in this universe and stratosphere. To think there is not some possible intelligent life-form out there is somewhat naive and narrow-minded.

After continued visits to Elaine's place, a beautiful condo in Rancho Bernardo, a northern San Diego suburb, she encouraged me to move in with her, which I did. After I did, it was time to meet my kids, all of them. I can't remember if I white-lied a little or Elaine didn't hear me clearly, but suddenly realizing there were four kids and not two was a bit of a jolt although she took it like a trooper. She had met Alex once but not the rest. The first time was for Christmas. We had to drive to LA to pick them up. Elaine had just gotten a brand-new car. She met them upon pickup and couldn't have been more warm and gracious. The kids all immediately took to her too because of her friendly, accepting demeanor.

Just after we passed from the 405 freeway to the 5 freeway, Jenny started throwing up in the backseat, heaving huge stomach fulls of vomit into a shallow cookie tray Elaine picked up. We couldn't help but laugh, and when Jenny was finally finished, she felt so bad she cried. After ten minutes, we pulled off the freeway and I cleaned up the worst of it and quickly got going again. Elaine had beautifully decorated her place for Christmas, and she owned a pet rabbit so the kids were very happy there. I went out to poor Elaine's new car and cleaned it perfectly. Christmas was wonderful and the kids' stay very positive.

After some outside sales and marketing training through TWA and disability, I took on a job, then another, then yet another. All bogus, hyped-up opportunities that didn't pan out. I was also getting counseling at a Vets center in San Diego to help with career guidance and personal issues. At different times, we took on Alex, Adam, and Chrissy as residents. Neither one stayed despite Elaine's welcoming arms for the same reasons that Alex never stayed, because of home and their siblings and friends. I left Elaine and moved back to Utah to be close to the kids so many times and then returned again to San Diego, it was a joke. I paid a dear price for all those moves both in my head and my bank account.

The only time I didn't was when I took an outside sales and marketing consulting position with United Parcel Service (UPS) in Salt Lake, under a one-year contract that paid quite well. I was one of only twelve people in the entire nation that was selected, which I took as a personal honor. Accept for weekly meetings and related paperwork, I was on my own. I had Alex and Adam move in and was a happy father for that time despite the cold shoulder from My Ex. I had the girls over frequently and every other weekend.

Just before the contract ran its course, I had closed a million-dollar new account and brought back some customers thought lost. I also sold another large account. As much as this was a huge success for me, without realizing it, by selling these accounts right under the nose of their existing field account managers, it raised serious questions on their coverage and abilities, including the facility sales supervisor. I did nothing wrong and everything right; however, without me having boots on, I stepped on a lot of feet and created animosity and jealousy. So much for being hired to expose flaws and recommend new inroads of sales and marketing approaches. I left under a dubious cloud of defensive, analytical criticism from them and extreme frustration and a feeling of injustice from me. It was just another successful failure of my life on the career front.

Despite wanting to stay in Utah for the kids' and having extreme feelings of rejection and frustration in the Salt Lake job market, I started my own little consulting contracts in sales, marketing, and public relations, but couldn't make a living, mainly because I was always so incredibly stressed over the kids and Ex-Wife. I once again packed up my car and headed back to San Diego. Driving down the 15 freeway between the two states always had me stop in Las Vegas. And nearly every time, I would make attempts to find that showgirl Marilyn Marx, going back to my stop in Vegas in 1967. It was going on thirty years now since that meeting, and while disappointing, I still had hope of somehow making contact. I just wanted to hug her, take her to dinner and thank her, but again, no luck. If I ever dropped $20 on gambling, I would have considered myself a big spender from the east.

On my trip to Salt Lake and subsequent stop in Vegas, en route to assume that UPS position, I stayed at the Sahara Hotel, my favorite casino. While strolling around the casino floor watching high rollers that I loved to do, I ran into a line for this free show, where they had some secondary singers and performers. I thought I'd take it in and relax. I realized that standing right in front of me was former heavyweight boxing champion, Ken Norton, wearing a cowboy hat, alongside an attractive blonde, who I would soon find out, was his wife. I introduced myself, and as we shook hands, I asked him if it was true that he was a former Marine, which he confirmed. We talked and laughed as we waited in line, really hitting it off.

When we got in, Ken asked me to sit with them and watch the show. He bought the first drink and I would buy the second. His wife, very sweet and quiet, seemed content to enjoy the show herself, as we just had a ball, joking, laughing, and talking just a bit about

Muhammad Ali and Norton breaking his jaw. The main performer was this washed-out singer character whom I had seen on the old talk show host *Mike Douglas Show*. His main performance was singing the recent huge hit, "My Achy Breaky Heart." Soon, after knocking down numerous drinks and talking Marine Corps stuff, we were virtually reeling, singing lightly along with the performer. Ken's wife was also joining in and having fun.

Toward the end of the show, a large group of breathtaking women came in and sat together across from Ken. It soon became apparent that they were predominantly lesbian, with the one in the center, seemingly their leader, having one of the most perfectly sculpted womanly faces I had ever seen. I had a little hard time keeping my eyes off her. Before long, several of the other women in the group were looking at me, especially this one in particular, who had pure hate and vengeance in her eyes. Ken noticed this and kept looking back and forth between me and them, grinning and apparently getting the biggest kick out of it.

"Hey, Marine, you better be careful, that one who has been staring you down looks like she could scratch your eyes out." Norton laughed. "I might have to intervene and defend your ass." We laughed so hard, with help from all the liquor, that we were nearly rolling on the floor.

Ken was a great, great guy, and it was a huge shot in my arm as I went back to Utah and my kids.

Back in San Diego, also where Ken lived, we had talked briefly of getting together because I felt I could help him a little in his upcoming business ventures (never happened). I was with Elaine again. I had helped her with many financial issues in her life, and she was glad to have me return, as I was to be there again. Before long, I flew on a buddy pass from Elaine back to Minnesota to visit family, old buddy Jerome, and spend time with Gary, reeling from separation and divorce challenges. Dad's health was going downhill, and as always, I tried to find an opening, no matter how small, to talk about his lifelong secret, prison time and everything related.

At one point when we were talking about his father who was shot over that horse race and when Dad went to the state capital to argue that the killer shouldn't be released just because of his reputation and won his argument with the parole board, I thought it was the perfect time. I had my opening. But I didn't have my opportunity. Mom was sitting in the kitchen and could overhear everything. I backed off again. I was so flustered by it I could have screamed. I did compliment Dad on his fight for justice, and he seemed to really appreciate that, as Mom had always probably heard her share and was not a sounding board for him much anymore.

Soon, after I returned to San Diego, daughter Jenny was on the phone crying, nearly out of control, over missing me, and wanted to come live with me and Elaine and the bunny. She was stressed over many things that were going on between her and her mother back in Utah. Since this situation was taking place, My Ex was more than happy to send Jenny on the next available flight out.

When she arrived, it took several days to calm her down, added by the fact that she was starting her menstrual cycle for the first time at twelve. Elaine helped her and in a few days things calmed down. For the next several weeks, we went out of our way to appease Jenny's every need. It helped to heal a lot of wounds but not bury them. When the date rolled around for Jenny to leave, she knew we would take her, but now she had to ask her mother. We didn't see that as much of a problem because My Ex wanted her gone anyway. I prepped Jenny on exactly what to say.

It was so sad seeing Jenny sitting on the edge of the bed and being torn between us and My Ex although that call was more for her siblings than her mother, I'm afraid. Some of the stories Jenny was conveying broke our hearts. It took a tremendous build-up of courage before Jenny could make the call, but she did. Probably because Jenny was now telling her mother she thought it was better that she stay with us and that she felt that "Elaine loved her. And was really nice." We overheard every word of the conversation and how quickly all of a sudden My Ex wanted her daughter back. They went back and forth, with My Ex telling her to come home immediately and Jenny crying her eyes out, losing her breath and shedding hankies full of tears. Jenny finally slammed the phone down, and we all talked out the situation. Jenny still clung to her desire to stay with us.

My Ex called back demanding Jenny to get ready to leave. I had Jenny try to ask My Ex to please talk to me, but it fell on deaf ears. When My Ex finally said she would call the police and file a kidnapping report, I told Jenny that since I made the mistake of my life and signed off on My Ex having full custody, I had no choice but to put her on the plane. Hours after she left, we got a call from Able Airlines saying Jenny was a minor and didn't have anyone to pick her up, so they asked permission if they could have an employee run her home since they couldn't get ahold of My Ex. Later, My Ex claimed that she forgot the day and time of arrival despite being the one who demanded and arranged it all.

One night when Elaine was due home from her trip, she was overdue so I was concerned since she never called me with a delay notice. No sooner had I thought that than I got a call from Elaine saying she was having dinner at George's on the Cove, in La Jolla. Then she said she met this guy on the plane who was celebrating getting a big book advance from a major publisher and wanted her to accompany him to La Jolla for dinner and champagne and then call me and invite me. But it was already 9:00 p.m. and I really didn't feel like leaving.

She kept begging me until the guy grabbed the phone and told me he heard I was also a writer and a former Marine who had served in Vietnam. He said he was a special intelligence officer in Vietnam and that was what the book was about. He literally begged me to come, and I continually turned him down until he said he was sending a limousine to pick me up and he wouldn't take no for an answer, even though I told him it was extremely foggy up in Rancho Bernardo at the time. I got up and got ready. The limo ride took forever because of the overcast and it was a risky night to be out, but after I got there, it was all worth it. I met the guy, and he was well on his way of being stone drunk.

I took advantage of his hospitality and, upon his insistence, ordered prime rib and lobster and a few side dishes. He ordered several hundred-dollar bottles of champagne and poured it out like water. As Elaine and I got pretty lit and enjoyed the expensive entrees, he told us his incredible story of being trained as the first psychic warfare officer, using paranormal mind manipulation and control, which was tied in with the CIA.

When the evening ended, after telling us about being raised in the area by wealthy parents, he gave us his phone number and his parents' phone number and wanted to get together again. But as he left, he said if he disappeared, we should not be alarmed. Or if we couldn't reach him by phone, we should just be patient. He actually gave me galley sheets for the first five chapters. We never were able to reach him, as all the phones were disconnected and never reinstated. His book did come out and got good press, then it disappeared just as quickly. Never could figure it out. Maybe it was para-abnormal?

The last time Alex came to stay with us, he got a job several blocks away at Domino's Pizza. He stayed long enough to save money to buy a beater van, and then for the same reason as always, he went back to Utah and My Ex to be with his siblings. Just before he left, he had an extensive heart-to-heart with his mother, and she was welcoming him back with open arms and saying she would help him. I felt really good about it, as much as I hated to see Alex leave—again.

Since I was not working for the time being, I decided to write a screenplay. I had always spent many hours on various movie sets talking to Jewish grandmothers, and with their sense of humor and stories, combined with my sincere willingness to listen, I learned an awful lot. I found my share of Holocaust survivors, most having great demeanors and willing to share. I created a Jewish heroine and had her survive the Holocaust at ten years old, lose her father, migrate to the States, and connect to extended family in New York, where she would later meet her very successful husband, get married, and have one daughter. Then the story unfolds in many different directions and makes more humorous twists than a pretzel.

I had entered the Academy Awards Screenwriting Contest for a $25,000 grand prize in Hollywood at the same time that I was getting antsy again and greatly missing the kids. So despite Elaine not understanding my constant moving, I packed my belongings and left again for Utah and the kids. I got an apartment and settled in to finish my screenplay titled, "Ned." I was having a difficult time wrapping up the script, but did so under great duress and made the contest deadline. Thereafter, I spent my days watching the O. J. Simpson trial and the ridiculous courtroom melodrama. It was like a cast of cartoon characters to me, especially when the defense team had OJ try on the glove and then slip that hat on his head, saying, "If it doesn't fit, you must acquit." Good for a cheap laugh, I suppose, but this was a serious murder trial. It could have been conducted with far less theatrics.

One of the first things I faced when I arrived in Salt Lake this time was hearing that My Ex had Alex arrested in her house first thing in the morning in bed after the night before was very positive between them. She told the police he was "out of control" and had to be removed. Alex had to sleep in his van for the next several weeks, and it caused him to lose his new job. I came to the rescue as usual and felt so bad for him. I was determined to make yet another attempt with My Ex to make amends.

She actually agreed to talk, and we ended up hugging and crying together. Later, we went to a movie. The next day, it was like nothing happened. All communications severed—again. Even though I did a little public relations for this guy in his small business, Salt Lake once again defeated me and sent me packing. More rounds of apologies, tears, and goodbyes with the kids.

One of the things I discussed with My Ex was child support. The Utah courts had made their determination, and I paid every month even though the amount was rather pathetic. I told My Ex that I wish I had been in a better position in work and career so the child support would have been more. I also said my life was made much more difficult because she wouldn't share anything with me about the kids, and I was a nervous basket case with raw nerves worrying about them all the time. It affected everything in my life, from mental to physical. She basically laughed at me and shut me down. When I brought up her throwing away designer clothes I had given the kids, the "daddy bear" tapes, and letters to the kids, it ended the rare discussion we had since the divorce. I also found out that she had destroyed most of our wedding photo album.

Chapter Sixty-One

Back in San Diego again, I got news that I didn't win the screenplay competition and was somewhat bummed. I went up to LA to resubmit my Writer's Guild *Ned* copyright, which I made some changes to. While there, I was determined to find an agent, which I did. She was a former actress and had been an agent for nineteen and a half years and took my screenplay on as her final project. She loved it and even thought of herself in the role since my character *Ned* was much older. That same day in LA, I also went to Leah (Adler) Spielberg's restaurant, *The Milky Way*. She was Steven Spielberg's mother and very friendly despite her saying she never talked Hollywood in her establishment. That day, it was well over one hundred degrees and mixed with the smog, very uncomfortable, and I had stumbled across her place during my day and was desperate for ice water, so I asked them. Mrs. Spielberg had this warm but confident manner, and I thought she would make the perfect Ned. I was probably delirious from an empty stomach and the heat. I had a cheap sandwich and left.

The agent nearly sold my screenplay to TV's Hallmark Hall of Fame and MTM (Mary Tyler Moore) Productions. The latter had a vice president change, and with his departure, all his considerations were swept off his desk when he left. And my hopes were gone with him. That's Hollywood. After that, my agent just gave up and retired. She said my script was the last one she would ever touch. She admitted she was totally burned out and wished me well. Another Hollywood casualty.

I secured a sales position with a financial processing company expanding into the West Coast from the East. One day, I got a call from Taylor Made Golf, whom I had made dozens of calls to with no positive response. The vice president said he had to call me back and invite me to come in and talk shop because I had been so persistent, yet professional, and he wanted to meet me. I went there, and between that meeting and a few more with our manager to explain the exacting technology, I sold an annual account worth 46.5 million, plus a tag-along growing account worth 1.5. It was the largest sale ever made in this 1,500-employee company's history. It blew the management away 'cause I didn't spend one dime to nail the account down. It was so big they didn't know how to pay me.

It took two months and a phone call from the president of the company to finally apologize and determine a proper payment, and that amount turned out to be very small in comparison to the profit the company made, especially as an annual account. Elaine and I had planned a trip to Europe, and this seemed like the perfect time to take a break and reward myself.

Because my dad had some previous cancer scares and had gotten quite weak, I was concerned for his well-being so I called my mom and asked her his true and accurate diagnosis since he never complained or discussed health issues much to us kids. She said he was not doing so well and his doctor was concerned, but he had just recently made a positive rebound and gave him more hope for an extended life. I then talked to Dad and he was pretty upbeat although his voice was quite weak. I told him of our plans to be gone for two and a half weeks as we were going to Greece. I asked him several times if he felt strong and if he thought he would be okay.

He repeated again and again that he was fine, doing better, and that we should go on our trip. He then spoke up and insisted I not worry and take the trip. There was a moment there when I quickly thought of a way to tell him I knew his secret, but realized it would be touchy, even risky, emotion and health wise. Also, Mom was right there, so I simply couldn't. My mom was still reeling somewhat from her mother's recent death—Grandma Hilda—as it was a great loss for the family. I had given the eulogy at her funeral and Dad even took it hard, so the emotions were fragile all around. It wouldn't have been right. Dad and I ended our conversation by sharing we loved each other. I had to say it, and I think he did too.

In preparation of this trip, I had determined to get in the best shape of my life so I could have my photos taken in front of the Greek ruins. Five months before, I had let myself get in my worst shape ever from the onslaught of near-constant family stress. I used this trip as an incentive to turn things around. First, I lost forty-three pounds in five weeks to rid myself of fat and my stomach. Then I concentrated on building muscle back I had lost in the dramatic weight loss with walking, sprints, and weight training. I dropped another five pounds of pure fat before our departure, plus refining my muscle definition and hardness. I reached a distinct deep six-pack and was ready for Greek photos—at just under fifty-two years old. My goal was to produce my own fitness course and market it later.

We would visit the Greek islands of Hydra, Aegina, and one of the most beautiful settings on earth, Santorini. But first, Elaine took photos of me in Athens where we were chased and yelled at for posing among the wrong part of the ancient ruins without understanding what we were doing wrong. Finally, this seemingly disposed, educated Greek philosopher, by his own admission, told me that while I had a body like a Greek god, it was illegal to pose flesh against those particular Greek ruins. So we were told I could go outside the protected area and pose in front of the gates.

After photos outside at the approved area, the Greek pointed out that perhaps the police thought we were still inside the protected area and were summoned, so he directed us to a back street to escape. We did get some great shots and resumed being normal tourists as we heard the sirens in the background. Wherever we went in Athens, we found the same touchy situation. The old ladies in black full-body robes would see us, make these sharp whistles, and then scream, directing us out of the protected areas. We still got many photos in the unrestricted areas, always being confused by the language barrier.

When we got to the other islands, especially the ancient historical city of Aegina, we asked permission; and to my amazement it was granted, so we had no problems getting photos and it completed our trip, along with much fun, especially in Santorini, where we stayed an entire week. On Elaine's travels, where she almost exclusively flew international, she met the female owner of a group of cave-like apartments and a restaurant, and that's where we stayed. The lady knew about my continued training, even there at a Santorini gym, and made me incredibly large breakfasts with eggs, meat, bread, veggies, and the most incredible, homemade plain Greek yogurt topped with walnuts, pistachios, and raw honey. That breakfast gave me incredible energy and power for the day, as I loved to run all the way down this endless brick stairway from the city to the ocean shore.

When the night came to pack and take a plane out the next morning, there was a major wind and rainstorm. A stray mother cat was at the bottom of our apartment's long stairway with eight newly born kittens over on the side, somewhat under the steps. Elaine had thought she heard some meowing, and there they were. The mother hauled every kitty up those stairs in the rain with Elaine actually supervising the whole thing. After she plopped down the final newborn on our bed, the mother jumped up and groomed them.

That mother cat somehow sensed Elaine's big heart and love of cats and instinctively knew her babies would be safe. Elaine laid down next to them all and helped the kittens hook up to the mother's breasts. It was one of the most touching scenes you could imagine. I joined them, but Elaine and that mother cat were just looking at each other and motherly bonding. The fact that we had to leave them first thing the next morning was heartbreaking, but we begged our Greek host to look out after them, at least until they could get settled somewhere.

As soon as we got home to San Diego, I rushed to a phone and called Mom. She told me that Dad had taken a turn for the worse and was given twenty-four hours to live, at the most. I took a deep breath and said I would be on the next flight home. I started my praying, especially asking for forgiveness for Dad's life and asking to save him because of all his good qualities.

I may not have made it back physically, but along with all my regrets and memories, I did mentally.

Epilogue

Survival is all about weathering the storms of life.
—JM

When I finished this memoir, it gave me a weird feeling of both elation and frustration. All of a sudden with the final stroke of a key, the book is more fun because it is done. At the same time, I wondered if I did myself, the book, and all the events and people in it justice. If justice is truth and honor, to the best of my recollection and memory, then I am satisfied. If justice is ambiguous and unanswered, then I will remain an enigma of myself. In the final analysis, I choose to let the story speak for my convictions.

When it comes to the spiritual experience I had in Beverly Hills, I labored over it something fierce, taking four months alone to determine exactly how to handle and write it. Just those few pages were harder to write than the entire remainder of the book. In the end, I wrote it exactly the way it happened, just as it was suggested to me it be done. It still was very difficult. I felt such an incredible wave of humility and the personal necessity to ensure it was accurate.

In the most symbolic biblical sense then, *the truth did set me free.*

So if I didn't convey the message in its unabridged simplicity, along with all the surrounding story elements, I will have to face and answer to the *Man* himself. That would be a tall order for any mortal being. But I accept it. Like all of mankind, I am a flawed human being. God didn't make cookie-cutter versions of one another. Everyone has their own unique DNA, and no one has the same fingerprint. Incredible. My personal indiscretions, of which are many, have certainly been exposed in this memoir and are mine to bare. All of humanity has some cross to bear; in an exposé sense, my memoir is mine. However, it also comes with a profound message.

Let there be no mistake; I also had my fun with the written word and my life's experiences, but never at the expense of truth. Yes, I was blunt; yes, I was open; yes, I spared no details, but I did so in the scheme of storytelling, with truth again prevailing, or at least the essence of truth. Sometimes I saw a green light when others saw red.

Other times I saw a red light when others saw green. Seldom did I see a yellow light or proceed with caution. I always responded to a light no matter what the color. I lived life in its fullest, with little thought to consequences although sometimes measuring them. It was this spontaneity that served me platters of good and bad portions of life and a literal smorgasbord of experiences. I savored it all in the amounts I could digest, seldom rejecting any. I am totally responsible and accountable for it all, even the parts in my life and memoir that surprised me about me.

If I hadn't lived through it myself, I would find my story hard to believe, in many aspects. But I did.

During the serious writing of this memoir in 2015, Gary and my Vietnam Ninth Engineer buddies also came to the forefront. Gary was suffering from cancer resulting from Agent Orange and is in pretty rough shape, but we planned for him to make the trip out to Arizona to spend several weeks with me, exactly upon completion of my book. Pistol Pete Kuhlmann from Ninth Engineers was a life-long smoker and was dearly paying the price, having been confined mainly to home on oxygen. We talk regularly. Lenny "OJ" Rinaldini, also from Ninth, who was suffering from Agent Orange and had an open claim with the VA and lives in the same area as Pete, finally had his claim determined and received his just compensation. It took years, but it was finally ruled in his favor and so nice to hear about and share with him.

Also, well before the book was finished, I got bad news from Barb Parmer that Harry had a stroke and was hospitalized in critical condition. He was paralyzed from the chest down, my old buddy from Camp Pendleton and Vietnam. Harry had retired from the Marines as a major and also led Marines in Desert Storm. It was a blow to hear that, especially since sometime before that Barb and Harry had divorced. The good news however quickly followed that when Harry survived and made a miraculous recovery, slowly regaining feeling in his mid-torso and slowly going down.

Just before Gary was due to fly out, he had a scheduled medical exam at the VA. His doctor gave him two big thumbs-down on any flying or even travel of any kind. We were both devastated. I would not be celebrating the completion of this memoir with my lifetime good buddy. I went out myself and had Mexican and four beers. I just toasted the piñata hanging up on the ceiling.

Some short memoir conclusions: Serving your country—couldn't be a more honorable thing.

Divorce (with kids): Couldn't be a more challenging thing.

Forgiveness: Couldn't be a more difficult, yet rewarding thing. Life is about the fight. The fight for what is deemed to be right.

The biggest lessons I've learned in life is about giving and forgiving. Although not perfect, I believe it is better to forgive some than none. Life is like a big test, and I am still trying to pass the best I can. I am certainly a work in progress.

I also had some rather strange thoughts and subsequent actions that I admittedly don't fully understand while writing certain parts of the book, especially after the Vietnam and the Marine parts. I sought out some Vietnamese and Asian women and gave them money, which they really had difficulty accepting. I found just the right ones with special needs and gave them collectively several thousand dollars—plus. It served me as much as them, making me feel great. I guess I still carry these profound thoughts that women and children suffer the most in any war. I assume it was my way of giving back.

While wars are sometimes unfortunately unavoidable, and if entered should be quickly won with a huge definitive offensive, and declared a victory, war is a basic waste of humanity. But as long as you have blood pumping through the veins of man, wars will never die, just its participants. Personally, before any countries engage in war, I think all the politicians from all sides should be locked together in an auditorium and be forced to fight it out, resolving all issues, with the only blood being shed, their own. It bears repeating: Besides the combatants themselves, innocent civilians—particularly women and children—are the biggest victims.

During the researching and writing of this memoir, I had my doubts about exposing myself and my torrid tales, losing gobs of hair in the shower from memories and stress. While I have my share of regrets in life, I *do not* regret writing my story. Now that I have finished my memoir, what do I think of myself? I don't know, I really don't? I will let the readers decide that for me and themselves.

In the end it matters not how I may define my life, as Vietnam is forever etched in my rear view mirror.

APPENDIX

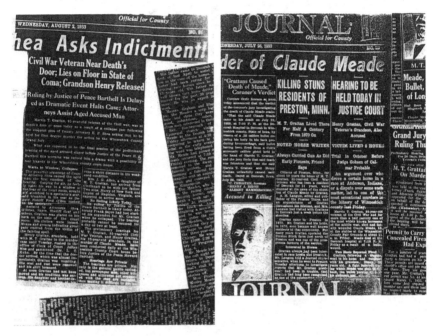

My never-met grandfather, Claude Meade, made front page news with his murder.
The facts of the case and the party's involved were the scandals of the day.

M. T. Grattan

Meade, Victim of Bullet, Horseman of Long Standing

Had Been Managing Graham-Blagsvedt Horses Here Since Last April.

Claude Meade, 53 years old, Minneapolis, killed Friday by M. T. Grattan, 85, Civil War veteran, in an argument over the driver of Hiph Celia, a horse owned by B. M. Graham and Ole Blagsvedt of Decorah, had been in charge of the Graham-Blagsvedt stable of race horses and had just returned from a circuit of races in Indiana, due to an injury to a horse.

Was Born in New York

Claude Meade was a native of New York, but had made Minneapolis his home for 28 years. He lived at 4355 Irving avenue, Minneapolis. His widow and three sons, Lester and John, of Minneapolis and Wesley of Decorah, survive. Mr. Meade was born in Randolph, N. Y. Two sisters, Miss Elizabeth Meade of Dunkirk, N. Y., and Mrs. Herbert Sill of Flushing, N. Y., also survive. Another son, Wesley, was associated with his father at the Graham-Blagsvedt stables here and was the driver in the races.

For more than 20 years Meade was an employe, principally as a teamster, for the City of Minneapolis. Later he had charge of the horses of the Northland Milk Co. in Minneapolis. Last April he joined his son, Wesley, here. Wesley had been in Decorah since last October.

After remaining at his father's bedside until his death at about 7 p. m. Friday, Wesley went to the home of his wife's parents, Mr. and Mrs. Albert Nelson, living near Ridgeway.

Funeral on Tuesday

The body was taken to Minneapolis in a funeral coach Saturday. Funeral services were to be held in Minneapolis Monday afternoon. Mr. Meade had been affiliated with St. Mark's Episcopal church. About an hour before his death, Rev. Allen O. Birchenough, rector of the Grace Episcopal church of Decorah, was called to the bedside of Mr. Meade.

Suffering intense pain from the bullet wound, which entered his back and passed virtually through

Interested in Horses

Grattan always had been interested in race horses and livestock. Mr. Langum told a Journal representative, when he went to Preston Tuesday afternoon to investigate reports that Mr. Grattan previously had been in trouble, that Grattan had long been recognized as one of the outstanding authorities of the nation on horse racing and that his articles concerning horse racing were eagerly sought by readers of that community.

For many years, including this spring, Grattan had been the Memorial Day speaker at the services held at Preston. He is one of the two survivors of the Civil War in that community. Grattan had a reputation of always having carried a gun on his person.

"You must remember", Mrs. Langum chimed in, "that 'Dad' Grattan was not a product of 1933. When Grattan came to Minnesota in the early seventies many persons carried guns—and they needed them."

Mr. Langum stated that Grattan was often involved in arguments with persons of that community, but stated that as far back as he could remember Grattan had been in no actual trouble. He stated that some 25 years ago he and a village marshal at Preston had been involved in a lengthy argument, but that there had been no arrests or anything more serious than arguments.

Had Five Children

The Grattans raised their family of five children in Preston. Three of the children are still living, Guyon, in Virginia; Harry in New York, and Jenny, in Cincinnati. Mr. and Mrs. M. T. Grattan reared two of their grandchildren in Decorah.

May Preside

Judge Thomas H. Goheen of Calmar is scheduled to preside at the October term of court. If M. T. Grattan is held for trial it is probable that Judge Goheen will preside at the trial of the aged Civil War veteran. It will be the first term of court at which the new Judge, elected last fall, will preside in his home county.

wound.

Two Shots Reported Fired

Grattan, following a dispute, went to his home and returned with his grandson, Henry, 22 years old. A fight followed during which Meade was shot in the back, the bullet passing through his abdomen and almost passed through his body, the bullet being visible from the front.

Fred Thomas, at the stables during the argument and fight, and Wesley Meade, son of the murder victim, rushed Meade to the Decorah hospital. Grattan and grandson drove to the office of Sheriff Mike C. Graf and gave themselves up and were held on a charge of attempted murder. Grattan had been released on $15,000 ball furnished by W. B. Ingvoldstad and G. E. Boland prior to Meade's death. Later Grattan was returned to jail as first degree murder is not bailable in such cases.

Hearing On Today

The preliminary hearing was held Saturday at 9 a. m. before Justice of the Peace H. F. Barthell. Both M. T. Grattan and grandson, Henry, face charges of murder in the first degree on information filed by Sheriff Mike C. Graf. The hearing was postponed until Wednesday (this) afternoon at 1:30 p. m. at the request of counsel for the accused. The Grattans were represented by Frank Sayre of Decorah and J. G. O'Brien of Waukon.

County Attorney E. P. Shea will represent the state.

The coroner's jury also has been selected and preliminary hearings held. The members of the jury, according to Coroner Orrie Iverson, are Henry Bidne, Albert Hammeraness and Clarence Christen. The inquest by the coroner's jury will be held this afternoon when the justice court hearing is completed.

Trial in October Likely

The trial of the Grattans probably will be in October if the grand jury returns the indictments which will be sought. The case will be considered by the grand jury at the term of court which will convene here October 2. Judge T. H. Goheen of Calmar is scheduled to preside at this term of court, which will be the first term of court he will have presided at in Decorah.

A great deal of interest in the probable trial has been expressed and indications are that there will be crowded courtrooms for the trial.

EYE-WITNESS STORY OF KILLING

Fred Thomas, a retired farmer who lives in West Decorah and who is a great lover of horses, was at the racehorse barns at the Winneshiek County Fair grounds and witnessed the entire affair leading up to the

Meade victim of bullet—The murder of my grandfather was reported to be the most controversial ever in county.

sons, Lester and John, of Minneapolis and Wesley of Decorah, survive. Mr. Meade was born in Randolph, N. Y. Two sisters, Miss Elizabeth Meade of Dunkirk, N. Y., and Mrs. Herbert Bill of Flushing, N. Y., also survive. Another son, Wesley, was associated with his father at the Graham-Blagsvedt stables here and was the driver in the races.

For more than 20 years Meade was an employe, principally as a teamster, for the City of Minneapolis. Later he had charge of the horses of the Northland Milk Co. in Minneapolis. Last April he joined his son, Wesley, here. Wesley had been in Decorah since last October.

After remaining at his father's bedside until his death at about 7 p. m. Friday, Wesley went to the home of his wife's parents, Mr. and Mrs. Albert Nelson, living near Ridgeway.

Funeral on Tuesday

The body was taken to Minneapolis in a funeral coach Saturday. Funeral services were to be held in Minneapolis Monday afternoon. Mr. Meade had been affiliated with St. Mark's Episcopal church. About an hour before his death, Rev. Allen O. Birchenough, rector of the Grace Episcopal church of Decorah, was called to the bedside of Mr. Meade.

Suffering intense pain from the bullet wound, which entered his back and passed virtually through his body, Meade was unable to talk much.

"The poor old man" was one expression which Rev. Birchenough was able to distinguish as he attempted to comfort Mr. Meade.

Praised as Horseman

Barney Graham and Ole Blagsvedt, who employed Meade as a trainer, praised highly his ability as a horseman. He had long experience as a horseman and was in charge of the Graham-Blagsvedt stables. He was given much praise for the victory of their horse, Martinique, Jr., that won the race at Dayton, O., in three straight heats July 4. The horse had been returned to Decorah and was being cared for by Meade, and his son, Wesley, 23 years old. Wesley has been a racehorse driver since he was 13. The father previously had driven. Martinique is being cared for now locally and Graham and Blagsvedt hope to enter him in races in Chicago in August.

ing, Guyon, in Virginia; Harry in New York, and Jenny, in Cincinnati. Mr. and Mrs. M. T. Grattan reared two of their grandchildren in Decorah.

May Preside

Judge Thomas H. Goheen of Calmar is scheduled to preside at the October term of court. If M. T. Grattan is held for trial it is probable that Judge Goheen will preside at the trial of the aged Civil War veteran. It will be the first term of court at which the new judge, elected last fall, will preside in his home county.

ings held...jury, according to Coroner Orrie Iverson, are Henry Bidne, Albert Hammersness and Clarence Chrisen. The inquest by the coroner's jury will be held this afternoon when the justice court hearing is completed.

Trial in October Likely

The trial of the Grattans probably will be in October if the grand jury returns the indictments which will be sought. The case will be considered by the grand jury at the term of court which will convene here October 2. Judge T. H. Goheen of Calmar is scheduled to preside at this term of court, which will be the first term of court he will have presided at in Decorah.

A great deal of interest in the probable trial has been expressed and indications are that there will be crowded courtrooms for the trial.

EYE-WITNESS STORY OF KILLING

Fred Thomas, a retired farmer who lives in West Decorah and who is a great lover of horses, was at the racehorse barns at the Winneshiek County Fair grounds and witnessed the entire affair leading up to the shooting of Claude Meade at about 11 A. M. last Friday. Mr. Thomas was there when the argument started and remained until after the shooting. It was Mr. Thomas and the son of the bullet victim, Wesley Meade, who carried Mr. Meade to the Thomas automobile and transported him to the hospital. Dr. Fritchen was called to care for the wounded man.

Argued About Horse Race

The following is Mr. Thomas' story about the affair as an eye witness:

"Grattan had a horse paper, with an article concerning who drove High Celia, a racehorse owned by Dan Alleman of Decorah, in a race in Indiana. Grattan insisted that Alleman had driven the horse and Meade declared that a Mr. Dagget had driven the horse. Grattan was using the horse magazine article to attempt to prove

his point and Meade said that he had witnessed the race and knew what he was talking about.

"The argument waxed fast and furious. Oaths were hurled at Grattan and both accused the other of being a liar. Grattan, angered, went to his home and his grandson, Henry Grattan, accompanied him back. Meade had ordered Grattan to leave the place.

"Grattan returned with Henry and wanted to have Henry beat Meade up. As I remember it, Henry Grattan started to attack Meade, who seized a pitchfork and attempted to strike Henry Grattan. Old Man Grattan was standing in back of Meade. He pulled a revolver from his pocket and fired twice, one shot going almost through Meade's body, entering at the back and coming out through the stomach, but not quite going clear through the body. The other shot went wild...

Eye-Witness story of killing.

Grand Jury; Bail Ruling Thursday

Preliminary Hearing Drags Out For 20 Days, Delayed By Veteran's Collapse

Twenty days after the killing of Claude Meade, 53 years old, Minneapolis, the preliminary hearing of Marvin T. Grattan, 85-year-old veteran of the Civil War drags on.

The hearing was postponed a week ago today until Monday following the dramatic collapse of Grattan following the powerful argument of County Attorney E. P. Shea asking for indictment on a charge of first degree murder and requesting that he be bound over to the grand jury.

Grattan Bound Over

A decision has been reached by Justice of the Peace H. F. Barthell to bind Grattan over to the Grand Jury, which convenes on October 2, when Judge T. H. Goheen will preside at his first term of court in Winneshiek County.

Justice of the Peace Barthell, however, has reserved until Thursday his ruling as to whether Grattan shall be admitted to bail. Arguments were completed Monday, O'Brian and O'Brien and Hart Brothers of Waukon and Frank Sayre of Decorah, the latter as chief counsel, representing the accused man.

Attorney J. A. Nelson of Decorah, a former county attorney, also has been retained as a lawyer to defend Grattan when the case comes before the district court.

Bail Question Undecided

Justice of the Peace Barthell summoned Drs. L. C. Kuhn, A. F. Barfoot and A. F. Fritchen to examine Grattan and report as to his physical condition. That Grattan was seriously ill at the time of his collapse last week is known, and he appears more feeble and crest-fallen than he did up to a week ago. It is reported that Dr. Kuhn considers Grattan a very sick man, that Dr. Fitchen reported his heart is now normal for a man of 85 and that Dr. Barfoot considered his condition not unusual for a man of his age.

Grattan's attorney pleaded that he be released on bail due to his physical condition and extremely advanced age. A motion, however, to have him returned to the Decorah hospital was denied and Grattan was sent back to a cell in the county jail.

The bail matter is the one question still remaining to be decided. Attorney Shea said that Iowa law forbids the release on bail of a person accused of murder where the proof of the crime is evident or the presumption great. County Attorney E. P. Shea contends Grattan should not be admitted to bail, as three eye witnesses testified as to the crime. Grattan did not take the stand.

Grand jury; bail.

Obituary of Claude Meade.

Claude Meade was 52 years, 4 months and 11 days of age, born in Randolph, New York, March 10, 1881. He was a son of George and Mabel Kingan Meade, the father being a native of Maine, and the mother of Galesburg, Ill.

Mr. and Mrs. Meade were married in Schenectady, New York, about 30 years ago, and shortly after their marriage established their home in Minneapolis where it has since been. The bereaved wife and two sons, Lester and John, reside in Minneapolis and one son Wesley in Decorah.

Wesley Meade came to Decorah last October, entering the employ of B. M. Graham and Ole Blagsvedt of this city, taking charge of and driving their race horses, Martinique Jr., Clover Blossom and Chestnut Frisco.

Wesley Meade is married to a Winneshiek county girl, daughter of Mr. and Mrs. Albert Nelson of Madison township. They met in Minneapolis and were married two years ago.

His father came to Decorah the first of last April to assist the son in the care of the horses. The latter had been caring for and driving race horses since he was 13 years old. The father was a well known race horse driver and trainer for the past 30 years or more. He was an expert in his work.

Messrs. Graham and Blagsvedt pay the Meades a very high tribute and state they were both good, industrious, sober, high class men interested in their work.

Rev. Birchenough of Grace Episcopal church visited Mr. Meade at the Decorah hospital.

The argument waxed hot and the elder Meade called Grattan a liar, it is reported. Meade ordered Grattan to leave the barn, which he did, starting for his home. He caught a ride with Robert Seegmiller, who had a horse and buggy and had driven to the grounds with his grandfather, John Seegmiller.

Grattan returned shortly afterward in a car with his grandson, Henry Grattan. When they arrived at the barn, they entered and walked up to the Meades, where they were working on a horse, Grattan remarking "Here is a man who can whip both of you Meades."

The elder Meade turned to Henry Grattan, told him to get out of the barn and stay out. Meade had a pitchfork in his hand and chased young Grattan out of the barn through an opening in the south door. When Meade reached the door he stopped and stuck his head out to see what had become of young Grattan.

The elder Grattan trailed Meade toward the door with an automatic pistol in his hand and when within about six feet of him fired twice. One shot missed, the second one entering Meade's back on the left side of his spinal column, traveling nearly through his body, the bullet stopping just under the skin to the right of the navel.

Meade turned to his son and said, "Wesley, he shot me," then walked to the north door of the barn, leaving the barn and walking to a little shack north of the new barn. Seeing no one in the shack he walked west toward the old barn and after traveling about 35 feet fell to the ground.

His son Wesley, Larry Keefe and Fred Thomas picked him up, placed him in the latter's car and rushed him to the hospital just across the street, west of the fair grounds. Dr. A. F. Fritchen and Dr. Stabo attended the wounded man, who was in great pain and suffering from shock. They gave him treatment to ease the pain, but decided his condition was too grave to stand an operation. He lingered on during the afternoon and early morning, passing away at 7:10.

After the shooting Grattan and his grandson got in their car and drove to the sheriff's office in the court house, arriving at eight

O'Boy and Constable Lange went to the Grattan residence on East Broadway, read the warrants to the Grattans, placed them under arrest and lodged them in jail at a quarter to nine Friday night. Deputy O'Boy told Grattan "It is too bad anything like this happened to a man of your age." He answered, "I am sorry the man died."

A coroner's jury composed of

Permit to Carry Concealed Firearm Had Expired

For a number of years, Mr. Grattan had had a permit to carry a firearm on his person. These permits are issued at the sheriff's office and are registered there. They are good for one year. Mr. Grattan's present permit was No. 44 and was issued March 1, 1932, therefore same had expired some months ago and there had been no request made to renew it. Had this request been made, Sheriff Graf states it would have been denied. There are 54 of these permits now in force, practically all of same for an entirely legitimate reason.

Ex-Sheriff Clarence Christen, former County Recorder Albert Hammersness and H. J. Bidne, retired hardware dealer, was empanelled by County Coroner Orrie Iverson to hold an inquest, which opened Saturday morning and was adjourned until Monday, when eleven witnesses were examined. The inquest was adjourned the second time until Wednesday so as to take the testimony of Wesley Meade, who took the remains of his father to Minneapolis on Saturday morning.

A post mortem was conducted Friday night by Drs. A. F. Fritchen and J. D. Hexom. The doctors found the bullet had punctured the left mesentery and cut a groove in the left kidney.

A preliminary information was filed by the county attorney charging the Grattans with murder. They were taken before Justice Barthell for a preliminary hearing Saturday morning which

(Continued on Page 6.)

Left, obituary of Claude Meade.

My Civil Air Patrol (CAP) stripes and service ribbon—55 years later.

My dog tags—50 years later.

Meeting in Tijuana with G.I.'s at famous Long Bar.

Meade Promoted
In S. Vietnam

DA NANG, VIETNAM (FHT NC) June 2—Marine Corporal Jon M. Meade, son of Mr. and Mrs. John F. Meade of 521 12th Ave. N.W., New Brighton, Minn., was promoted to his present rank while serving as a member of the Ninth Engineer Battalion, First Marine Division based near Da Nang, Vietnam.

His promotion was based on time in service and rank, military appearance, and his knowledge of selected military subjects.

His battalion supports the division through road and building construction, and the laying of land mines. Engineers are also trained in the use of explosives and demolitions.

Field promotions were very common.

My Geneva Conventions I.D. Card (in event of capture—POW).

461

MARINES COMPLETE TRAINING COURSE — Marines from the Marine Barracks, NAS Lemoore, recently completed a Marine Corps Institute Course entitled "Operations Against Guerrilla Units." The course, which began in early July and ended late last month, was taught by SSGT R. G. Anderson, Guard Chief of the Marine Barracks. It was part of the overall Annual Training Requirements necessary for completion by Marines annually. Topics covered in this refresher course included: History and Evolution of Guerrilla Units, Counter-guerrilla Operations, Immediate Action Drills and Ambushes, Attacking Guerrilla Camps, Clearing Villages and Elimination of Guerrilla Forces, Security and Population Control and recent changes in Tactics and Techniques. Ninety percent of the men enrolled successfully completed the course. They are: SSGT Anderson and (from L to R) CPL E. A. Strawhacker, SGT J. A. Black Jr., PFC D. W. Copenbarger, CPL R. D. Gilbertson, CPL J. R. L. Lucero, LCPL D. C. Mager, CPL D. D. Martinez, CPL J. M. Meade and CPL G. M. Peacock. (Back row L to R) LCPL J. Williams, LCPL D. C. Wilson, SGT C. L. Sullivan, CPL J. P. Cooley, SGT J. J. Gonzalez, SGT L. Turner, LCPL L. A. Dinew and CPL R. Boyce. Nine Marines who passed the course but who were not present for the photo are: CPL S. J. Zanolini, CPL D. Spence, LCPL D. B. Jolley, CPL F. A. Lopez, CPL D. R. Phenneger, LCPL J. Capps Jr., LCPL J. G. Castillo, CPL G. S. Thacker II and CPL C. F. Price. CPL Strawhacker was the leading student in the course with his final exam grade being 100%.

MCI training course, "Operations Against Guerrilla Units." I am second from right in front.

BksBul 1510
26 Aug 1968

TRAINING SCHEDULE 2 SEPT-13 SEPT 1968

DAY/DATE SECTION	HOURS FROM/TO	SUBJECT	LOCATION	INSTRUCTOR	REFERENCE	UNIFORM EQUIPMENT
MON&WED 26&4 SEP STBD & PORT	0845-0945	PHYSICAL TRAINING	AS REQ	TRNG NCO	MCO 6100.3E	U,W/O SHIRT
TUES & THURS 3&5 SEP PORT & STBD	0800-0845	PHYSICAL TRAINING	AS REQ	TRNG NCO	MCO 6100.3E	U,W/O SHIRT
	0905-0930	COD	PL	TRNG NCO	LPM	U,M1
	0935-1155	MCI GROUP STUDY (FINAL)	CR	SSGT ANDERSON	MCI 03.24	U
	1300-1350	INTERIOR GUARD	AS REQ	SGT SCARPINATO	LPM	U
	1400-1425	CO's TIME	BksCubes	C.O.		WINTER SERVIC
	1450-1530	UNIFORM INSPECTION	BksCubes	C.O.		
FRIDAY 6 SEP	0845-0945	STBD-PHYSICAL TRAINING	AS REQ	TRNG NCO	MCO 6100.3E	U,W/O SHIRT
	1300-1400	PORT-PHYSICAL TRAINING	TRNG TK	TRNG NCO	-do-	PT GEAR
MON&WED 9 & 11 SEP PORT & STBD	0845-0945	PHYSICAL TRAINING	AS REQ	TRNG NCO	MCO 6100.3E	U,w/o SHIRT
TUES&THURS 10 & 12 SEP STBD & PORT	0800-0845	PHYSICAL TRAINING	AS REQ	TRNG NCO	MCO 6100.3E	U,W/O SHIRT
	0905-0930	COD	P.L.	TRNG NCO →*REHEARSED* LPM		U,M1
	0935-1000	HAND TO HAND COMBAT	S.Bks	CPL. MEADE *(ON USEP)*	NAVMC 1146	U
	1005-1055	BAYONET FIGHTING	S.Bks	CPL. PEACOCK	FM 1-1	PUGIL STICKS
	1105-1150	M-60 MACHINE GUN	S.Bks	CPL FORE	G3 Chap 36	U
	1300-1350	MCI GROUP STUDY	CR	1/LT GRAVES	MCI 03.17	U
	1400-1415	VN.-AMBUSHES&PATROL	CR	SGT CARTER	AS REQ	
	1420-1435	VN.-MINES &B-TRAPS	CR	SGT CARTER	TC 5-31,Ch 1	U
	1440-1455	VN.-CIVIC ACTION	CR	SGT CARTER	AS REQ	
	1500-1530	HIST.&TRAD.ofMC	CR	CAPT DIEDRICH	AS REQ	U
FRIDAY 13 SEP	0845-0945	PORT- PHYSICAL TRAINING	AS REQ	TRNG NCO	MCO 6100.3E	U,W/O SHIRT
	1300-1450	STBD- PHYSICAL TRAINING	AS REQ	TRNG NCO	MCO 6100.3E	U,w/o SHIRT

Training schedule for my hand-to-hand combat at Marine Barracks.

ORIGINAL ORDERS

TRANSPORTATION ENDORSEMENT
(2ND NOTT 1/66 (9-66)

E. z 8Nov67

FROM Passenger Trans Officer, Marine Barracks,
Treasure Island, San Francisco California

TO (NAME-LAST, FIRST, INITIAL) NEADE, JON M.

SERVICE NO.

NAME CPL

DESTINATION Minneapolis, Minn.

I CERTIFY THAT THE FOLLOWING TRANSPORTATION HAS BEEN FURNISHED THIS DATE:

TR #PO,483,458 Drawn on Western Airlines for one mixed class air fare from San Francisco,Calif to
Minneapolis, Minn. and return to Fresno, Calif. VIA: WA-Y-SFO-MSB;WA-Y-MSP-LAX;
UA-T-LAX-FAT COST: $196.85

DECEASED   Transportation for deceased covered under government bill of lading

MILITARY ESCORT FOR THE REMAINS OF LCPL DANA A. PITTS,   USMC

SCHEDULE

DEPART				ARRIVE		
PLACE	TIME	DATE	VIA	PLACE	TIME	DATE
San Francisco, Calif.	1800	8Nov67	WA 528	Minneapolis, Minn.	2304	8Nov67
RETURN RESERVATIONS MUST BE MADE BY TRAVELER						

Upon completion of travel, report to the Passenger Transportation Officer at destination all unused tickets, transportation requests, meal tickets, and change of service of a lesser value than authorized by the tickets. If your basic orders direct the use of Government Air, where available, endorsement(s) must be obtained at your TAD Stations as to the availability of Government Air.

NAME A. E. MOORE JR., SSGT, USMC

SIGNATURE (BY DIRECTION)

TA FOR F. A. ANDERSON, CWO, USMC
Passenger Transportation Officer

Original orders for the military escort of L/Cpl. Dana A. Pitts.

O. E. Larson Mortuary

ESTABLISHED 1896

2301 Central Avenue N. E.

Telephone: ST. 9-3571
Area Code 612

Minneapolis, Minnesota, 55418

November 9, 1967

TO whom it may concern:

    We, O. E. LARSON MORTUARY, 2301 Central Avenue,
N.E., Minneapolis, Minnesota 55418 received the remains
of LCPL. Dana A. Pitts, USMC.

Wayne Bateman
O.E. LARSON MORTUARY

Jon M. Meade
Escort of remains

Mortuary letter: Receipt of L/Cpl. Dana A. Pitts remains.

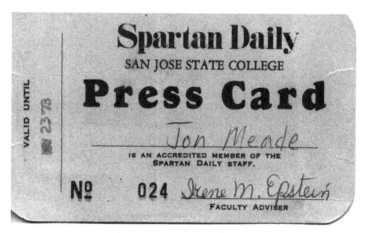

My college newspaper press card.

HERB CAEN

It Takes All Kinds

DO YOU SOMETIMES get the feeling that Arthur Hoppe and his fellow satirists, Art Buchwald and Russell Baker, are writing the news? I had that distinct impression earlier this week upon reading two wire service squibs from Washington, one upon the other . . . First this: "Julie Nixon Eisenhower will be the main speaker at the June 14 graduation ceremonies of the American School of the Deaf in Washington" . . . Then this: "An 'Insect Zoo' scheduled to open June 1 at the Smithsonian Institution has been postponed because, officials said, recent heavy rains have caused a shortage of bugs in the Washington area" . . . The world is going mad.

★ ★ ★

READING THE papers for fun & items: "First Woman ROTC Graduate Feels No Different From Male Cadets," reads the San Jose State Spartan headline over a piece by Jon Meade, apparently an investigative reporter who digs deep . . . Page one headline in the P'Alto Times Monday: "Stanford Researcher Finds Differences In Men and Women" (well, Meade?) . . . Sanford Feinglass found this in the N.Y. Daily News: "The Veterans Administration has no power to round up frug-addicted victims and force them to submit to treatment" (invite 'em to the Waltz Ball), whereas Paolo's restaurant in San Jose announced a cut in prices via an ad in the San Jose Merc that reads "We are in our own way trying to set a precedent that might bring a little relief to the barassed dining public" . . . If that's not a typo it's one of the great coinages.

★ ★ ★

JOHN MAYBURY, rooting around in the '59 edition of the International Celebrity Register, by Cleveland Amory and Earl Blackwell, discovers "Richard Nixon. Political enigma, press agent's dream, misunderstood patriot, boy gladiator. 'I wanted to be a sportswriter. I found out I could become Vice President faster than I could become a newspaperman'" . . . So THAT'S why he stopped hanging around the Press Club.

Making Herb Caen's famous column in the San Francisco Chronicle was a privilege.

First woman AFROTC graduate feels no different from male cadets

By JON MEADE

In 1971, San Jose State University's Air Force ROTC program accepted Joan Kerst, a 20-year-old senior in criminal justice, as its first woman cadet.

Miss Kerst, a cadet Lt. Colonel, will be standing in the ranks of 28 men as the first woman to graduate and be commissioned from SJSU's AFROTC Department.

Being the first woman to be commissioned does not make Miss Kerst feel uneasy or even different. She just likes to be thought of as another cadet. "More often than not I feel that I'm just graduating," said Miss Kerst, "not that I'm the first female graduating."

Miss Kerst, who was born in Pennsylvania and migrated to California with her parents in 1958, graduated from Saratoga High School one year ahead of her class in 1967.

She then went on to SJSU to pursue her interest in law. She first thought about joining ROTC while she was a junior.

"I felt very proud of the guys in the campus ROTC program," she stated. "It made me feel a responsibility to my country. I guess it's just like something that grows, like loving your family. I wanted to do my part."

Miss Kerst didn't actually think about herself joining the ROTC until she saw an ad in the Spartan Daily.

"I saw an announcement in the school paper which read: The ROTC will be testing for cadets. Women can apply," she said.

"I was really shocked," she admitted. "I didn't think women could apply."

Miss Kerst, who has three sisters that have mixed feelings about her decision to join the service, believed joining the ROTC was a way in which she could show she cared.

"Often times a person can support something with words," she said, "but it means more to support with actions."

Miss Kerst, who believes more in the defense of her country than the defense of womens lib, says women have the same advantages as men in the ROTC and military. That's why she joined.

"We have most of the advantages men have," said the sandy haired blonde, "including education and franchise, so we should share the responsibility of serving."

Admitting that many people have preconceived ideas about why girls join the military, Miss Kerst said "The idea that all girls join because they are lonely and want to find a man is absurd . . . I'm not."

Filling her leisure time, which is hard as she is working on her masters, Miss Kerst finds chess, ballet, art, reading, cooking and skiing her most enjoyable and relaxing pleasures.

Although Miss Kerst has held the position of inspector general while a cadet, she believes the leaders of the country and home should be men.

"I really feel if a woman is qualified she'll be treated equal, maybe better than male counterparts," she said.

"If women were equal to men in all respects I would prefer the men to be the leaders and have the final word.

"I think it's wrong for a woman to go through life with a chip on her shoulder, complaining about injustices and how they have been mistreated."

Miss Kerst, an honor student who said she didn't know a lieutenant from a sergeant before she joined the ROTC, published a cadet handbook that answered "everything the cadet did not know and was afraid to ask."

She has also been president of Alpha Phi Sigma (honor society) and of the Student Affairs Committee of the School of Applied Arts and Sciences.

Miss Kerst's dedication in her job as cadet inspector general is best reflected by the time she invited some long haired cadets into the orderly room for a hair trimming session.

Lt. Col. Albert Tarvin, AFROTC commander, said her position in the corps was a very demanding one, even for the strongest of men.

"Joan has been tremendously active in her two years of AFROTC," the colonel said. "She will definitely be designated as a distinguished military graduate from SJSU.

"She is also a hard worker who tends to be a perfectionist. Joan is very patriotic, idealistic and determined."

Dave Huckaday, another cadet who will be commissioned along with Miss Kerst in June, said, "She's very energetic and competitive. She is also a stickler for detail, very able to get jobs done."

Looking forward to a law degree sometime in the future, Miss Kerst most people don't understand appreciate the military and R enough.

She said cadets who are missioned as officers face far responsibility than the average co graduate.

Cadet Lt. Col. Joan Kerst

This is the article which drew attention to Herb Caen's famous column.

Jon Meade

Ali shuns fight talk

By JON MEADE
Sports Writer

Muhammad Ali, AKA Cassius Clay, former Heavyweight Boxing Champion of the World, spoke last Friday, May 21, before a sun-drenched crowd of approximately 3,000 at Stanford's Frost Amphitheater.

Ali's "main" topic was "The Intoxication of Life," but before his presentation he enlightened the crowd with his philosophies on today's black man and his plight with the "whitie" world around him.

"'Right on brother,' don't

mean a damn thing 'less you know who you're real leader is. The Honorable Elija Muhammed is the black man's real leader. Elija Muhammed is 'the man' not all the dead black leaders like Malcolm X or Martin Luther King. That's the trouble with most black brothers and sisters today — they follow DEAD people."

Ali, who looked a bit on the tired side, went on to condemn many blacks for what he called "cheapening their women." He shouted, "stop prostituting your women, stop lovin' white gals and start respectin' your own sisters; stop smokin' and carrin' on with dope and things; take pride with yourself or you'll wind up like lots of them winos and junkies on the streets!"

With that finished, Ali said, "now for my speech," the crowd roared with laughter and gave the ex-champ a standing ovation.

Most of the questions asked were the usual, even the one of yours truly, "Is the Chamberlain fight on or off?" Ali smiled for a minute and said, "don't really know, all I know is TIMBER."

It wasn't easy getting Ali to answer my question, but I finally got my answer—"TIMBER!"

468

April 5, 1973, Page 3

Vet conference endorses amnesty

'Viet vets poorly treated'

By JON MEADE

The Vietnam veteran truly faces tremendous problems. He is inadequately treated and receives almost no attention, charged Sen. Alan Cranston, D-Calif.

Speaking to a group of over 50 veteran affairs representatives, including San Jose State University's Tom Alvarado, Sen. Cranston, an extremely tall, slim and confident legislator, made the above statement at the Northern California Veterans Conference recently in San Francisco.

The conference, which was attended by campus representatives as far south as Fresno and as far north as Shasta, met to discuss veteran affairs with Sen. Cranston and other related officials, including San Francisco Director of the Veteran Administration, E.J. Mullins.

Sen. Cranston, a WW II veteran and long time supporter of VA affairs, talked at length about what he called "vets missing in America."

The senator said the grassroots level of vets, on the college campuses are the only avenues of approach through which the various problems can be handled.

"That's what the campus veteran offices are all about," declared Cranston. "They help the veteran and help open doors to better understanding between the VA, administration, and veterans."

One of the issues decided at the conference was that of an amnesty and our office. It's merely an experiment in teamwork."

Another issue voted on was the amnesty situation, an issue a few notches cooler and POWs and most prison.

Alvarado, who is also president of the California Veterans Association, said the entire group, with exception of a few, voted in favor of not prosecuting amnesty violators.

"Several things should be pointed out however," said Alvarado. "If men are not to be prosecuted for amnesty, they should not be prosecuted for bad conduct, drug use, alcoholism and other related problems that cause the issue of bad conduct discharges.

"It's not fair," Alvarado charged. "A guy does not deserve a bad conduct discharge for something that service or war induced him to do.

A veteran who did not serve does not deserve such funk, regardless of what has done, does not deserve anything. It is true, but what the vet deserves is help and quick

In response to the discharge issue Cranston related to the drug treatment bill he helped introduce.

The senator said many drug addicts who had previous habits of $5 or $10 in Vietnam come back to the states and face $125 to $175 a day.

"The vet turns to crime and vice to support his habit," related Cranston with comes of remorse in his manner.

The was given less than an honorable discharge the vet gets no help. The new drug treatment bill will change that in the light of the circumstances and help the vet solve his drug problem and do something with his life.

Sen. Cranston, who admittedly was on a personal crusade "not finding an end," said he plans to follow up on how the Administration and Congress handles VA affairs.

"Beside the Nixon Administration cutting disabled veterans benefits by 50 per cent," claimed Cranston, "they have also failed to follow up on the recent vets employment bill.

The Administration has failed to hire any veteran employment advisers. They have not attempted to enact their promises," he asserted.

Lou Encinger, SJSU graduate veteran advisor, who also attended the conference, told Cranston he thought vets met such difficulty when trying to get their problems solved by the VA.

"Let's face it," Encinger said, "the VA is just not fulfilling its dedicated people in the VA, there are also those who just pick up their pay check," answered Cranston.

Encinger, who later said Cranston impressed the hell out of me, also asked the senator why there are so many WW II VA employees and so few Vietnam employees.

"After all," Encinger said, "What the vet needs today is someone who can relate to him. In other words a Vietnam VA advisor, counselor, or whatever."

Cranston replied, he recognized the problem and understood the complications. He said ever since he occupied his senate seat he has tried to resolve that very situation, but to no avail.

Cranston has been a senator for one term now and plans to campaign for another when election time rolls around in a couple of years.

It will be interesting to see how many veterans will unite together to support the man who has given so much of his time and effort to support them.

I was proud to be the sole reporter covering the Veteran's beat.

April 27, 1973, Page 3

Commissioned from AFROTC ranks

First Black cadet to graduate

By JON MEADE

When June rolls around at SJSU's AFROTC program as a Air Force ROTC will have its first Black cadet standing in ranks waiting to graduate and be commissioned as a second lieutenant.

Cadet Williams, who was selected as cadet commander for the present semester, has always professed a love for flying and airplanes.

"When I was a young kid," said Williams, "I used to wait at the planetarium off and land for hours. I just dug airports."

Enjoying his hobby of plane watching was convenient for him as he lived next to Brooks Field in Oakland. Williams attended and graduated from Skyline High School.

So intense was his love for flying that he took lessons while in high school. He earned his private pilots license one day before he graduated.

Recently married, Williams financed his own lessons by working as a store clerk. His parents also pitched in but and helped.

Although Williams thought about being a policeman or fireman when he was in his formative years, he eventually took his parents' advice "to get an education and go to college."

After looking into several college aeronautics programs, Williams finally decided upon SJSU, "the only solid aeronautics program in the area," according to Williams. He ended up, however, changing his mind slightly about his future plans.

"When I got to State," admitted Williams, a member and past president of Alpha Phi Alpha, "I realized it was

sophomore, La Forrest Williams, 21, has worked hard and looked forward to the time when he will have the shiny bars secured on his shoulders.

Ever since he enrolled in too expensive to train as a private pilot, so I joined the AFROTC program."

Williams, the third eldest of five children, believes the Black person has come a long way in his quest for equality, but has further to go.

"It seemed to be hard for Blacks to qualify as officers years ago because of the Air Force Officers Test," related Williams.

"The test was culturally biased. Or Blacks supposedly couldn't take the attitude and so on. Things have changed though. I personally have not encountered any form of prejudice to my knowledge since my days as a cadet began.

"Today," Williams said positively, "the military has changed. It's more open-minded.

"Matter of fact, right now is the prime time for Black people to take advantage of a military career or any career.

"I'm not pushing anything onto any brother," he said. "I say let them do their own thing, that's what it's all about."

Williams, whose second love is jogging, with young people also enjoys horseback riding and movies.

Williams, who says he didn't feel out of place one bit as SJSU's first Black AFROTC cadet, given much credit to the

Communities Education opportunity program, for the betterment of education for Blacks and other ethnic groups.

"I think the EOP has done a fantastic job," said Williams, "in giving minorities the chance for improvement and education. We're graduating from colleges all over."

Lt. Col. Albert Tarvin, AFROTC commander and professor of aerospace studies, had high praise for Williams and thinks he has a bright future in store for him.

Johnson, who said he would like to be accepted as an officer and not "a Black officer," summed up cadet Williams' time here at SJSU. "I would like to believe that cadet Williams has been accepted not because he is a Black cadet but because he is a cadet."

Cadet Commander, La Forrest Williams

My Veteran beat was a trail blazer in many crucial areas.

ROTC commanding officer

Dedicated serviceman not a 'Patton'

By ION MEADE

Whenever a person meets a career military man, it is sometimes difficult to see past the uniform. Everything is so straight, neat and spit polished.

Col. Glenn A. Davis, San Jose State University's seventh Army ROTC commanding officer and professor of military science, is no exception. His military bearing is quite evident.

Col. Davis looks, acts, and carries himself like a strict, professional military man. His tall, erect statue-like posture radiates confidence and pride. His voice crackles with confidence and his face, with its stiff upper lip and strong, slightly jutted jaw reflects persistence and prevalence. Some liberals may label him as the "typical Patton type," but he's not. Not entirely, that is.

Col. Davis, 52, is a dedicated career serviceman, 30 years worth. He is also a dedicated husband and father of eight children.

He is a lover of classical music, chess, bridge and literature, "fiction and non-fiction dealing with the near-

design in 1953, has a heavy load of "cabbage, as military talk goes, on his chest.

His awards include: Legion of Merit (two oak leaf clusters), Bronze Star Medal, Army Commendation Medal (two OLC), Air Medal, Purple Heart, and the Vietnamese Armed Forces Honor Medal.

Bwsides his numerous military education courses, Col. Davis has a M.S. degree in civil engineering from Texas A&M University (1956).

SJSU's Army ROTC program is the first such duty for Col. Davis. He has definite thoughts regarding his new ROTC post.

"Two of my sons recently completed Army ROTC at Texas A&M," the colonel said with a proud grin. "Another son, who is a sophomore at the University of Virginia, is now applying for the two-year ROTC program.

"This personal experience makes it easier for me to relate to the cadets here at SJSU. And, I believe the 'relating' is mutual."

'Open Door' policy for cadets

Col. Davis, who has an "open door" policy for cadets, was viewed by Maj.

month or $1,000 per year. Students are classified as not signing the contract and are not subject to six-weeks summer camp and pay allowances."

ROTC cadets attend regularly scheduled classes in military science. The cadet goes on to more intensive military and leadership training such as rifle teams, drill teams and other related

Col. Glenn Davis

academic degree. The program builds qualities that are an important part of leadership that contributes to success in any kind of career."

Col. Davis pointed out a definite relationship between success and an ROTC education.

"An analysis made in the late 1960's indicated that from the relatively small number of college graduates who receive an ROTC education (approximately 4 per cent, 14 per cent congress members, and 22 per cent key business and industrial executives earning between $100,000 and $300,000 per year."

A resident of Sunnyvale with his wife and two youngest children. Col. Davis sees little effect on students concerning the hair and uniform issue.

"Students who are enrolled in ROTC courses for academic credit only are not required to wear the uniform, and are thusly not affected. Cadets on the other hand, take pride in the uniform and wear it to classes.

Hair is no problem

ended and the all-volunteer Army is around the corner, the decision to participate in ROTC is entirely a voluntary one."

Col. Davis, who taught first-year college math at the College of Columbus in 1959, looks forward to spending the rest of his military days as PMS at SJSU.

"I plan to remain in my current position until retirement, subject to concurrence of the Army and university."

Until then, Col. "the old man" Davis, will have his door open...and a stiff upper lip.

The colonel was very appreciative of the coverage they got.

Thursday, March 15, 1973

Spartan Da

Serving California State University at San Jose Since 193

Didn't want post

Alvarado heads Cal Vet

By JON MEADE

Tom Alvarado, San Jose State University's director of veterans affairs, returned from a state-wide veterans symposium in southern California last Monday with more than an empty pen and notes...he returned as the new president of California Veterans Affairs.

The symposium, held at the University of California at Los Angeles, voted Alvarado president after considerable discussion concerning what part of the state would be the "vocal point," and delegation of authority for veterans affairs.

"To tell you the truth," Alvarado admitted, "Things were getting out of hand, everyone was arguing and nothing was really being accomplished."

"I simply got sick of it and told and group that we all came here to get organized, learn proper veteran procedures, not argue and fight over such petty issues as who's going to do this and who's going to get that."

Although Alvarado claimed to be seeking no presidential or authoritative post, the other veteran's affairs directors apparently had different ideas as they cast their votes and Alvarado emerged president.

"I really didn't want such a position," Alvarado said. "I merely spoke up and gave my opinion and the next thing I know, I'm the Man."

The highlight of the symposium, according to the SJSU VA director and CVA president, was the introduction of a drug treatment bill, as introduced by Senator Alan Cranston, D-Calif.

Although the bill, which is for all veterans, regardless of type of discharge, must be passed by Congress Sen. Cranston, one of the speakers at the symposium and long time mediator of VA affairs, voiced his support of the measure with strong convictions.

Cranston talked about various GI-related bills that have been passed and others that were introduced,

particularly the drug treatment bill.

Cranston emphasized the failure of the Nixon Administration, Alvarado stated, "to fulfill the growing needs of the veteran."

Cranston also made it clear that the administration's new budget that cut into the veterans' program was unfair, particularly in the case of disabled vets.

Alvarado said Cranston referred to neglected veterans as, "Vets Missing in America."

Regarding the drug treatment bill more specifically, Alvarado declared it was an issue which should have been handled long ago.

"Previously, only honorably discharged veterans were treated for drug problems. With this new bill, it will allow all veterans, even if they were dishonorably discharged, to have treatment."

Alvarado pointed to a recent Newsweek article, "The Vets: Heroes as Orphans," when relating some of the discussions that took place at the symposium.

This top headline Vets story made my day.

Page 6, May 15, 1973

AFROTC commander leaves SJSU, changes places with Alabama Colonel

By JON MEADE

A rather unique event involving military marted chairs will be place at the end of this semester as San Jose State University's Air Force ROTC Department.

Lt. Col. Albert L. Tarvin, professor of aerospace studies and SJSU AFROTC commander, will be leaving his post June 7 to assume a new duty assignment at the Air War College in Alabama.

Tarvin's replacement

Tarvin's replacement, Col. Mark D. Gale, will be leaving his present assignment at Alabama's War College in late August to assume his new post and chair at SJSU's AFROTC commander.

Col. Tarvin, 44, who is often referred to in military largon as a "messenger," has explained that when you look far away through the ranks to officer, enlisted in the Air Force in 1948 after graduating from high school in Georgia.

In a period of six years, Col. Tarvin made the rank of Master Sergeant. Shortly after he went to Officers Candidate School where he was commissioned a Second Lieutenant, graduating as a distinguished candidate.

Col. Tarvin attended the universities of Maryland, Hawaii and Utah State to attain his B.S. in business and social studies in 1965.

In 1966 Tarvin went to Germany

as part of a University of Southern California program. He left there with his Masters in education in 1968.

During his stay in Germany Tarvin was promoted to the rank of Major. His achievement was classified as a "below-the-primary-zone promotion" or promotion sooner than the average.

Col. Tarvin, a communications-electronics officer and father of four, has seen duty in Canada, Japan, England, Germany an Turkey, as well as cities throughout the United States prior to his ROTC-teaching assignment at SJSU in 1970.

The 25-year, soft spoken veteran, who was also promoted "below-the-zone" as Lieutenant Colonel recently, believes the so-called "service-brat" (child whose father is in the military) benefits from such a life of world-wide travel when growing up.

"I don't think travel hinders the child's development," said the colonel.

"If anything, travel broadens a youngsters development. It gives the kids' real life adventures first hand rather than just reading about them."

Although not a flying officer, Col. Tarvin's most vivid memory concerned flying in Turkey where he was supervisor for the installation of Air Force satellite communications systems.

"While waiting to take off in a C-

119 cargo plane, one of the propellers spun off and dug its edge into the side of the plane, causing alot of fright but no injuries."

Residing with his wife, Quimby, and four children in San Jose, Col. Tarvin looks at his time at SJSU as a position "totally different than any regular job in the Air Force but very rewarding. To be able to work so closely with the real leaders in education such asPro. Brandel, Dean R.J. Moore and numerous others," said Tarvin, "has been a real education in itself.

"Regardless of the fact that they hold high degrees they are real people, people who care."

Tarvin admitted the fury of Vietnam controversy and demonstrations on campus will remain uppermost in his mind, especially over particular incident.

One incident he remembers

"A group of students were running through the halls (MacQuarrie Hall Building) yelling, ripping off papers and causing total disruption," recalled Tarvin.

"One lad, about 6'2" was about to mash in one of the glass cases when Dean Moore stopped him with mere general persuasion, right in the midst of all the action.

"It took a hell of a lot of courage," admitted Tarvin. "Dean Moore is not a big man, in terms of size, but he handled the situation with a lot of cool."

Tarvin, who says he doesn't believe in violence and admits there is always potential unrest when the United States carries out foreign policy, said the only thing the '70 and '71 riots caused was bad records and jail terms for its participants.

"Just look at those students arrested during that time," recalled Tarvin. "Most of them are still hunting for jobs. They just hurt themselves with various personal consequences. It's too bad."

Tarvin was selected by an Air Force board in Washington to attend the War College, believes the ROTC program offers many personal rewards to the student.

"The program teaches the cadets responsibility, integrity and a sense of personal and patriotic pride," said Tarvin.

Cadets get better grades

"For the record," AFROTC cadets have better GPA's than the average student and are better socially developed and determined as to what they want out of life," Tarvin summed up the AFROTC program by saying, "If they fall on their ass here it's better than doing it while flying a million-dollar airplane."

SJSU and Col. Tarvin's AFROTC program has doubled in the last several years while the national ROTC level has declined. The program now boasts it ranks number one across

the nation in enrollment and commissioning of officers.

Lt. Col. Billy J. Winfield

Between the time of Tarvin's departure in June and Col. Gale's arrival in August, however, Lt. Col. Billy J. Wingfield, AFROTC instructor, will occupy the chair that Col. Tarvin has occupied the past three years.

The military musical chairs in the SJSU AFROTC Department will become stalemate once again when the new commander takes the east of Lt. Col. Albert Tarvin.

Lt. Col. Albert L. Tarvin

I managed to constantly keep the ROTC on campus in the news.

473

The National Family Gazette was suppose to eventually compete with the Enquirer
—only non-scandalous.

NATIONAL FAMILY GAZETTE

The World's Fastest Growing Church is "The Church of Jesus Christ of the Latter — Day Saints"

"You no speaka English?"

No problem.

The Visitors Center of the L.D.S., 10777 Santa Monica Boulevard, Los Angeles, is open daily from 9 a.m. til' 10 p.m., except Christmas. They have 21 translations of "The Book of Mormon" available and in print. Translations include Africans, Chinese, Danish, Dutch, English, French, Finnish, German, Indonesian, Italian, Japanese, Korean, Norwegian, Portuguese, Rarotonga, Samoan, Spanish, Swedish, Tahitian, Tonganese and Thailand.

(If you are not in Los Angeles just write Department NFG, 50 East North Temple St., Salt Lake City, Utah, 84150, in your native language.)

"Why should you read this book?"

No problem.

Jews read the Old Testament of the Bible; Christians read the Old Testament and the New Testament of the Bible; and Mormons read the Old Testament, the New Testament *plus* The Book of Mormon.

In contrast the Mormon Church is embracing a dramatically increased membership.

Leaders of other church denominations are carefully studying the missionary work success of the Mormons. Because along with members who have been born under the covenant of the church many high-income persons have sought out and aligned with the Church of Jesus Christ of Latter-Day Saints.

Next April the church will celebrate their 150th anniversary. Yet their laid-back style makes them subject to many misbeliefs.

One myth is that the church doesn't accept Blacks or Jews. Wrong.

Some highly educated and financially successful Blacks and Jews are joining their brethren in the Mormons.

Another myth is that the intensely family-oriented Mormons won't accept the unmarried. Wrong.

Among the Stake divisions is included a Singles Ward.

Still a third myth persists that the Mormons won't extend themselves past the American Indian industries.

barred from the eternal kingdom. This offers much solace to bereaved families.

The Mormons believe that God and Jesus are alive; therefore they don't have crucifixes, religious symbolism etc. And since they understand that God is alive, so does he have living prophets. Religions sometimes face stultification in theorizing that religion is ancient history. The Mormons offer an alternative choice with living prophets who receive new revelations to cope with a challenging world. They ask, "If God so loved the world . . . would he abandon us now?"

Mormons place much emphasis upon communal self-reliance and the work ethic. Thus the church becomes an extended family and each member rallies to the aid of each other and all Mormons are expected to be honest, diligent, cheerful employees.

Small wonder that industrialists such as Howard Hughes have beefed up their corporate staffs with Mormons.

Wrong.

I went to a Mormon square dance and they were all alert, in

mons. Also Hughes once told this writer that he admired their loyalty in upholding the secrecy of their temple rites.

Church tours never include Mormon temples. Mormons worship in their churches but even newcomers to the faith spend a year of probation after their baptism by total immersion before they can enter the Mormon Temples for such holy ordinances as the solemn assembly, marriage for eternity and baptism of the dead.

Recently another attraction of the Mormon Church surfaced when the movie "Roots" became a hit. The Mormon's revere and practice the study of genealogy and are rumored to have the most voluminous family-tree archives in the world secreted in their mountain vaults.

All Mormons are expected to maintain one-year's food supply for their families inside of their homes. Scientists opine that even an atomic searing of the earth would cool off in such a time frame.

And the silliest of all myths is that since th Mormons don't drink.

HOT POTATO
by Jon Meade

Rank	Denomination	Members	Number of Churches
1)	Roman Catholic	49,325,752	18,572
2)	Southern Baptist	13,083,199	32,255
3)	United Methodist	9,785,534	38,744
4)	American Lutheran	4,160,955	4,832
5)	Church of Jesus Christ of Latter Day Saints	4,060,462	6,917
8)	Church of Christ	3,760,849	21,378
7)	Eastern Orthodox	3,654,761	1,275
8)	Episcopalian	3,070,349	7,494
9)	United Presbyterian	2,569,437	8,656
10)	Assemblies of God, Pentecostal	1,302,318	9,208

Christian membership figures above are carefully compiled. Below estimates of Jewish Congregations is made from a more casual approach:

Union of American Hebrew Congregations (Reformed)	1,100,000	720
Union of Orthodox Jewish Congregations of America	250,000	500
United Synagogue of America, (Conservative)	225,000 (families)	830

And there are 38,000 pairs of elders of the Church teamed around the globe to explain this doctrine through six home lessons.

"How does one qualify?"

No problem.

Just plan to adhere to the Mormons' Code of Health, abstaining from alcohol, tobacco, drugs, coffee and tea. Then you must tithe.

"Tithe?" "What is tithing?"

No problem.

Just contribute 10% of your gross income.

Despite these stringent requirements, The Mormons, as the public popularity refers to the members of The Church of Jesus Christ of Latter-Day Saints, this group enjoys the fastest growth enrollment of all churches in the World.

Despite the population explosion, some denominations are beset with diminishing membership rolls.

The Los Angeles Second Branch is Korean Speaking and both the Third and Fourth Wards are Spanish Speaking.

Interviews with recent converts seem to be summarized by saying that having unfilled needs in other religions the converts "didn't like the harvest of their years and decided to change their seed." Thence they found a home among the Mormons.

The church's successful attraction includes the fact they are theocratic instead of democratic. Although the church will bless an infant, the child doesn't qualify for baptism until the age of accountability (Age-8).

The church has a rite for baptism after death. An example of their rationale is . . . how could an infant taken in death possibly have accrued any sins and therefore be

Upon my visit to Seattle I learned first-hand what Hilda hospitality really means.

Like many old-country hospitable grandmothers, Hilda spares nothing to ensure a guest's every culinary whim. And my culinary whims are not slim! And neither was I after I left her dinner table.

At one point I thought I had found a few in Hilda by thinking her judgment-was disoriented, because I swore she cooked enough for an army.

Perhaps this attitude about Hilda, herself, enjoys eating so much. She seems to consider it a sin to leave any morsels of food clinging to China, rather than her stomach.

The plates before me were adorned with corn on the cob, green beans, fresh bread, smoked salmon, pork chops, applesauce, baked potato, and apple pie ala-mode, not to mention other delicacies.

After I had eaten most of the delicious meal, Hilda noticed that my baked potato was gone so she insisted I have another! At this point I nearly said 'uncle', but I couldn't convince her that I wasn't still hungry.

Actually, I have to admit, even though Hilda's going to find out, I just could not eat that baked potato, so, behind her back, I stuffed the lukewarm potato in my sock until I could think of a way to dispose of it later.

MUCH later!

First, I had to get through the second baked potato and apple pie ala-mode.

Simultaneously, as I forced my mouth open for the last bite, my free hand went, immediately, to my

belt. My sigh of relief was two-fold, I had just eaten a meal fit for ten kings, and given my poor stomach room to stretch.

It was at this point, although I had tried a dozen times to convince her to do so earlier, Hilda finally sat down and ate. It was also at this point that I excused myself from the table and went down to the third floor of the high-rise to examine the facilities, and more precisely find a place to ditch the potato.

What happened next would fit into a Woody Allen movie!

I went to the laundry room where I found a garbage can, rolled up my pant leg, slipped the baked potato out and quickly dropped it into the garbage can.

But it wasn't quick enough.

I got caught in the act by a well-dressed elderly lady and mumbled my awkward explanation. Her expression said 'I don't believe this', but she said I was cute, and wished me a good evening. What else could she say?!

I learned a valuable lesson from all of this. First and last, never empty a plate before Hilda has sat down. If you do, never stick a baked potato in your sock and expect not to get caught dumping it so Hilda won't know you didn't eat it! Very awkward!

Stick it in your pocket, your jacket, the toilet, anything, but not your sock. They really radiate warmth, just like Hilda. She's one-in-a-million.

Hot potato or not, ya gotta love Grandma Hilda.

Joe's mysterious coverage of "World's Fastest Growing Church," of which I had no part nor knowledge.

Jon Meade

GAGNE, the Legend

by Jon Meade

Dateline—Minneapolis

The sports field has many legends. But few with the enduring stature of Verne Gagne, professional wrestler. This past summer marked the 30th anniversary of this man's remarkable career.

He's more than just another former world champion who earns a six figure salary. He is a personality with a multi-faceted record of athletic achievements. The Gagne reputation is practically more magnanimous than the sport itself.

In the midwest and his home state of Minnesota, his name is synonymous with not only wrestling, of all kinds, but with the whole spectrum of sport. But it doesn't stop there. New Yorkers recognize him, too.

The man is gargantuan!

At 53 years of age he is still without a peer. He has encountered many rivals over the years with few defeats. And among his friends are a wide gamut of famous people, including the late General Douglas MacArthur and Hubert Humphrey.

When you consider his longevity in what almost has to be the most demanding contact sport around, not to mention the showmanship that shares the spotlight, Mr. Gagne, sometimes referred to as "Gags" by close friends, is a rare athlete.

Not even the greatest lib and jab man of all time, retiring heavyweight boxing champion Mohammad Ali, could out the mustard past 37. And

Hunter Roberts
Actor-Screenwriter
S.A.G.-A.F.T.R.A.

463-2263

HOLLYWOOD, CALIFORNIA

Maxine Bell
CONCERT PIANIST · COMPOSER
MASTER TEACHER OF CLASSIC PIANO

PHONE
559-4659

9115 1/2 NATIONAL BLVD.
LOS ANGELES, CA 90034

DR. ALFRED R. BECKER
CONTACT LENS
SPECIALIST

OFFICE GRANITE 9-2111
RES. WEBSTER 9-6334

10899 WEYBURN AVE.
WESTWOOD VILLAGE
LOS ANGELES, CALIF. 90024

CREAM Court Reporters

competent, reliable, experienced
accurate, mature reporters

Dorothy East #1

Second page, NFG, featured Verne Gagne, a great champion and loyal friend.

National Family Gazette publications Inc. Chairman, President Jon Meade. Second class postage paid in Las Vegas, Nevada and at additional mailing offices.

Publishing address is National Family Gazette, P.O. Box 36159, 5350 Wilshire Blvd., Los Angeles, California, 90036.

Subscription rate $16 per year, $18 in Canada. Foreign $22.

Advertising policy — Does not accept tobacco, alcohol, coffee, tea, or patent medicine advertising.

All classified advertising responses should be directed to the publishers postal box unless specifically designated otherwise.

Billie Jean King is hanging in there around her mid thirties, as is 41-year old pitcher Gaylord Perry, and Pete Rose is flirting with forty, but these sports do not take the physical toll that professional wrestling does. Although still handsome, Gagne wears the tatoos of his trade from the top of his cauliflowered ears to the bottom of his shattered shins.

Just recently, a major publishing house has come out with a hard-cover book on professional wrestling, looking at the sport with in-depth colored glasses. The title is "Main Event" and it centers much of its color around Verne Gagne. And this past summer many papers and magazines picked up on the growing Gagne legend. No doubt because Gagne's life could make many volumes of books. Books that would unveil a truly unique individual.

In the next issue of Family Gazette we will have an exclusive, in-depth story of Verne Gagne, complete with pictures. His career, his background, his family, his hobbies and his charitable and community involvement, will all be painted in that very likeable Gagne color.

Wrestling fan or not, if you appreciate well rounded, unique people you won't want to miss . . . . Gagne, as the legend continues.

(Bottom part, Gagne article)Joe's blackened-out business card and ownership box below page, citing my name.

477

Jon Meade

HILDA'S HIDEAWAY

by Jon Meade

Dateline—Seattle, Washington

Should a 73-year old lady fall into the pattern of comfortable acceptance of senior citizen living or dare she carve out a life-style comparable to our founding fathers?

MOST of the residents of the senior citizens' highrise in Seattle are content to relax and enjoy the amenities of the new, multimillion dollar building.

MOST of the seniors feel security in their convenient life-style shared with people of their own age.

MOST feel the facilities provided an ease of life that is much appreciated after a lifetime of working and raising a family.

MOST. Not all!

Hilda Grant, is one exception.

She was considered one of the lucky ones when she received notice that she would be able to move into the beautiful housing complex within only minutes of Seattle's Space Needle and a free bus ride to shops and stores.

Because of minimal earnings, Hilda qualified for very reasonable rent and other lesser expensive services. She moved her somewhat modest belongings into the project and settled down on the 17th floor.

The third floor was the social floor which had various games, arts and crafts, group gatherings, a fireplace, and laundry facilities. Hilda went down there on occasion but felt that it was too cloistered.

She has a gorgeous view of Seattle from her window—even a glimpse of Mt. Ranier on a clear day—but the newness of the building, the _____ _____ ___ ___ _____ __ the government subsidized complex all contributed to a dislike of her new home and eventual unhappiness.

She started working more hours at Costello's Drapery Shop and spent much of her time away from her four-room apartment at the Bingo parlors. When it became a drudgery to return home she decided it was time for a change.

So, at an age when many people are well into retirement and content to reminisce and rest, she did the unthinkable. After living in the complex for less than a year, she packed her bags and tried to depart quietly. As it turned out, however, it wasn't so quiet. When her fellow residents and family back in Minnesota learned of her plans they tried everything they could to convince her to stay in her secure 'cocoon.' It wasn't so much that she wanted out of the highrise that bothered them, but rather what her moving plans were.

She wanted to move into her one-room cabin on one acre at Port Orchard. Port Orchard is a serene and quiet community across from Seattle via Puget Sound and is accessible by ferry only. Much like her background on her farm in North Dakota, the community is both relaxed and rural. And like those rugged earlier years, her living quarters are rugged and basic.

There was no electricity, water or plumbing and other modern conveniences which we all take so much for granted.

But it was hers. Free and clear. She paid the taxes herself and did not have to fill out monthly government rental subsidy forms. Uncle Sam was a good 'uncle' but she didn't like him in her home month after month. She owned the wooden structure that she and her husband built in the early sixties and she could do whatever she wanted, whenever she wanted. She felt young and rarin' to make a garden, take a hike to the out-house and build a fire in the cast iron stove with her own freshly-chopped wood.

Hilda Grant with Jon Meade.

Hilda, the proud mother of three daughters, nine grandchildren, and five great-grandchildren, reiterated: "I just had to get out of that place. It was so darn big but there wasn't really any 'room'. It was stuffy, too. There were a lot of nice people there, but I just didn't like sitting around or having things provided for me by 'Big Brother'. Too many people just sat around, complained and gossiped. I guess I don't like being around a bunch of old people . . . at least they don't have to act so old."

After getting settled, about the only thing she missed was convenient transportation. She doesn't drive, so her former husband, Bob Grant, who's been driving for no less than 60 years, came to her aid and acted as her 'chauffeur'. He also commuted back and forth to her property from his apartment in Seattle, in order to fix up the cabin, cut firewood, and utilize his expert carpentry skills to do handiwork on what some relatives affectionately call, "Hilda's hideaway."

It is now nearing a year since Hilda pulled up her roots and she doesn't regret it one bit. She still even commutes by ferry to Seattle and makes extra money sewing drapes. And she still drops by the old Bingo hall to re-kindle 'old acquaintances and try her luck.

She exclaimed, "What's nice about it all is that I can always go into town and look forward to returning to the cabin. I'm always doing something, it seems, and I'm happy. I know some of the seniors think I'm crazy, but I'm happily 'crazy.' I wouldn't go back, I don't think, for anything. My family and friends can visit me just as well out here, and the kids always have so much more fun on the acre.'

With the help of Bob, and some money from one of her daughters, Hilda now enjoys electricity. She immediately bought a stove and refrigerator, and froze many vegetables from her garden. She's planted fruit trees and has made many improvements to the cabin and acre. Soon, she will have water and plumbing.

Despite having painful arthritis throughout the lower portion of her body, and steel pins holding her knees together, Hilda works as a _____ ist with great vigor. Everything she does is with rigor and void of complaint. Her tireless pace and unrelenting ambition would make most young people envious. Her own family and friends marvel at her attitude and love of life.

For example, even with a pronounced limp from the chronic arthritis, and a hearty Norwegian frame, she drags her visitors up and down the steep hills of Seattle like a good-natured 'sargeant,' setting the pace with faltering cadence. Family legend has it that one should bring corn plasters and an extra pair of shoes when visiting Grandma Hilda in Seattle.

Hilda is among those senior citizens who thrives among younger people. Life doesn't evolve around Hilda, Hilda evolves around life! The breaths she takes are alive with appreciation. She tackles work vivaciously and faces each day with a fresh challenge.

Many things change with age, including people, but this senior citizen is not about to let the years dampen her spirits. She's a fine wine and an imported cheese, aged to perfection!

That's Hilda Grant!

Hilda is living testimony that age should not corral senior citizens into retirement pastures.

Also see "Hot Potato" page 7.

My feature article on my own grandmother, Hilda, my mom's mother.

478

Some of the leftover 250,000 copies of National Family
Gazette, in Joe's underground garage.

Even more NFG copies in my trunk.

PAUL CARUSO
ATTORNEY AT LAW

March 21, 1980

███████████████████████

Los Angeles, California   90036

Re: Jon Meade

Dear Sir:

This office represents Jon Meade.

It is my professional opinion that you are a fraud, crook, and a liar. Thus far, I'm being polite. It is my intention to the District Attorney and the bunko squad to institute criminal proceedings against you unless by 1 April, 1980, I receive the amount of $4,500.00.

I realize that in writing this letter, I am wasting the price of a postage stamp plus my secretary's time plus the parchment enclosed in my stationery (which is far too good for you).

If you have any doubts concerning my feelings in this matter, please feel free to call me collect.

Disrespectfully yours,

PAUL CARUSO

PC:ka
cc: ✓Jon Meade

Famous celebrity attorney's incredible letter to Joe on my behalf.

Muscle Digest masthead.

—— STAFF ——

PUBLISHER
Donald Wong, M.D.
DIRECTOR
John Williams
EDITOR
Jon Meade
CONTRIBUTING EDITORS
Dave Johns
Serge Nubret
Robby Robinson
Kal Szkalak
Sharon Wells
GRAPHIC DESIGNER
Claude Chatel
CIRCULATION MANAGER
Christine Clifford

ADVERTISING DIRECTOR
Debbie Serradell
(213) 695-0702

—— COVER ——

KAL SZKALAK
photo by Joe Valdez

MUSCLE DIGEST ISSN 0164-7792 is published
bi-monthly by Muscle Digest, Inc., a California
Corporation. © 1980 by Muscle Digest, Inc. All
rights reserved. Offices are located at 10317 E.
Whittier Blvd., Whittier, California 90606. The
subscription rate is as follows: 6 issues, $10.00; 12
issues, $18.00; single-copy newsstand price is $2.00.
Contributions should be mailed to Editor, Muscle
Digest Magazine, 10317 E. Whittier Blvd., Whittier, California 90606. Controlled circulation postage paid at Whittier, CA 90602 (ISSN 0164-7792),
Olive Branch, MS 38654 and Grants Pass, OR
97526. Unsolicited materials must be accompanied
by return postage. This magazine will assume no
responsibility for loss or damage thereto. Any
material accepted is subject to such revision as is
necessary in our sole discretion to meet the requirements of this publication. Upon publication, payment will be made at our current rate, which covers
the author's and/or contributor's right, title and
interest in and to the material mailed, including but
not limited to manuscripts, photographs, drawings,
charts and designs which shall be considered as
text. The act of mailing a manuscript and/or
material shall constitute an express warranty by
the contributor that the material is original and in
no way an infringement upon the rights of others.
Reproduction of this magazine, in whole or in part,
is prohibited without written consent. POST-
MASTER: Send address changes to MUSCLE
DIGEST, 10317 E. Whittier Blvd., Whittier, CA
90606.

Magazine staff credits, including my editorship.

Jon Meade

Muscle Digest table of contents: My Arnold interview/article reference.

This was Arnold Schwarzenegger in 1975, the last year he won the Olympia. Does he feel that he matched this shape for his 1980 Olympia win?

ARNOLD ANSWERS
IN REBUTTAL TO THE OLYMPIA CONTROVERSY

(Ed note: Refer to page 22 for Olympia report.)

MD—Years ago you said that you had retired, what prompted you, and at what point was it, that you made a decision to compete in this thing? We understand it wasn't until the last minute.

AS—*Right. I started training when I came back from my vacation in Europe, which was the end of July, beginning of August. We had a meeting for the rescheduling of Cohan—the movie—and decided to start shooting in October, in London and Spain. We looked at the shooting schedule and it was at the time when Conan was suppose to be 40 and 60 years old. Both times when he's already king, and at that time he was very huge and well fed because he had all the food he wanted as king, and he's very muscular. So, the question from the director was, could you get—by October—weighing around 230, although I have been asking you all along to weigh 215. And I said well, yeah I can be 230, but I should be in as good of shape as possible . . . he said I don't really need contest shape, but muscular and big looking because in the film your weight will change. By October, I want you to be 230 or 240. So I trained very hard. Once a day in the beginning, then twice a day, then harder and harder, and then when it came very close to the competition, Weider and Franco kept saying to me, why don't you compete in the Mr. Olympia contest, you're getting in all this terrific shape and I think by that time you can be cut up enough. You'd make a great Mr. Olympia for a change.*

MD—Who said that? Franco and who?

AS—*And Weider—Joe—Joe Weider. Yeah, they kept saying why don't you get in there, you will make a great Mr. Olympia for a change, this and that. That was three weeks before the contest. I kept saying, no, I really don't want to do it, I'm retired, I'd risk too much. One day I woke up and somehow had this gut feeling of jumping into the contest . . . you know, there was no rationale behind it, of course.*

MD—Weren't you scheduled to go to the Olympia to guest pose?

AS—*No, I was scheduled to be a judge over there.*

MD—When did you make the final decision?

AS—*The final decision was like two or three weeks before the contest.*

MD—You told no one, right?

AS—*Right, I told no one because I didn't know if I'd pull it together. I wanted to go in with an open mind, without calling Paul Graham and saying put me down as one of the competitors, because I didn't know for sure. I tried very hard. The last two weeks I got a lot of injuries because of overworking the body, and I had to get cortisone shots for the shoulders. It really screwed me up in a way for the competition, because*

cortisone retains water in your system. I went over there with my ankles swollen, and puffy, but Franco told me those were the side effects of cortisone, and said I should pose the whole day and sweat it out. I posed the whole day on Friday and got more and more defined. I then called Ben Weider and asked him to tell Bill Pearl that I would in fact be competing in the contest.

MD—When did you do that?

AS—*Friday night, the day before the competition.*

MD—There weren't any delay tactics on your part? Were they surprised?

AS—*I really don't know about the reaction because I was staying in a different hotel. I was staying where Dennis Tinerino and some of the other guys were, downtown Sydney. The others were staying around the Sydney beaches. I had no communication with any of the other guys except Dennis Tinerino, that was it. I didn't see anybody until I walked into the Sydney Opera House on Saturday, noon time. I saw Frank and Christine Zane. They both smiled and shook hands and said something to the effect . . . welcome back to the club type of a thing . . . Christine said, 'We wish the best of luck because you really need it today,' and I said 'yet, you're right.' Then we had meetings about weight classes and judges—should there be one weight class or two and should there be any judges excluded from the competition. That's the time they announced Bill Pearl pulled out as judge because of Chris Dickerson and Bill Drake pulled out because of me. But, I really don't know the reaction of the guys there . . . I sensed there was a certain coldness, but that's always the case on the day of the competition.*

MD—We would like to put forth certain questions to you that we've heard from people—their names are unimportant. On one side of the fence, we've heard that you were the best on that given night, although you weren't in your best shape . . . and that it was so close you didn't know you were going to win until the very last moment?

AS—*Yeah, I'd have to say that was pretty accurate. It was a tough battle. I felt I really screwed up at the posing. I didn't know there was music until someone told me and it really threw me off. I thought there were several guys whose posing was better than mine.*

MD—Didn't anyone tell you about needing your own music?

AS—*No, I said, well, do you have a tape here of Exodus because I posed to that in 1975. Another athlete there had selected Exodus too, so I used it.*

MD—Another rumor we heard was that when the compulsory posing came, you

(continued on page 74)   MUSCLE DIGEST **35**

MD—What is your opinion of your victory in the Olympia contest?

AS—*Well, I was very happy when I won the competition. First, because it was winning it the seventh time. You know, breaking my own records and on top of it, it meant beating a lot of new guys who came up in the last five years, whom I've never competed against. So it was a great feeling beating all the new guys. But, at the same time, I have to say that due to the time that I had available for training, and because of my late decision to enter, I did not come in the kind of shape that maybe I was in '75. At least this is what some of my close friends said and what I could say also, looking at the pictures and so on. But it was good enough to beat those guys and win the competition. It was very close and I thought that the guys were in top shape and it made for a very rough competition, much more so than any other time that I have competed.*

MD—What percent of the greatest shape were you in for this contest?

AS—*I thought that I was near 90%.*

MD—90%? What parts were lacking?

AS—*I think that the overall definition was a little bit lacking. Also, experience, basically; I mean there were guys there who worked so much on their posing and were so in tune to the music and into the professional behavior on stage and so on. Whereas, I have not been on the stage for 5 years; this was really the first time that I was really in front of people again posing. It was a total surprise to me posing at the pre-judging with music all of a sudden and I really had to pull my things together to win, and I worked very hard on it.*

Arnold Answers: First page of My Arnold interview/article reference.

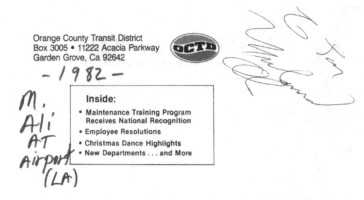

Orange County Transit District
Box 3005 • 11222 Acacia Parkway
Garden Grove, Ca 92642

- 1982 -

M. Ali AT Airport (LA)

Inside:
- Maintenance Training Program Receives National Recognition
- Employee Resolutions
- Christmas Dance Highlights
- New Departments ... and More

Muhammad Ali meeting and autograph at LAX.

Magazine masthead of Sportstyle, my original idea.

Hat from *Saved by the Bell* wrap party.

					42716350
ENTERTAINMENT PARTNERS	EPSG TALENT SERVICES 2835 N NAOMI ST 2nd FLOOR BURBANK CA 91504				
		Check Date	05/30/1999		
		Invoice No	RCA 00242830		
		EP Reference	5099/00000005/R43422		

PRODUCT INFORMATION

CLIENT NAME:	N.B.C. PRODUCTIONS, INC.
SHOW NAME:	SAVED BY THE BELL
EPISODE NAME:	CLOSE ENCOUNTER OF THE NERD KI
EPISODE NO:	6327
PRODUCT TYPE:	MADE FOR TELEVISION
PRINCIPAL PHOTO DATE:	09/25/1989
EP PRODUCT NO:	00000005-1202-6327
SIGNATOR	NBC STUDIOS, INC.

REUSE INFORMATION

MARKET/RUN	REUSE DATE
DOMESTIC SYNDICATION 32ND RUN	04/06/1999

Unemployment Data:
Employer: EPSG
Wage Request: 2835 N NAOMI ST
BURBANK , CA 91504
Telephone: (818) 955-6000
Unemployment State: CA
State Unemployment No 439796240000

Claim Filing Instr: If you become unemployed you may be eligible for benefits. You should go to the nearest Unemployment or Dept. of Labor office
Documents Needed:This check stub, record of prior claim, employment location, social security card and ID.

Name	Tax ID	Res State	M/S	Dep	Union/Local	Period
JON MEADE		CA	S	01	A DRAM-61310	05/29/1999
		Wrk Tax Day(s) Wrkd		Wrk State	Chk Date	Chk Number
Job Title: AFTRA-TV FREE LANCE		00 00		CA	05/30/1999	42716350

Earnings			Taxes			Deductions		
Descr	Hours	Amount	Descr	Amount	YTD	Descr	Amount	YTD
SYND	.0	9.90	FED.	2.77	8.31			
			FICA-SSA	.61	1.84			
			FICA-MED	.14	.43			
			VPDI CA	.03	.09			
			RES ST CA	.59	1.77			

Total Gross		9.90	Total	4.14	12.44	Total	.00	.00
Total Net		5.76	Comments: 32ND RUN CLOSE ENCO					
Subject FIT		9.90	* Please verify address. Mail or fax *					
YTD Payments		29.70	* corrections. Fax No:(818) 848-0254 *					
YTD subject FIT		29.70						

NBC pay stub for residuals: Saved By The Bell, voiceover, Close Encounters of Nerd kind.

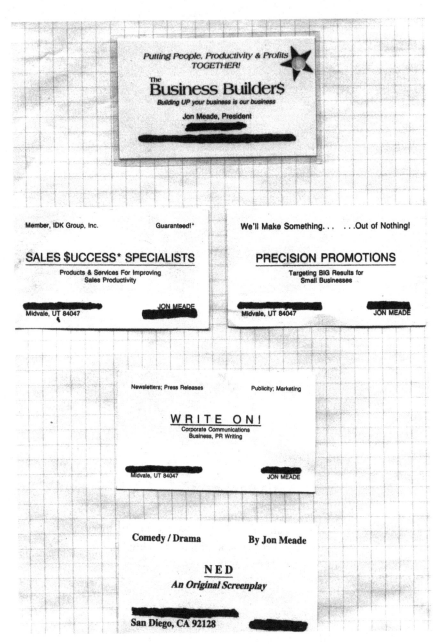

Business Cards: Just a few of my ideas and business starts.

Global Communcations
11 East 30th Street (4R), New York, NY 10016

FOR IMMEDIATE RELEASE   MEDIA CONTACT: TIM BECKLEY (212) 685-4080

SAN DIEGO TO HOST NATIONAL NEW AGE
& TRUTH ABOUT UFOS CONFERENCE
10,000 YEAR-OLD CRYSTAL SKULL
TO BE FEATURED

Believers in UFOs and extraterrestrials will get to find out all the latest information from over twenty-five leading authorities when they gather on March 15, 16 and 17 at the Clarion Hotel, 2223 El Cajon Blvd., in San Diego for the National New Age & Truth About UFOs Conference sponsored by Inner Light Publications.

"Many of the some 25-plus authorities have had former government connections, others have traveled all over the world documenting the existence of alien visitors on our cosmic shores," notes conference coordinator Timothy Green Beckley, who has personally been involved in this field for more than two decades and is editor of **UFO UNIVERSE,** the nation's only regularly published glossy newsstand publication on the topic.

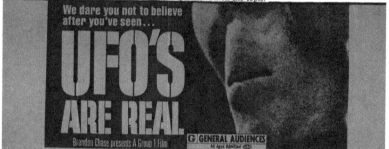

My proposed research and writing project by a LA
couple at the San Diego UFO Convention.

My infamous baseball bat, which I am glad I never used as planned.

Printed in the United States
By Bookmasters